XBOX 360 Forensics

XBOX 360 Forensics

A Digital Forensics Guide to Examining Artifacts

Steven Bolt

Samuel Liles
Technical Editor

ELSEVIER

AMSTERDAM • BOSTON • HEIDELBERG • LONDON
NEW YORK • OXFORD • PARIS • SAN DIEGO
SAN FRANCISCO • SINGAPORE • SYDNEY • TOKYO

Syngress is an imprint of Elsevier

Acquiring Editor: Angelina Ward
Development Editor: Heather Scherer
Project Manager: Sarah Binns
Designer: Kristen Davis

Syngress is an imprint of Elsevier
30 Corporate Drive, Suite 400, Burlington, MA 01803, USA

Library of Congress Cataloging-in-Publication Data
Application submitted

British Library Cataloguing-in-Publication Data
A catalogue record for this book is available from the British Library.

ISBN: 978-1-59749-623-0

Printed in the United States of America

11 12 13 14 15 10 9 8 7 6 5 4 3 2 1

Typeset by: diacriTech, India

For information on all Syngress publications visit our website at *www.syngress.com*

I would like to dedicate this work to my wife, for believing in me and pushing me to follow my dreams, and to our children, who bring so much joy to our lives. Looking into my children's eyes stirs such wondrous emotions, only a parent would understand the desire to protect that innocence and wonder. I would do anything to protect my family. And I know that same passion is shared within the law enforcement community.

As a former law enforcement official, I was taught that I should strive to make my part of the world better than the way I received it. My hope is that with this book, I am placing the tools and information into the hands of the officials who continue the fight and continue to strive to improve their part of the world and protect the most innocent, the children.

Contents

Acknowledgments

This project was an interesting undertaking. What I mean by this is that there is little understood about the artifacts of the console, how it stores information, what format the information is stored in, and how to extract that data and make sense of it. This lack of knowledge is, of course, in comparison with the more mainstream digital storage media, such as a Windows-based PC hard drive or an Apple Mac hard drive. In any event, there was concern on my part about either overlooking an important step or inadvertently generating artifacts from a process that was run or a game that was executed.

With all these factors to be concerned about, I decided that there were several initial steps that needed to be taken. The first, of course, was that I needed to ensure I had the right forensic software to work with. For this, I reached out to several companies that decided to assist in this research. The first company was Guidance Software, the makers of EnCase. Guidance provided me with a licensed copy of EnCase to use for the research. The second company was X-Ways Forensics, which is another respected company within the forensics community. Two more companies provided their assistance to this project: Paraben Corporation provided their P2 Commander, and Wiebetech provided several write blockers so that a wide variety of the necessary forensic hardware and software was present. I want to express my gratitude to these companies for their assistance, without which this project would never have been possible.

My colleagues at the Department of Defense Cyber Investigations Training Academy (DCITA) have been supportive and have provided me with guidance when the effort seemed almost too much, and I render my heartfelt thanks to them.

This project would never have happened if not for my wife. She is my inspiration and she supports me in every endeavor I pursue. With her, all things are possible.

About the Author

Steven Bolt is a computer forensics leader employed by the Computer Sciences Corporation (CSC) with the Department of Defense Cyber Investigations Training Academy (DCITA). He serves as the network intrusions track manager, a role in which, along with his team, he is responsible for the development and delivery of course material and real-world scenarios for network intrusion analysis. Steven has presented material at many national and international conferences, including the Department of Defense Cyber Crime Conference, the High Technology Crime Investigation Association (HTCIA), and Internet Crimes Against Children (ICAC). He currently holds a CISSP, CEH, CHFI, EnCE, and ACE certificates.

CHAPTER

The XBOX 360: Why We Need to Be Concerned

1

INFORMATION IN THIS CHAPTER

- Introduction
- The XBOX 360
- Criminal uses of the XBOX 360
- Poor man's virtual reality simulator

INTRODUCTION

In this chapter, we will discuss the video game console market as well as the distribution of the Microsoft XBOX 360. This will provide the digital media analyst the needed information to understand why these gaming consoles can prove to be of interest as well as the need to understand the location of the digital artifacts, decipher their meaning and determine what can be extracted and its relevance to a case. Finally, we will explore some of the criminal activities that have been developed by the criminal element that takes advantage of social network aspects of the online gaming portal called XBOX Live.

THE XBOX 360

The XBOX 360 is Microsoft's second production game console and is the evolution of the original XBOX. Released to the North American retail market on November 22, 2005, the unit met with such success that it sold out almost immediately. Since its release, the console has continued to evolve to meet market demands, adding more features not only to the console but also to the associated online portal. This console is one of three that are considered to be the seventh generation of consoles, and each competes for market share. Included in this category are the Microsoft XBOX 360, the Sony Play Station 3,[1] and the Nintendo Wii.[2] Market share is a constantly flowing dynamic, but because of the business nature, there are statistics that show the relative numbers. Table 1.1 shows some statistics that detail the market share of each console and the total sales by a yearly breakdown.

The dates covered are as follows:

2007 – (Week beginning December 31, 2006 to March 24, 2007)
2008 – (Week beginning December 30, 2007 to March 22, 2008)
2009 – (Week beginning December 28, 2008 to March 21, 2009)
2010 – (Week beginning December 27, 2009 to March 20, 2010) [1]

Although the market share displays a percentage of the total, it is not sensational if compared with the actual numbers of sales and the total number of units that have been sold. There are many figures for each retail region of the globe, but for the purposes of this book, it is important to focus on the North American region. Table 1.2 details the total number of sales within the same time frame as Table 1.1.

Lifetime sales provide yet another picture of each console and the sheer numbers of units that have been shipped and that are scattered throughout the world. Table 1.3 provides some hard figures for each of the seventh generation consoles. Pay particular attention to the lifetime sales figures showing the total number of sales for each console.

Table 1.1 The Market Share Breakdown between the XBOX 360, Wii, and Play Station 3

	Market Share (Same Periods Covered)			
	2007	**2008**	**2009**	**2010**
360	24.03%	21.51%	26.12%	22.75%
Wii	49.94%	50.88%	50.58%	47.36%
PS3	26.04%	27.61%	23.30%	29.89%

Table 1.2 Total Sales of the XBOX 360, Wii, and Play Station 3

	2007	**2008**	**2009**	**2009 versus 2008**
360	1,292,149	1,553,430	2,323,492	49.57%
Wii	2,685,642	3,674,125	4,499,189	22.46%
PS3	1,400,391	1,993,838	2,072,718	3.96%
Total	5,378,182	7,221,393	8,895,399	23.18%

[1]Play Station 3 is a trademark of the Sony Corporation.
[2]Nintendo Wii is a trademark of the Nintendo Corporation.

Table 1.3 Lifetime Sales of the XBOX 360, Wii, and Play Station 3

	Wii	360	PS3	Total
2007	16,387,941	7,878,345	7,621,891	31,888,177
	51.39%	24.71%	23.90%	100.00%
2008	24,425,467	11,008,653	9,687,882	45,122,002
	54.13%	24.40%	21.47%	100.00%
2009	22,520,863	10,593,216	12,739,243	45,853,322
	49.12%	23.10%	27.78%	100.00%
2010	4,495,763	2,158,998	2,837,233	9,491,994
	47.36%	22.75%	29.89%	100.00%
Lifetime	69,272,095	38,898,576	33,315,566	141,486,237
	48.96%	27.49%	23.55%	100.00%

Digital forensic analysts and high-tech crime investigators are well versed in the media analysis of all the major operating systems, network devices, and a whole host of small devices that are encountered on a regular basis. However, there is an entire class of digital media that may be overlooked because of the perception that they are merely toys. It is incumbent on those of us in the community to educate others that with the technological advances that have been made during the last several years, almost anything can and, usually, does contain a piece of electronics that can contain memory. This memory may contain artifacts that are relevant to the analysis at hand and may provide the missing link to a puzzle. Game consoles are no longer toys to be played with by social outcasts; they have developed into a multibillion dollar industry that spans racial, economic, and generational hurdles [2].

High-tech investigators need to ensure that if there is a console involved in a case, then it is seized and searched just as any other piece of digital evidence would be, considering the best practices for the seizure of media.

TIP

For all intents and purposes, a modern gaming console is a computer; guidelines for the seizure of a computer should be adhered to. Best practices for search and seizure of digital media should be considered before the seizure of a console, and some of these guides can be located at www.cybercrime.gov/ssmanual/index.html.

In "video game play" there is a great deal of preference between gamers and their platform of choice, and this book focuses on the XBOX 360. In time, there will be an analysis of each console as well as any other that develops and will be released to the public for wide acceptance and use.

As with any other new device or technique that is developed and released to the general public, there are perpetrators who will not only attempt to use that technology to commit crimes but also tend to develop methods and usage for the technology that the designers never dreamt their devices would be used for. The XBOX 360 and XBOX Live are no different.

CRIMINAL USES OF THE XBOX 360

This section will discuss some of the known uses of the XBOX 360 and the XBOX Live online portal to assist in a wide range of criminal activity. In addition, there will be a discussion of hypothetical situations that may shed some light on current and future criminal uses for this machine.

Known Criminal Uses of Video Games

There have been a few instances in which the XBOX 360 game console and, in particular, the XBOX Live service have been used as a conduit between a perpetrator and a victim. A few of the cases that have come to light all involve the use of the communication functionality within the XBOX Live service and a perpetrator contacting a victim, which later leads to an in-person meeting and illegal activity.

The case that started this research involved a 26-year-old man who, back in 2006, used the XBOX Live service to make initial contact with his victim while playing a game over the XBOX Live service [3]. Figure 1.1 provides a snapshot of the news release.

Another example provides information that the FBI is aware of the game consoles being used for the exploitation of children and has investigated some cases. The article suggests that the XBOX Live service is being used by pedophiles to lurk and seek out individuals to victimize. Figure 1.2 provides a snapshot of the new article.

Although not comprehensive, these examples provide some insight into the way the game console has been used to commit crimes. Expanding on these examples, it is not a stretch to consider that the console and its associated network functionality will continue to be of concern to the forensic community.

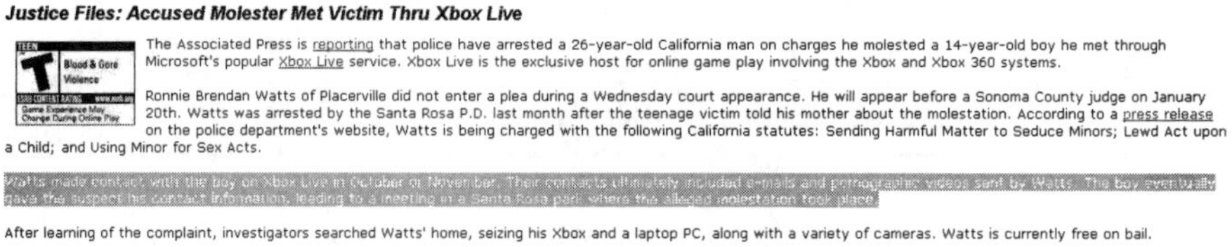

Justice Files: Accused Molester Met Victim Thru Xbox Live

The Associated Press is reporting that police have arrested a 26-year-old California man on charges he molested a 14-year-old boy he met through Microsoft's popular Xbox Live service. Xbox Live is the exclusive host for online game play involving the Xbox and Xbox 360 systems.

Ronnie Brendan Watts of Placerville did not enter a plea during a Wednesday court appearance. He will appear before a Sonoma County judge on January 20th. Watts was arrested by the Santa Rosa P.D. last month after the teenage victim told his mother about the molestation. According to a press release on the police department's website, Watts is being charged with the following California statutes: Sending Harmful Matter to Seduce Minors; Lewd Act upon a Child; and Using Minor for Sex Acts.

Watts made contact with the boy on Xbox Live in October or November. Their contacts ultimately included e-mails and pornographic videos sent by Watts. The boy eventually gave the suspect his contact information, leading to a meeting in a Santa Rosa park where the alleged molestation took place.

After learning of the complaint, investigators searched Watts' home, seizing his Xbox and a laptop PC, along with a variety of cameras. Watts is currently free on bail.

FIGURE 1.1

News release from http://gamepolitics.livejournal.com/171996.html detailing one case of XBOX Live criminal use. Note the highlighted area.

Sexual Predators Exploit Xbox 360 to Target Children

By: MY BASEPAGE
Feb. 13th. 2008 8:56 am
Share This Article

ChannelCincinnati.com reports that Xbox Live has become sexual predators' new playground as the online gaming service for the Xbox 360 allows pedophiles to lurk online and communicate with children through headsets and instant messages. WLWT Cincinnati reports:

The FBI has investigated cases in southern Ohio, where sexual predators have used game systems such as Xbox 360 to target children.

"A pedophile is talking to a child, they are gaining their trust and understanding, and then tries to engage in that next level, which is taking them from the cyber world to the physical world," said Douglas Roden, an FBI forensic examiner.

Investigators said a 30-year-old Dayton woman used an Xbox 360 game system to send nude photos of herself to a 16-year-old Arizona boy, and then convinced him to send her nude photos of himself.

Authorities said the risk is not limited to Xbox 360, because Nintendo Wii and Playstation 3 also contain some online capabilities.

FIGURE 1.2

Yet another news article that discusses a way in which the XBOX Live service has been used for a crime.

The article can be located at http://news.teamxbox.com/xbox/15701/Sexual-Predators-Exploit-Xbox-360-to-Target-Children/

Ways the XBOX 360 Is Used by Criminals

Criminal use of technology and, specifically, networked communications through the Internet is not new; however, the device that gets connected is ever changing. The digital forensic community is constantly trying to understand each device and how it stores data once these devices are released to the public, from the Apple iPhone to new network devices and game consoles.

The criminal element uses technology much in the same way that the rest of society does. They use their computers to surf the Internet for directions from their home to a drug deal, robbery location, family member's house, fence stolen property, locate information on how to make drugs, weapons, hide evidence, destroy evidence, and chat with their social network, including other criminals. Other ways in which the dual-use technology can be used by the criminal element includes the following:

- Regular usage
  - Send and receive e-mails, chat with criminal members, and surf the Web for information.
- Play games
  - Many criminals pass the time as the rest of society does, by playing video games.

- Engage in other activities
  - Research methods on how to make drugs, sell drugs, launder money, or commit counterintelligence against law enforcement officials.
  - Research information on law enforcement units and its members who are pursuing them.
- Use the machine as a conduit for streaming illicit material
  - The XBOX is designed to be the center of home entertainment, no matter what that entertainment is. In some cases, it is family photos or slide shows; in others, more illicit activities, which might include the streaming of contraband material and child exploitation. The console is simply designed to stream the media, and there is no filter preventing an end user from streaming such horrible media as described.
- How law enforcement investigators have apprehended suspects gaming with a stolen machine.
  - If a console is stolen and the thief uses the console to log onto the XBOX Live service, Microsoft maintains a record of the connections. An investigator can obtain those records from Microsoft and determine the ISP, which in turn could provide the subscriber information for that connection.
  - Contact Microsoft to get subscriber information. The subscriber information is maintained at Microsoft for a period of time. Because each Gamertag is unique, similar to an e-mail account, the information is unique to an individual and, therefore, the information provided might provide the vector back to a person.

In addition to the known ways in which the consoles can be used to assist in the commission of other crimes, there are also many ways in which this machine and its associated online portal can be used directly in crimes, but no proof has been located because of the unique nature or the media.

Covert Channel of Communication

The XBOX 360 is designed as a gaming device; however, the functionality of the machine has evolved to the point that it is a conduit for communication that many investigators may not be aware of. It is the network connections and associated communications channels that may not be common knowledge. The console and its associated portal have social networking, e-mail, voice mail, and streaming media capabilities that may be overlooked. E-mails are accessed through the console, but the end user is provided with a notification that there is an e-mail through the online portal. Streaming video chats require a camera, so the investigator must take an assessment of the console and surrounding media to make a determination of the capabilities that may be utilized by the end user. Social media is a trend that links many people together and can be a gold mine for certain investigations. The XBOX 360 Live online portal provides a functionality for the linkage to several social media Web sites, which may provide logs of communication.

POOR MAN'S VIRTUAL REALITY SIMULATOR

Virtual reality is a reality in the modern technological world. Governments are utilizing this concept and associated software and hardware to provide training to their military members to better pilot airplanes, deal with situations, and train their soldiers in a safe environment. With the advent of the gaming console, the ability to provide training of this nature in a variety of ways is now in the hands of the common consumer. Although the quality of the training would be dramatically different, the end result is the same; a user is placed into a situation that is attempting to mimic a real-world situation so that training can occur. Combing the first-person shooter games with the video streaming and chat capabilities of the XBOX Live service, a group of people could easily "train" on group move and shoot tactics common to the military and law enforcement communities. The information could be easily located online and practiced in the virtual world, providing a covert training facility to these small groups that could be overlooked.

SUMMARY

This chapter provided an introduction to the XBOX 360 console and the way in which it has been and could be used as a device for criminal behavior. Gaming consoles are a part of modern life and are, in fact, application-specific computers, meaning that they are computers that are designed for a specific task. Given the market penetration that game consoles have been blessed with, it is only a matter of time before a forensic examiner is provided with a gaming console for a forensic exam. In many cases, a game console may be the only computer in a household, and with the network functionality, the console may be the only computer needed.

References

[1] Williams, Brent. "2010 Year on Year Sales and Market Share Update to March 20th." http://gamrfeed.vgchartz.com/story/7595/2010-year-on-year-sales-and-market-share-update-to-march-20th/ (accessed 14.10.10).

[2] http://industrygamers.com/news/npd-video-game-and-pc-game-industry-totals-20.2-billion-in-09/ (accessed 7.10.10).

[3] http://gamepolitics.livejournal.com/171996.html (accessed 7.10.10).

CHAPTER

XBOX 360 Hardware

2

INFORMATION IN THIS CHAPTER

- Getting started with the XBOX 360
- Technical specifications
- Hard drive disassembly

GETTING STARTED WITH THE XBOX 360

The XBOX 360 is available in several different retail packages that are categorized by the size or lack of a hard drive. Upon its initial release in November 2005, the XBOX 360 was available in two retail packages. The first model was called the Arcade or Core, as seen in Figure 2.1; it was provided with no removable hard disk drive and touted the ability to play the games locally, but if the end user wanted to go online with XBOX Live, then they needed to purchase a hard drive or a memory card. The Arcade version dropped off the market for a time and has reemerged as a retail option.

The next retail model was the Pro or Premium model. Initially included with this model was a detachable 20GB hard drive that was housed in its own custom case with its own custom interface to the XBOX 360 console. Later models of the Pro version included an upgrade in hard drive space to 60GB. Figures 2.2 and 2.3 provide images of the Pro model and the detachable hard drive, respectively.

The hard drive is designed to be easily removed from the console and is also standardized so that it can be interchangeable between consoles; if, for instance, a user purchased a console with a 20GB unit, they could purchase an upgraded hard drive, available as a separate retail package, and connect it to their console, giving themselves more storage. It should be noted to avoid confusion that only one Microsoft XBOX 360 hard drive can be connected at a time. This interchangeability is for functionality purposes to enable a user to take game saves as well as Gamertag identification (a unique identifier on the XBOX Live Network) from one console to another. We shall see that there are digital artifacts that can provide indications that a console was not bundled with a hard drive or the subject of an investigation has used multiple hard drives on the system.

FIGURE 2.1

Advertisement from Xbox.com Great Britain depicting the XBOX 360 Arcade version. Note the absence of a hard drive on the top of the machine.

FIGURE 2.2

This is a picture of the Pro system.

Image available from www.walmart.com/ip/Xbox-360-60Gb-Console/10207697

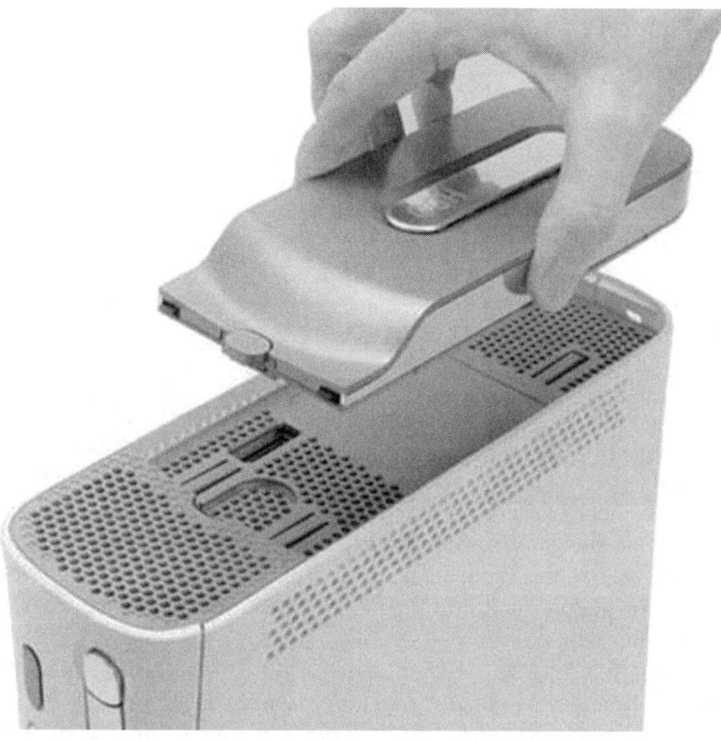

FIGURE 2.3

This image depicts the removal of the hard drive from the console.

Image available from www.theregister.co.uk/2005/12/05/review_xbox_360/print.html

Over time, the XBOX 360 has undergone an evolution. Since its release, there have been many technical changes to the box, including a wide variety of motherboards and added functionality that comes with each revision. In part, the motherboard evolution was because of the "red ring of death," which was caused because of excessive heat between the graphics processing unit (GPU) and the central processing unit (CPU) [1]. Table 2.1 provides a listing of the numerous motherboard variations and some associated notes and technical specifications.

Although an entire chapter could be devoted for discussing motherboard evolution, it is not of primary importance to the artifact analysis for the XBOX 360 console as it pertains to digital examinations. Some might argue that the ability to store information on the machine has increased with the addition on later models of the console with onboard storage chips of 256 MB and 512 MB, this storage location is not easy to manipulate and is believed to hold the console's operating system. Many organizations that are attempting to run Linux on the console are trying to access this onboard storage and have met with varied success.

Table 2.1 Listing of the Different Motherboard Evolutions

Motherboard Code Name	Release Date
Xenon	November 2005
Zephyr	July 2007
Falcon	September 2007
Opus	June 2008
Jasper	September 2008
Valhalla	June 2010

Ref: http://gamrconnect.vgchartz.com/thread.php?id=56521

Current guidelines for search and seizure of digital media include the capturing of volatile data, including network connections, running processes, and the system's RAM. Unfortunately, because of the security measures that have been put into place by Microsoft, the standard methods for capturing volatile data from the machine is not an option at this time. There are some features to determine the console Internet Protocol address and use that information to collect network connections by interrogating the associated router.

In addition to the hard drive options that are available with the retail console and for separate purchase, there is also a custom memory card available. The memory card is available in several different storage capacities including:

- 64 MB
- 256 MB
- 512 MB

Figure 2.4 provides an image of the retail package of one of these memory cards. This is something that investigators and responders need to look for, when a console is believed to be involved in a case or is part of an investigation.

The console requires a memory device, either a hard drive or a memory card, before the end user can connect to the XBOX Live service and engage in cooperative play. It is this connection to the XBOX Live network that has been a major selling point to the end user and has drawn the attention of the high-tech investigations community.

Table 2.2 provides a good overview of the current and past XBOX 360 consoles with their associated storage capabilities.

TECHNICAL SPECIFICATIONS

The XBOX 360 has been described as an application-specific computer. What is meant by this is that the machine is designed to run one specific type of application: video games. However, this is somewhat of a misconception because the console was designed to incorporate the network component to allow for cooperative play since

FIGURE 2.4

The custom memory cartridge available for the XBOX 360. It is available from www.amazon.com/Xbox-360-Memory-Unit-512MB/dp/B000062OS6.

Table 2.2 An Overview of the Various Available Models of XBOX 360

Model	Drive Storage Capacity	Release Date
Slim	250GB HDD/4GB internal	June 2010
Elite	250GB HDD/120GB HDD	October 2009/April 2007
Arcade	512 MB/256 MB Onboard	June 2009/December 2008
Pro	60GB HDD/20GB HDD	September 2008/November 2005
Core	None	November 2005

Ref: http://gamrconnect.vgchartz.com/thread.php?id=56521

its inception. Although the technical specifications read like computer specifications, it is important to include them so that the high-tech investigator or forensic examiner may get a better understanding about why the system is important to such an examination. The machine is built for network communication and to transfer data – a lot of data – very fast. These characteristics make the XBOX 360 an ideal machine for a server. This hardware, if the security mechanisms can be overcome, would provide for a very inexpensive server platform. There is a large community that is attempting to accomplish this task and, in fact, there are applications available from this community that will be discussed or addressed in later chapters.

BACKGROUND

The original XBOX console was reverse engineered by Andrew "Bunnie" Huang and his research allowed the home brew community to eventually run Linux on the console.

Figure 2.5 provides the technical specifications for the XBOX 360 gaming console. The information reads like a description of a high-end PC.

The inputs and outputs shown in Figure 2.6 for the console provide some interesting information. Of particular interest is the inclusion of the memory unit ports; these ports are the custom memory cartridges mentioned earlier. There is still support for these cards even though their capacity does not support a great deal of data. The ports are located at the front of the machine and covered with a spring loaded flap. The console's CPU is PowerPC based and its specifications are detailed in Figure 2.7.

The PowerPC-based CPU provides some guidance on deciphering the file system and the operating system. The CPU has undergone several iterations since the XBOX 360 was released. Table 2.2 provides an evolution of the different CPUs that have been or are currently available.

The console has an advanced ATI Graphics chip that has evolved in parallel with the CPU to meet the demands of the market. The evolution of the ATI chip was driven by the need for a more realistic game simulation engine. An examination of the ATI Graphics chip provides some details as to the extreme bandwidth the console was designed for.

On a purely hardware level, ATI's XBOX 360 Graphics Processing Unit (codenamed Xenos) is quite interesting. The part itself is made up of two physically distinct silicon integrated circuits (IC). One IC is the GPU itself, which houses all the shader hardware and most of the processing power. The second IC (which ATI refers to as

Xbox 360 Technical Specifications

General

General Power requirements:	Refer to ratings plate on power supply unit
Dimensions (approximate):	310 x 80 x 260 mm (12 x 3 x 10 in)
Mass (approximate):	3.5 kg (7.7 lb)
Operating temperature:	5°C to 35°C (41°F to 95°F)

FIGURE 2.5

General power and physical specifications for the XBOX 360.

Inputs/Outputs

- Memory Unit ports (2)
- USB ports (2 front, 1 rear)
- Ethernet port
- AV port
- HDMI port
- DC IN power port
- IR remote receiver
- Wireless: 2.4 GHz Digital Spread Spectrum (up to four players)

FIGURE 2.6

Input and output for the XBOX 360 console.

Custom PowerPC-based CPU

- 3 symmetrical cores running at 3.2 GHz
- 2 hardware threads per core (6 hardware threads total)
- 1 MB L2 cache
- 2.7GHz Front Side Bus

FIGURE 2.7

PowerPC-based CPU specifications.

Custom ATI Graphics

- Processor 500 MHz clock speed
- 10 MB embedded DRAM (256GB/s)
- 48-way parallel floating-point dynamically scheduled shader pipelines
- Unified shader architecture

FIGURE 2.8

Custom ATI graphics.

the "daughter die") is a 10MB block of embedded DRAM (eDRAM) combined with the hardware necessary for z and stencil operations, color and alpha processing, and antialiasing. This daughter die is connected to the GPU proper through a 32GBps interconnect. Data sent over this bus will be compressed, so usable bandwidth will be higher than 32GBps. Inside the daughter die, between the processing hardware and the eDRAM itself, bandwidth is 256GBps [2]. Figure 2.8 provides the technical specifications of the ATI Graphics card.

HARD DRIVE DISASSEMBLY

We have already discussed the different hard drive capacities that are available with the XBOX 360 console. To provide a brief review, the console is available with a "married" 20, 120, or 250GB hard drive. These hard drives appear to be from a limited number of manufacturers, such as Samsung and Western Digital. Deciphering some of the information on the drives and, in fact, getting access to certain portions of the drive itself are problematic; however, research indicates that the firmware of the drive is altered in some fashion to further add a level of complexity. If the data on the console are altered to any great extent in an attempt to inject code or otherwise change the information that is permitted, the XBOX Live server security checks may locate the alteration and ban the console from network play.

Drive disassembly is a straightforward process. The drives are all standard Serial Advanced Technology Attachment, or SATA laptop 2.5-in. hard drives that are housed in their own custom cases complete with custom interfaces to the console.

Because of the custom interface, it is necessary to remove the drive from the housing. This is a matter of eight screws that need to be removed before the drive can be extracted for forensic imaging.

Figures 2.9 through 2.15 will provide more guidance on this process.

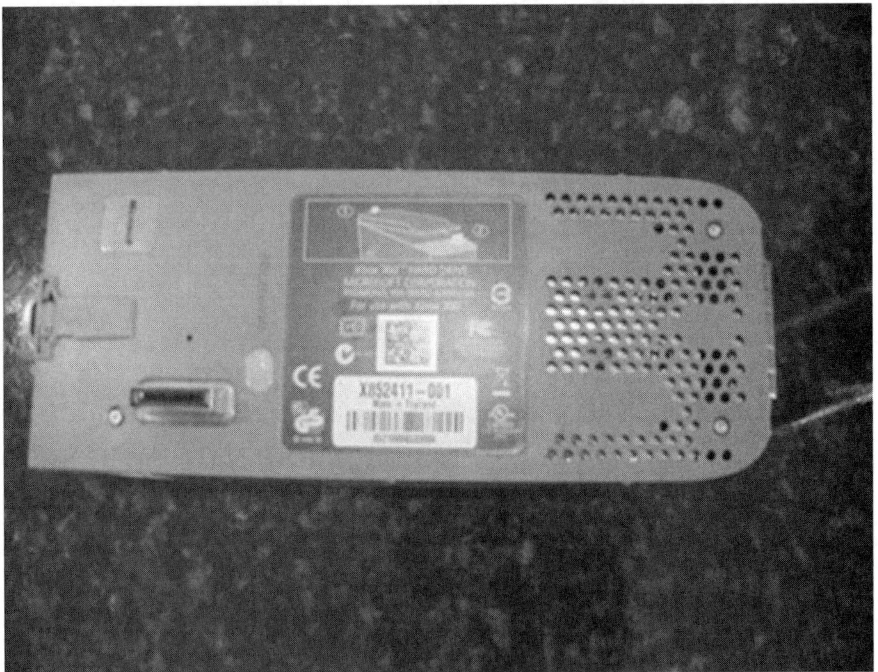

FIGURE 2.9

The underside of the hard drive case showing the custom interface.

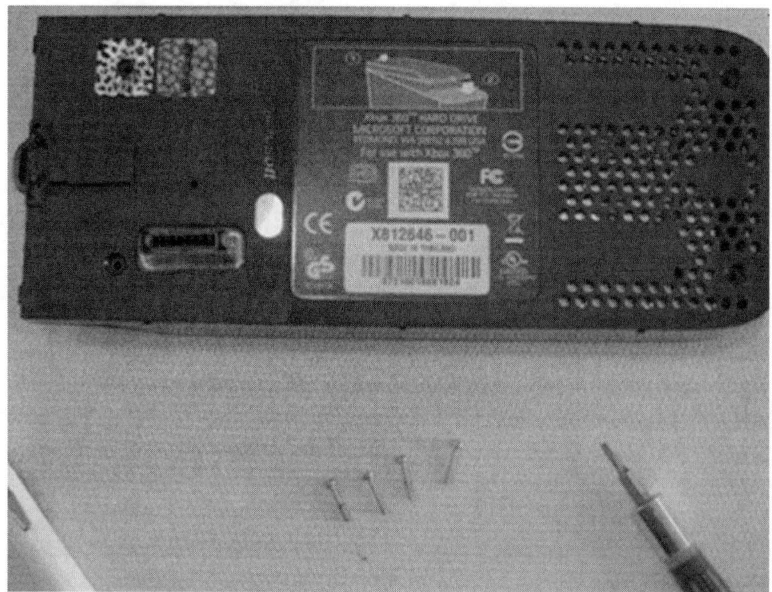

FIGURE 2.10

Image depicting the four case-housing screws removed and the Microsoft sticker relocated.

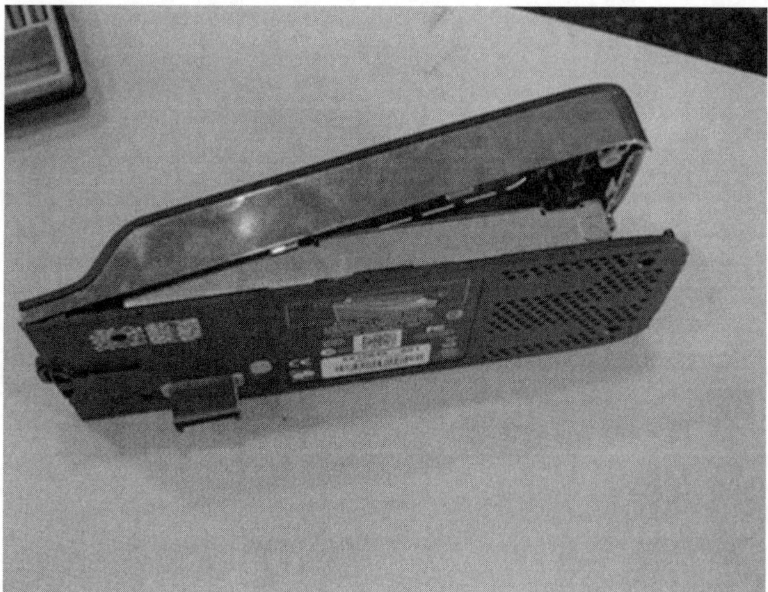

FIGURE 2.11

The outer housing being disconnected from the inner housing.

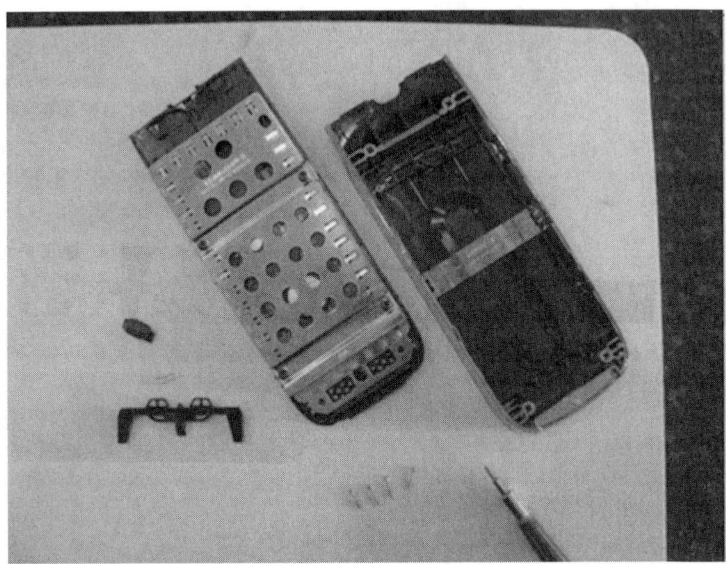

FIGURE 2.12

Showing the exterior housing removed and the spring loaded latch components for connection to the console.

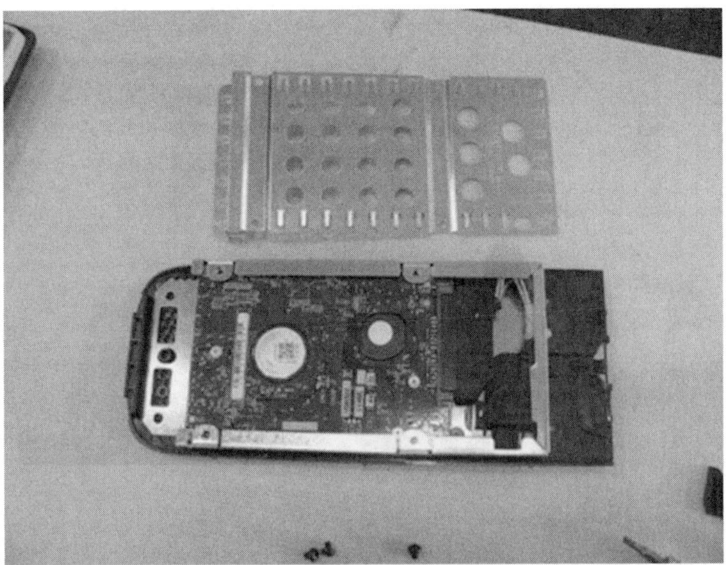

FIGURE 2.13

Image of the interior housing removed to reveal the SATA drive and the custom SATA interface.

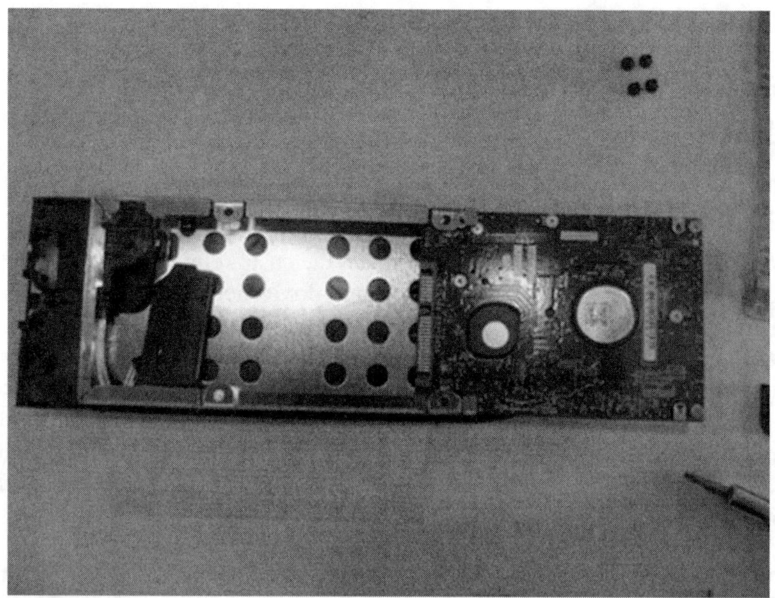

FIGURE 2.14

The disconnected drive being removed from the internal housing.

FIGURE 2.15

The isolated drive along with the custom interface removed from the hard drive case.

The hard drive for the XBOX 360 comes in its own customized case. If the console was purchased with the hard drive married to it, then the retail package will have the drive already attached to the console. However, there is also a retail package (an individual hard drive) for users who wished to have more storage or upgrade from the drive capacity they originally purchased.

Once the drive has been identified and obtained for imaging, it is a matter of removing one sticker and eight screws to isolate the drive.

Step 1: Flip the custom drive case so that the custom interface is facing up. Figure 2.9 provides an image of the hard drive enclosure with the custom interface facing the end user.
Step 2: Remove the Microsoft sticker to reveal the fourth screw that secures the case around the SATA drive. Remove these screws to begin the process of drive extraction. It should be noted that standard precautions for dealing with digital hard drives must be adhered to, in order to limit the potential for elector static damage. Figure 2.10 provides a snapshot of the screws and the case after the removal of the screws.

> **TIP**
>
> Removal of the Microsoft sticker and the removal of the drive from the case may violate the warranty. Precautions should be taken to limit any damage to the drive.

Step 3: This step is the removal of the case to reveal the inner housing. As with many electronics, the Microsoft XBOX 360 hard drive is a collection of plastic, metal, and integrated circuits, so it is imperative that the examiner be careful when removing the housing. In the front of the exterior housing, the end closest to the custom interface, there is a lip that the examiner needs to be cautious of; if the removal of the housing is forced, the plastic lip area may be damaged. Figure 2.11 provides an image, depicting the case being disassembled.
Step 4: In this step, the inner housing is removed, another four screws are removed, and the internal SATA drive is exposed to enable removal. Once the screws are removed, the drive is still connected to the custom interface to enable connection to the console. The drive is easily disconnected from this interface and removed by sliding the drive out the back of the interior housing. Figures 2.12 through 2.15 provide images depicting the drive disassembly and removal from the custom case.

Now that the drive is removed, it is ready to be imaged in accordance with standard forensic practices. The drive will be connected to several Wiebetech write blockers to ensure that no operating system data is being written to the target drive.

During the initial research, back in 2006, we had a 20GB hard drive to work with and used various forensic software tools to image the drive. The current research is no different in the procedures that are going to be utilized for imaging and artifact analysis. The details will be laid out in later chapters.

SUMMARY

Within this chapter, we presented the various retail packages that have been and are currently available for the XBOX 360 gaming console. Storage for the console consists of either a hard drive in its own custom enclosure or a custom memory cartridge. Other external media can also be connected through the three USB 2.0 ports that are integrated into the console. Removing the hard drive from the custom enclosure is a simple enough task, which is accomplished by the removal of eight screws. Once removed from the custom case, the drive can be forensically imaged just as any other piece of digital media.

References

[1] http://squidoo.com/what-causes-red-ring-of-death (accessed 23.08.10).

[2] Microsoft's XBOX 360, Sony's PS3 – A hardware discussion – AnandTech :: Your source for hardware analysis and news. Home – AnandTech :: Your Source for Hardware Analysis and News. N.p., n.d. www.anandtech.com/show/1719/7 (accessed 23.08.10).

CHAPTER

XBOX Live

3

INFORMATION IN THIS CHAPTER

- Introduction
- What is XBOX Live?
- Creating an XBOX Live account
- Getting connected

INTRODUCTION

XBOX Live is a two-prong Web portal that provides a portal for online gamers to connect, socialize, and interact with one another over the game console. It is two pronged in that there is a Web portal as well as the portal that the gamers use to connect using their XBOX 360 console. These two vectors to access the portal work together to notify the end user that there are messages to be read, listened to, or otherwise provide a reason why the end user needs to log onto the portal. Most messages, such as e-mails, can only be reviewed through the console interface and the end user will be prompted through an e-mail to his or her associated Gamertag, to log into his or her console through the Web portal under these circumstances. Games that are sold for use in the console are enabled to connect to the network for cooperative or competitive game play. In addition to console games, there are several games that are provided for use on Windows-based PCs that allow gamers on computers and consoles to experience the network cooperative or competitive game play.

To illustrate the need for an examiner or investigator to be concerned about this console and network game play, we have already addressed some of the criminal activity that has occurred using the XBOX Live service as the network communication vector. It is always nice to have facts to back up assertions, and while these news clips were provided regarding the criminal activity, it is not known how wide spread the use of the paid service is on XBOX Live and just how many of these consoles are in circulation. A news article from January 6, 2009 on Gamespot News provides

FIGURE 3.1

The initial page for XBOX Live.

some very interesting statistics on the number of XBOX 360 consoles that have been sold. According to the report, there are 28 million XBOX 360 consoles that have been sold, with an estimated 17 million users of the XBOX Live service [1]. This statistics shows that although there are many consoles sold, not every console will be connected to the Live service. With this many users and this many consoles in the "wild," it is only a matter of time before the devices and their functionality combine to add to the list of devices that forensic examiners must contend with.

The Web portal can be found at www.XBOX.com/en-US/live/ and is the starting point to connect the console to the XBOX Live portal. Figure 3.1 provides a screenshot of the XBOX Live portal home page.

WHAT IS XBOX LIVE?

There is no better description of what the XBOX Live service is than the one that is provided by the makers of the console. Figure 3.2 provides the description of the service as it is provided on the Web portal.

In short, XBOX Live can be considered an online portal that can be accessed through Windows-based PCs, original XBOX consoles, XBOX 360 consoles, and research indicates that Microsoft has plans to expand access to include Windows-based smart phones. This new initiative is called Live Anywhere and was introduced in late 2006. The company has long-term plans for the development of Live Anywhere. "Gates was on hand to introduce XBOX Live Anywhere, the company's

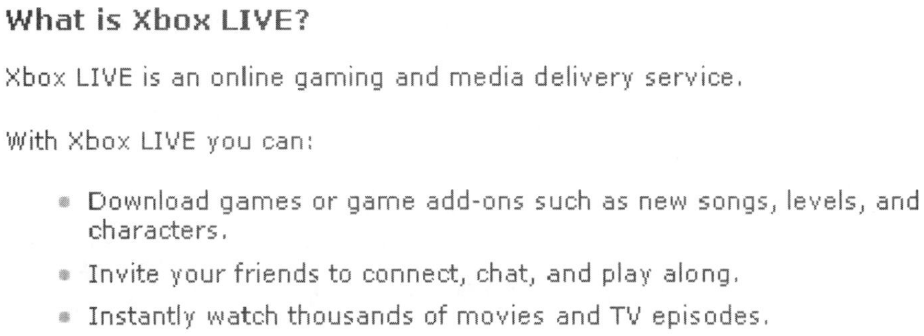

What is Xbox LIVE?

Xbox LIVE is an online gaming and media delivery service.

With Xbox LIVE you can:

- Download games or game add-ons such as new songs, levels, and characters.
- Invite your friends to connect, chat, and play along.
- Instantly watch thousands of movies and TV episodes.

FIGURE 3.2

XBOX Live description from the XBOX Live portal.

new initiative to unite your gaming opportunities across multiple platforms. XBOX Live Anywhere, according to Gates, will be cross-platform, regardless of the device you're using" [2].

The point is that gaming is no longer a pastime simply for the socially inadequate (no offense to the gamer world). Gaming has evolved with each generation, and it is now perfectly acceptable for someone, in his or her 20s who is waiting in line at a bank, doctor's office, restaurant, or amusement park to be playing a video game of some sort to pass the time.

From the perspective of a high-tech crime investigator, this interconnectivity provides a wealth of information for network connections, personal contacts, e-mail lists, and digital artifacts that may not make a case, but may provide the necessary vector or initial contact that may be the missing link or missing puzzle piece to an investigation or examination.

TIP

Gaming consoles of today are being explored by many organizations for their social networking capabilities. In addition, the virtual reality world of gaming has evolved into a recruitment tool for several organizations. Several organizations, such as the United States Army, have developed games to assist in their recruiting efforts.

The XBOX Live portal provides users with at least four networking features. Once the account is created, users are able to take advantage of these features. However, it must be mentioned that XBOX Live is available in two formats, a free service and a commercial service, referred to as Silver and Gold memberships, respectively. The Silver membership is currently free with the purchase of a console and provides several features such as game downloads and voice and text chatting. In order to get the most out of the portal, meaning all the functionality that is offered, a user will have to pay for a Gold account. XBOX Live requires a user to pay for a subscription, although only a modest $49.99 fee, which includes all game map updates and other downloadable material that is on a paid-for basis with other game console portals. Figure 3.3 provides a synopsis of the differences between the Silver and Gold memberships.

Another perspective of the services offered for each of the memberships is provided in Table 3.1. Although this is not a comprehensive list of all the services, it does provide an overview of some of the major network functions.

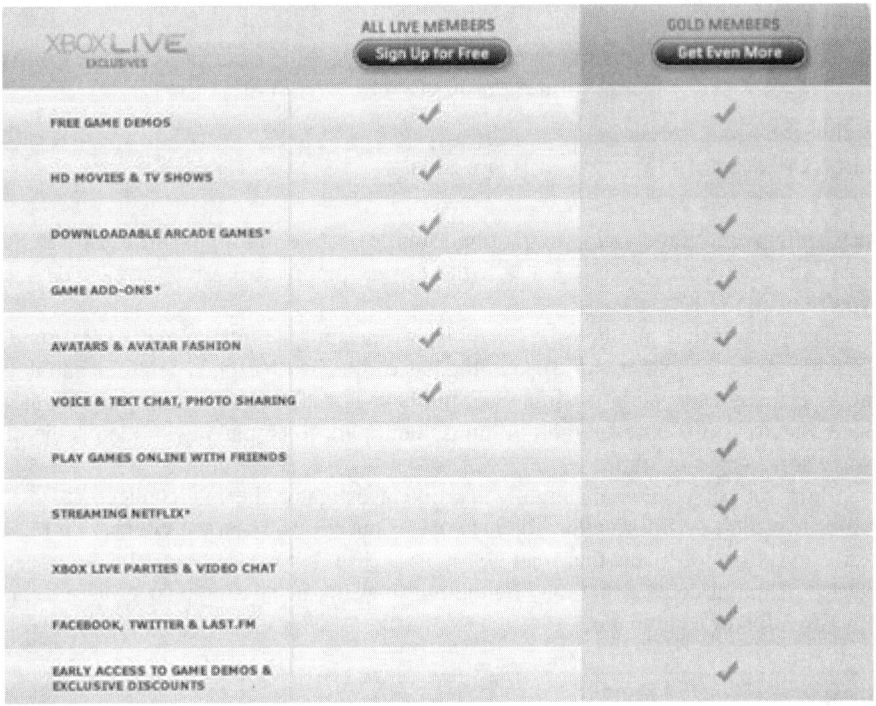

XBOX LIVE EXCLUSIVES	ALL LIVE MEMBERS Sign Up for Free	GOLD MEMBERS Get Even More
FREE GAME DEMOS	✓	✓
HD MOVIES & TV SHOWS	✓	✓
DOWNLOADABLE ARCADE GAMES*	✓	✓
GAME ADD-ONS*	✓	✓
AVATARS & AVATAR FASHION	✓	✓
VOICE & TEXT CHAT, PHOTO SHARING	✓	✓
PLAY GAMES ONLINE WITH FRIENDS		✓
STREAMING NETFLIX*		✓
XBOX LIVE PARTIES & VIDEO CHAT		✓
FACEBOOK, TWITTER & LAST.FM		✓
EARLY ACCESS TO GAME DEMOS & EXCLUSIVE DISCOUNTS		✓

FIGURE 3.3

Comparison between Silver and Gold memberships.

Table 3.1 Comparison of Some of the Functions Available with the Silver and Gold Memberships

Functionality	Silver	Gold
Voice chat	Yes	Yes
Video chat	No	Yes
Downloadable content	Yes	Yes
Multiplayer gaming	No	Yes
Netflix	No	Yes
Facebook	No	Yes
Twitter	No	Yes

CREATING AN XBOX LIVE ACCOUNT AND GETTING CONNECTED

To get connected to the portal, a user must first sign up for the service, similar to creating a Web-based e-mail account. This initial process is done through the Web portal, not on the console, and simply involves following the steps provided through the process. All that is required is an e-mail account. This e-mail account is linked to the XBOX Live account for records tracking, which can be used for investigations and information requests that can be sent to Microsoft for logs pertaining to the account. Research indicates that the original IP address at the date and time of the initial sign up are archived by Microsoft.

TIP

In order to have Microsoft pull its logs for investigations of this nature, there is a fee that accompanies the request. Although Microsoft is helpful to the law enforcement community, they need to recoup the costs associated with the logging and retrieval of information. Contacting Microsoft for these records can be accomplished by calling, e-mailing, or faxing the request. The contact information is located in several places; one location is at www.search.org/programs/hightech/isp/default.asp#189, and it can also be found under Microsoft or Hotmail searches.

The XBOX Live service has undergone changes throughout its life span. The service itself was released in conjunction with the original XBOX console back in November of 2002. Since that time, the service has evolved to include functionality updates and aesthetic upgrades to provide the user with a more social look and feel. Figure 3.4

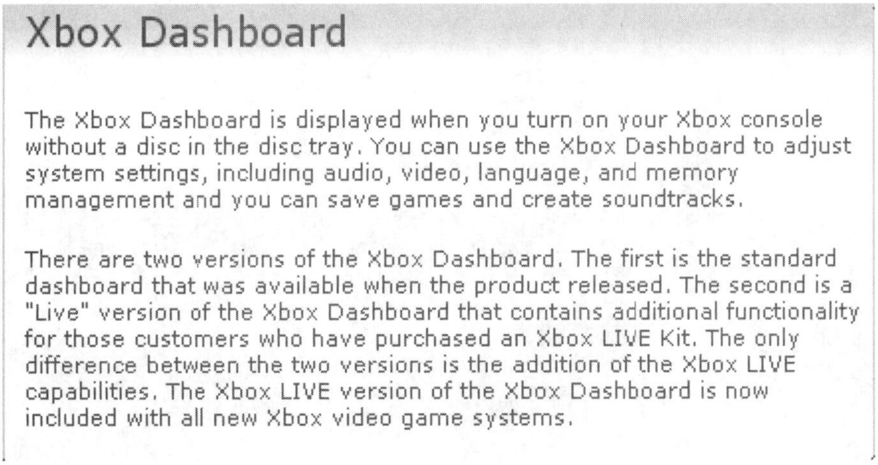

Xbox Dashboard

The Xbox Dashboard is displayed when you turn on your Xbox console without a disc in the disc tray. You can use the Xbox Dashboard to adjust system settings, including audio, video, language, and memory management and you can save games and create soundtracks.

There are two versions of the Xbox Dashboard. The first is the standard dashboard that was available when the product released. The second is a "Live" version of the Xbox Dashboard that contains additional functionality for those customers who have purchased an Xbox LIVE Kit. The only difference between the two versions is the addition of the Xbox LIVE capabilities. The Xbox LIVE version of the Xbox Dashboard is now included with all new Xbox video game systems.

FIGURE 3.4

XBOX Dashboard descriptions [3].

provides a description of the Dashboard. The current user interface for the XBOX Live console is called the dashboard. The dashboard is available in two versions: the original version, which was supported with the original XBOX console that provided the ability to adjust system settings, and the new Live version of the dashboard provides, which support for the advanced functions of the Live service already mentioned. According to Microsoft, the new Live version of the dashboard is included on all new XBOX 360 consoles.

Social networking has been a wealth of information for high-tech investigators for many years now, and the ability of the XBOX 360 console to connect to these sites through the XBOX Live service was realized in November 2009 with an XBOX Live update. Although not all the features of a regular Web interface are provided with the XBOX Live application, the basic functionality is still there, leaving artifacts for the examiner to contend with.

There are three social networking applications that are available for the XBOX 360, two of which have been known to the high-tech investigations and examination community for years: Twitter and Facebook. The third social networking application is the XBOX Live service itself. Like their desktop counterparts, the Twitter and Facebook applications for XBOX Live attempt to create more network linkage over this hardware device by providing search features so that the gamer or end user can search to find his or her "friends" who are also on XBOX Live. Figure 3.5 provides a screenshot of the Twitter application as it is used over the XBOX Live service. Figure 3.6 provides a screenshot of the Facebook application as seen on XBOX Live.

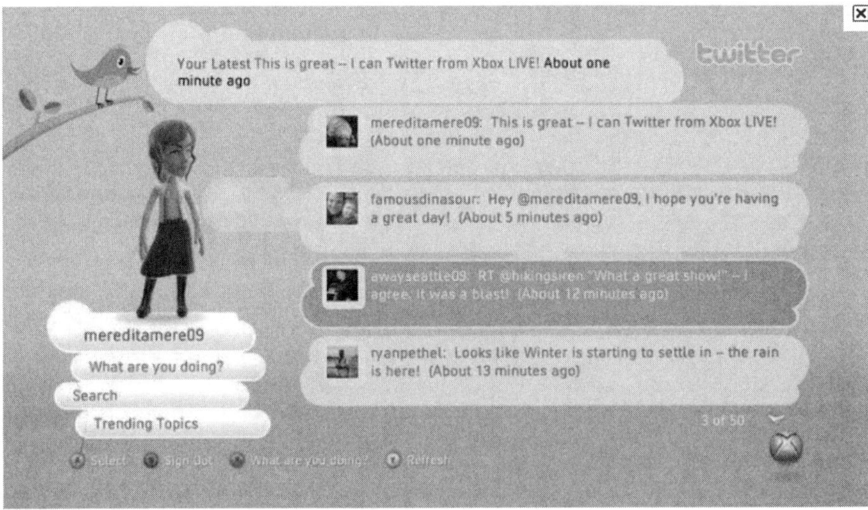

FIGURE 3.5

Depiction of the Twitter application for the XBOX 360 console [4].

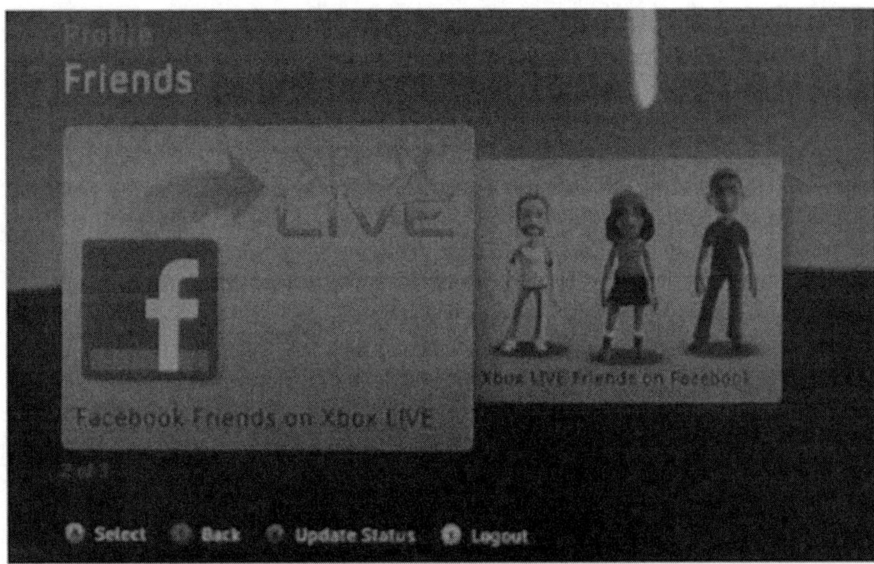

The friend linker tool can help you figure out which of your Facebook friends has an Xbox Live account and vice versa. (Credit: Josh Lowensohn/CNET)

FIGURE 3.6

Depiction of the Facebook application for the XBOX 360 console [5].

CREATING A LIVE ACCOUNT

As of publication of this writing, the first step to creating a Live account is to navigate to the Web portal. The portal is available at www.XBOXlive.com, and the creation of an account is akin to creating a Web-based e-mail account. Once an account is created, the user is then prompted to configure his or her console and log on with the XBOX Live account that is created through this portal. This prompting is done through a confirmation e-mail that is sent to the entered e-mail account to confirm registration.

The main page, depicted in Figure 3.7, provides more information as to the functionality, displaying these features in call-out bubbles:

- Free game demos
- Social networking
- Customized avatars
- Streaming HD movies

The first step in the process of creating an account is to select **Experience** XBOX Live from the main page in Figure 3.7. Once selected, the process begins by prompting the user for some information, including date of birth, region, and an e-mail account. Figure 3.8 provides a screenshot of this Web page for sign up.

FIGURE 3.7

XBOX Live main Web page.

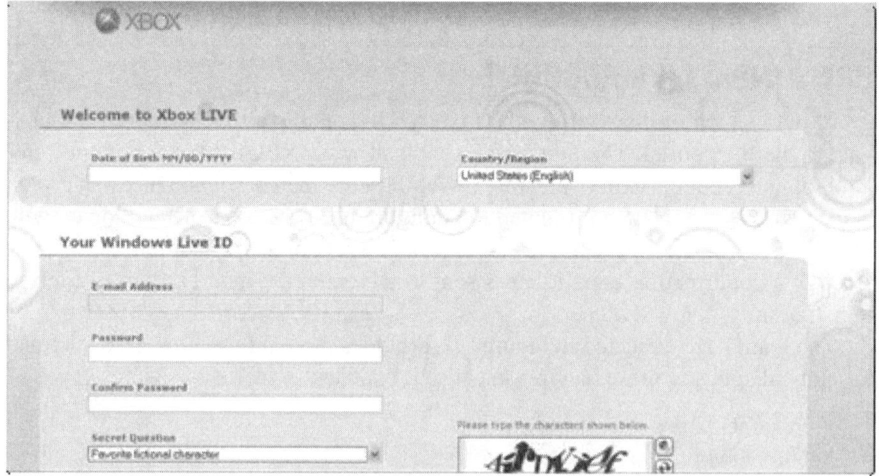

FIGURE 3.8

Initial sign-up page of XBOX Live account.

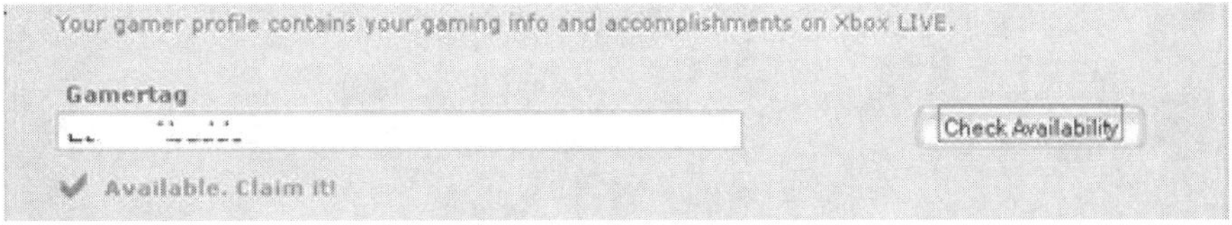

FIGURE 3.9

The Gamertag that was created while writing this book.

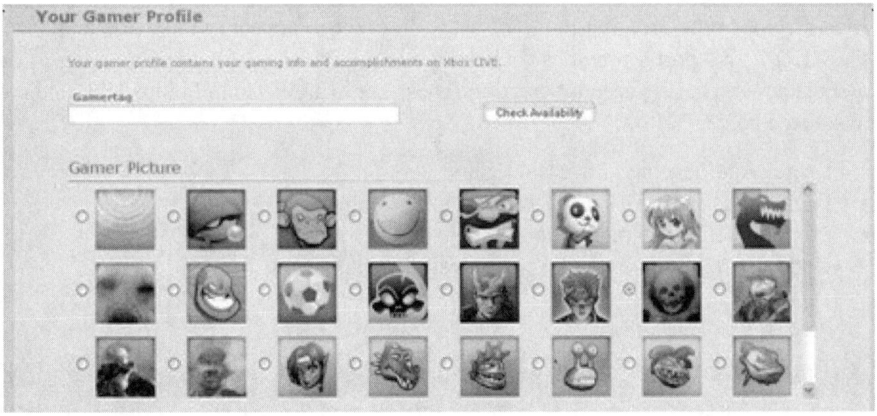

FIGURE 3.10

Default avatar selection.

The next step in the process is to determine the Gamertag that will be used. This Gamertag is a unique identifier, similar to an e-mail address that is created by the user and is tied back to their e-mail, as well as being the log-in credentials that will be used on the console.

Because of the number of users, Microsoft XBOX Live account creation prompts the user to determine if the selected Gamertag is available for use (See Figure 3.9).

Personalization of the Gamertag is the next step in account creation. Each Gamertag has an avatar associated with it, that is, a picture representing the gamer. There are several default images that can be used for this avatar. As the user interacts with the portal and other users more, he or she may earn enough points on the XBOX Live portal to further customize his or her avatar. Figure 3.10 provides an overview of some of the default avatar images available to the end user.

Because of the nature of the XBOX Live portal, there will be a wide range of users that the portal will appeal to. In fact, it would only make for a good business decision for Microsoft if they attempted to market the XBOX 360 console and the XBOX

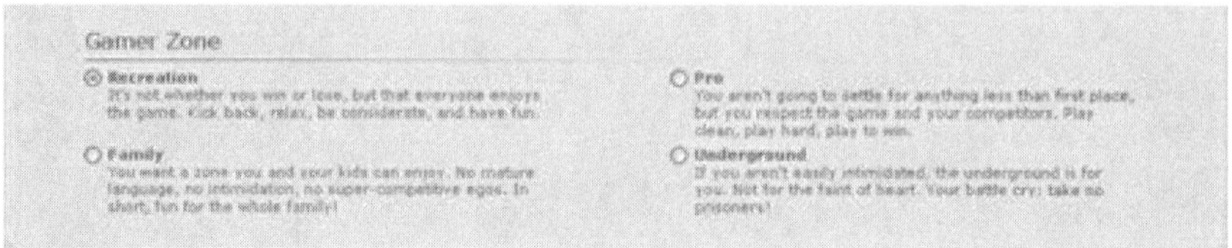

FIGURE 3.11

Gamer zone selection.

Live service to the broadest range of users. In order to appeal to this wide audience, the XBOX Live portal provides four distinct gamer "zones" for the Gamertag to be associated with during account creation. These zones are listed in Figure 3.11, and are also listed here as follows:

- Recreation: designed for casual game play
- Family: designed for family fun and entertainment
- Pro: competitive gamer action
- Underground: gaming at the next level of competition

SUMMARY

This chapter introduced the concept of the XBOX Live portal and its associated user-interaction capabilities. The gamer needs to create an account through the normal Web interface using a standard Web browser. The process for Gamertag creation is straightforward, and once it is completed and the information is confirmed, the end user has opened the door to a gaming social network. The functionality of the console, once an XBOX Live account has been created, is where the interests of a high-tech investigator or forensic examiner should be piqued. The functionality of the console from this point forward is akin to a networked computer, complete with social networking capabilities, streaming media, voice and text chat, and e-mail and video.

References

[1] Thorsen, Tor. 28 million XBOX 360s sold, 17 million on XBOX Live – news at GameSpot. GameSpot is Your Go-To Source for Video Game News, Reviews, and Entertainment. N.p., n.d. www.gamespot.com/news/6202733.html (accessed 23.08.10).

[2] Today @ PC World Gates Intros XBOX Live Anywhere at E3. PC World. N.p., n.d. http://blogs.pcworld.com/staffblog/archives/002023.html (accessed 23.08.10).

[3] Description of the original XBOX console Dashboard. XBOX NXE Hardware, XBOX LIVE, Games & Media Support | XBOX Support. N.p., n.d. http://support.XBOX.com/support/en/us/XBOX/kb.aspx?ID=817028&lcid=1033&category (accessed 10.10.10).

[4] http://erictric.com/2009/11/12/zune-video-store-facebook-twitter-and-more-coming-to-xbox-live-on-november-17th/ (accessed 19.11.10).

[5] http://news.cnet.com/8301-27076_3-10375398-248.html (accessed 10.08.10).

CHAPTER

Configuration of the Console

4

INFORMATION IN THIS CHAPTER

- Introduction
- Getting started
- Network configuration and Gamertag recovery
- Tour of the dashboard, profile creation and Gamertag configuration
- Connecting to XBOX Live
- Joining XBOX Live

INTRODUCTION

The network connectivity of the XBOX 360 presents some unique social networking features that may contain one piece of the investigative puzzle for a high-tech crime investigation. Any forensics examiner has no doubt come across social networking artifacts during the course of any dead box analysis. The XBOX 360 has the functionality to connect with many of the mainstream social networking applications that can be accessed through a normal Web browser. Accessing these sites through the applications on the XBOX 360 console is facilitated through the XBOX Live service. In order to connect to the XBOX Live service, the end user must complete his or her registration and link his or her previously created Gamertag to the console.

GETTING STARTED

It is necessary to detail all the aspects of this linkage to the XBOX Live service in order to get a better understanding of the process to assist in the determination of digital artifacts location. There are two locations in which a user can create an XBOX Live account: from the Web site mentioned earlier, or through the console interface. In either case, the finalization of the XBOX Live account, as well as the Gamertag, is completed on the XBOX 360 console.

It is this account creation that provides the end user of the console with access to the XBOX Live portal and the networking functionality that places artifacts on the storage media. It is this communication vector that provides interest for the digital media forensic professionals for investigations and examinations.

Account creation is a straightforward process. A user must first create an account on either the XBOX 360 console or on the XBOX Live Web portal. Once this account is created, the process must be completed using the console.

A user logs into the console and is immediately prompted to configure the machine for initial use. One of the first settings presented is the language configuration. Because of the widespread market that the console enjoys, there are several different languages that are supported. Figure 4.1 provides a screenshot of the language set up page.

The next setting to configure is the locale. As with the language support, there are many different markets for the console, and as such there are several different locales that can be configured. The locale is a setting that can be changed in the future if a user relocates. Changing the locale does not change the regional coding for games. Figure 4.2 provides a screenshot of the locale selection for the console.

The next settings are for the HDTV settings to optimize video output. Figure 4.3 provides an image of the selection options for HDTV.

Family settings are configuration settings that allow a parent to have more control over the types of games that the family will play, based on Entertainment Software Rating Board, (ESRB) ratings. However, the settings go beyond the types of

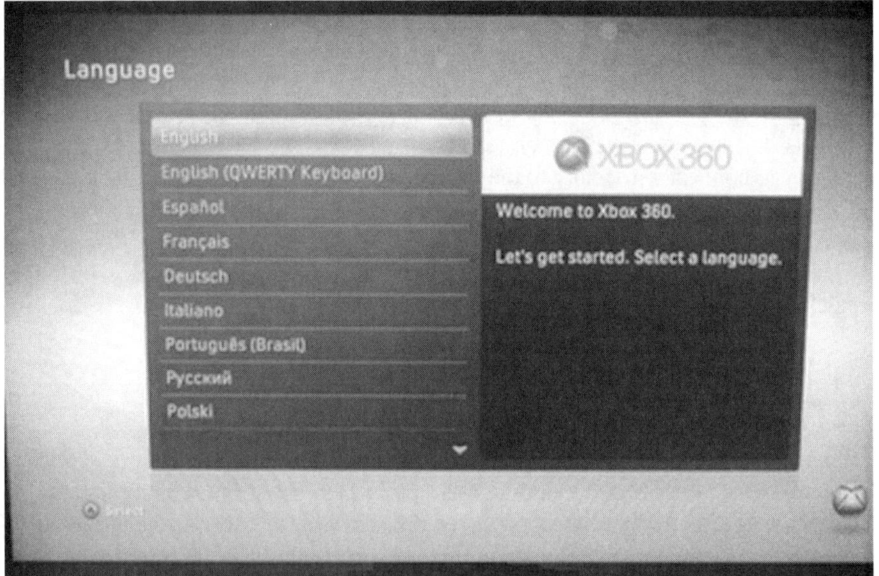

FIGURE 4.1

Configuring default language settings.

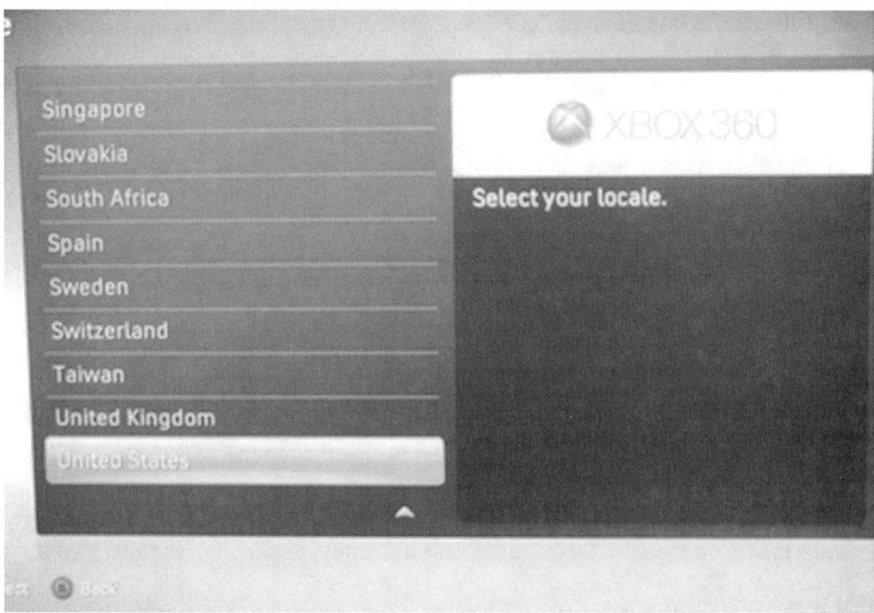

FIGURE 4.2

Setting the locale.

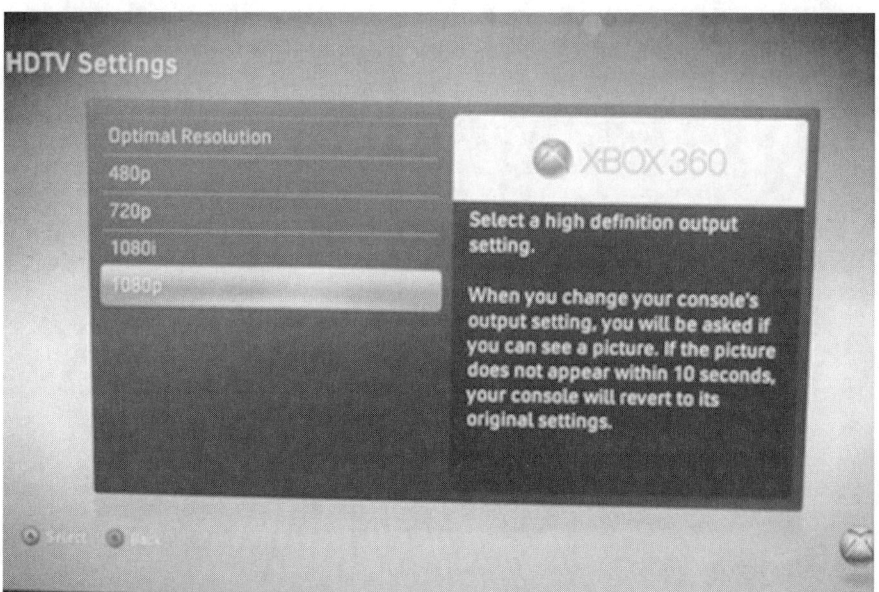

FIGURE 4.3

Configuring HDTV settings.

games that are allowed and include settings for a variety of features. The following setting descriptions were taken from www.xbox.com/en-US/support/familysettings/console/xbox360/consolefamilysettings.htm:

Game Ratings: Select the games you want your child to play, from EC (Early Childhood) to M (Mature)
Video Ratings: XBOX 360 recognizes ratings encoded into movies, TV shows, and other videos
Access to XBOX Live: Allow or prevent the console from connecting to XBOX Live
XBOX Live Membership Creation: Decide whether to allow or prevent the ability to create new XBOX Live memberships from the console
XBOX Live Marketplace Content: Decide whether you want to be able to see restricted content while browsing XBOX Live Marketplace. This setting also affects access to the Inside XBOX news feed from the XBOX Dashboard
Family Timer: Set the amount of time that the console can be used on a daily or weekly basis
Set Pass Code: Limit who can access or change the Family Settings on your console
Turn off Family Settings: No kids? No problem! Shut down Family Settings!

Following the video, locale, language, and family settings, the user is almost done with the initial console configuration. The next dialog box that appears informs the user that the initial console set up is complete and that the user is now ready to enjoy the "Ultimate in Games and Entertainment." Once all the setting have been configured, the Setup Complete dialog box appears, as depicted in Figure 4.4.

FIGURE 4.4

Completing the console configuration.

NETWORK CONFIGURATION AND GAMERTAG RECOVERY

Now that the initial console configuration is complete, a user could conceivably play games on the console the old-fashioned way, meaning that he or she could insert the game DVD and play the game in story mode where it is only a local game. However, the true power of the seventh generation game consoles, and the main reason that digital media analysts need to be concerned, is the network connectivity that is integrated.

For my research console, a wireless network adapter was connected before initial configuration of the console. Once the configuration was completed, the USB wireless adapter was automatically detected, and the console's operating system prompted for network configuration. Although with this particular setup, the console interface prompted for network configuration, there are manual steps that can be taken to connect the console to a network. Figure 4.5 provides an image of the dialog box that notifies of the wireless network adapter.

Configuration of the network settings for the console is, again, a straightforward process. As with most settings for the console, there is a wizard that walks the end user through these configuration settings. The network setup can consist

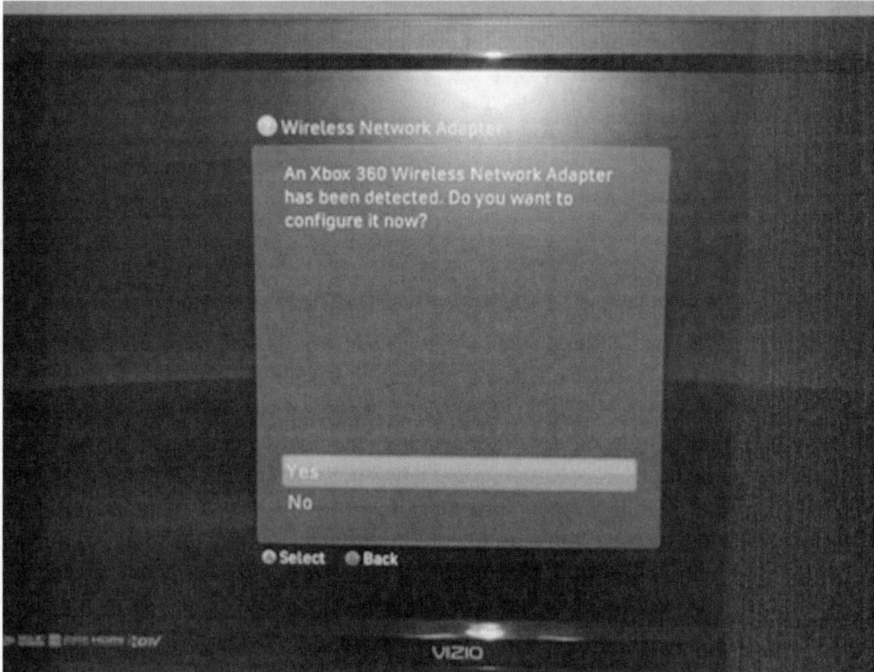

FIGURE 4.5

Screenshot of autodetection of the wireless USB.

of many different options, as the console is geared toward being connected to any of the following:

- The Internet
- XBOX Live
- Other consoles
- A Windows-based PC

With all these options for networking connections, the accompanying functionality again reiterates that this console is simply another network node that must be considered as a source of digital media for analysis.

The initial step in network connectivity is to select the LAN settings. This is the first step that is presented to the end user with the network configuration wizard.

As you can see from the diagram in Figure 4.6, there is a multistep process to test connectivity. The first step provides for a local connection diagnostic, then there is a connection attempt to the Internet, and finally, a connection is established with the XBOX Live service. To begin the process of configuring the network connections, the user needs to select the **Configure Network** option from the network settings configuration wizard. This selection will launch the basic configuration tab of the network configuration. In addition to the **Basic Settings** tab that is launched, there is

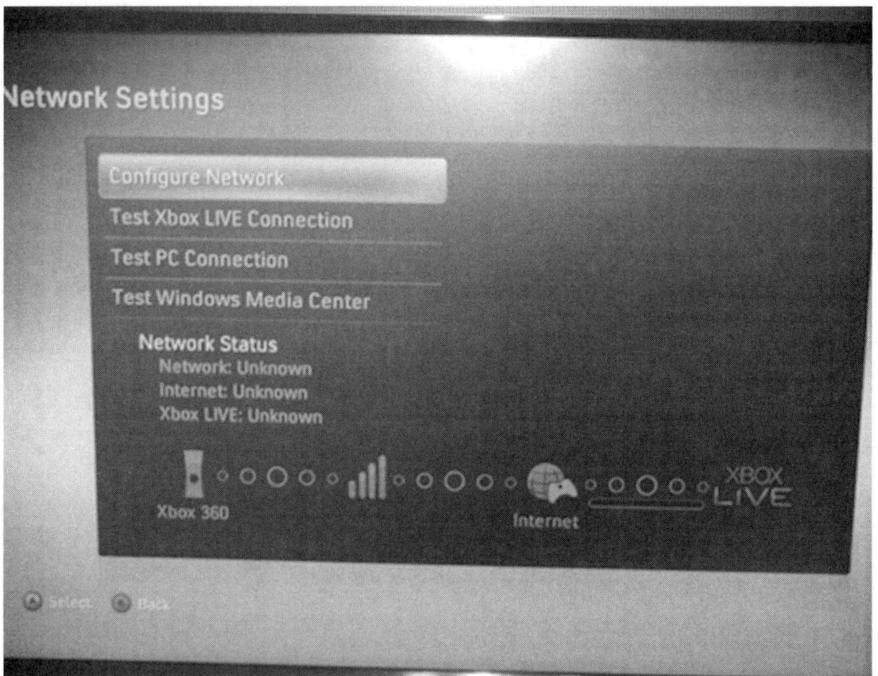

FIGURE 4.6

Network settings wizard.

an **Additional Settings** tab that provides more detailed options. Figure 4.7 provides a screenshot of the **Basic Settings** tab.

The green area on the screen, highlighted below, indicates the selection that is made by the end user. By moving the joysticks on the controller, the end user is able to navigate each page and make the necessary selections. In this specific case, because the wireless network adapter was connected, it was chosen to be configured in wireless mode. By highlighting this area in green and pressing the **X** button on the controller, we are presented with the next dialog box. The next screen prompts the end user to scan for wireless networks, similar to any other USB or integrated wireless NIC, Network Interface Card. Figure 4.8 provides a screenshot of this options window.

Once this option is selected, it is no different than scanning for wireless networks from a PC. The wireless networks that are within range and that are "visible" to the console will be displayed for the user to connect to. Selecting the appropriate network will then prompt the user to provide more information to finalize the connection, such as the network key. The next series of figures are screenshots depicting the list of available wireless networks near the XBOX 360, the on-screen keyboard that is presented for data input, as well as the network configuration screen from Figure 4.7, but with the information that was input to connect.

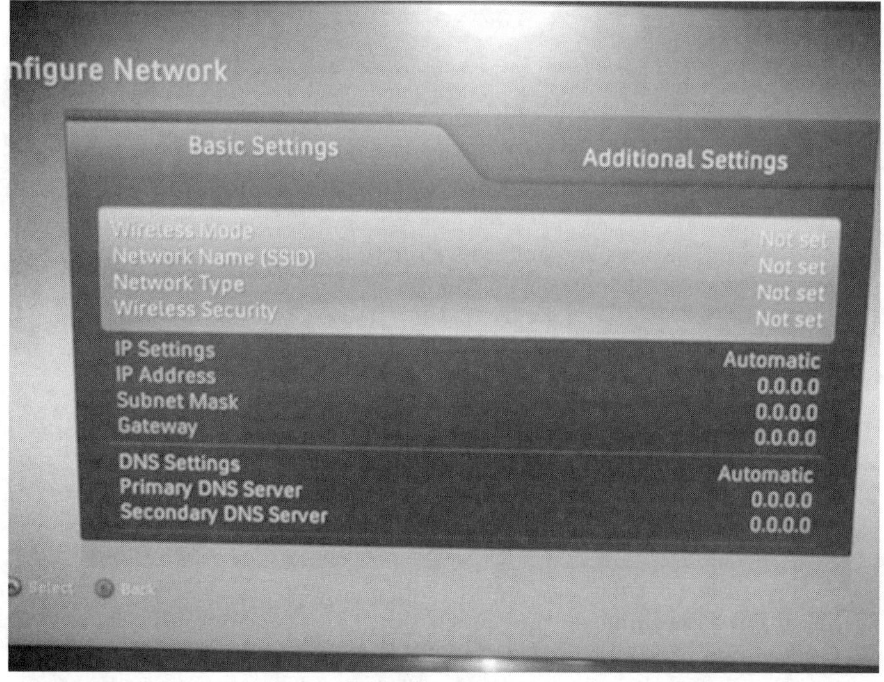

FIGURE 4.7

Basic network settings.

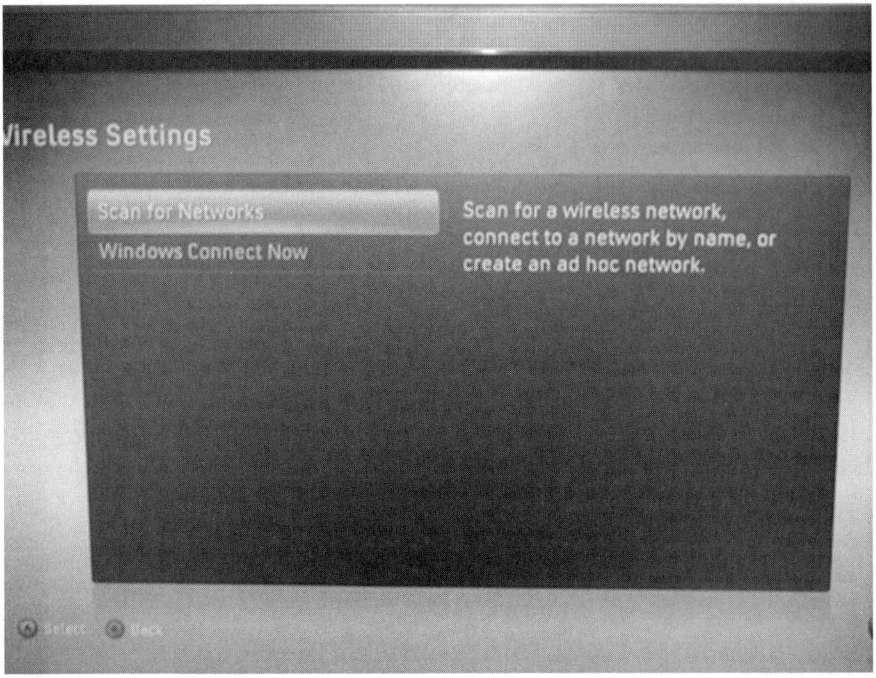

FIGURE 4.8

Scanning for wireless networks.

The **Windows Connect Now** feature allows a user to input their network settings from his or her Windows-networked PC. In order to use this feature, users would have to save their network settings from their Windows PC to removable media, such as a USB drive. The steps are outlined well from the support portal for the XBOX 360 and can be located at http://support.xbox.com/support/en/us/nxe/kb.aspx?ID=962966&lcid=1033&category=xboxlive.

The following steps are from the Web page on how to use this feature on the XBOX 360 console:

1. Select **System Settings**.
2. Select **Network Settings**.
3. Select **Configure Network**.
4. Select **Wireless Information**.
   Note: Make sure that your wireless adapter is connected to the rear of the console. Otherwise, this option will not be available.
5. **Select Windows Connect Now**.
6. Connect your USB flash drive to the USB port on your XBOX 360 console. When you receive a message that states "*Windows Connect Now Settings have been found*," select **OK** to apply your wireless settings.

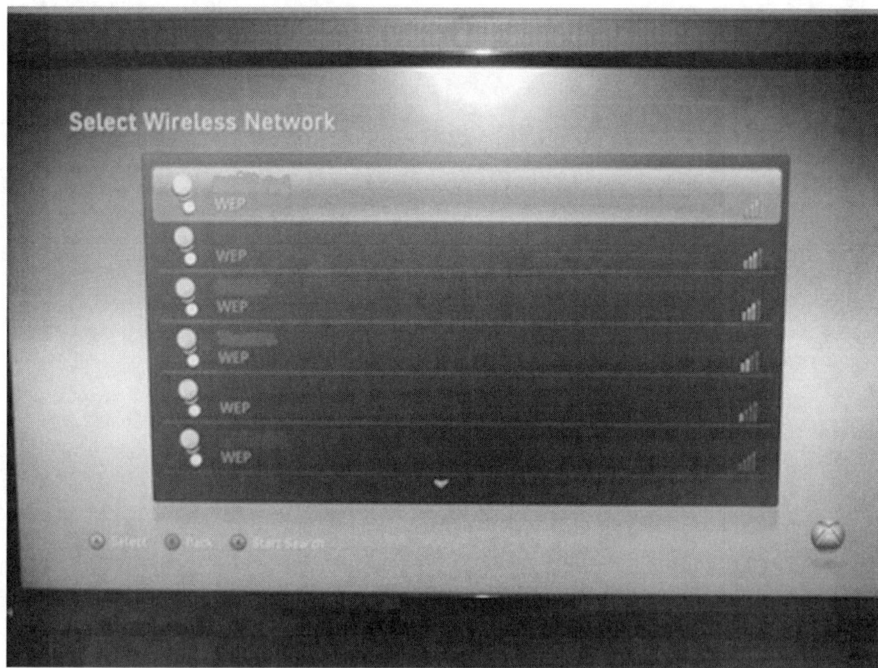

FIGURE 4.9

Wireless network list.

Figure 4.9 provides a screen capture of available wireless networks. Figures 4.10 and 4.11 also provide images of the next configuration steps that are required.

The **Additional Settings** tab provides more detailed configuration if required by the specifics of the LAN. Included in this tab are PPPoE, (Point to Point Protocol over Ethernet) as well as other advanced settings. Figure 4.12 shows the options that are available under this tab. Configuring them is no different than configuring the wireless network settings. Simply highlight the selection and press the **X** button on the controller and follow through as the wizard prompts for end user input.

After configuring the console with the appropriate connection settings and ensuring that the connections are active, the next step is to connect the console to the XBOX Live service. In doing so, there is a dialog box that appears informing the end user that there is "information that must be added to the console in order to connect to XBOX Live." The details of this information are not specified, and without a storage device connected, this initial connection attempt will fail. In the chapter on forensic analysis of the console, there will be an examination of the hard drive to determine what this information is. Figure 4.13 shows a screenshot of this dialog box.

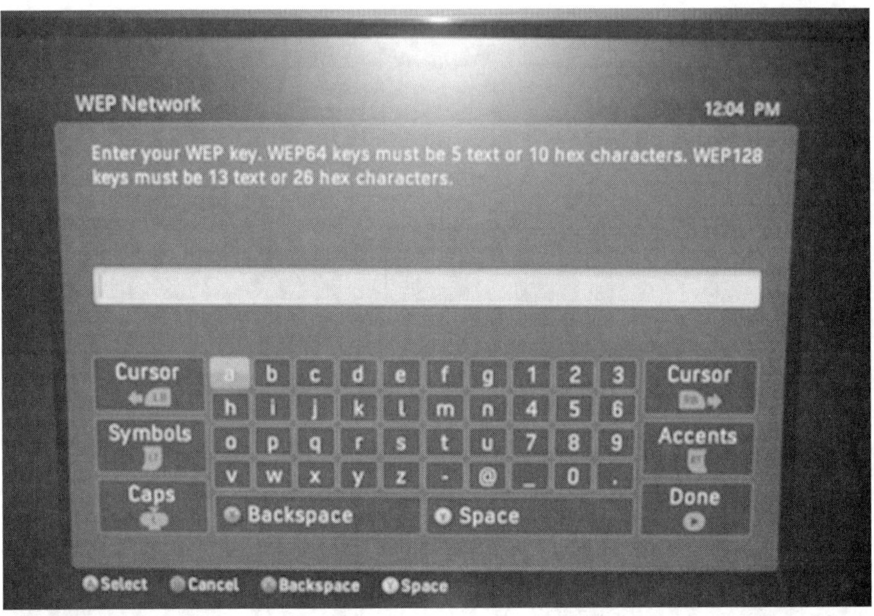

FIGURE 4.10

The on-screen keyboard for data entry.

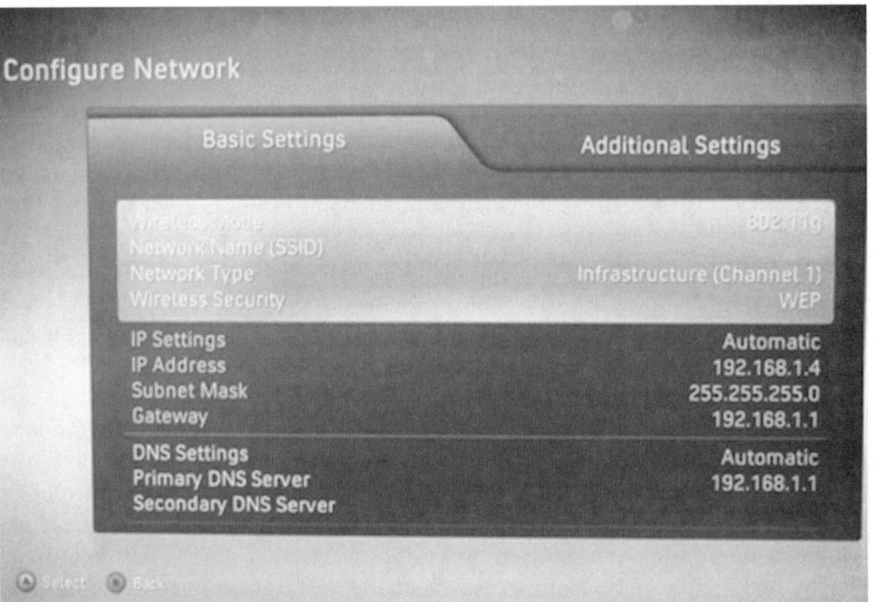

FIGURE 4.11

Depiction of the network settings with the specifics of the SSID and DNS IPs removed.

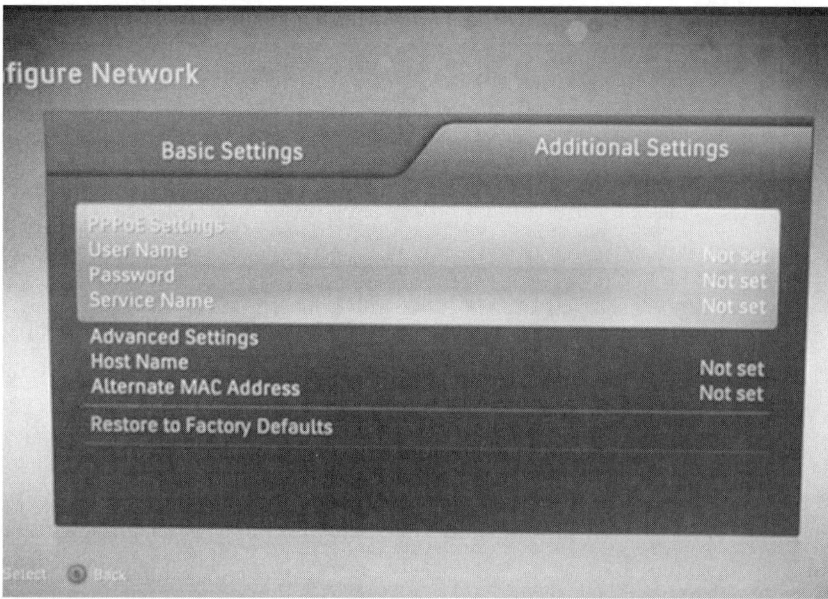

FIGURE 4.12

Advanced settings.

FIGURE 4.13

Initial connection to XBOX Live.

Once the end user accepts this addition of information to the console, the **Yes, continue** option in Figure 4.13, the next screen that appears is a diagram of the network test that is being performed. The test is similar to that of an Internet Control Message Protocol (ICMP), Echo request, also known as a PING test. The console first determines if the local connect is up and running. Once that test is complete and passes, then the next test is to determine if the console can connect to the Internet. If that test passes, the console continues on and attempts to connect to the XBOX Live service. Figure 4.14 provides a screenshot of the network test.

As with the previous example of the XBOX Live service pushing data down to the console, the end user is again presented with a forced download from Microsoft XBOX Live. In this case, the download is billed as a system update, and if the end user declines the update, he or she will not be able to connect to the XBOX Live service. Research indicates that these two downloads are an exchange of information that is actually registering the console to the XBOX Live service as a security measure. It is thought that there is some sort of hash calculation done on the console and the hash value is sent to a database at Microsoft. This measure is thought to be a security control to prevent hacking of the hardware to circumvent the console's operating system. Figure 4.15 shows a screenshot of the update dialog box, and Figures 4.16 and 4.17 show a failed update and a successful update notification, respectively.

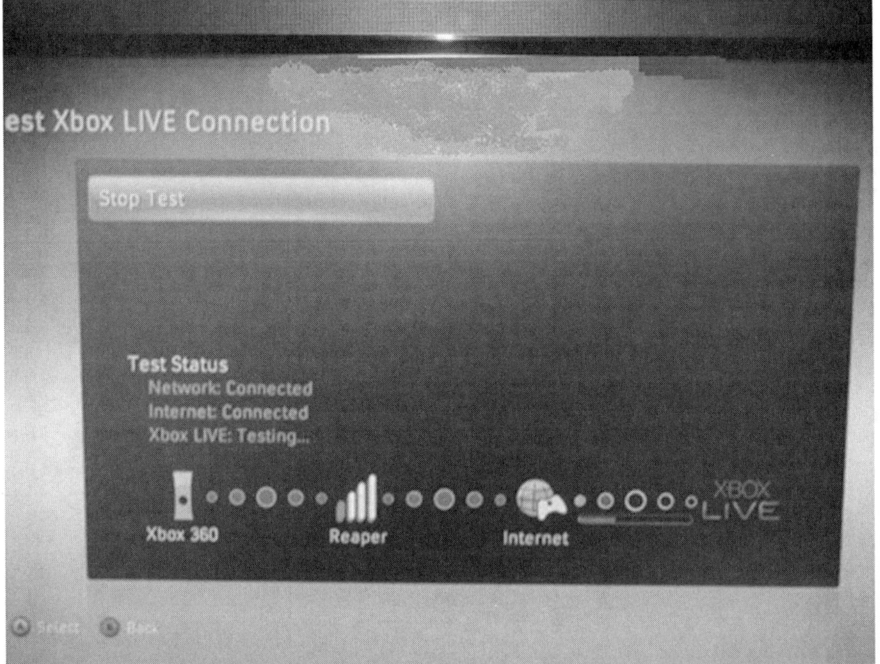

FIGURE 4.14

Screenshot of the network connection tests.

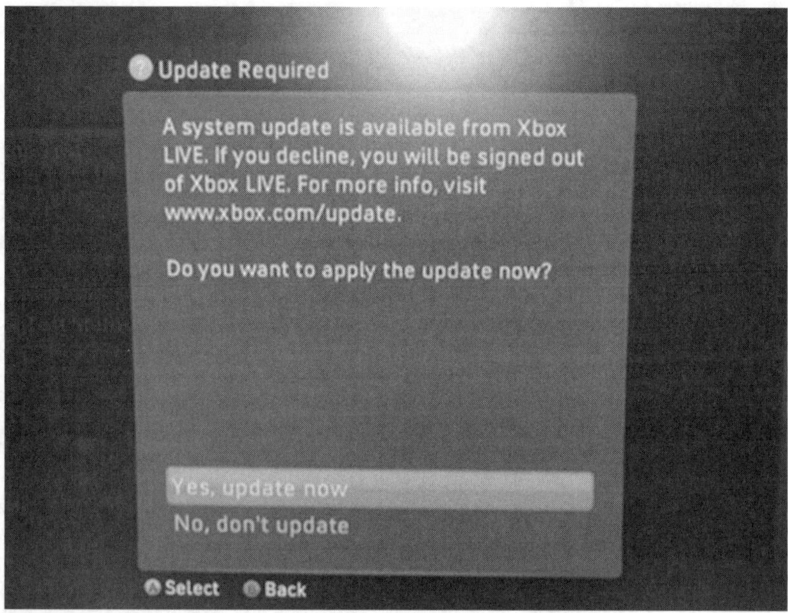

FIGURE 4.15

System update.

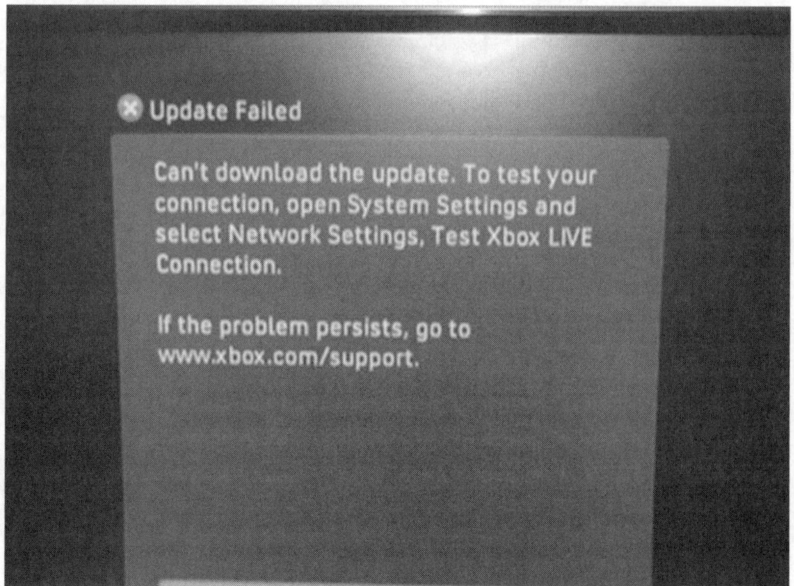

FIGURE 4.16

Update failure notification.

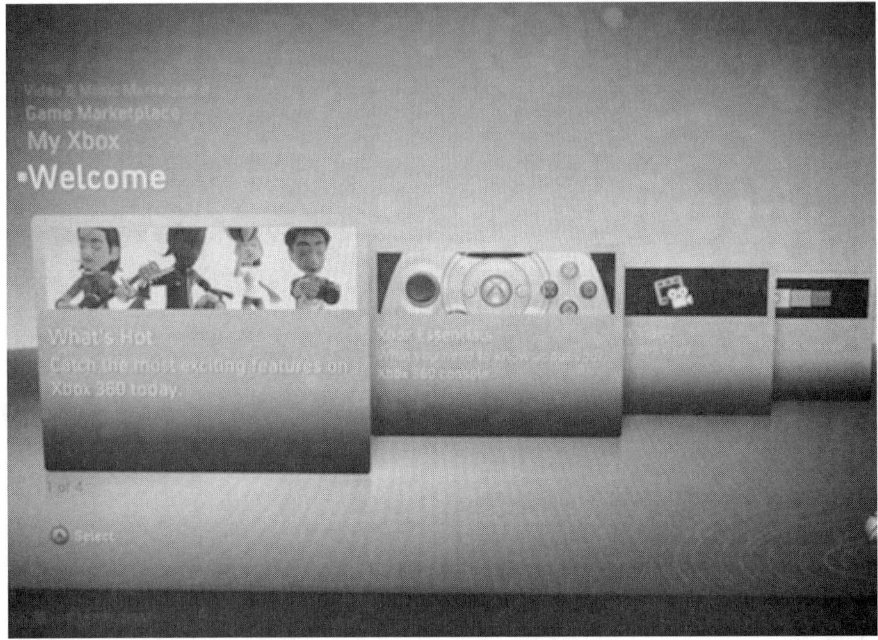

FIGURE 4.17

Home page of the XBOX 360 Dashboard after system upgrade.

On a successful update to the system, a reboot is forced and the end user is displayed with the default dashboard of the console. At this point, the console has been updated and the console has initiated its test to ensure connection to the network and XBOX Live. As was mentioned earlier, the functionality of the console to connect to a network and be another network node is integral to getting the most from the console and its features. The wizards make the connection a simple matter to add the console to a LAN and get it connected to the Internet and finally to the XBOX Live service.

TOUR OF THE DASHBOARD, PROFILE CREATION, AND GAMERTAG CONFIGURATION

Now that the console is configured and it is able to connect to the XBOX Live service, there are several features that must be addressed. The first is the dashboard that is presented to the end user. This is the interactive screen that is displayed in Figure 4.17. The dashboard is the main system interface, akin to the desktop of a Windows-based PC. The dashboard interface has undergone several updates and functionality changes since its inception and seems to be evolving. The older version of the interface consisted of up to five "blades" that were umbrella categories that a user would navigate to in order to perform the desired functions.

In November 2008, the dashboard underwent an upgrade and from that point forward was referred to as the "New XBOX Experience" or the "NXE." The upgrades to the dashboard removed the blade interface and provided an interface that is more interactive and similar in look and feel to the Windows Media Center. The console supports streaming audio, streaming video, cooperative network game play, social networking, and a wide variety of other features that are all accessed through the dashboard interface. Continuing on from the main page of the dashboard, as shown in Figure 4.17, each category has specific functionality and system settings that can be accessed through each broad category.

As the user navigates through each category, the number of subcategories is displayed in the lower left-hand corner. Each one of these subcategories is accessed by using the controller and moving the joystick in the direction of the desired category. The available panels and associated options change depending on whether the console is connected to the XBOX Live service or not. There are seven panels that are available through the NXE dashboard.

The seven panels are as follows:

- Welcome: Provides information on current happenings and hardware information.
- My XBOX: Displays information about the local machine and data storage
- Game Marketplace: Online game shopping
- Video and Music Marketplace: Online music and video shopping
- Friends: Connect to friends through Facebook, Twitter, Friends list, and so on
- Inside XBOX: Sign up for information regarding the most current XBOX 360 events
- Events: Current events on XBOX Live

The Welcome panel or home panel is the default panel that is presented to the end user on start up. Figure 4.18 shows a screenshot of this panel. Figures 4.19 through 4.24 provide screenshots of the panels as they are navigated.

Several of these panels require the end user to have an XBOX Live account, and when an attempt it made to access the panel without being signed into XBOX Live, a dialog box appears prompting account creation and activation for XBOX Live. Each one of these options can provide digital media artifacts that will be explored in future chapters.

CONNECTING TO XBOX LIVE

Connecting to XBOX Live requires the Gamertag that was created earlier. Once the user turns on the console, there are two ways in which to log into the console. The first route is to create a profile; the series of steps includes the creation of a unique identifier, the Gamertag. The second route is to have a Gamertag created through the Web site and to "recover" the Gamertag through the console interface.

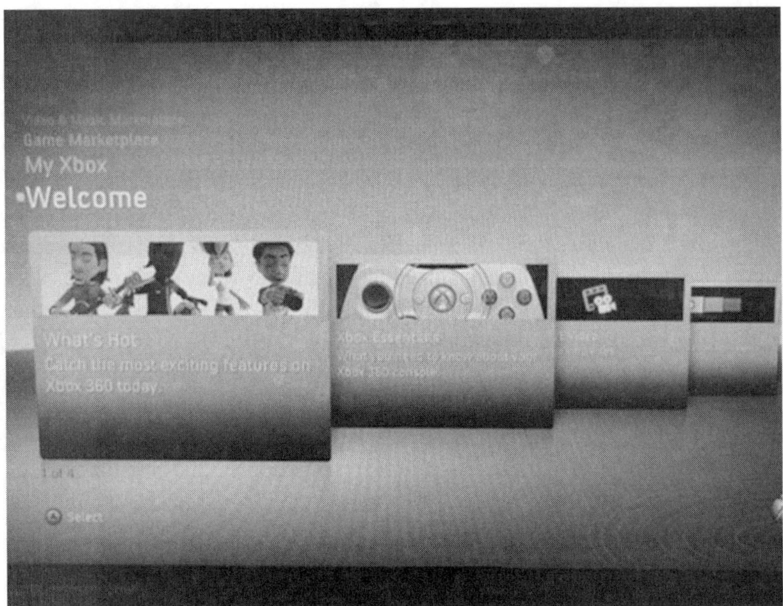

FIGURE 4.18

Welcome panel.

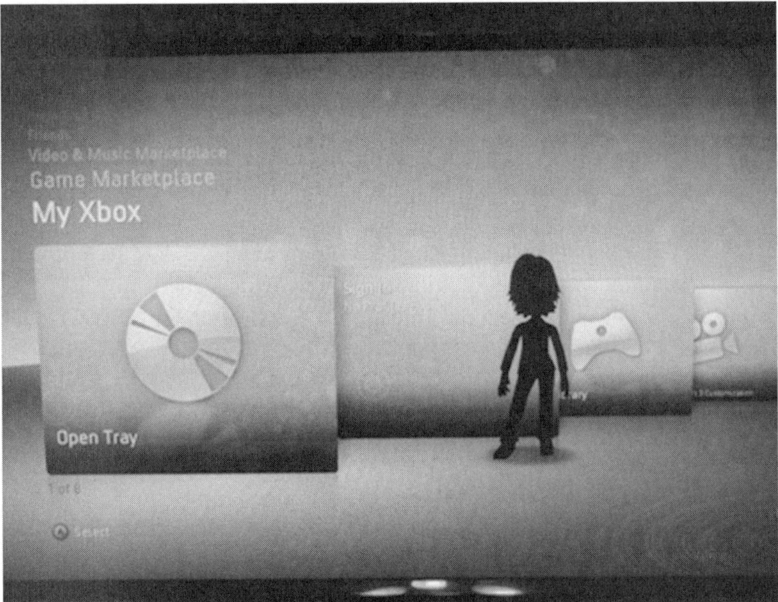

FIGURE 4.19

My XBOX panel.

FIGURE 4.20

Game Marketplace panel.

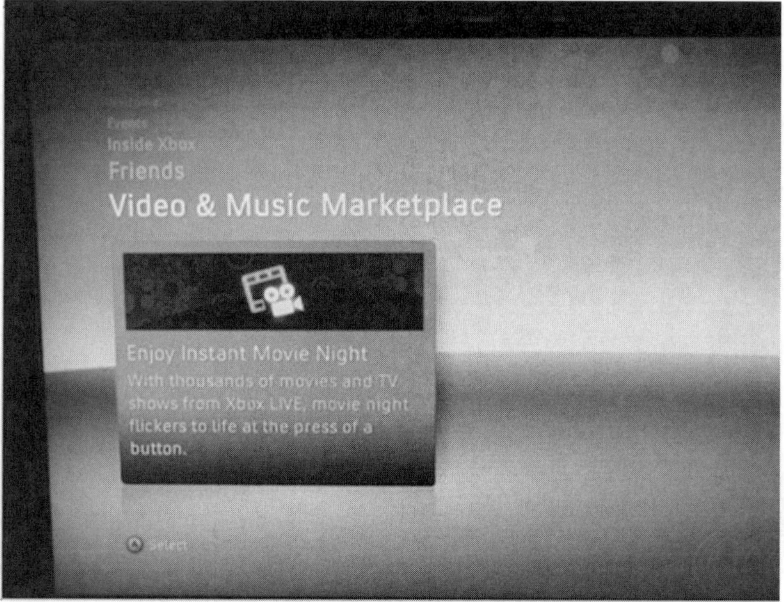

FIGURE 4.21

Video and Music Marketplace panel.

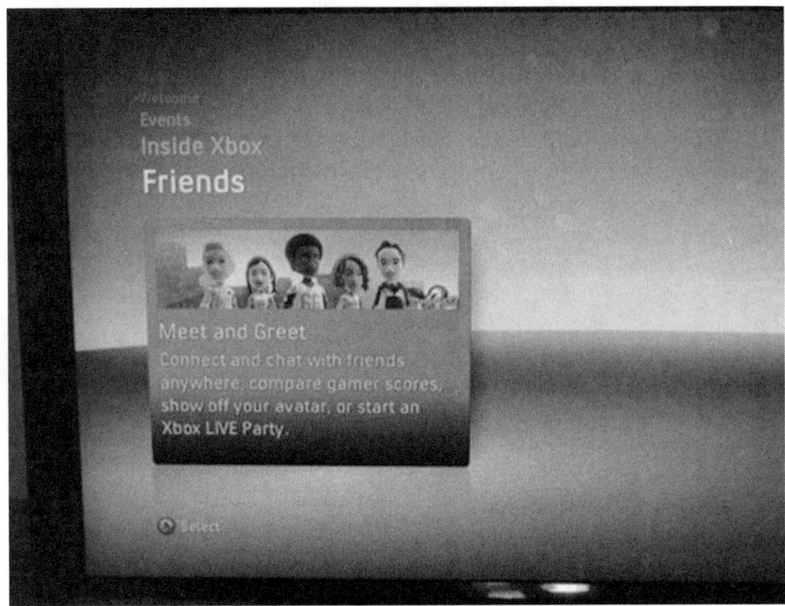

FIGURE 4.22

Friends panel.

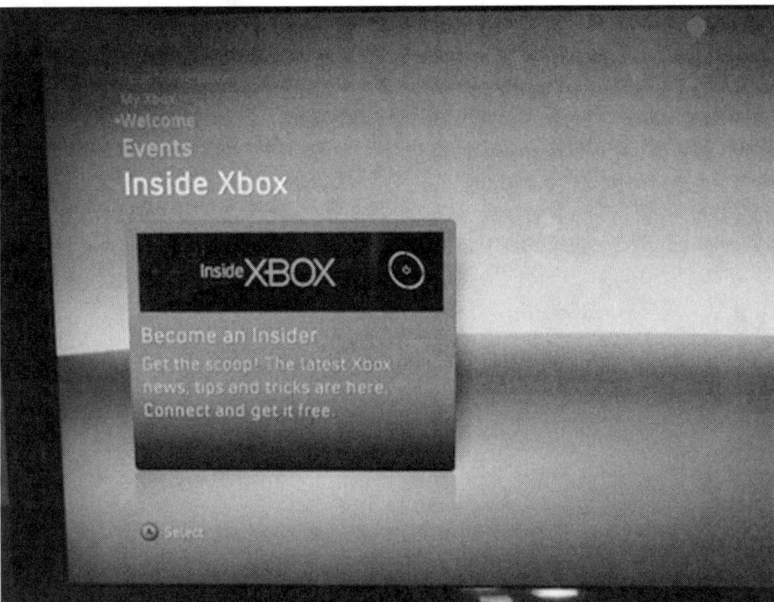

FIGURE 4.23

Inside XBOX panel.

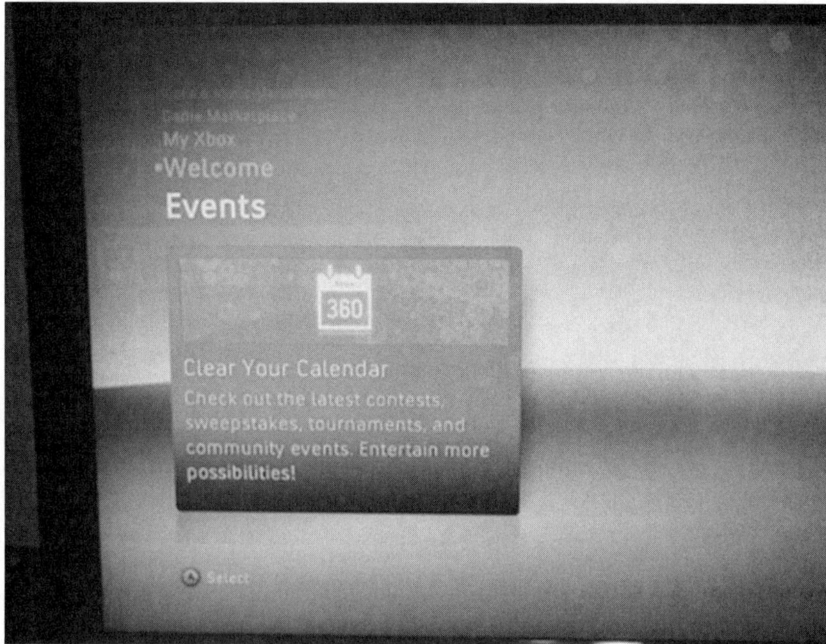

FIGURE 4.24
Events panel.

The two options are displayed in panel format to remain consistent with the interface. It is a simple matter of navigating to the desired option and following the prompts from the wizard. Screenshots of the two options are provided in Figure 4.25.

In creating a profile or recovery of a Gamertag, the end user is configuring the console with more specific information that may be stored on the associated hard drive or other removable media that was connected during the time of configuration. In this particular case, we have already created a Gamertag. A Gamertag is a unique identifier that is created either through the console or through the associated Web portal. It can be assumed that the information that is provided during this creation is captured and archived by Microsoft, a similar practice that has been documented with Web-based e-mail providers. The information is limited but may include the initial IP address, date, and time.

To create a new profile for the console and a new Gamertag through the console, the first option from Figure 4.25 would be selected. The second option from Figure 4.25 is **Recover Gamertag**. Either option launches a wizard that walks the end user through the process.

Part of the process of the Gamertag creation or linkage of a Gamertag to the console is the creation of an avatar. This avatar is created through the customization of standard templates that are provided. Figures 4.26 and 4.27 provide screen shots of the Avatar selection and customization options. Once the avatar is selected, customization can proceed, again through a wizard and user-selected choices.

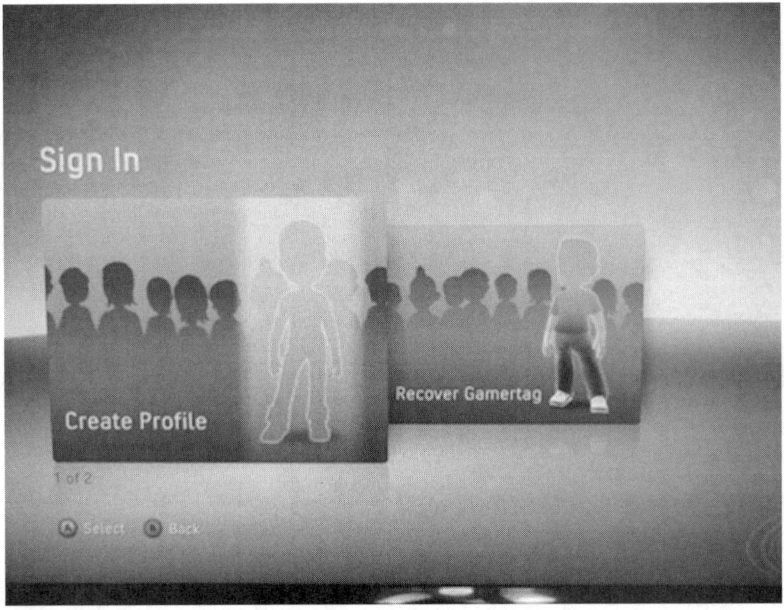

FIGURE 4.25

Create or recover.

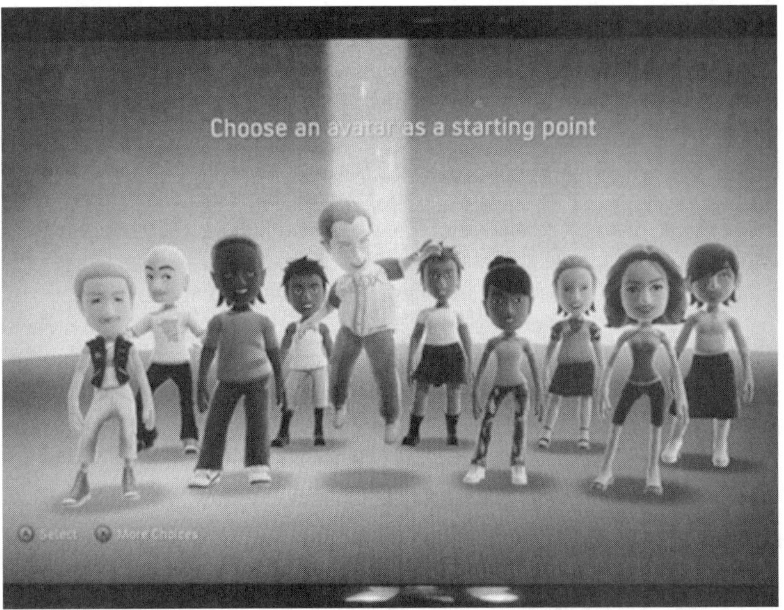

FIGURE 4.26

Selection of the default avatar.

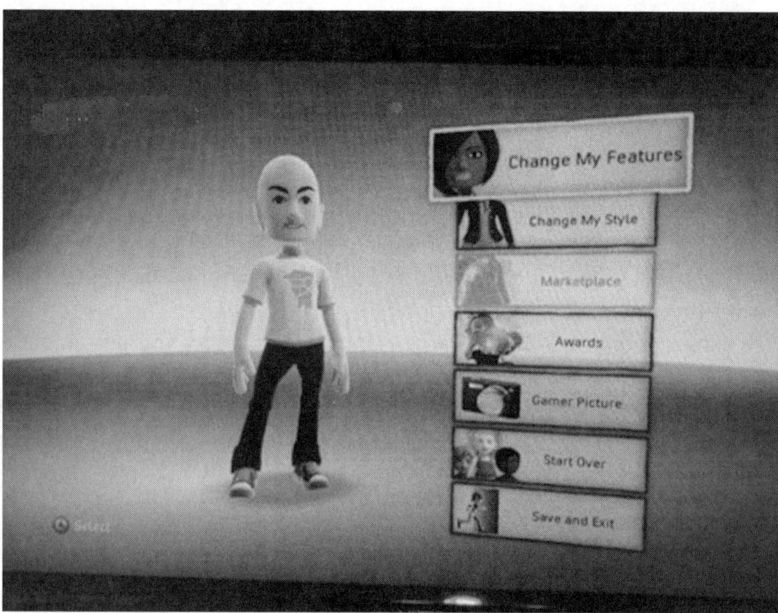

FIGURE 4.27

Customization selection screen for the avatar.

The next selection is the customization of the avatar. Avatar selection can be a concern, when there are online proactive investigations. The argument of entrapment is oftentimes a defense in cases of this nature, and some can argue that an avatar was suggestive in nature. Of course, these types of investigations are the type in which an investigator has his or her own Live account and is actively participating in the online community. This can be a concern in high-tech investigations as there tend to be certain policies and procedures that require avatars to be of a certain type, dress a certain way, or even appear a certain way. Investigations that may involve the avatar should at least address the need to customize the avatar to a certain extent to match the persona.

JOINING XBOX LIVE

Once the Gamertag has either been created or associated to the console, then the connection to XBOX Live can be configured. The initial page details the four main steps that are required for this process. The four steps are as follows:

- Create account
- Choose a membership
- Create your gamer profile
- Pick your gamer picture

Creating an account is pretty straightforward and consists of entering an e-mail, one that is connected to a Live account. The next step is to determine the locale, something that is automatically filled from the console configuration. Finally, the end user needs to accept the End User License Agreement or EULA.

The next step in the process is to determine the membership. This was addressed in earlier chapters providing more detail than is needed here. The two memberships that are available are the Silver and Gold memberships. The Gold membership is also broken up into several different options to allow the end user to determine the amount of time they are willing to pay for. As of this writing, the first option is a full 12-month subscription, which is a retail value of $49.99. The next option is a 3-month subscription for $19.99. The last option is a **Pay as you go** option and is broken down to $7.99 a month.

Entering any payment information in this screen will provide digital artifacts for the high-tech investigator. Whether those artifacts are on the local machine, on removable media, or stored at Microsoft is a subject for future chapter. Figures 4.28 through 4.31 provide screenshots of the steps mentioned earlier.

Now that the EULA has been accepted and the type of account has been chosen, the next step is to determine whether or not the end user wishes to accept advertising e-mails from XBOX and other third-party vendors. This would again link the account to these e-mails and perhaps provide another vector for digital artifact creation and examination.

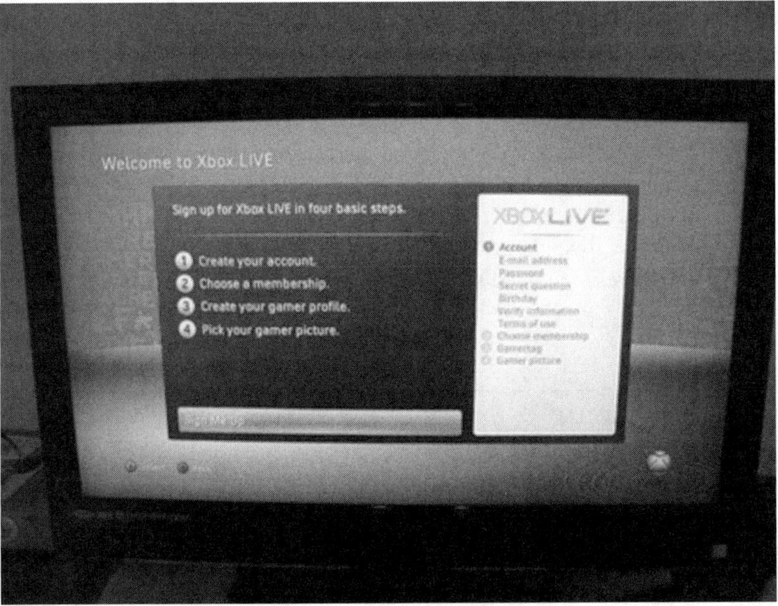

FIGURE 4.28

Welcome to XBOX Live.

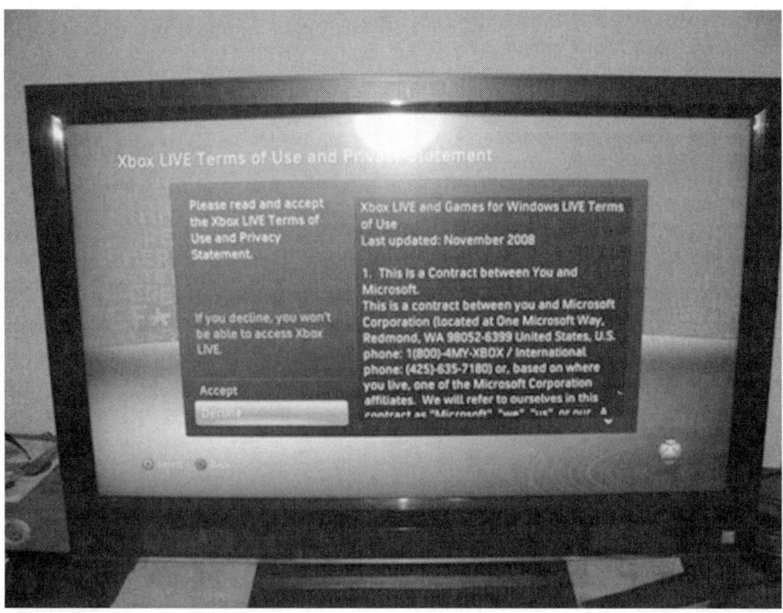

FIGURE 4.29

Accepting the EULA.

FIGURE 4.30

XBOX Live marketing.

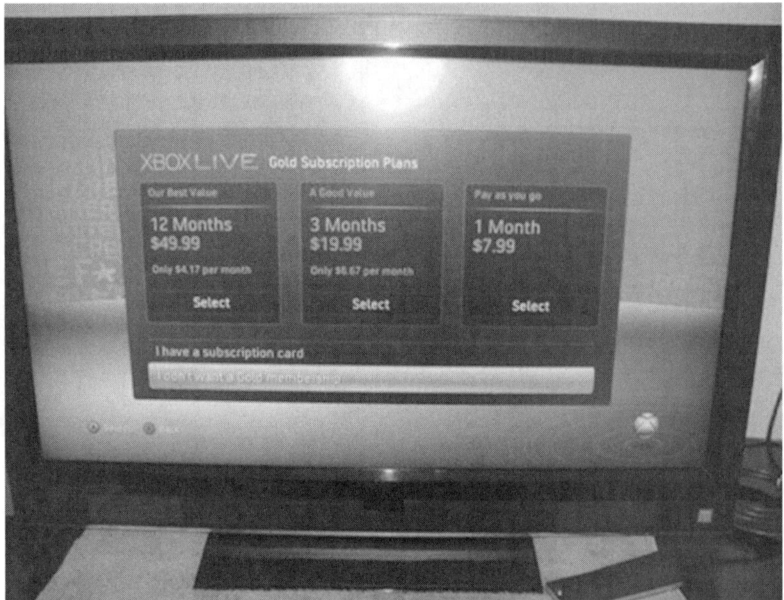

FIGURE 4.31

Gold subscription options.

The next phase is the selection of the gamer zone. Each zone is designed to optimize the gaming experience for the end user. For instance, a person who is a novice would not want to play a game with professional video game players, as they would not do very well and it would jade their experience. There are four gamer zones, which are as follows:

- Recreation
- Family
- Pro
- Underground

The **Recreation** zone is designed for casual gamers, the **Family** zone for family oriented games, the **Pro** zone is geared toward competitive gamers, and the **Underground** zone is for a no-holds-barred experience.

The final steps include setting the time zone, entering the date of birth for ESRB ratings, and finally entering a Gamertag. Figure 4.32 shows the gamer zone selection. This entire process is for creating the Gamertag without having one already created over the Web portal. To link a Gamertag to the console, the user would use the **Recover Gamertag** option. With this option, the user is prompted to enter his or her Microsoft Live ID that was created through the XBOX portal. Once this information is entered, all the profile entries that were entered on the portal are configured on the console.

The entry of the data is conducted over the on-screen keyboard, which is a fundamental interface for navigating through the various screens. Figure 4.33 shows the on-screen keyboard.

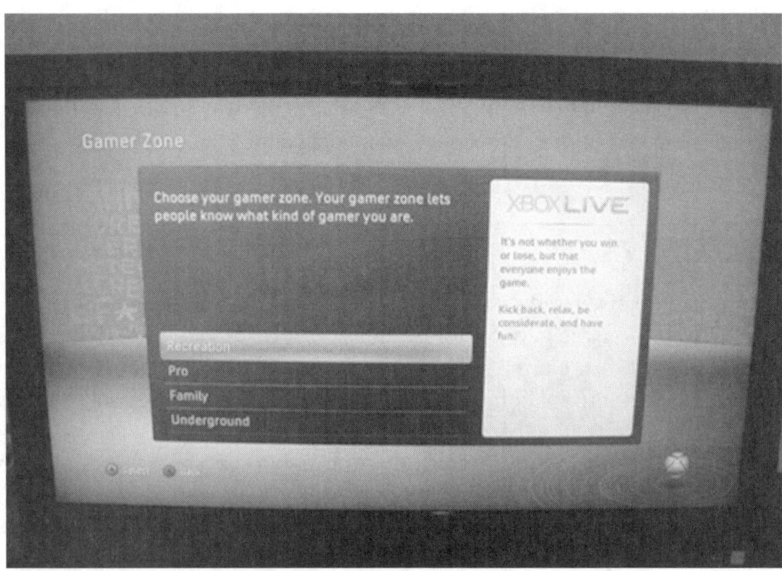

FIGURE 4.32

Choosing the gamer zone.

FIGURE 4.33

On-screen keyboard.

Once all these processes are completed and all the wizards have been worked through, the console is ready for XBOX Live content or local machine game play. Many of these features can be altered as needed and on occasion need to be altered. Each console can have multiple profiles on the machine, and each profile can be associated to a different Gamertag. This is similar to the way in which Windows is a multiuser system and each user account is independent of the others.

SUMMARY

In this chapter, we discussed several initial steps that must be taken by the end user of the XBOX 360 console in order for the console to be functional and to connect to the XBOX Live service. During this process, several fields are required that include personal identifying information. This information does not undergo any sort of verification, akin to the creation of a Web mail account. However, there may be some fields in which the end user enters truthful information that can be verified. Among these fields, the initial IP address may be archived by Microsoft, there may be financial information present if the end user linked his or her XBOX Live account to a credit card. Once the Gamertag is linked, then Microsoft can track the IP address that the Gamertag logs in from, giving a high-tech crime investigator another avenue to pursue.

The next few chapters will detail the steps taken for the forensic imaging and examination of the console's associated hard drive.

CHAPTER

Initial Forensic Acquisition and Examination

5

INFORMATION IN THIS CHAPTER

- Imaging the console hard drive
- A first look at the contents of the drive
- Additional information located on the drive

IMAGING THE CONSOLE HARD DRIVE

The steps for imaging the hard drive were not too complex of a process. Once the drive was removed from the case, all the necessary precautions were taken to lessen the chances of damage to the drive. The main issue from a research perspective was to ensure that the processes were all documented and repeatable so that other researchers and examiners could follow the process. The imaging was an issue in which there needed to be some starting point, meaning that a baseline needed to be determined. This method of research was in an effort to ensure that all the processes that could leave digital artifacts could be launched on the console, tracked, detailed, and the artifacts could be identified. Each time a process was run, the hard drive was removed and imaged. Although this was a time-consuming effort, it was necessary in order to attempt to track the changes that were made to the box during the course of normal operation.

In keeping with this process outlined above, the first order of business was to image the hard drive as it existed when it was initially pulled from the retail package. The console unit was removed from the package, and the hard drive case was removed from the console. The hard drive was extracted from the casing as outlined in Chapter 2, "XBOX 360 Hardware."

Imaging the drive presented no serious issues that have not been encountered with other digital media and no forensic imaging that has not been experienced by examiners. The research used Guidance Software's EnCase v. 6.16.2 and Access Data's FTK Imager v.2.7.0.33 to image the drive. The issues that were experienced had more to do with the drive not being recognized because of the equipment that was

FIGURE 5.1

Hitachi drive fresh from the custom hard drive case.

used. One method of imaging the drive was using a Wiebetech USB Write Blocker (Figure 5.1). However, there were mixed results, with the drive consistently being identified and read by both EnCase and FTK Imager. In both cases, an error message, if received, indicated that there was a read error and the imaging could not be completed. Switching the type of write blocker that was used and moving forward with a Wiebetech Forensic UltraDock, no further issues were experienced. However, the problems with the USB Write Blocker were researched, and it was determined that the issue was with the power draw by the attached drive. Wiebetech offers an additional power connector for the USB Write Blocker that overcomes this issue by providing a secondary USB connection for additional power.

The retail package that was purchased for this project was a special edition, Final Fantasy XIII. Once the drive was extracted from the custom case, it was determined that it was simply a Hitachi[1] 2.5" SATA drive. The markings on the drive are provided in Figure 5.1. The research began by connecting the hard drive to a power supply from a USB adapter kit. Once this was completed, the drive was then connected to the Wiebetech write blocker. Figure 5.2 provides a snapshot of configuration with the write blocker and the attached drive.

[1]Hitachi is a registered trademark of the Hitachi Corporation

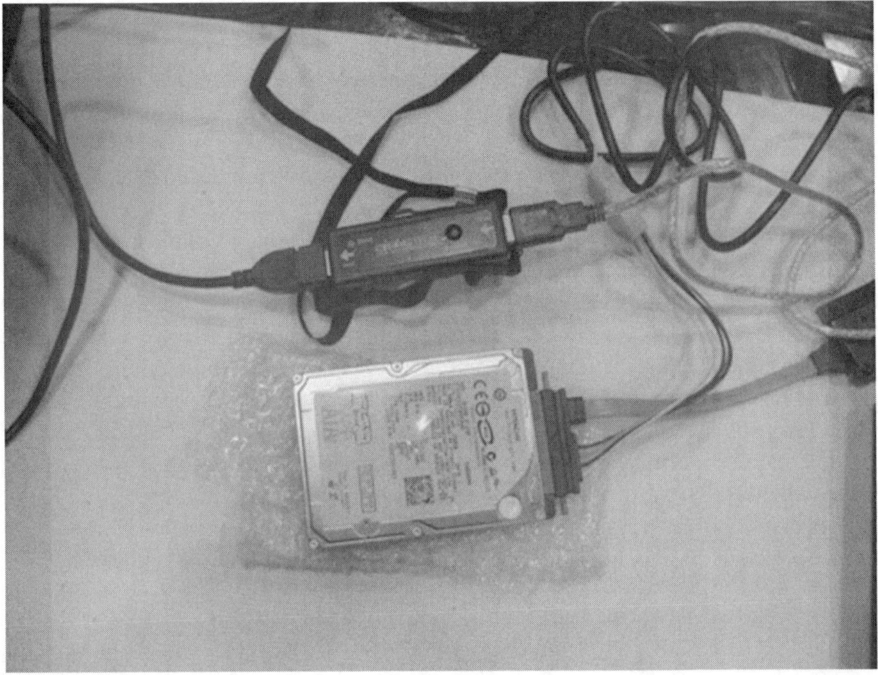

FIGURE 5.2

The USB write blocker set up that received mixed results. Note: There is no additional power supply which is thought to be the cause of this particular issue.

The first attempt with this particular set up met with no setbacks. The drive was connected to the examination machine, and FTK Imager was utilized. Initially, there was a desire to determine if Imager could recognize the drive and any artifacts that may have been present. Research from 2006 located artifacts that were resident on the hard drives. Located on the drive were several interesting artifacts, including some short movies, gamer pictures, and some themes for customization of the dashboard. Microsoft and specifically the XBOX 360 team deemed these preloaded items as XBOX "extras." These extras included the following:

- Preloaded gamer pictures
- Dashboard themes
- XBOX Live arcade freebies
- Instant play lists
- Four short films

As mentioned, these were the extras that came preloaded on the XBOX 360 hard drive when the research began in 2006. We are working off of the assumption that loaded on all hard drives that are shipped for the console, there are some sort of "extra" files or group of files that would be included on the drive. It appears that the content that is included on each drive depends on the console, the size of the drive, and in particular the shipping date. There are also several special release consoles on the market that are bundled with specific games that have customized consoles with the associated drive content as well. This would include specialized themes, avatars, movie trailers, and game trailers.

In order to test the theory that each console comes with preloaded data, a baseline image was required. The first step was to isolate and connect the target media through a write blocking device to an examination machine. Having accomplished this task, the next step was to have a forensic application or imaging application recognize the drive and successfully image it. Again, there were some issues using the Wiebetech USB Write Blocker without the additional USB power adapters. However, this issue was intermittent and switching to the UltraDock alleviated all these issues.

The first step was to load FTK Imager and ensure that the drive could be identified. Imager was able to recognize the drive as a physical device attached to the examination machine. The first step was to either add an "evidence file" or "create a new disk image" from the file menu selections of FTK Imager. Figure 5.3 provides a screenshot of how this information was presented.

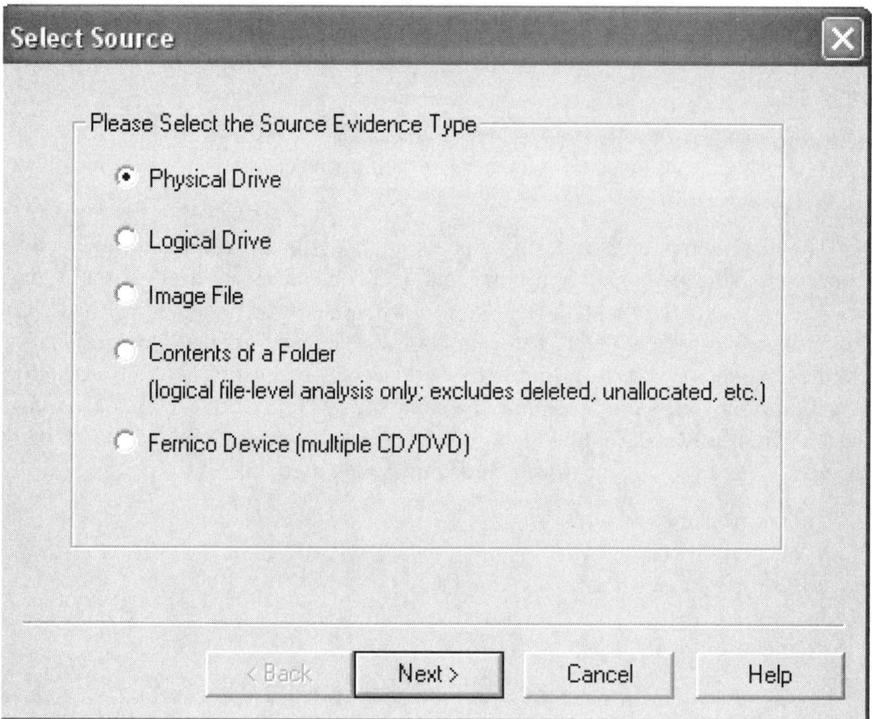

FIGURE 5.3

Creating a disk image.

Now that a physical device has been selected, an attached drive must be identified. In this particular case, we have already seen that the drive we want to specify is a Hitachi drive that is 250GB in size. Again, there were inconsistencies in the drive being recognized by the software. Several times when attempting to identify this drive, FTK Imager would report that a drive was present, but the size of the drive was reported as being 0 bytes. Figure 5.4 provides a sample.

Following drive identification, the next steps were to determine the location to store the image files, what name to give the file, and the format the file would be created in, either E01, SMART or a RAW image. Because of space concerns, the E01 format with compression was selected and the imaging proceeded. Figure 5.5 shows the dialog for selection of the image format, and Figure 5.6 shows the progress bar as reported by FTK Imager during the imaging process.

The drive acquired successfully, and FTK Imager reported the drive and acquisition information. Figure 5.7 provides a screenshot of the FTK Imager text file that is generated.

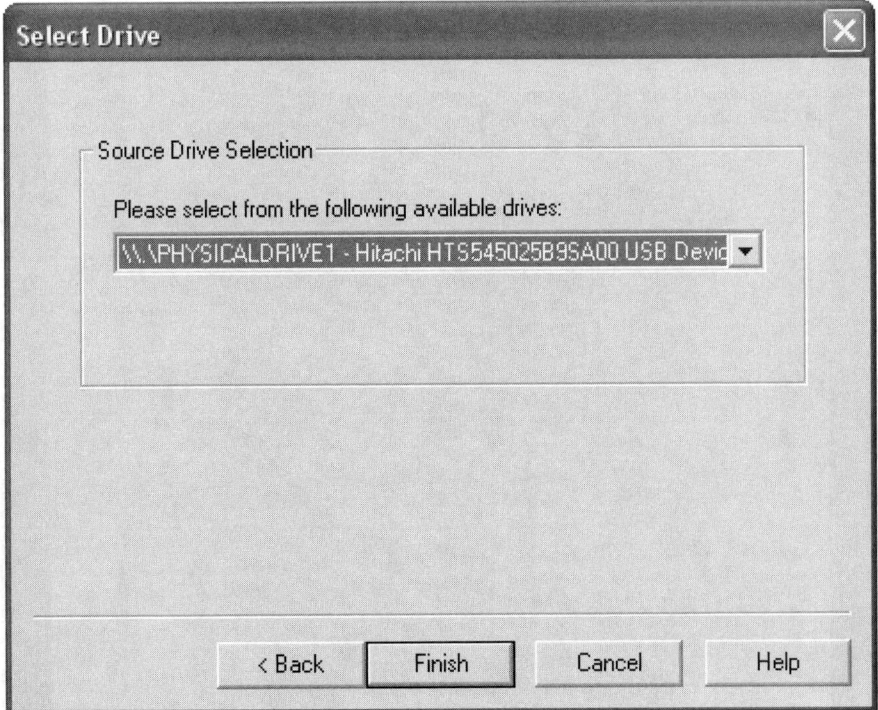

FIGURE 5.4

First initial steps for imaging the XBOX 360 hard drive.

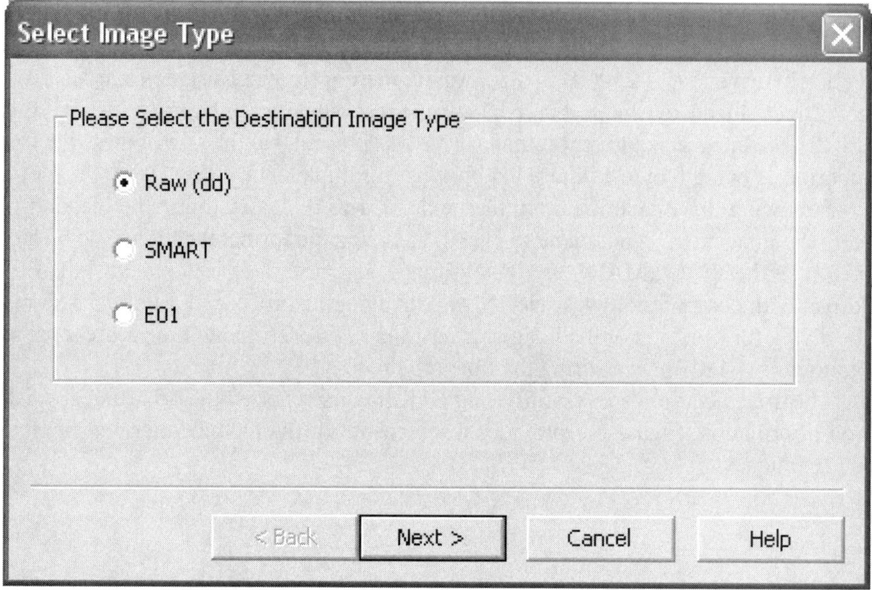

FIGURE 5.5

Image type selection.

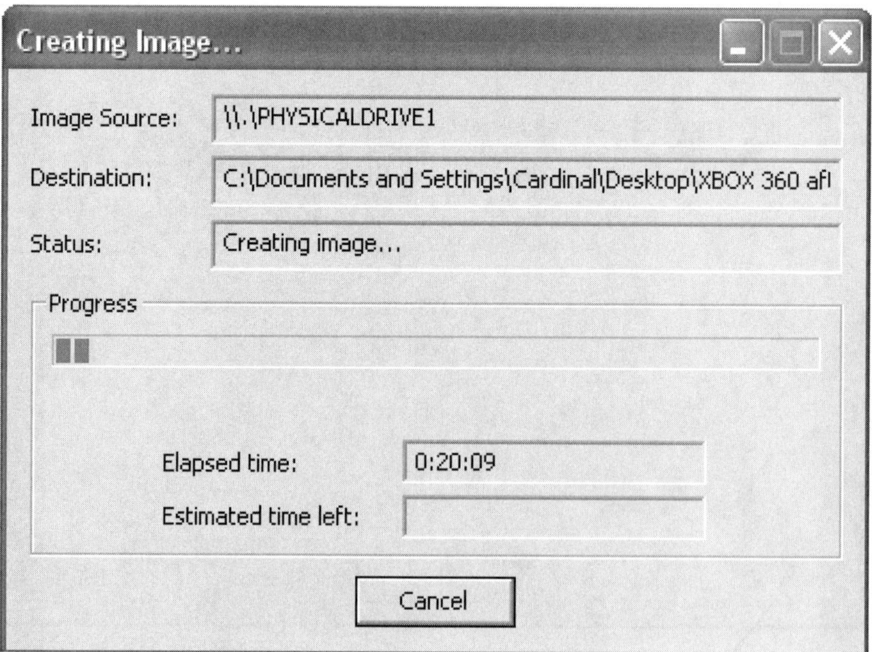

FIGURE 5.6

Progress bar progression during image generation.

```
Created By AccessData® FTK® Imager 2.7.0.33 091119

Case Information:
Case Number: 1
Evidence Number: 1
Unique description: 360 Final Fantasy
Examiner: sb
Notes: FF

--------------------------------------------------------------

Information for C:\Users\Steve\Desktop\XBOX 360 250 gig\Final Fantasy 360:

Physical Evidentiary Item (Source) Information:
[Drive Geometry]
 Cylinders: 30,401
 Tracks per Cylinder: 255
 Sectors per Track: 63
 Bytes per Sector: 512
 Sector Count: 488,397,168
[Physical Drive Information]
 Drive Model: Hitachi HTS545025B9SA00 USB Device
 Drive Serial Number: 0
 Drive Interface Type: USB
 Source data size: 238475 MB
 Sector count:    488397168
[Computed Hashes]
 MD5 checksum:    050076fd2b52e5176738545d63b24cf0
 SHA1 checksum:   adfe7700cca80a3c6638bd7597ceb69db4cc2827

Image Information:
 Acquisition started:   Tue Jul 27 13:12:06 2010
 Acquisition finished:  Tue Jul 27 22:52:24 2010
 Segment list:
  C:\Users\Steve\Desktop\XBOX 360 250 gig\Final Fantasy 360.E01

Image Verification Results:
 Verification started:  Tue Jul 27 22:52:25 2010
 Verification finished: Tue Jul 27 23:30:02 2010
 MD5 checksum:    050076fd2b52e5176738545d63b24cf0 : verified
 SHA1 checksum:   adfe7700cca80a3c6638bd7597ceb69db4cc2827 : verified
```

FIGURE 5.7

FTK Imager report.

A FIRST LOOK AT THE CONTENTS OF THE DRIVE

After having successfully imaged the "preplayed" drive, it was time to load it into a forensic application and see what information, if any, was present. In the previous research, from 2006, there was information, the so-called XBOX extras, but that data did not begin where expected. There was no information at physical sector 0 of the XBOX 360's associated hard drive, which after further review and research should have been expected. Traditional digital media storage has information located at physical sector 0, generally in the master boot record, because most hard drives store not only the file system but also the operating system as well. It is clear through this research that the digital storage is simply organized storage. The operating system of the console does not appear to be located on the drive. Evidence of this observation is provided with the ability of the console to function normally without an associated storage card or hard drive. The storage device provides several additional functions, including an alternate dashboard, the graphical user interface, for online content, and storage of network and game artifacts. The normal boot sequence of a Windows-based PC starts with the BIOS initialization. This process, if it completes successfully, seeks information from the master boot record (MBR), which, through industry standard, is located at physical sector 0 on a boot volume. The issue here is that the hard drive of the XBOX 360 is not a boot device; therefore, no data should be located at sector 0.

In the normal boot process of a personal computer, the master boot record is located at physical sector 0 and tells the system the number of partitions available and where to locate the operating system files, usually a jump instruction to physical sector 63. Figure 5.8 shows how EnCase reports the information from the first sector.

The first instance of data that is present on the drive is located at physical sector 4. This information contains some interesting plain text, including a date and a name, but the significance is elusive. The data contains the name "Josh" and a date of "01-18-10," as well as what may be a revision number of "X-852266-001." The data block spans two sectors and is 640 bytes in length. Figures 5.9, 5.10, and 5.11 depict how this data is displayed using EnCase, X-Ways, and Access Data's FTK Imager.

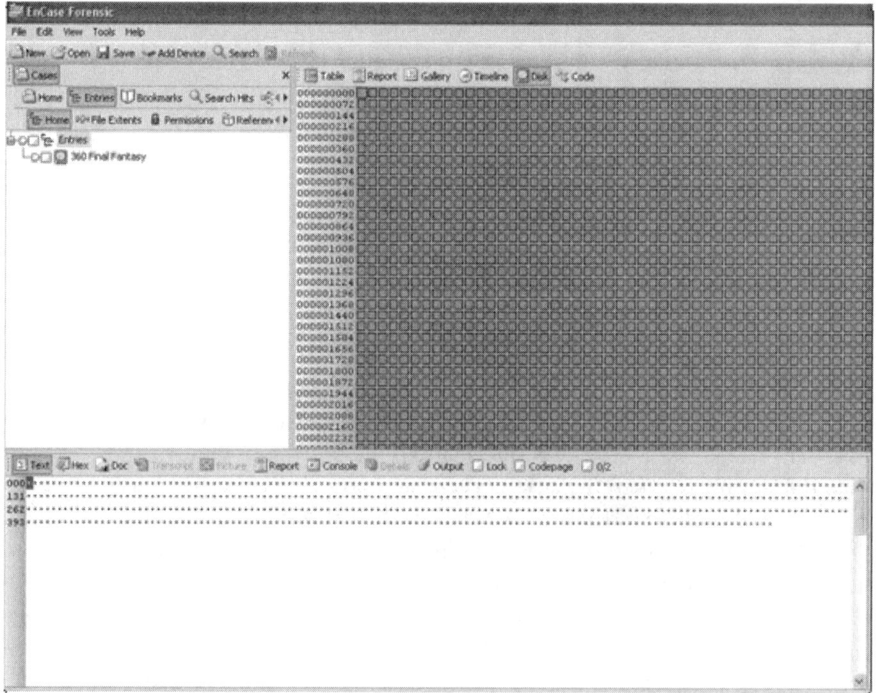

FIGURE 5.8

Physical sector 0 with no information listed.

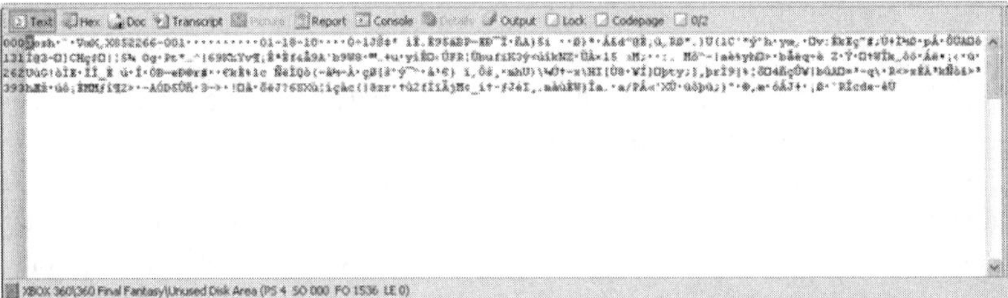

FIGURE 5.9

EnCase interpretation of data at PS 4.

Offset	0	1	2	3	4	5	6	7	8	9	A	B	C	D	E	F	
00000007E0	00	00	00	00	00	00	00	00	00	00	00	00	00	00	00	00	
00000007F0	00	00	00	00	00	00	00	00	00	00	00	00	00	00	00	00	
0000000800	4A	6F	73	68	01	A8	01	56	9C	58	82	58	38	35	32	32	Josh ¨ V▮X▮X8522
0000000810	36	36	2D	30	30	31	00	00	00	00	00	00	00	00	00	02	66-001
0000000820	30	31	2D	31	38	2D	31	30	00	01	00	01	D6	F7	31	4A	01-18-10 Ö÷1J
0000000830	8A	87	B2	09	EC	CB	2E	CB	39	35	E4	42	50	97	45	D0	▮▮² ìË.Ë95äBP▮EÐ
0000000840	AF	CF	0E	F1	41	7D	35	69	A0	14	01	DF	29	AA	0B	C2	¯Ï ñA}5i ß)ª Â
0000000850	A3	64	94	40	C8	A1	FC	82	52	DF	2A	2E	29	55	28	6C	£d▮@È¡ü▮Rß*.)U(l
0000000860	43	27	2A	FD	BA	68	11	79	9C	82	19	90	76	3A	C9	6B	C'*ýºh y▮▮ ▮v:Ék
0000000870	45	E7	98	23	3B	DA	2B	CC	BD	DF	14	70	C2	18	D4	DC	Eç▮#;Ú+Ì½ß pÂ ÔÜ
0000000880	41	9D	F4	CE	40	33	96	8F	5D	43	48	E7	24	9D	7C	A6	A▮ôÎ@3▮▮]CHç$▮|¦
0000000890	35	BE	20	30	67	0C	50	74	2A	85	5E	7C	36	39	4B	89	5¾ 0g Pt*▮^|69K▮
00000008A0	59	76	B6	A1	CA	AA	C8	66	26	E5	39	41	27	62	39	57	Yv¶¡ÊªÈf&å9A'b9W
00000008B0	38	04	99	85	2B	75	1D	79	ED	CA	9D	8B	DA	46	52	A6	8 ▮▮+u yíÊ▮▮ÚFR¦
00000008C0	DC	62	75	66	69	4B	33	FD	3C	FA	EE	6B	4E	5A	0C	D9	ÜbufiK3ý<úîkNZ Ù
00000008D0	C0	D7	6C	35	0A	9B	4D	3B	1B	05	3A	2E	0D	4D	F4	93	À×l5 ▮M; :. Mô▮
00000008E0	2D	7C	61	E8	25	79	68	8F	3E	11	62	E5	EB	71	F7	E8	-|aè%yh▮> båëq÷è
00000008F0	09	5A	1B	DD	15	8F	86	57	CE	6B	84	F4	F6	1A	C1	EB	Z Ý ▮▮WÎk▮ôö Áë
0000000900	95	A1	8B	19	FC	0C	55	F9	47	21	F2	CC	45	17	CF	CE	▮¡▮ ü UùG!òÌE ÏÎ
0000000910	5F	C8	20	FA	07	CD	B7	D6	42	97	65	D0	A9	72	23	1D	_È ú Í·ÖB▮eÐ©r#
0000000920	07	80	6B	C8	25	6C	63	A0	D1	EB	CC	51	F2	28	AD	E2	▮kÈ%lc ÑëÌQò(-â
0000000930	BD	2D	C0	0F	E7	D8	5B	9A	BA	FD	AF	93	07	E2	B9	80	½-À çØ[▮ºý¯▮ â¹▮
0000000940	7D	A0	EF	82	D4	9A	B8	1C	6D	68	55	29	5C	BC	DA	86	} ï▮Ô▮¸ mhU)\¼Ú▮
0000000950	AD	78	5C	48	49	5B	D9	38	1D	A5	CD	5D	81	FE	74	79	-x\HI[Ù8 ¥Í]▮þty
0000000960	3B	5D	2C	FE	72	CC	39	90	25	A6	F5	8D	34	F1	E7	DB	;],þrÌ9▮%¦õ▮4ñçÛ
0000000970	A5	7C	62	FB	41	90	3D	B3	2D	71	5C	0C	52	3C	3E	78	¥|bûA▮=³-q\ R<>x
0000000980	C9	C4	B3	6B	D1	F2	A3	3E	B3	68	C6	9E	1C	FA	F4	A1	ÉÄ³kÑò£>³hÆ▮ úô¡
0000000990	C8	4D	4D	83	EE	B6	32	3E	1F	AD	41	D3	44	35	DB	F1	ÈMM▮î¶2> -AÓD5Ûñ

FIGURE 5.10

X-Ways interpretation of the data at PS 4.

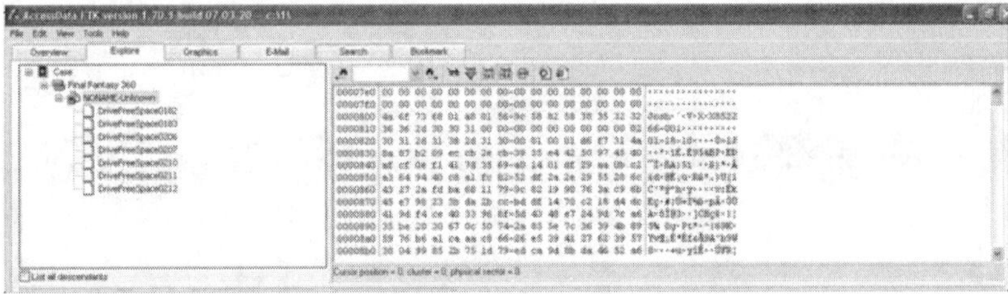

FIGURE 5.11

Sector 4 as rendered by FTK v. 1.70.1.

Further research into sector 4, or "Josh," indicates that the cryptic data that is listed after "Josh" is the console security certificates that assist in the verification of the authenticity of the drive. This information was located at www.free60.org/fatx. Table 5.1 provides a summary of the sector offsets and the data that can be located there.

The next data located on the drive is found at physical sector 16. The information contains the hard drive make and model, and it is connected to the console that the drive was bundled with. This information does not extend beyond this sector. This could be an indicator that there is more than one drive to examine and perhaps there is more digital media to be seized. Figures 5.12 and 5.13 provide some examples of how the drive data is interpreted by EnCase and X-Ways.

The researchers at www.free60.org have termed this sector the "security sector," as it contains the necessary information so that the drive can be verified or authenticated as a legitimate Microsoft hard drive for the XBOX 360 console. They have been able to detail the information contained within this sector, which includes several security hashes, firmware revision, the drive serial number, and the number of sectors that are present on the drive. Attempts have been made within the "mod or modification," to add a larger third-party hard drive to their system as the main storage drive. They have been met with limited success, and some clues can be found within this "security sector." At offset, 0 × 58 of the security sector is a value that defines the number of sectors for the drive. This information dictates to the console how to interpret the drive size. If a third-party hard drive were to be utilized in an

Table 5.1 Josh Sector Information

Offset	Length	Type	Information
The "Josh" sector is located on the fourth sector (0 × 800). Its purpose is currently unknown. It may be used just to identify the XBOX that previously formatted it.			
0 × 0	0 × 4	ascii string	"Josh" magic
The Console Security Certificate then Follows, Continuing With a Pair of Entries, the Format of Which Is Given Below			
0 × 0	0 × 8	(un?)signed long	Unknown (ID of some kind?)
0 × 8	0 × 14	bytes	Unknown (0 × 14 bytes... SHA1 hash?)
0 × 1C	0 × 4	(un?) signed int	Unknown
0 × 20	0 × 4	(un?) signed int	Unknown
The Sector then Ends with the Following Format			
0 × 0	0 × 4	(un?) signed int	Unknown
0 × 4	0 × 4	(un?) signed int	Unknown
0 × 8	0 × 4	(un?) signed int	Unknown
0 × C	0 × 4	(un?) signed int	Unknown

From www.free60.org/fatx

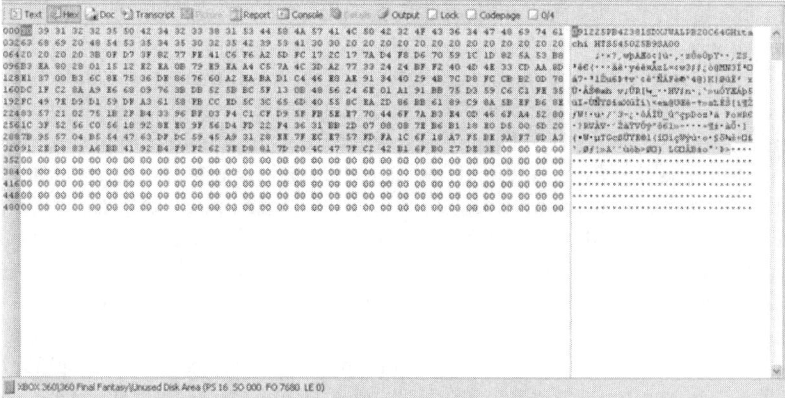

FIGURE 5.12

EnCase view of the information located at physical sector 16.

```
Disk | File | Preview | Details | Gallery | Legend | Sync
Offset      0  1  2  3  4  5  6  7   8  9  A  B  C  D  E  F
0000001FD0  00 00 00 00 00 00 00 00  00 00 00 00 00 00 00 00
0000001FE0  00 00 00 00 00 00 00 00  00 00 00 00 00 00 00 00
0000001FF0  00 00 00 00 00 00 00 00  00 00 00 00 00 00 00 00
0000002000  30 39 31 32 32 35 50 42  34 32 33 38 31 53 44 58  091225PB42381SDX
0000002010  4A 57 41 4C 50 42 32 4F  43 36 34 47 48 69 74 61  JWALPB2OC64GHita
0000002020  63 68 69 20 48 54 53 35  34 35 30 32 35 42 39 53  chi HTS545025B9S
0000002030  41 30 30 20 20 20 20 20  20 20 20 20 20 20 20 20  A00
0000002040  20 20 20 20 3B 0F D7 3F  82 77 FE 41 C6 F6 A2 5D      ; ×?▮wþAÆö¢]
0000002050  FC 17 2C 17 7A D4 F8 D6  70 59 1C 1D 82 5A 53 B8  ü , zÔøÖpY  ▮ZS¸
0000002060  B3 EA 80 28 01 15 12 E2  EA 0B 79 E9 EA A4 C5 7A  ³ê▮(   âê yéê¤Åz
0000002070  4C 3D A2 77 33 24 24 BF  F2 40 4D 4E 33 CD AA 8D  L=¢w3$$¿ò@MN3Íª▮
0000002080  E1 37 00 B3 6C 8E 75 36  DE 86 76 60 A2 EA BA D1  á7 ³l▮u6Þ▮v`¢êºÑ
0000002090  C4 46 E8 AE 91 34 40 29  4B 7C D8 FC CB B2 0D 78  ÄFè®'4@)K|ØüË² x
00000020A0  DC 1F C2 8A A9 E6 68 09  76 3B DB 52 5B BC 5F 13  Ü Â▮©æh v;ÛR[¼_
00000020B0  0B 48 56 24 6E 01 A1 91  BB 75 D3 59 C6 C1 FE 35   HV$n ¡'»uÓYÆÁþ5
00000020C0  FC 49 7E D9 D1 59 DF A3  61 58 FB CC ED 5C 3C 65  üI~ÙÑYß£aXûÌí\<e
00000020D0  6D 40 55 8C EA 2D 86 BB  61 89 C9 8A 5B EF B6 8E  m@U▮ê-▮»a▮É▮[ï¶▮
00000020E0  83 57 21 02 75 1B 2F B4  33 96 BF 03 F4 C1 CF D9  ▮W! u /´3▮¿ ôÁÏÙ
00000020F0  5F FB 5E E7 70 44 6F 7A  B3 E4 0D 46 6F A4 52 80  _û^çpDoz³ä Fo¤R▮
0000002100  1C 3F 52 56 C0 56 18 92  8E E0 9F 56 D4 FD 22 F4   ?RVÀV '▮à▮VÔý"ô
0000002110  36 31 BB 2D 07 08 08 7E  B6 B1 18 E0 D5 00 5D 20  61»-   ~¶± àÕ ]
0000002120  7B 95 57 04 B5 54 47 63  DF DC 59 45 A9 31 28 EE  {▮W µTGcßÜYE©1(î
0000002130  7F EC E7 57 FD FA 1C 6F  18 A7 F5 BE 9A F7 8D A3  ▮ìçWýú o §õ¾▮÷▮£
0000002140  91 2E D8 83 A6 BB 41 92  B4 F9 F2 62 3E D8 81 7D  '.Ø▮¦»A'´ùòb>Ø▮}
0000002150  20 4C 47 7F C2 42 B1 6F  B0 27 DE 3E 00 00 00 00   LG▮ÂB±o°'Þ>
0000002160  00 00 00 00 00 00 00 00  00 00 00 00 00 00 00 00
0000002170  00 00 00 00 00 00 00 00  00 00 00 00 00 00 00 00
0000002180  00 00 00 00 00 00 00 00  00 00 00 00 00 00 00 00
Sector 15 of 488397168    Offset:    1FDA    = 0  Block:
```

FIGURE 5.13

X-Ways depiction of physical sector 16.

attempt to increase the storage capacity, this value would need to be altered to reflect the sector count. If the value is not altered, the drive would only report the smaller storage capacity.

Once again, the researchers at www.free60.org have done a good job of detailing the information located within this sector. In order to verify some of the information located within this table, the raw hex information for the sector count was compared to the count that was reported by FTK Imager. Table 5.2 shows the sector offsets for the data.

As a verification of the information located within the table, the data found at sector 16, offset 0 × 58 (decimal 88), for a length of 4 bytes was highlighted and provided value of 70 59 1C 1D (hex). However, because there is evidence that the data is stored as Big Endian, this data has to be read right to left, giving the value of 1D 1C 59 70. Converting this hex number to a decimal value of 488397168 and comparing this value to the value reported by FTK Imager, we see that there is verification. Figures 5.14 and 5.15 show this sector offset within EnCase, as well as a verification of the converted value and the reported sector count by FTK Imager.

In sector 17, there exists more data, this time a portable networks graphic, PNG file. The data has some padding in the header, which makes its rendering within forensic applications problematic. The data was able to be manually carved from the image and exported. Once the image file was exported from the drive image, it was able to be opened without issue. Research indicates that a hard drive for the XBOX 360 console must have these two pieces of information for it to be considered valid by the XBOX 360 console:

Table 5.2 Sector Offsets for the Security Sector Located at Physical Sector 16

Offset	Length	Type	Information
0 × 0	0 × 14	ascii string	Serial number
0 × 14	0 × 8	ascii string	Firmware revision
0 × 1C	0 × 28	ascii string	Model number
0 × 44	0 × 14	bytes	MS logo hash
0 × 58	0 × 4	unsigned int	Number of sectors on drive
0 × 5C	0 × 100	bytes	RSA signature
0 × 200	0 × 4	signed int	MS logo size
0 × 204	MS logo size	Image	MS logo

FIGURE 5.14

Value for the sector count at offset 0 × 58.

```
Physical Evidentiary Item (Source) Information:
[Drive Geometry]
 Cylinders: 30,401
 Tracks per Cylinder: 255
 Sectors per Track: 63
 Bytes per Sector: 512
 Sector Count: 488,397,168
[Physical Drive Information]
 Drive Model: Hitachi HTS545025B9SA00 USB Device
 Drive Serial Number: 0
 Drive Interface Type: USB
 Source data size: 238475 MB
 Sector count:    488397168
[Computed Hashes]
 MD5 checksum:    050076fd2b52e5176738545d63b24cf0
 SHA1 checksum:   adfe7700cca80a3c6638bd7597ceb69db4cc2827
```

FIGURE 5.15

Verification of the sector count value from the FTK Imager report at the time of acquisition.

Microsoft

FIGURE 5.16

Manually carved Microsoft logo from sector 17.

1. Plain text drive information located at physical sector 16 (the so-called security sector).
2. Microsoft Logo (PNG file located from physical sectors 17 to 22).

If these two pieces of information are not present, then the drive is not recognized by the console and will not be usable. Research indicates that there are three drive manufacturers who have been supplying drives for Microsoft and the XBOX 360 console. These drive manufacturers are as follows:

- Samsung[2]
- Hitachi
- Seagate[3]

This may be another avenue of examination to determine if the drive being examined is linked to the console, an aftermarket purchase, or a home brew hack that enabled a third-party drive to be utilized on the console.

Extraction of the PNG file was a simple matter of finding the normal PNG header and footer and highlighting the data within EnCase. Once the start and stop locations were located, the file was carved from the image file and opened with Irfanview. Figure 5.16 shows the manually extracted file.

[2]Samsung is a registered trademark of the Samsung Corporation.

[3]Seagate is a registered trademark of the Seagate Corporation.

Examination of the "padding" revealed that this information is actually a report of the size of the file. Highlighting the data and converting the values between hex and decimal provide that the hex value, 0A C2, gives a file size of 2754 bytes. This information is verified once the extracted file properties are reviewed. Figures 5.17 and 5.18 show the data as displayed in the EnCase Hex viewer.

From physical sector 23 to physical sector 1023, 1000 sectors, there is data, but it is the hex value of 0 × CD repeated for the entire 1000 sectors. As previously mentioned, this research was not an exercise in reverse engineering, but research shows that Microsoft has, on occasion, reserved space for a variety of "future" uses. It is unclear what the function of these 1000 sectors of 0 × CD is, but it is a block of data that is present on the drive and therefore its boundaries must be marked to determine if it changes as the consoles undergo more usage. Figures 5.19 and 5.20 provide views with two different forensics tools of this data.

Sector 1024 contains the first instance of XTAF, indicating that the file system for the XBOX 360 console is FATX; remember that this information is stored in Big Endian. FATX is a unique file system that has only been documented to exist on the XBOX consoles. It is similar to the FAT file system but there are slight differences. The information located within this sector provides the layout of the FATX drive. The researchers at www.free60.org have once again done a good job of interpreting the data within this sector. The information with this sector contains the "magic name" of XTAF at the start of the sector. Immediately following the XTAF is information that is the partition ID, consisting of 4 bytes. The next 4 bytes in this sector provide the sector count per cluster, which is once again defined by a 4-byte value. Finally, the last value defined in the sector is the root directory cluster, which is once again a 4-byte value.

Figures 5.21 and 5.22 provide information regarding the partition locations on a drive, as well as a table from www.free60.org that details this information quite well.

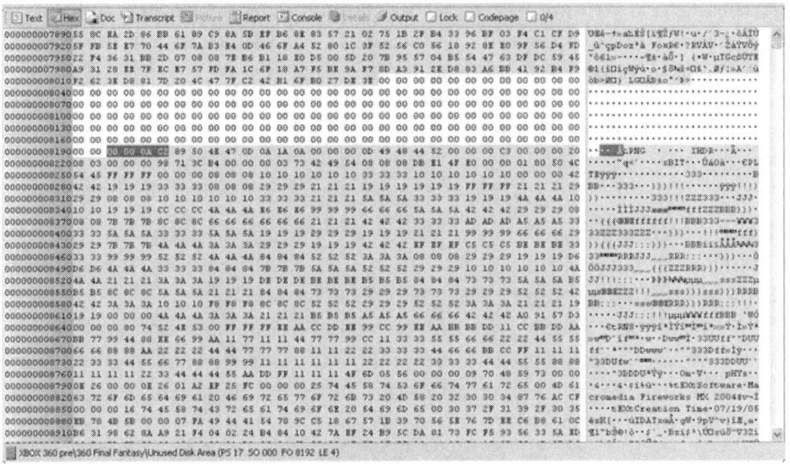

FIGURE 5.17

Sector offset showing the "padding" that is actually the size of the PNG file.

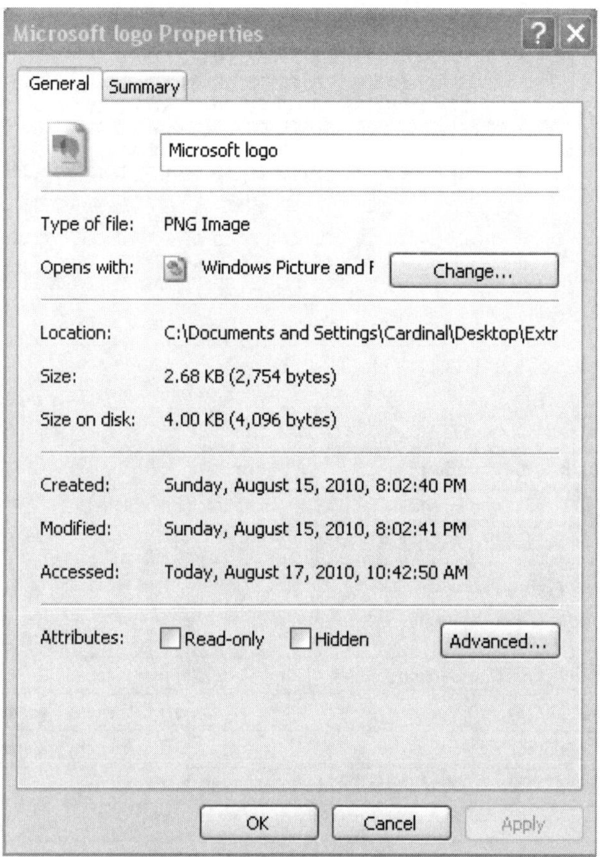

FIGURE 5.18

PNG file properties detailing that the file size padding accurately reports as the size of the file (2754 bytes).

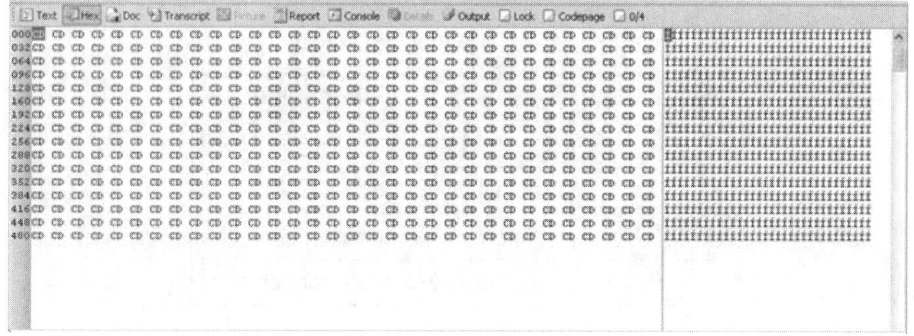

FIGURE 5.19

EnCase snapshot of section of the 0 × CD data that extends from physical sector 23 to physical sector 1023.

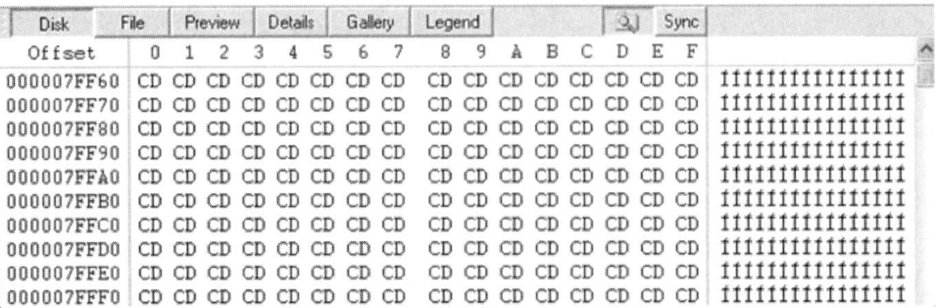

FIGURE 5.20

X-Ways screenshot of the 0 × CD data.

Memory Unit

Offset	Length	Information	Format
0x0	0x7FF000	System Cache	STFC (Secure Transacted File Cache)
0x7FF000	end of drive	Data	FATX

Xbox 360 Hard Drive

Offset	Length	Information	Format
0x2000	0x204 - 0x80000	Security Sector	Binary
0x80000	0x80000000	System Cache	STFC (Secure Transacted File Cache)
0x80080000	0xA0E30000	Game Cache	STFC (Secure Transacted File Cache)
0x120eb0000	0x10000000	Xbox 1 Backwards Compatibility	FATX
0x130eb0000	end of drive	Data	FATX

FIGURE 5.21

Partition locations for a memory unit as well as a hard drive.

Partition Header

For each offset, add the offset of the partition.

Offset	Length	Type	Information
0x0	0x4	ascii string	Partition magic (XTAF)
0x4	0x4	unsigned int	Partition ID
0x8	0x4	unsigned int	Sectors per Cluster
0xC	0x4	unsigned int	Root directory cluster

FIGURE 5.22

Table detailing the information contained in sector 1024 identifying and defining FATX on the drive.

Deciphering this information from the research drive provides the following values:

- Partition "magic" value is still XTAF.
- Partition ID is 0 × 15 B6 41 70 or in decimal value 364265840.
- Sectors per cluster value is 0 × 00 00 00 10 or a decimal value of 16.
- Root directory cluster is a value of 0 × 00 00 00 01 or a decimal value of 1.

Figures 5.23 and 5.24 provide system screenshots depicting the information as it is interpreted by both EnCase and X-Ways.

Detailing the information on this drive in this manner would take a great deal of time, because the drive is reporting in all forensic applications as 233 to 238GB of unallocated space, depending upon the application that is reading the data. There is

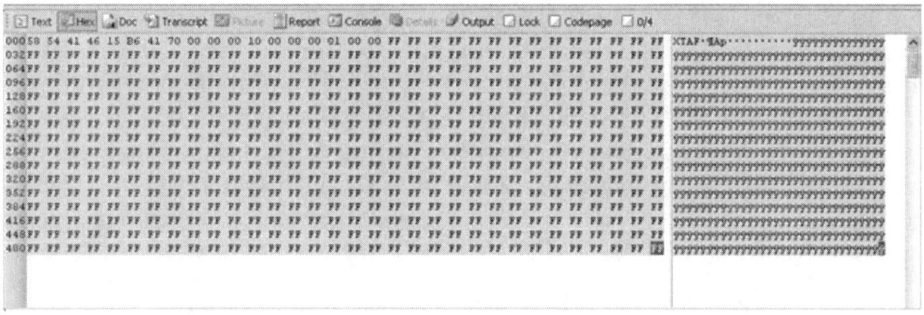

FIGURE 5.23

EnCase screenshot depicting sector 1024 and the XTAF information, or FATX.

0000080000 58 54 41 46 15 B6 41 70 00 00 00 10 00 00 00 01 XTAF ¶Ap
0000080010 00 00 FF FF FF FF FF FF FF FF FF FF FF FF FF FF ÿÿÿÿÿÿÿÿÿÿÿÿÿÿ
0000080020 FF FF FF FF FF FF FF FF FF FF FF FF FF FF FF FF ÿÿÿÿÿÿÿÿÿÿÿÿÿÿÿÿ
0000080030 FF FF FF FF FF FF FF FF FF FF FF FF FF FF FF FF ÿÿÿÿÿÿÿÿÿÿÿÿÿÿÿÿ
0000080040 FF FF FF FF FF FF FF FF FF FF FF FF FF FF FF FF ÿÿÿÿÿÿÿÿÿÿÿÿÿÿÿÿ
0000080050 FF FF FF FF FF FF FF FF FF FF FF FF FF FF FF FF ÿÿÿÿÿÿÿÿÿÿÿÿÿÿÿÿ
0000080060 FF FF FF FF FF FF FF FF FF FF FF FF FF FF FF FF ÿÿÿÿÿÿÿÿÿÿÿÿÿÿÿÿ
0000080070 FF FF FF FF FF FF FF FF FF FF FF FF FF FF FF FF ÿÿÿÿÿÿÿÿÿÿÿÿÿÿÿÿ
0000080080 FF FF FF FF FF FF FF FF FF FF FF FF FF FF FF FF ÿÿÿÿÿÿÿÿÿÿÿÿÿÿÿÿ
0000080090 FF FF FF FF FF FF FF FF FF FF FF FF FF FF FF FF ÿÿÿÿÿÿÿÿÿÿÿÿÿÿÿÿ
00000800A0 FF FF FF FF FF FF FF FF FF FF FF FF FF FF FF FF ÿÿÿÿÿÿÿÿÿÿÿÿÿÿÿÿ
00000800B0 FF FF FF FF FF FF FF FF FF FF FF FF FF FF FF FF ÿÿÿÿÿÿÿÿÿÿÿÿÿÿÿÿ
00000800C0 FF FF FF FF FF FF FF FF FF FF FF FF FF FF FF FF ÿÿÿÿÿÿÿÿÿÿÿÿÿÿÿÿ
00000800D0 FF FF FF FF FF FF FF FF FF FF FF FF FF FF FF FF ÿÿÿÿÿÿÿÿÿÿÿÿÿÿÿÿ
00000800E0 FF FF FF FF FF FF FF FF FF FF FF FF FF FF FF FF ÿÿÿÿÿÿÿÿÿÿÿÿÿÿÿÿ
00000800F0 FF FF FF FF FF FF FF FF FF FF FF FF FF FF FF FF ÿÿÿÿÿÿÿÿÿÿÿÿÿÿÿÿ
0000080100 FF FF FF FF FF FF FF FF FF FF FF FF FF FF FF FF ÿÿÿÿÿÿÿÿÿÿÿÿÿÿÿÿ
0000080110 FF FF FF FF FF FF FF FF FF FF FF FF FF FF FF FF ÿÿÿÿÿÿÿÿÿÿÿÿÿÿÿÿ
0000080120 FF FF FF FF FF FF FF FF FF FF FF FF FF FF FF FF ÿÿÿÿÿÿÿÿÿÿÿÿÿÿÿÿ
0000080130 FF FF FF FF FF FF FF FF FF FF FF FF FF FF FF FF ÿÿÿÿÿÿÿÿÿÿÿÿÿÿÿÿ
0000080140 FF FF FF FF FF FF FF FF FF FF FF FF FF FF FF FF ÿÿÿÿÿÿÿÿÿÿÿÿÿÿÿÿ
0000080150 FF FF FF FF FF FF FF FF FF FF FF FF FF FF FF FF ÿÿÿÿÿÿÿÿÿÿÿÿÿÿÿÿ
0000080160 FF FF FF FF FF FF FF FF FF FF FF FF FF FF FF FF ÿÿÿÿÿÿÿÿÿÿÿÿÿÿÿÿ

FIGURE 5.24

X-Ways screenshot of physical sector 1024 depicting XTAF, or FATX.

a third-party tool that is available online to help interpret the information present on the drive. The tool itself appears to be designed to assist the gaming community in manipulating their game accomplishments, but it can be used for the forensic community to interpret the data on the XBOX 360 drive.

The application is called Xplorer360, and it is available for download at www.xbox-scene.com/xbox1data/sep/EEFAZAlEpAHLgaWKhN.php. Xplorer360 will load a FATX formatted drive or an image of a drive. In this case, the drive was connected to the research machine through a write blocker, a similar set up as before, and loaded the connected drive through Xplorer360. Using another XBOX 360 hard drive that was available, this time a 120GB drive, the application was executed and the drive was loaded into Xplorer360. Xplorer 360 reported that there were three FATX partitions, and Partition 2 reported there was already some information resident on the drive. Figure 5.25 provides a screenshot of Xplorer360 with the drive loaded.

Working with the information that is provided from Xplorer360, a keyword search was conducted specifically searching for the locations of the three FATX partitions. In addition, a keyword search was conducted for the term "xtaf," and results were able to locate all three of the mentioned partitions. The first partition begins at physical sector 1024 and ends at sector 9205119. Taking this information and multiplying by 512 bytes in order to convert to the proper size, the FATX partition appears to be roughly 4.4GB in size.

$$
\begin{aligned}
\text{PS } 9205119 \text{ PS } 1024 &= 9204095 \text{ sectors} \times 512 \text{ bytes} \\
&= 4712496640 \text{ bytes} \\
&= 4.38 \text{ GB}
\end{aligned}
$$

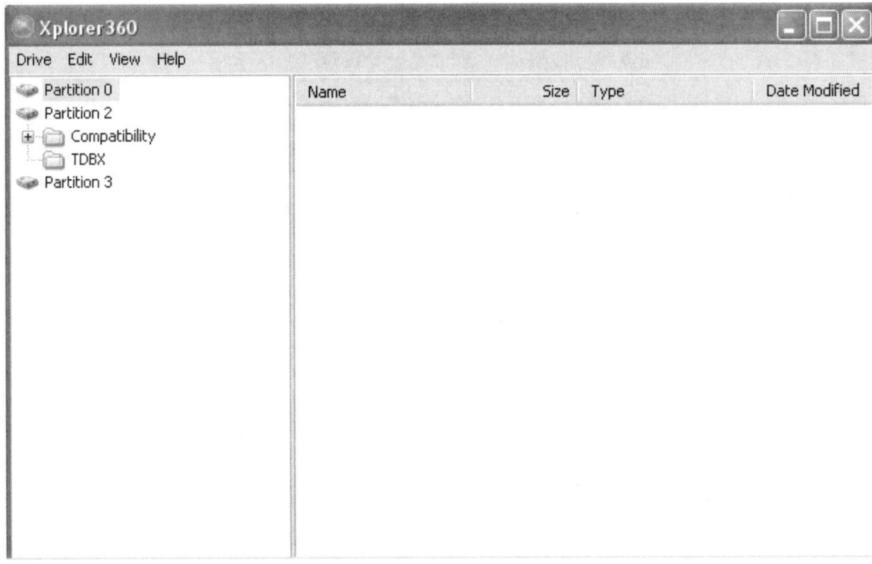

FIGURE 5.25

Xplorer360 with a FATX-formatted drive loaded.

The second instance of "XTAF," and therefore the second FATX partition on the hard drive, is located at physical sector 9205120 and ends at physical sector 9467123. Following through with the same calculation as before, this partition is approximately 125MB.

The next XTAF partition on this drive starts at physical sector 9467264 and ends at physical sector 9991551, for a partition size of approximately 255MB. Still another XTAF partition was located on the research drive. This fourth XTAF, FATX, partition starts at physical sector 9991552.

A summary of the FATX partitions that have been located will provide a better understanding and perhaps a clearer picture of the information. After locating the first partition manually and deciphering the contents within the partition header, it was decided to run a keyword search in EnCase to determine if there were any more partitions. The results revealed that there were a total of four FATX partitions resident on the drive. Figure 5.26 shows the keyword search hits from EnCase, and Figure 5.27 shows the same information, however, from X-Ways.

As mentioned, the drive that had been obtained for this research is a 250GB drive with very little information already stored on it. As such, there is a tremendous amount of empty space, obviously reserved for storage as the console is used and games are saved. The next series of figures are screenshots showing the physical location of the FATX partitions; this is provided simply to show that the partition ID's are different. Figures 5.28 to 5.31 provide images of the FATX partitions, as they are represented in various forensics utilities.

The partition information, once deciphered, details the specifics for each partition. Taking the information from the partition header information previously detailed, the first two partition's information is as follows:

- Partition 1
  - Start sector 1024
  - Stop sector 9205119
  - Partition ID = 0 × 15 B6 41 70
  - Sectors per cluster = 0 × 00 00 00 10 or a decimal value of 16
  - Root directory cluster = 0 × 00 00 00 01 or a decimal value of 1

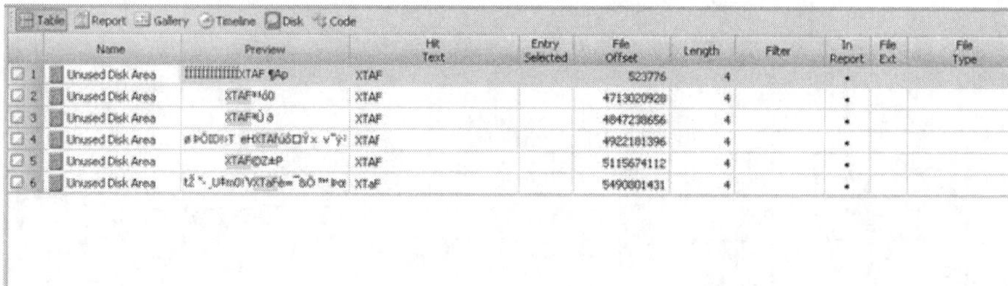

FIGURE 5.26

Screenshot of the search hits on the keyword of XTAF or FATX.

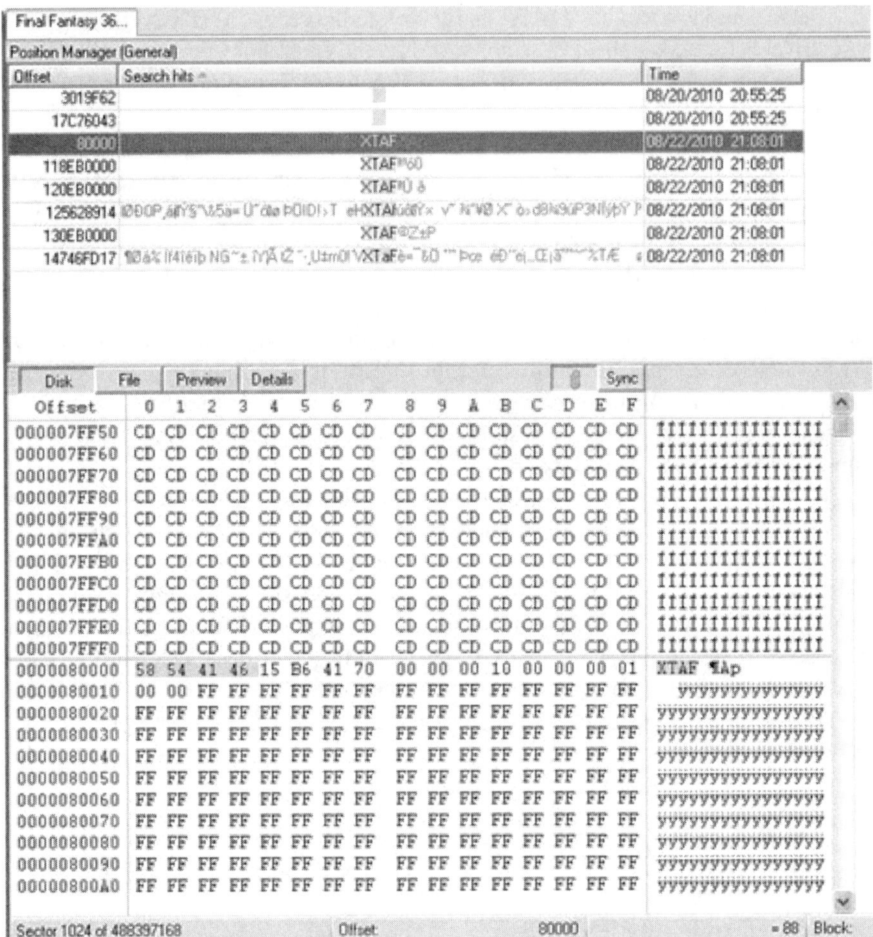

FIGURE 5.27

Screenshot of the search hits for XTAF using X-Ways; the term was located six times using X-Ways.

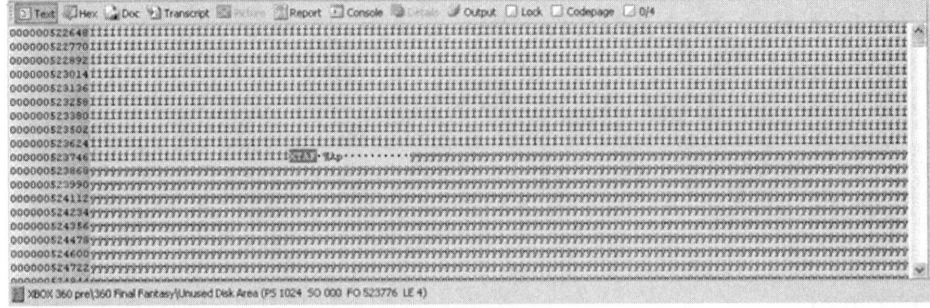

FIGURE 5.28

First FATX partition on the drive, located at physical sector 1024.

FIGURE 5.29

The second FATX-partition that was located on the drive, located at physical sector 9205120.

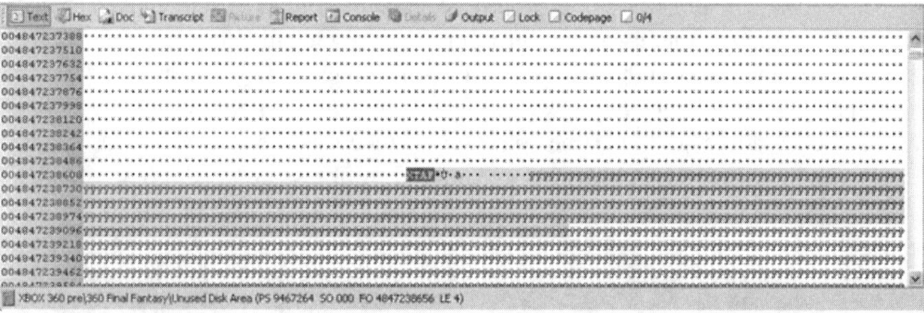

FIGURE 5.30

The third FATX-partition is located at physical sector 9467264.

FIGURE 5.31

The fourth partition on the drive is located at physical sector 9991552.

- Partition 2
  - Start sector 9205120
  - Stop sector 9467263
  - Partition ID = 0 × AA D9 13 F0
  - Sectors per cluster = 0 × 00 00 00 20 or a decimal value of 32
  - Root directory cluster = 0 × 00 00 00 01 or a decimal value of 1

There are still additional partitions on the drive, but the idea here was to show that each partition has its own ID and sectors per cluster count. Each partition can be dissected in this way to provide the details as needed.

ADDITIONAL INFORMATION LOCATED ON THE DRIVE

Previous research provided information that there exists on each hard drive what Microsoft has termed XBOX 360 extras. These extras include game and movie trailers, music, full-length games, and dashboard themes. Although the previous research was several years ago, it was a safe bet that there still existed on the new drives some residual data.

In order to test this theory, the console was once again connected with the hard drive. After waiting the appropriate amount of time for the console to recognize the drive and automatically sign in with a profile, each panel was then navigated to in an effort to determine if there was any information stored locally.

Navigation was a straightforward process once logged into the console. After the log-in process, the Games panel was navigated in order to determine if any games were listed. In doing so, the Games panel confirmed that there were six games, one full game called Hexic HD, previously identified from research in 2006. Figure 5.32

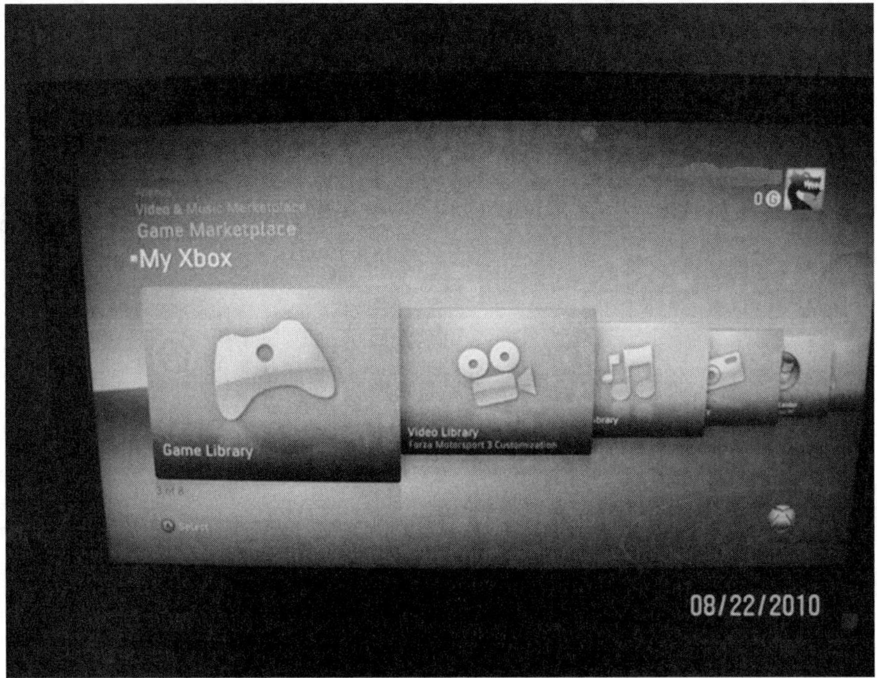

FIGURE 5.32

Screenshot of the Games Library panel.

FIGURE 5.33

This screenshot shows the title of the games that are already on the hard drive.

provides a screenshot of the Games Library panel. The other games were new to this particular hard drive, as were all game trailers; each is listed next, and a screenshot of the games' list is provided in Figure 5.33.

- Pinball FX G
- Peggle
- Geometry Ways Evolved
- Galaga Legions
- SWOS

After reviewing the default game installations, the next step was to try to identify any videos that may be on the hard drive. The Video Library panel was the next panel to be explored, and there were two videos listed, the Forza Motorsport 3 and a welcome video. The video library screens and video downloads are depicted in Figures 5.33 to 5.36.

Because the console is designed to network to other devices there is the functionality listed by which to connect to a computer for videos. The **Downloaded Videos** option was selected.

Following this procedure, each panel was navigated in sequence, seeking more information that could be documented for the default data that is resident on the drive. In doing so, there was no new information revealed that suggested there were other media artifacts on the drive. The next steps were to take the information that was located and generate a keyword list to search for. EnCase and X-Ways were used to search for these keywords, and the results from each utility were similar.

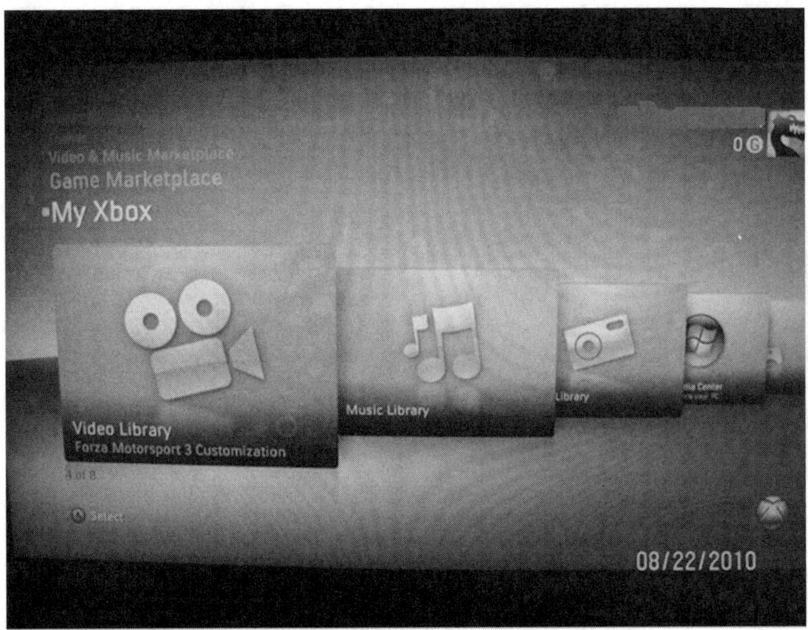

FIGURE 5.34

Video Library panel.

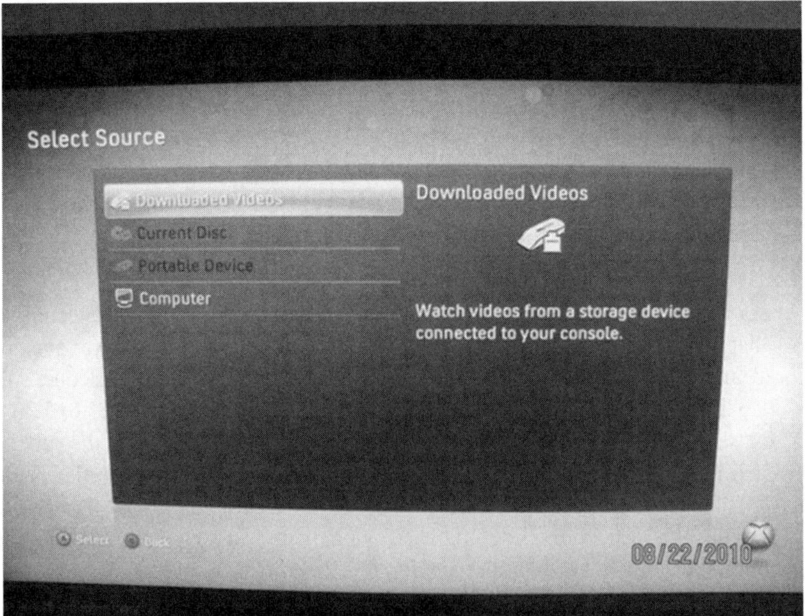

FIGURE 5.35

Video source selection.

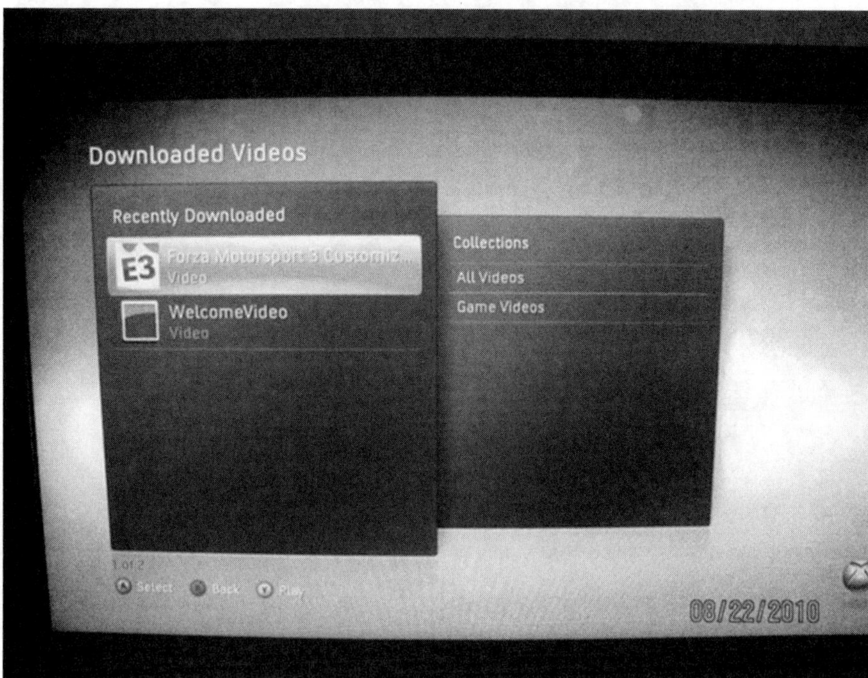

FIGURE 5.36

Screenshot detailing the two videos that were listed in the video library downloaded content.

Conducting a keyword search for Forza Motorsport 3 using EnCase, seven entries were located. Forza Motorsport 3 is a video game, and this video file seems to be a trailer advertising the game. Figure 5.37 depicts the information that was located.

The next video to look for was the welcome video that is launched once the console is turned on and boots properly. The video is a short video that introduces the console and details some of the functions and XBOX Live. A keyword search for the term "welcome" provides 40 search hits, but none of them were for the welcome video, Figure 5.38. Additional searches for Windows Media Player[4] were conducted that located videos, which were extracted, but they were not able to be played with a media player. Every search hit in the list provided information pertaining to the games that are located on the drive. Some of the search hits were game text, and others were a welcome message to the game itself, in this case Peggle.

The next items that were chosen to search for were the games that were preloaded on the hard drive. In order to look for the data for each of these games, a new keyword list was created in EnCase, and the search was launched with this list checked as the keywords. The information was interesting to say the least. The number of hits per keyword was larger than had originally been expected, but then it was remembered that the console is marketed in several countries and many of these games have to

[4]Windows Media Player is a registered trademark of the Microsoft Corporation.

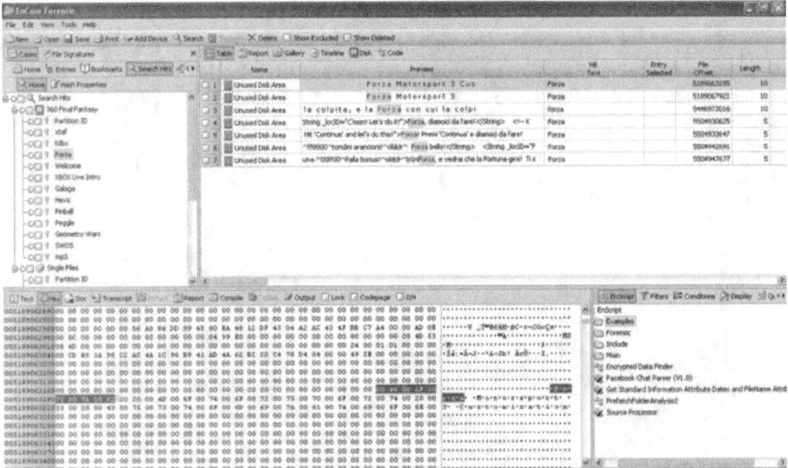

FIGURE 5.37

Screenshot showing the seven search hits on Forza Motorsport 3.

	Name	Preview	Hit Text	Entry Selected	File Offset	Length
21	Unused Disk Area	IN YOUR NEW JOB WELCOME %a, WE LOOK FOR	WELCOME		5447506307	16
22	Unused Disk Area	NEW PARTNERSHIP WELCOME %a, WE HOPE YOU	WELCOME		5447506445	16
23	Unused Disk Area	E CAREER******* WELCOME TO OUR CLUB %a,	WELCOME		5447511833	16
24	Unused Disk Area	TNERSHIP******* WELCOME TO OUR CLUB, WE	WELCOME		5447512013	16
25	Unused Disk Area	UNGER MAN****** WELCOME TO OUR CLUB, WE	WELCOME		5447515713	16
26	Unused Disk Area	IN YOUR NEW JOB WELCOME %a, WE LOOK FOR	WELCOME		5447637379	16
27	Unused Disk Area	NEW PARTNERSHIP WELCOME %a, WE HOPE YOU	WELCOME		5447637517	16
28	Unused Disk Area	E CAREER******* WELCOME TO OUR CLUB %a,	WELCOME		5447642905	16
29	Unused Disk Area	TNERSHIP******* WELCOME TO OUR CLUB, WE	WELCOME		5447643085	16
30	Unused Disk Area	UNGER MAN****** WELCOME TO OUR CLUB, WE	WELCOME		5447646785	16
31	Unused Disk Area	</String> <String _locID="Welcome to Peggle!">Sei gegrÃ¼Ãt! Willkomm	Welcome		5495371778	8
32	Unused Disk Area	el</String> <String _locID="Welcome to Peggle!">Greetings! Welcome to t	Welcome		5499765185	8
33	Unused Disk Area	ID="Welcome to Peggle!">Greetings! Welcome to the Peggle Institute.</String>	Welcome		5499765216	8
34	Unused Disk Area	String> <String _locID="Welcome to Peggle!">Â¡Hola! Te doy la bienv	Welcome		5501469246	8
35	Unused Disk Area	</String> <String _locID="Welcome to Peggle!">Salutations ! Bien	Welcome		5503304104	8

FIGURE 5.38

Screenshot of the keyword "Welcome"search hits.

have multilingual support, which may account for the large number of hits. The following is a list of the video game keywords and their search hit count:

- Galaga: 634 hits
- Hexic: 179 hits
- Pinball: 36 hits
- Peggle: 917 hits
- Geometry Wars: 28 hits
- SWOS: 185 hits

Figure 5.39 provides a screenshot of how the search hits for Hexic are represented within EnCase. This sample is provided to show how the information is located on the drive in multiple locations.

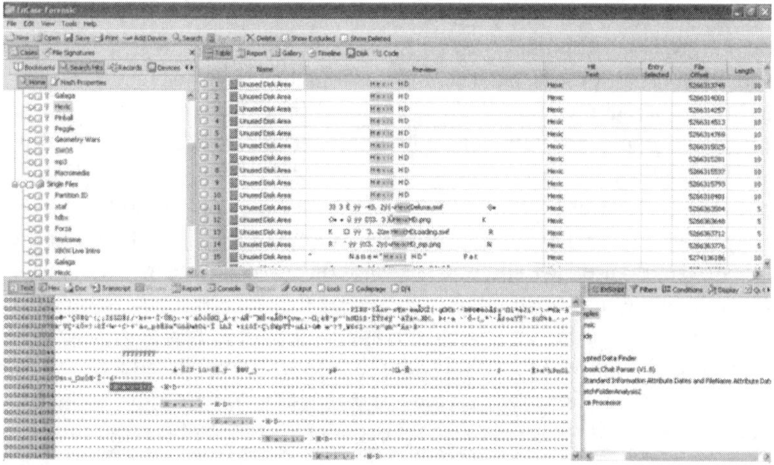

FIGURE 5.39

Depiction of how Hexic is reported after a keyword search within EnCase.

Additional searching of the drive using some of the keywords that were utilized in the past, as well as due to continued research, provided several search hits that are of interest. Once again, there are instances of the terms "macromedia fireworks" and "MP3." While searching the drive for information, there was a long list of information that we learned could be utilized as keywords to search. Making sense of some of the data was still elusive, but the artifacts were present.

Examining the information located on the game Hexic, there is some more information that needs to be detailed. This game has a sound track that plays along as the game progresses, as most modern games do. The music for the game is stored on the drive, as well as the audio tracks for the console and all associated introductions and multimedia that is played from the stored content.

Knowing that there are PNG files on the hard drive, it was decided to attempt a data carve with EnCase to see if the information could be extracted from the image. Unfortunately, the PNGs were not able to be extracted through the EnCase data carve process; this could be due to a variety of reasons, so if at first you don't succeed, try again. The data carves were able to be manually carved once the headers were located. For an automated data carve process, both X-Ways, Forensics and Access Data's FTK were used, and each successfully extracted image files. This information was used to create a hash set of the standard images located on the drive.

One of the first steps to recover files was to load the image into Access Data's FTK and conduct a default data carve for files; this was able to extract a great deal of information from the drive. FTK, as with all other mainstream forensic utilities, cannot interpret the FATX file system, so the drive was reported as unallocated space. After the data carve completed, the total number of files was a little surprising. The "graphics" that were reported numbered 4427 image files and a report of 1012 duplicate items. Reviewing the images, it appears that many of the images seem to be the same image in various languages, once again theorized to be because of the retail markets, in which the console is marketed in. Figure 5.40 shows an example of the information, as it was reported with FTK.

In addition to using FTK to data carve the drive image, it was loaded into X-Ways to determine what, if anything, X-Ways could interpret from the image. Once again, the application could not sufficiently interpret the file structure, so the drive was reported as unallocated space. Using one of the tools under the **Specialist** menu option, a data carver was performed on the drive. X-Ways only reported a fraction of what was reported by FTK. X-Ways reported a total of 197 PNG files that it carved from the image. Figure 5.41 shows a snapshot of the data as reported in X-Ways.

Researching the information that is stored on the drives provided some expected results. It seems that the information that is stored on the hard drive is dependent upon which version of the drive is bundled with the console or purchased as an aftermarket drive. Some special edition consoles have special game trailers, other retail packages are released at the time that a new game is coming to market, and so on. However,

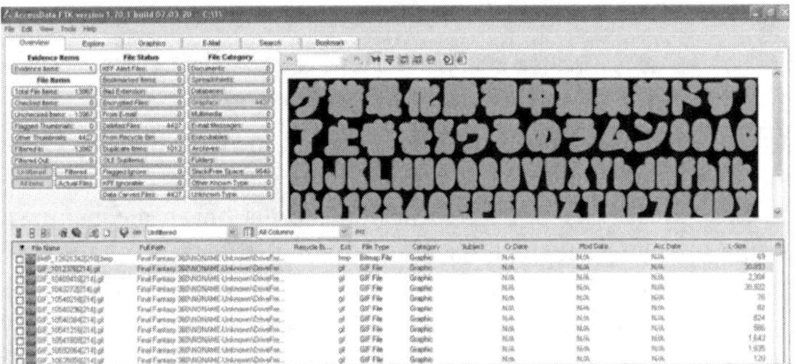

FIGURE 5.40

FTK screenshot showing the graphics count and duplicate items.

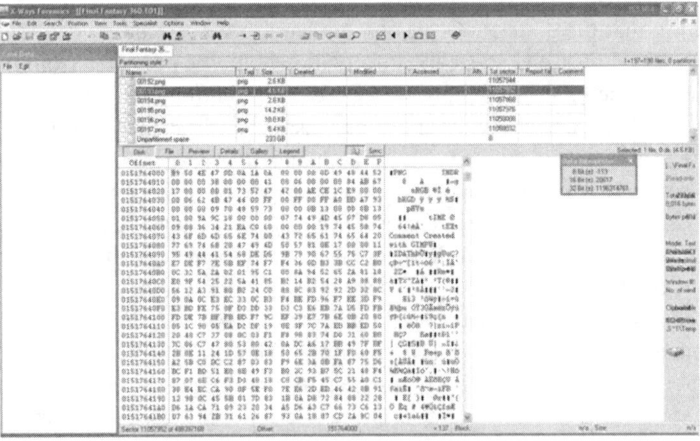

FIGURE 5.41

X-Ways forensic report of recovered PNG files.

there seems to be some classifications of content that can be applied to the type of information that is preloaded. The generic content umbrella classifications that can be said to be included on the drives are games, demos and full versions, videos, movie trailers, welcome videos and game trailers, and finally audio tracks. One Web site that was located during the research detailed some information that they believed could be located on the 120GB hard drive. Without a drive to confirm this information, it cannot be said for certain that this information is present, but it is provided here in case an examiner encounters a drive of this nature. Figures 5.42 to 5.44 provide lists of the data that can be located on the hard drive. (List retrieved from: www.gearlive.com/news/article/q207-list-of-pre-loaded-content-on-xbox-360-120-gb-hard-drive/.)

Trailers:
Forza 2 customization and damage videos
Halo Wars
Fable 2
Halo 3 TV Ad
Halo 3 Trailer
Halo 3 et tu brute video
Accessories TV Spot
Wireless World Video
Holiday '06 Accessories Video

Full Games:
Hexic HD

FIGURE 5.42

Partial list of XBOX 360 120GB drive preloaded content.

Playable Demos:
Assault Heroes
Cloning Clyde
Geometry Wars
Marble Blast Ultra
Small Arms
Feeding Frenzy
Uno
Pac-Man
Street Fighter II
Lumines Live!
Zuma
Heavy Weapon
Lego Star Wars II
Lost Planet (multiplayer Live)
Madden '07
Fusion Frenzy 2
Call of Duty 3

Plus several themes and gamer pics

FIGURE 5.43

Partial list of XBOX 360 120GB drive preloaded content.

If you pick up an Xbox 360 Elite, you get these additional peices of content, which are mostly just promotional videos:

Videos:
Step into Liquid
Justice League
The Goal 2/3
Adidas Clip #1
Adidas Clip #2
UFC All Access
Viva Piñata
Warren Miller - Extreme Sports

Full Games:
Hexic HD

Playable Demos:
Lara Croft Tomb Raider™ LEGEND
Kameo™: Elements of Power™ (2nd Demo)
Burnout Revenge™

Plus several themes and gamer pics

FIGURE 5.44

Partial list of XBOX 360 120GB drive preloaded content.

SUMMARY

A great deal of information was covered in this chapter. Imaging the hard drive is a straightforward process that is easily conducted with a write blocker and your choice of forensic application. An initial review of the hard drive and the stored information reveals that the drive is formatted FATX and that there is some preloaded content on the drive. From games to trailers to Gamertag images, the data that is preloaded needs to be documented so that examiners have the known values to deal with.

References

[1] www.free60.org/fatx (accessed 23.08.10).
[2] Free60. http://www.free60.org (accessed 23.08.10).
[3] XBOX-Scene. "Xplorer360 v0.9: Read/Write access to XBOX 360 HD, Mcard." http://www.xbox-scene.com/xbox1data/sep/EEFAZAlEpAHLgaWKhN.php (accessed 23.08.10).
[4] XBOX-Scene News: Xplorer360 v0.9: Read/Write access to XBOX 360 HD, Mcard *UPDATED* Beta2. Xbox-Scene.com–XBOX 360 XBOX360 Modchips Xecuter3 Xenium SmartXX X-Chip X-B.I.T Xecuter2.6 Xodus–Gamesave Dashboard exploit–EvolutionX Avalaunch MXM Dashboard UnleashX–X2 & EvoX bios–Copy XBOX Hacks & Cracks tutorials faq–Cheapmod. N.p., n.d. http://www.xbox-scene.com/xbox1data/sep/EEFAZAlEpAHLgaWKhN.php (accessed 22.08.10).

CHAPTER

XBOX 360–Specific File Types

6

INFORMATION IN THIS CHAPTER

- XBOX content

XBOX CONTENT

Some of the information on the XBOX 360 console is provided through downloads through the XBOX Live service. Generally, there are three types or general classifications of downloads that are pushed to the machine during the course of online activities. These classifications can either be system software updates, game updates, including map updates, or XBOX firmware updates. Each of these classifications of compressed data can be distinguished by its signature. Once again the researchers at www.free60.org have done an excellent job of dissecting the information within these files. The three file signatures, or magic bytes, are CON files, PIRS files, and LIVE files.

CON Files

The CON files seem to be console-specific files, such as cache files, profiles, and game saves. This information is very sparse on the image from the hard drive that was pulled from the retail package. Running a keyword search for "CON" provided several hits, but the way in which the data was coded in the keyword was the issue. There were more than 15,000 hits on the word "CON," but that included terms such as content, context, and so on. Figure 6.1 is a screenshot showing my mistake, but it also provides the investigators more details as to the data that is included on a nonused hard drive for the console.

Figure 6.1 provides a very good look at the additional keywords, located in the upper left-hand corner, that were used to search the drive. With the search hits for the word "CON," there are many instances of the word in plain text, providing the clear evidence that the drive is full of data fresh from the box.

The CON files that we are searching for, the files that are specific to the console are lacking on this drive at this stage of the research. In fact, there is only one

FIGURE 6.1

Example of the keyword search hits for the word "con."

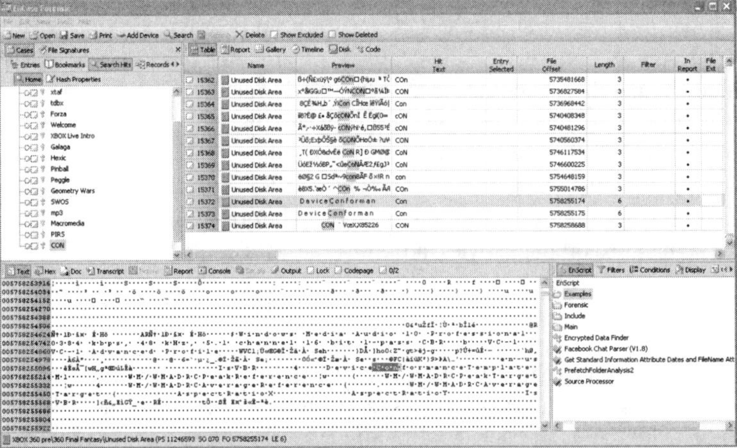

FIGURE 6.2

Con file within EnCase.

instance of this type of file on the hard drive, and it just so happens that it was the last hit on the search list. This file appears to be one that is signed by a specific console, which could indicate whether or not a hard drive with an associated gamer profile was removed and added to another console because the drives are interchangeable between consoles. The saved game information may provide the vector of communication between a suspect and victim or between two or more suspects, or provide information to refute such a connection. Figure 6.2 is a screenshot of a CON file as it is displayed within EnCase.

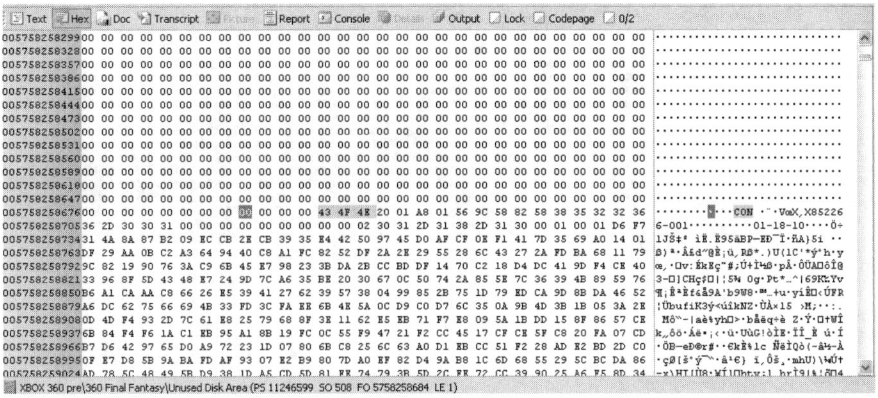

FIGURE 6.3

A more detailed look at the CON file through a hex editor.

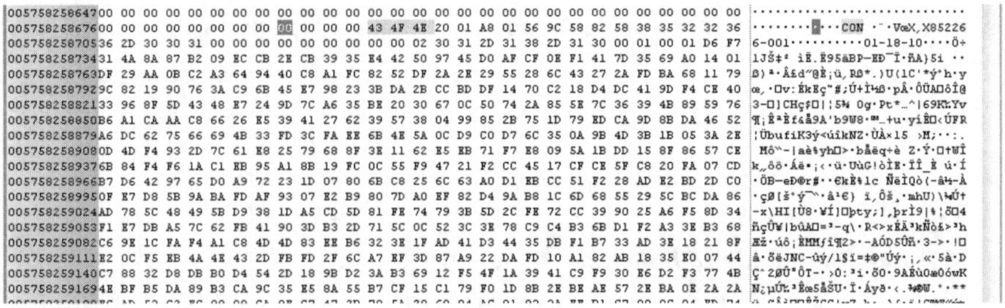

FIGURE 6.4

CON security certificate.

Figure 6.3 (details through a hex editor) provides a little more detail in regard to the information found within the CON file. These files are digitally signed using the console security certificate. This is evidenced by reviewing the details from sector 4, the security sector, and the CON file that is located in a physical sector 11246600. Figure 6.4 provides an example of the data as viewed through EnCase.

Although Figures 6.4 and 6.5 provide hex views of the security certificates; a better look at these two areas provides a good comparison as shown in Table 6.1.

The next step is to dissect the information that was located within the CON file and compare it to the console security sector. Research indicates that the CON files use the same digital signature that the security sector uses, thereby linking the console to the CON files. This might be a verification process that Microsoft uses for one reason or another. Having read that many attempts have been made to modify the console, these attempts, if detected, prevent the end user from connecting to the Live service once a software modification has been made; perhaps this information sheds some light on the subject.

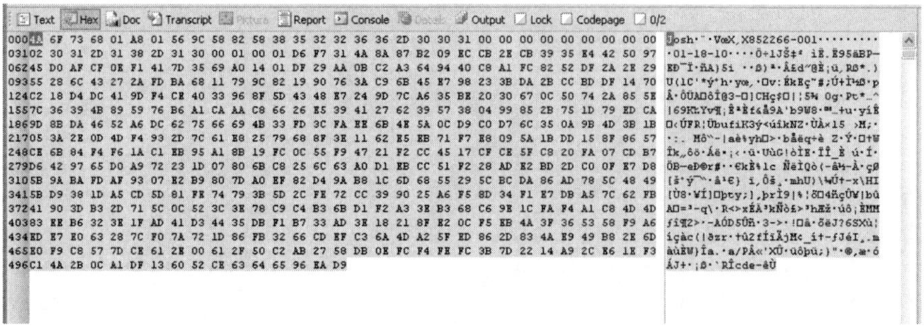

FIGURE 6.5

Console security certificate.

Table 6.1 Data Contained within the Security Certificates

Offset	Length	Type	Information
Console Security Certificate			
0 × 0	0 × 8	(un?)signed long	Unknown(ID of some kind?)
0 × 8	0 × 14	Bytes	Unknown(0 × 14 bytes … SHA1 hash?)
0 × 1c	0 × 4	(un?)signed int	Unknown
0 × 20	0 × 4	(un?)signed int	Unknown
The Sector Then Ends with the Following Format			
0 × 0	0 × 4	(un?)signed int	Unknown
0 × 4	0 × 4	(un?)signed int	Unknown
0 × 8	0 × 4	(un?)signed int	Unknown
0 × C	0 × 4	(un?)signed int	Unknown

Reference www.free60.org

As a spot check to ensure that the information that is contained within this physical sector and CON file does use the console security certificate, some verification needed to be conducted. In order to verify this information, the console security sector from physical sector 4 was compared with the information located with the CON file. The first 8 bytes of information are thought to be an ID of some sort and include the plain text name of "Josh."

From the security sector:

0 × 4A 6F 73 68 01 A8 01 56

From the CON file:

0 × 4A 6F 73 68 01 A8 01 56

Table 6.2 First Eight PIRS Search Hit Plain Text Information

Physical Sector[a]	Plain Text Information
9205392	Community Games Player Pack
9241618	Live Utilities Update
9244848	Avatar Asset Package
9272208	Avatar App Pack
9304688	Dictionary Pack
9306832	Certificate Pack
9306992	Dash Pack
9328912	Migration Pack

[a]*This pattern continues throughout the first eight entries of the PIRS search hits that were performed. The information below details the physical sectors of these first eight entries along with the plain text that is associated with it.*

The next information that is presented for comparison is a hash of some sort; it starts at offset 0 × 8 and is 14 bytes in length, and it also matches from between the security sector and the CON file.

0 × 9C 58 82 58 38 35 32 32 36 36 2D 30 30 31

In plain text this is "œX,X852266-001."

Without dissecting the entire file, it is clear that the security sector, which includes the console security certificate, is reused with the CON files, providing a linkage of sorts between the cache files, the profiles on the console, saved games and perhaps more information. For an investigator or examiner, this information could provide the linkage between a particular console and a Gamertag or show that a gamer played a particular game on a particular console.

PIRS and LIVE Files

The next two classifications of XBOX compressed files are the PIRS and LIVE files. Research indicates that the PIRS files are files that are signed and delivered by Microsoft but not delivered through the XBOX Live services, including such items as system updates. A search of the pre–system update drive, fresh from the retail package, for the keyword "PIRS" reveals that there are 23 instances of the word on the drive. Many of these PIRS instances are associated with the preinstalled games that were identified earlier. Examining the information gives some insight as to what the information that may be stored within this file format relates to.

The first eight instances of the PIRS file on the drive seem to be specific to more network functionality rather than the preloaded games, shown in Table 6.2. The first instance occurs at physical sector 9205392. Along with the search hit for PIRS, there is some plain text that indicates the information within this file is responsible for the community games that can be played over the XBOX Live service. It is unclear exactly what the function of this file is; it could be either a storage location for later content download from the Live service or a code that is only unpacked and executed when the gamer connects to the Live service and plays in the community games that are located there. Figures 6.6 and 6.7 provide views of this information through EnCase and X-Ways Forensic.

Similar information is presented in the next seven hits on the search term "PIRS." The next entry in the search results provides plain text entries for "Live Utilities Update," which is clearly an indicator of XBOX Live utilities, and the data is stored

004713159782 ÿÿ
004713159891 ÿÿ
004713160000 ÿÿ
004713160109 ÿÿÿPIRS`3N·ƒS·KRFF...
004713160218 [illegible]
004713160327 [illegible]
004713160436 [illegible]
004713160545 ···
004713160654 ···ÿÿÿÿÿÿÿÿ······
004713160763 ···
004713160872 ···
004713160981 [illegible]
004713161090 [illegible]
004713161199 ·······························C·o·m·m·u·n·i·t·y· ·G·a·m·e·s· ·P·l·a·y·e·r· ·P·a·c·k·····················
004713161308 ···
004713161417 ···
004713161526 ···

FIGURE 6.6

View of the first search hit on the keyword "PIRS"; note the plain text data referencing Community Games Player Pack.

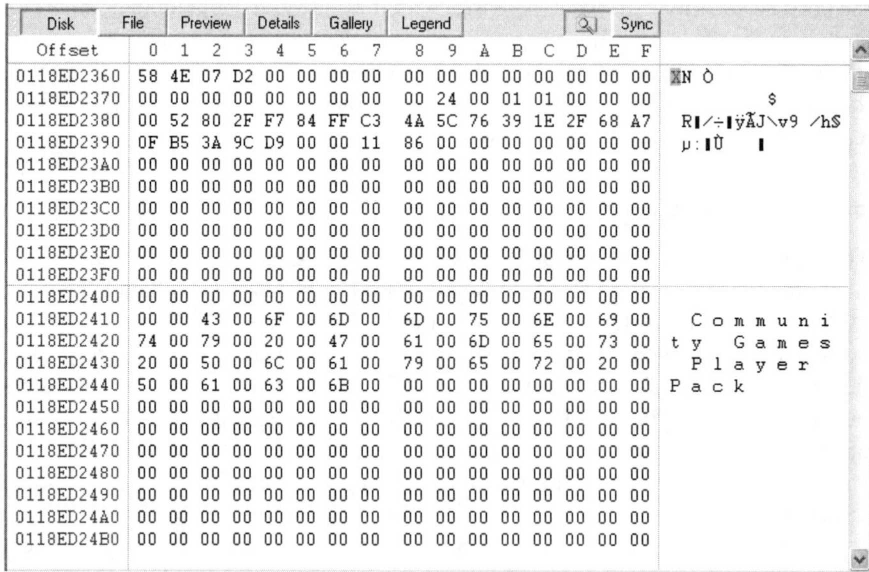

Disk | File | Preview | Details | Gallery | Legend | Sync

Offset	0	1	2	3	4	5	6	7	8	9	A	B	C	D	E	F	
0118ED2360	58	4E	07	D2	00	00	00	00	00	00	00	00	00	00	00	00	XN Ò
0118ED2370	00	00	00	00	00	00	00	00	00	24	00	01	01	00	00	00	$
0118ED2380	00	52	80	2F	F7	84	FF	C3	4A	5C	76	39	1E	2F	68	A7	R /÷ ÿÃJ\v9 /h§
0118ED2390	0F	B5	3A	9C	D9	00	00	11	86	00	00	00	00	00	00	00	µ: Ù
0118ED23A0	00	00	00	00	00	00	00	00	00	00	00	00	00	00	00	00	
0118ED23B0	00	00	00	00	00	00	00	00	00	00	00	00	00	00	00	00	
0118ED23C0	00	00	00	00	00	00	00	00	00	00	00	00	00	00	00	00	
0118ED23D0	00	00	00	00	00	00	00	00	00	00	00	00	00	00	00	00	
0118ED23E0	00	00	00	00	00	00	00	00	00	00	00	00	00	00	00	00	
0118ED23F0	00	00	00	00	00	00	00	00	00	00	00	00	00	00	00	00	
0118ED2400	00	00	00	00	00	00	00	00	00	00	00	00	00	00	00	00	
0118ED2410	00	00	43	00	6F	00	6D	00	6D	00	75	00	6E	00	69	00	C o m m u n i
0118ED2420	74	00	79	00	20	00	47	00	61	00	6D	00	65	00	73	00	t y G a m e s
0118ED2430	20	00	50	00	6C	00	61	00	79	00	65	00	72	00	20	00	P l a y e r
0118ED2440	50	00	61	00	63	00	6B	00	00	00	00	00	00	00	00	00	P a c k
0118ED2450	00	00	00	00	00	00	00	00	00	00	00	00	00	00	00	00	
0118ED2460	00	00	00	00	00	00	00	00	00	00	00	00	00	00	00	00	
0118ED2470	00	00	00	00	00	00	00	00	00	00	00	00	00	00	00	00	
0118ED2480	00	00	00	00	00	00	00	00	00	00	00	00	00	00	00	00	
0118ED2490	00	00	00	00	00	00	00	00	00	00	00	00	00	00	00	00	
0118ED24A0	00	00	00	00	00	00	00	00	00	00	00	00	00	00	00	00	
0118ED24B0	00	00	00	00	00	00	00	00	00	00	00	00	00	00	00	00	

FIGURE 6.7

The X-Ways interpretation of the same data that is represented in Figure 6.6.

in physical sector 9241618. It is theorized that the information that is stored within these PIRS files is executed once the end user navigates to the particular functionality that would call the referenced information. Figures 6.8 and 6.9 depict the information located within this sector.

The ninth search hit on PIRS does not appear to be a PIRS file header and is simply the phrase "pirs" buried within other text. Figure 6.10 provides a screenshot of this information.

The next several hits on PIRS are directly related to the preinstalled information such as the preloaded games. The information located within these next few files can be summed up in Table 6.3. The way in which the information is displayed in EnCase and X-Ways is no different than it was earlier displayed.

There were four PIRS keyword hits that did not conform to the standard listed in the two tables. Three of the four appear to be simply a matter of the phrase matching the search pattern. In each of these three cases, the PIRS code is listed, but it is not a header and is buried within the text of other data. Although this suggests it

FIGURE 6.8

PIRS file from sector 9241618 depicting the plain text of Live Utilities Update.

Offset	0	1	2	3	4	5	6	7	8	9	A	B	C	D	E	F	
011A082400	00	00	00	00	00	00	00	00	00	00	00	00	00	00	00	00	
011A082410	00	00	4C	00	69	00	76	00	65	00	20	00	55	00	74	00	L i v e U t
011A082420	69	00	6C	00	69	00	74	00	69	00	65	00	73	00	20	00	i l i t i e s
011A082430	55	00	70	00	64	00	61	00	74	00	65	00	00	00	00	00	U p d a t e
011A082440	00	00	00	00	00	00	00	00	00	00	00	00	00	00	00	00	
011A082450	00	00	00	00	00	00	00	00	00	00	00	00	00	00	00	00	
011A082460	00	00	00	00	00	00	00	00	00	00	00	00	00	00	00	00	
011A082470	00	00	00	00	00	00	00	00	00	00	00	00	00	00	00	00	
011A082480	00	00	00	00	00	00	00	00	00	00	00	00	00	00	00	00	
011A082490	00	00	00	00	00	00	00	00	00	00	00	00	00	00	00	00	
011A0824A0	00	00	00	00	00	00	00	00	00	00	00	00	00	00	00	00	
011A0824B0	00	00	00	00	00	00	00	00	00	00	00	00	00	00	00	00	
011A0824C0	00	00	00	00	00	00	00	00	00	00	00	00	00	00	00	00	

FIGURE 6.9

A snapshot of the same PIRS file as depicted in Figure 6.8.

FIGURE 6.10

PIRS search hit that is not a PIRS file.

Table 6.3 Additional Physical Sectors and the Associated Plain Text

Physical Sector	Associated Plain Text Information
10109224	System Update
10124680	Fusions Title Update
10134888	Forza Motorsport 3 customization
10285768	Hexic HD
10398600	Pinball
10500104	Sensible World of Soccer
10640168	Peggle
10849768	Galaga Legions
11051048	Geometry Wars
11133608	Welcome Video

is not of importance to the listing of the other PIRS file headers, it was decided to include a snapshot of the data to demonstrate the context in which the information rests. Figure 6.11 provides a screen capture of the PIRS search hit as it exists in these search hits.

The last false search hit on the term "PIRS" as a file header occurs at search hit number 18 within my EnCase case. In this particular instance, the information is once again not a file header but appears to be a name. The data is located within an area of data that appears to be a set of names. A search of the surrounding sectors provides no clues as to the nature of the list of names. Speculation is that this might be a list of the programmers from a preloaded game or video. Another theory is that this could be a list of characters from within a video game that is preloaded on

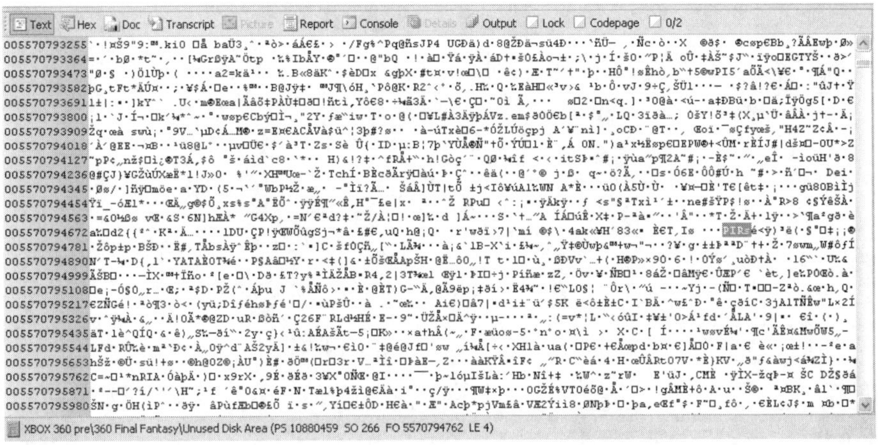

FIGURE 6.11

Screenshot depicting a search hit on PIRS that is not a file header.

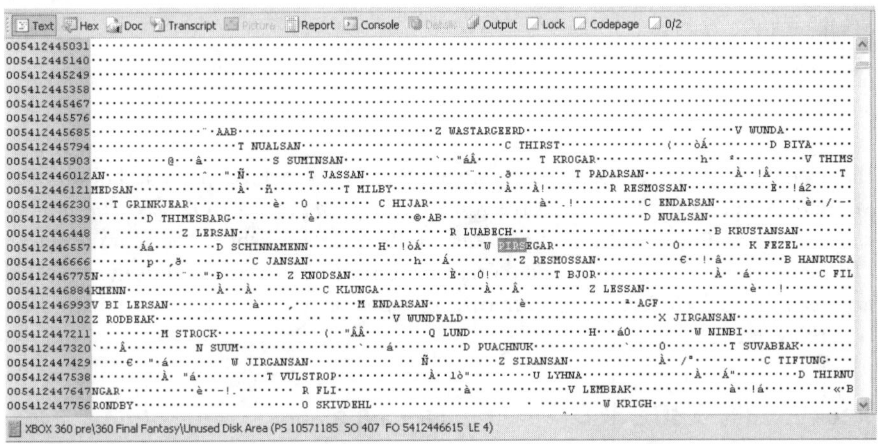

FIGURE 6.12

PIRS search hit number 18, what appears to be a last name and a first initial.

the hard drive. In an effort to make sense of the information, several searches were conducted on the Internet using a variety of search engines and search terms and using several variations of the name in conjunction with Microsoft or XBOX 360 and XBOX Live, but nothing was returned that provided any further information. Figure 6.12 provides a screenshot detailing the information.

The last XBOX 360–specific file type is the file with the LIVE header. A keyword search of the pre–system update drive did not return any hits with "LIVE" as

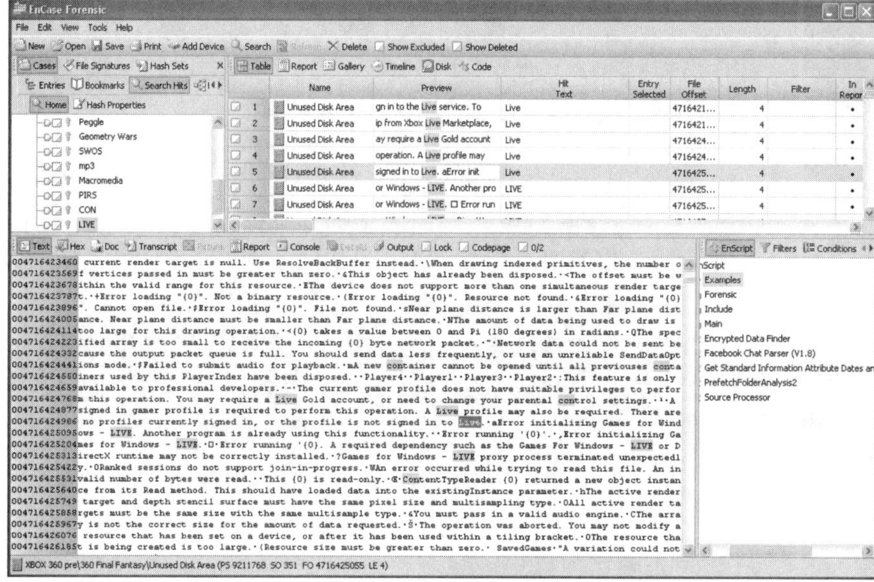

FIGURE 6.13

Keyword search hits on the word "LIVE." There were no hits with LIVE as a file header.

the header. There were many search hits with the keyword live present, but this was simply text referencing XBOX Live content or signing into XBOX Live, or indicating that the end user was not signed into XBOX Live. In short, the search hits for "LIVE" on this pre–system update drive were messages to the end user, regarding connections to XBOX Live. Figure 6.13 provides an example of the data and how it is represented.

Recap of the XBOX 360–Specific File Types

There is a great deal of data that is present on the hard drive of the XBOX 360 upon shipping. This information includes preloaded videos, games, and trailers for both movies and games, as well as a wide variety of text messages that are streamed to the end user, during game play or as part of the log-in process to the XBOX Live service. The three XBOX 360–specific file types are the CON, PIRS, and LIVE files. These files appear to be of a custom compression format for the console and each contains specific data that may assist an examiner.

The CON files contain cache files, profiles, and game saves, and each contains the console security certificate that is initially located at physical sector 4. With the functionality of the hard drive to be moved from console to console, this information may provide a linkage between two or more consoles as well as two or more gamers. If CON files exist on a hard drive and there is more than one console certificate, this is an indication that the drive has been connected to more than one console.

PIRS files contain a security certificate signed by Microsoft and are considered to be information that is downloaded to the console through non-XBOX Live functions. This information could be system updates or, in some cases detailed earlier, the preloaded games that are on the hard drive.

The last XBOX 360–specific file is the file that contains LIVE as the header. LIVE files are signed by Microsoft and are delivered through the XBOX Live service. Previously, the functionality of XBOX Live was documented, and there were many different areas in which an end user could choose to download information. If a user downloads information from the XBOX Live service, it will be formatted and have LIVE and the file header.

Each of these files has a specific purpose and may provide a linkage between a suspect and a victim. For instance, certain games require the downloading of a map package before the game can be played online. If the game in question is a game that a victim stated was the vector of communication, then there should be artifacts on the victim and suspect's XBOX 360 storage media that would indicate the same map pack. This is but one example, and there are certainly many more. Each of these files has a specific format and each contains much more specific information. The researchers at www.free60.org have detailed the format of these files; some of the information is included here in Figures 6.14 through 6.16, and a complete reference is located at www.free60.org/XContent.

XContent Header

Offset	Length	Type	Information
0x0	0x4	unsigned int	Signature Type

The signature type can be one of the following:

Signature Type	Information
"CON "	Signed by a console. Found on many files such as cache files, profiles, saved games.
PIRS	Signed by Microsoft. Found on files delivered by Microsoft through non-Xbox Live means such as system updates.
LIVE	Signed by Microsoft. Found on files delivered over Xbox Live such as items from the Marketplace like themes.

For console signed ("CON ") packages, the Console Security Certificate is used.

For remotely signed (LIVE/PIRS) packages, the following format is used:

Offset	Length	Type	Information
0x4	0x100	bytes	Package Signature
0x104	0x128	bytes	Padding

The Package Signature is generated using the value at 0x32C (Content ID/Header SHA1).

FIGURE 6.14

Description of the XBOX 360–specific files, deemed XContent by www.free60.org.

XContent Metadata

Offset	Length	Type	Information
0x22C	0x100	license entries (see below)	Licensing Data (used to check package owner)
0x32C	0x14	bytes	Content ID / Header SHA1 Hash
0x340	0x4	unsigned int	Entry ID
0x344	0x4	signed int	Content Type (see below)
0x348	0x4	signed int	Metadata Version (see below)
0x34C	0x8	signed long	Content Size
0x354	0x4	unsigned int	Media ID
0x358	0x4	signed int	Version (system/title updates)
0x35C	0x4	signed int	Base Version (system/title updates)
0x360	0x4	unsigned int	Title ID
0x364	0x1	byte	Platform (xbox/gfwl?)
0x365	0x1	byte	Executable Type
0x366	0x1	byte	Disc Number
0x367	0x1	byte	Disc In Set
0x368	0x4	unsigned int	Save Game ID
0x36C	0x5	bytes	Console ID
0x371	0x8	bytes	Profile ID
0x379	0x1	byte	Volume Descriptor Structure Size (usually 0x24)
0x37A	**Volume Descriptor Structure Size** - 1	structure	Volume Descriptor
0x379 + **Volume Descriptor Structure Size**	0x4	signed int	Data File Count

FIGURE 6.15

An abbreviated descriptor of the metadata within the XContent files. A complete detail is available at www.free60.org/XContent.

Content Types

Value	Description
0xD0000	Arcade Title
0x9000	Avatar Item
0x40000	Cache File
0x2000000	Community Game
0x80000	Game Demo
0x20000	Gamer Picture
0xA0000	Game Title
0xC0000	Game Trailer
0x400000	Game Video
0x4000	Installed Game
0xB0000	Installer
0x2000	IPTV Pause Buffer
0xF0000	License Store
0x2	Marketplace Content

FIGURE 6.16

An abbreviated detail of the content types found within the XContent files. This information could provide a vector of communication or a linkage between groups.

SUMMARY

This chapter introduced the custom compressed files that can be located on the XBOX 360 storage media. The files are called PIRS, CON, and LIVE, and each can be located through keyword searches using the forensic utility of choice. Each one of these files populates the drive through specific actions that an end user must initiate in order to obtain the files. The examination of the files is an ongoing process, and as the research continues within the community, more details will be provided.

References

[1] Free60. www.free60.org (accessed 14.10.10).
[2] XContent – Free60. Free60. XContent. www.free60.org/XContent (accessed 14.10.10).

CHAPTER

XBOX 360 Hard Drive

7

Documenting the Artifacts after the Initial System Update and Live Account Creation

INFORMATION IN THIS CHAPTER

- Initial differences
- Examination of the post–system updated drive
- PIRS files after the initial system update
- CON and LIVE file examination
- New images added after the system update
- Other artifacts

INITIAL DIFFERENCES

As was mentioned in earlier chapters, one of the main marketing points of the XBOX 360 console is the ability to connect to a network. This network connection allows users to play online in cooperative or competitive modes against other end users, connect through social networking, stream videos and music, and a whole host of other features. In order to accomplish this vast array of networking functionality, the console must be configured with a Gamertag. The Gamertag can be configured ahead of time on the Web portal or it can be created at the time of the console configuration. This Gamertag is then utilized during the initial XBOX Live configuration on the console to connect to the XBOX Live servers and finalize the account. Finalization of the account consists of several items, but the crucial item is the acceptance of the terms of use of the XBOX Live service. If this end user license agreement (EULA) is not accepted, then the configuration is not allowed to continue. In addition, the end user is not allowed to connect to the XBOX Live service, and the console is only functional as a local gaming console. Once the EULA is accepted, the console configuration proceeds, and there is a TCP/IP session established and an update pushed to the attached storage device.

In order to examine the information that is downloaded, there needed to be a baseline image. This is the image that was being examined in earlier chapters. The first step was to insert the drive back into its housing and connect it to the console. The next step was to walk through the process of configuring the XBOX Live account and Gamertag recovery in order to associate the Gamertag and then connect to the Live service and accept the EULA. Once the download was completed and the XBOX Live account associated to the console, the drive was removed and imaged using the version of EnCase mentioned earlier. In order to distinguish between the two drives, it seemed logical to name one pre–system update and the other post–system update. Each drive was imaged using FTK Imager and the resultant hash values were verified once examination began. One issue with the hash analysis for verification was that the drive was being written intentionally to document the artifacts through the use of the console. So the hash values were only appropriate for the initial acquisition and the subsequent verification before examination.

EXAMINATION OF THE POST–SYSTEM UPDATED DRIVE

Knowing the steps that needed to be taken in order to configure the console with an XBOX Live account, one of the first steps was to determine if the Gamertag that was created is something that is associated and stored on the hard drive. This information is akin to a Windows Registry entry that provides the registered owner of a Windows-based PC.

As mentioned earlier, the Gamertag that was selected during the console and XBOX Live configuration is a unique name that allowed for an easy search term. In any event, this information was used as a keyword search to determine if the configuration Gamertag is stored on the drive. There were two search hits using the Gamertag, both located at physical sector 10108489, but there is surrounding data that is different, indicating differing functionality. Remember that the console can have several profiles associated to it, similar to a multiuser Windows PC, so this may be an indicator of the privileges of the account. Additional theories include this area of the drive being the generic storage location of all profiles and accounts placed and saved to the drive. Figure 7.1 provides the screenshot of EnCase showing the details of the location of the Gamertag. Figure 7.2 is the same information displayed with X-Ways. The information listed from the screenshot using X-Ways appears as though this is a table with the entry locations reserved for future profiles and Gamertags, but this is just a theory.

For comparison, Figure 7.3 provides a snapshot of the data as it is viewed using EnCase. This is a screenshot of the same location on the pre–system updated drive detailing that the location is populated by "ÿÿÿÿÿÿÿ" values.

In addition to the information that is listed above, there is a detail that should be noted. In Chapter 5, "Initial Forensic Acquisition and Examination," we discussed the application Xplorer 360 from 360 Gamesaves as another alternative to view the information contained on the storage media. Although not an application designed for forensic analysis, this application has proven to be one of the few tools available that interprets the FATX file system.

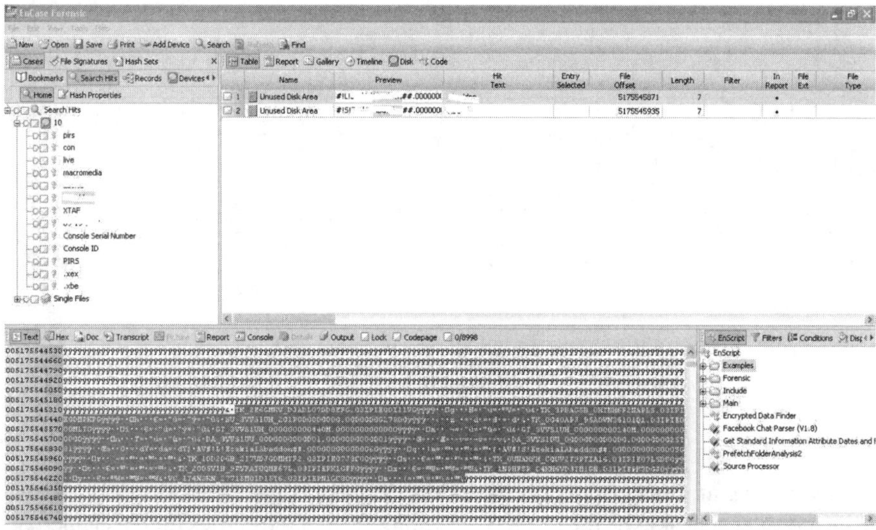

FIGURE 7.1

Screenshot from EnCase detailing the drive location of the stored Gamertag.

```
Disk  File  Preview  Details  Gallery  Legend        Sync

Offset      0  1  2  3  4  5  6  7   8  9  A  B  C  D  E  F
01347C9200  24 00 41 56 23 21 4C 21  45 7A 65 6B 69 61 6C 41  $ AV#!L!
01347C9210  62 61 64 64 6F 6E 23 23  2E 30 30 30 30 30 30 30       ##.0000000
01347C9220  30 30 30 30 30 30 36 47  FF FF FF FF 00 00 8D 71  0000006Gÿÿÿÿ  q
01347C9230  00 00 21 A4 3D 02 99 01  3D 02 99 01 3D 02 99 01    !¤=  =  =
01347C9240  24 00 41 56 23 21 53 21  45 7A 65 6B 69 61 6C 41  $ AV#!S!
01347C9250  62 61 64 64 6F 6E 23 23  2E 30 30 30 30 30 30 30       ##.0000000
01347C9260  30 30 30 30 30 30 53 47  FF FF FF FF 00 00 8D 72  000000SGÿÿÿÿ  r
01347C9270  00 00 0D 7E 3D 02 99 02  3D 02 99 02 3D 02 99 02    ~=  =  =
01347C9280  26 00 54 4B 5F 31 4F 44  32 4F 36 42 5F 32 49 37  & TK_1OD2O6B_2I7
01347C9290  55 44 4A 47 4F 4D 48 54  46 32 2E 30 33 49 50 49  UDJGOMHTF2.03IPI
01347C92A0  45 4F 37 4A 38 43 4F 30  FF FF FF FF 00 00 8D 73  EO7J8CO0ÿÿÿÿ  s
01347C92B0  00 00 07 80 3D 02 99 08  3D 02 99 08 3D 02 99 08     =  =  =
01347C92C0  26 00 54 4B 5F 30 55 4E  41 48 53 48 5F 43 51 55  & TK_0UNAHSH_CQU
01347C92D0  56 32 54 39 50 54 49 41  31 36 2E 30 33 49 50 49  V2T9PTIA16.03IPI
01347C92E0  45 4F 37 4C 35 44 53 30  FF FF FF FF 00 00 8D 74  EO7L5DS0ÿÿÿÿ  t
01347C92F0  00 00 07 80 3D 02 99 08  3D 02 99 08 3D 02 99 08     =  =  =
01347C9300  26 00 54 4B 5F 32 30 4F  35 56 31 42 5F 39 52 56  & TK_20O5V1B_9RV
01347C9310  46 41 54 55 51 4D 45 36  37 4C 2E 30 33 49 50 49  FATUQME67L.03IPI
01347C9320  45 50 4B 31 47 46 46 30  FF FF FF FF 00 00 8D 78  EPK1GFF0ÿÿÿÿ  x
01347C9330  00 00 07 80 3D 02 99 57  3D 02 99 57 3D 02 99 57     = W= W= W
01347C9340  26 00 54 4B 5F 31 4E 50  48 46 53 52 5F 43 34 4B  & TK_1NPHFSR_C4K
01347C9350  48 36 56 44 33 54 4D 31  47 4E 2E 30 33 49 50 49  H6VD3TM1GN.03IPI

Sector 10108489 of 488397168    Offset:    1347C9200    = 36  Block:
```

FIGURE 7.2

X-Ways screenshot showing the details of the same drive location. The information appears to be in more of a table format when viewed with the plain text view.

FIGURE 7.3

Detailing the location of the Gamertag before configuration and linkage of the account to the console.

Taking the information from the hex view provided by both EnCase and X-Ways, there are what appear to be file headers preceding each of the entries for the Gamertag. In the case of this example, there are

- **AV:** Preceding each of the entries for my Gamertag.
- **TK:** This entry appears several times, almost as a place holder, but may be a token file of sorts.

Using the Xplorer360 application, we see this same information stored on the drive under the Cache folder. But we are getting ahead of ourselves a bit. There needs to be some background information provided on this tool and the information that is presented with it. Previously, Xplorer360 was used to view the information on a pre–system update drive, and there were several FATX partitions displayed, although those displayed did not include the two partitions that are reserved for the secure transactions. When reviewing the data that was displayed, there were some folders that contained data and some that did not. The details of these differences are depicted in Chapter 5.

Investigating these Gamertag headers a bit further, we can navigate to the Cache folder within the directory tree of the XBOX 360 hard drive for further review. In doing so, the examiner can immediately see that there is far more data displayed once the initial system update is accepted. Navigating Partition 3 using Xplorer360, there are several subfolders that are displayed. The one that is of current interest is the Cache folder. Figure 7.4 provides a snapshot of this navigation.

Opening up the Cache folder presents several files that can be extracted using the extraction function of Xplorer360. However, there is an immediate linkage between the files stored here within the Cache folder and the data surrounding the Gamertag from Figures 7.1 and 7.2. The "file header" or "header information" is clearly listed within the Cache folder. Figure 7.5 provides a screenshot with these listings.

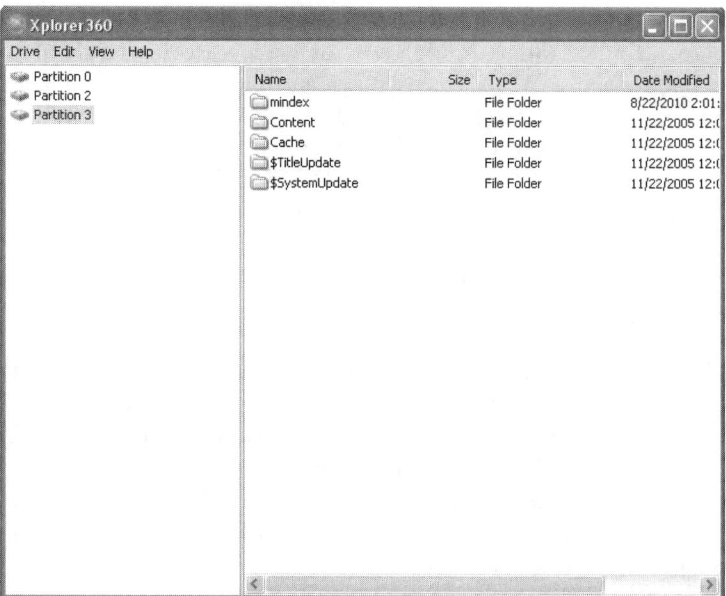

FIGURE 7.4

Partition 3 subfolders.

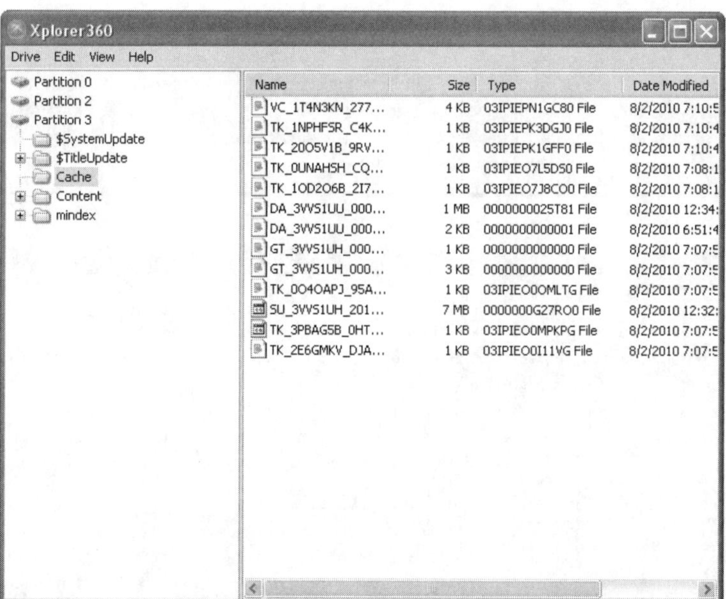

FIGURE 7.5

Listing of the files that are present in the Cache folder under Partition 3.

Each of these folders was extracted and examined for information that could be used to provide more artifacts during an examination. Reviewing the information from the EnCase and X-Ways screenshots, it appears that there is a TK file that is close in proximity to the Gamertag, named TK_1OD206B. However, a review of the file, or any of the files listed here, did not reveal the Gamertag created during the XBOX Live configuration and linkage to XBOX Live.

There was some data of interest within each of these text cache files. For example, the GT files began with the console security certificate that has previously been detailed. In addition, these files had some plain text references to Macromedia Fireworks MX and end in a unique signature (IEND®B`). Figure 7.6 provides a snapshot of the text of the file.

The next files that were examined were the TK files. Each one of these files is full of data, and there are some listed in plain text. The file header, or what appears to be a file header, or the "magic name," is PROD. It is unclear what this PROD magic name is or its function. Figure 7.7 provides an example.

There is one VC file that was examined. Once again, this file contains the console security certificate, and the remainder of the data appears to be encrypted. Figure 7.8 provides an example of this data.

There were two DA files that were of interest. One is an XBOX executable, and the other is full of data that is not represented well in Notepad. One thing that should be mentioned about all these cache files is that their size varies; the larger size files

> **WARNING**
>
> Using WordPad provided its own unique challenges that an examiner needs to be aware of. Opening these files in WordPad was only a preliminary step. WordPad does not interpret certain data well, which in turn may "hide" data. These files were later imported into EnCase, in order to view the file in its entirety.

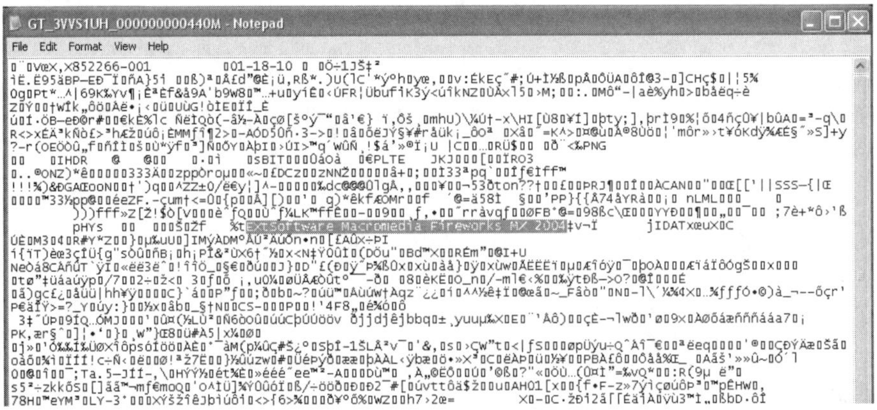

FIGURE 7.6

Example of a GT file.

FIGURE 7.7

TK file example.

FIGURE 7.8

Example of a VC file.

were opened using WordPad. Figures 7.9 and 7.10 provide screenshots of the information located within the files.

Examining the second of the two DA files, the XEX DA file, was interesting. At first, there were some issues experienced with trying to open this file using Notepad. Due to the file size, the application would crash and would have to be restarted. Opening the file in WordPad allowed some visual review of the data contained within it. Carving through this 1 MB file was daunting, but there were some plain text references within it. My next step was to use Strings by Microsoft Technet to carve through the file to search for ASCII or Unicode text. My initial search, using the defaults of the application, was not very successful, and it appeared as though every three-letter text was being displayed. In an effort to change this and obtain something useful, the default size was changed to search for a four-character string and the results were more useful; these results are displayed in Figure 7.11.

FIGURE 7.9

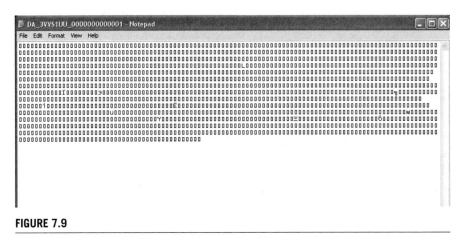

This is the screenshot of the smaller of the two DA files. It is unknown what this data is for.

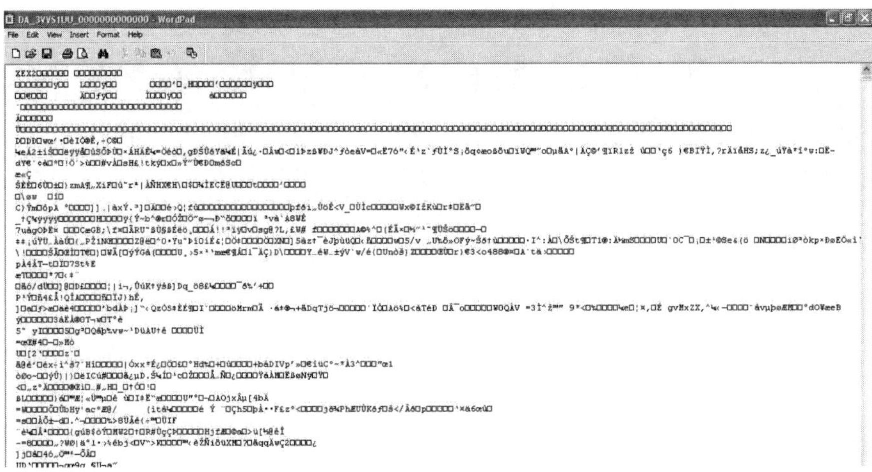

FIGURE 7.10

DA XBOX 360 executable file, with the header of XEX.

The last file that was examined here was titled the "SU" file. The initial theory is that this is a system update file, but it is not located in the System Update folder. So a comparison was done between the two files, and they are not the same. This SU, which was a system update file, was extracted from Xplorer360 and opened in both WordPad and then Strings. WordPad was somewhat daunting, as examination was restricted to manual review and keyword searching. Strings, with some adjustment of the length of the default search length, provided some useful information. This examination revealed another file extension that was new to me up until this point. The new extension is .xexp, and there were many files with this extension. The system update has a list of

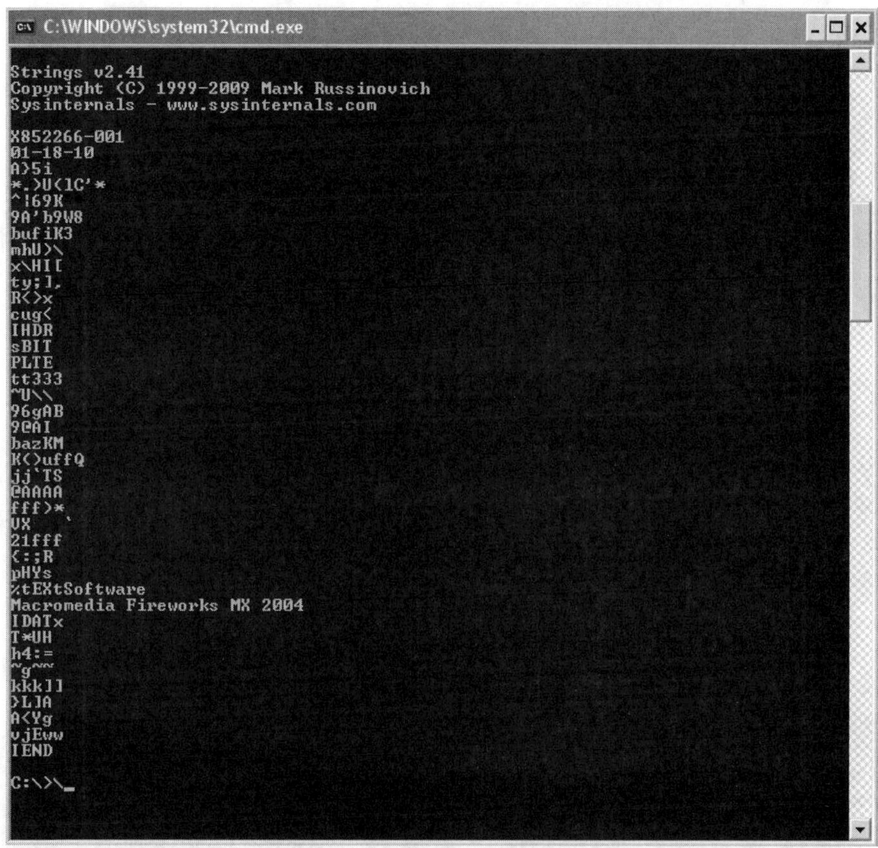

FIGURE 7.11

Strings run against the same DA file as was depicted in Figure 7.10. The first hit is an indicator that the console security certificate is used again.

files that appear to be a path to the files either reading or writing to the Flash memory of the console. Figure 7.12 provides the results using Strings.

The names of some of the files found within this SU file give some clues as to their usage or purpose. Some examples include the following:

- $flash_signin.xexp
- $flash_bootanim.xexp (assume the boot animation)
- $flash_dash.xex (dashboard executable)
- $flash_deviceselector.xexp (unclear what device, perhaps storage media)

This is by no means a complete review of the information listed here, but it gives a good example of the types of files that are being called in this SU file and, perhaps, their storage location or the location to which they are being written (the more likely option).

```
C:\WINDOWS\system32\cmd.exe

C:\>strings -n 13 "C:\Documents and Settings\Cardinal\Desktop\SU_3VVS1UH_201R000
000000.0000000G27RO0"

Strings v2.41
Copyright (C) 1999-2009 Mark Russinovich
Sysinternals - www.sysinternals.com

System Update
$flash_aac.xexp
 $flash_bootanim.xexp
 $flash_createprofile.xexp
 $flash_dash.xex
 $flash_deviceselector.xexp
 $flash_gamerprofile.xexp
 $flash_hud.xexp
 $flash_huduiskin.xex
 $flash_mfgbootlauncher.xexp
 $flash_minimediaplayer.xexp
 $flash_nomni.xexp
 $flash_nomnifwm.xexp
 $flash_signin.xexp
 $flash_systemupdate.xex
 $flash_updater.xexp
 $flash_vk.xexp
 $flash_xam.xexp
 $flash_XenonCLatin.xttp
 $flash_XenonJKLatin.xttp
 $flash_ximecore.xex
 $flash_ximedic.xexp
 $install_extender.xex
q<>=g5$,/#i'^
\Device\Flash\dash.xex
k9r¦n>>.bi9x>
;n,VK,_q#>H/r
jpOb:wy8%0d-j
\esDTL<Bxs>csJ>
~,E H%&#]h<jo
Wg8=v6"8c^3/
<BNnlzpxy?]Tm`
1*1+1,1-1.101112b bhbjblbn
1*1+1,1-1.101112b bhbjblbn
bTbVbXbZb\b`bbbd
 \Device\Flash\huduiskin.xex
]G%1@ I^<*hLu#
5P5H5P5X5`5h5p5x5
$\Device\Flash\systemupdate.xex
systemupdatefc.exe
<11>G<r4++'A>K
%N%6%8%:%>$@Cf
>74&¦o5r¦KHT\
>89\vbYMLiMBD
gP@`A+Bj-t2E>c
r*/ty<"Y[mjSm5
 \Device\Flash\XIMECORE.xex
installsuc.dll
$<YX,&VLH8rB#

C:\>_
```

FIGURE 7.12

Strings run against the SU file. Note the new file extensions such as .xexp and .xttp.

PIRS FILES AFTER THE INITIAL SYSTEM UPDATE

One of the console-specific file types that are located on the XBOX 360 is the PIRS file, as mentioned earlier. This is a file that has custom compression, akin to zipped files, and is found in many places. It was decided to review the PIRS files that are located on the pre- and posthard drive images to determine if there were any changes made. The first thing that was noticed was that there were fewer search hits on the post–system update drive, which was a surprise. The pre–system updated drive revealed that there were 23 search hits using "PIRS" as the search term. The post–system updated drive only had 22 search hits using the same search term. My current working theory is that this "missing" PIRS file is executed and deleted once the TCP IP connection is made to the XBOX Live servers. This is similar to the way in which code is uncompressed to a temporary folder, executed, and then the temporary files are deleted. Figure 7.13 provides a screenshot detailing the pre–system updated listing of PIRS files, and Figure 7.14 provides the details from the post–system updated PIRS files search hits.

In attempting to determine the PIRS file that was lost during the process, a comparative analyst of the two sets was conducted. Something interesting was

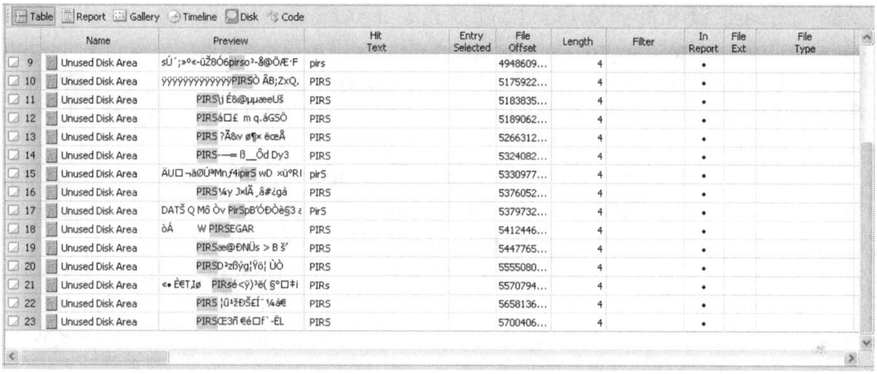

Table | Report | Gallery | Timeline | Disk | Code

	Name	Preview	Hit Text	Entry Selected	File Offset	Length	Filter	In Report	File Ext	File Type
9	Unused Disk Area	sÚ´;»º«-üŽ8Ó6pirso³-å@ÖÆ·F	pirs		4948609...	4		•		
10	Unused Disk Area	ÿÿÿÿÿÿÿÿÿÿÿÿÿPIRSÒ ÂB;ZxQ,	PIRS		5175922...	4		•		
11	Unused Disk Area	PIRS\j É&@µµæeUš	PIRS		5183835...	4		•		
12	Unused Disk Area	PIRSá□£ m q.áGSÖ	PIRS		5189062...	4		•		
13	Unused Disk Area	PIRS ?Ã&v ø¶× ëœÅ	PIRS		5266312...	4		•		
14	Unused Disk Area	PIRS-—= ß__Ôd Dy3	PIRS		5324082...	4		•		
15	Unused Disk Area	ÄU□¬äØÚªMnƒ4ipirS wD ×ü°RI	pirS		5330977...	4		•		
16	Unused Disk Area	PIRS¼y J×lÃ¸â#¿gà	PIRS		5376052...	4		•		
17	Unused Disk Area	DATŠ Q Mô Òv PirSpB'ÓÐÒè§3 ż	PirS		5379732...	4		•		
18	Unused Disk Area	òÁ W PIRSEGAR	PIRS		5412446...	4		•		
19	Unused Disk Area	PIRSæ@ÐNÜs > B š'	PIRS		5447765...	4		•		
20	Unused Disk Area	PIRSD²zßýg¦Ÿö¦ ÙÒ	PIRS		5555080...	4		•		
21	Unused Disk Area	«• È€T,Iø PIRsé<ÿ)³ë(§°□‡i	PIRs		5570794...	4		•		
22	Unused Disk Area	PIRS ¦û¹žÐŠ£Í¨ ¼à€	PIRS		5658136...	4		•		
23	Unused Disk Area	PIRSŒ3ñ €é□f`-ËL	PIRS		5700406...	4		•		

FIGURE 7.13

A listing of search hits on the pre–system update drive. Note that there are 23 search hits.

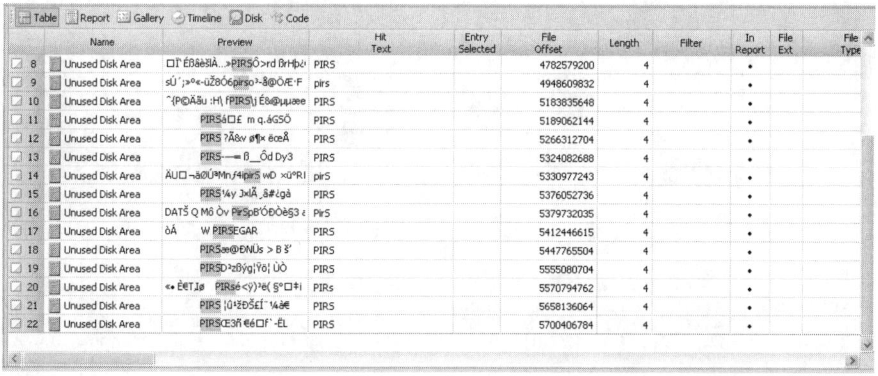

Table | Report | Gallery | Timeline | Disk | Code

	Name	Preview	Hit Text	Entry Selected	File Offset	Length	Filter	In Report	File Ext	File Type
8	Unused Disk Area	□Ï`ÉßâèšlÀ...»PIRSÔ>rd ßrHþ¿	PIRS		4782579200	4		•		
9	Unused Disk Area	sÚ´;»º«-üŽ8Ó6pirso³-å@ÖÆ·F	pirs		4948609832	4		•		
10	Unused Disk Area	^{P©Ääu :H\ fPIRS\j É&@µµæe	PIRS		5183835648	4		•		
11	Unused Disk Area	PIRSá□£ m q.áGSÖ	PIRS		5189062144	4		•		
12	Unused Disk Area	PIRS ?Ã&v ø¶× ëœÅ	PIRS		5266312704	4		•		
13	Unused Disk Area	PIRS-—= ß__Ôd Dy3	PIRS		5324082688	4		•		
14	Unused Disk Area	ÄU□¬äØÚªMnƒ4ipirS wD ×ü°RI	pirS		5330977243	4		•		
15	Unused Disk Area	PIRS¼y J×lÃ¸â#¿gà	PIRS		5376052736	4		•		
16	Unused Disk Area	DATŠ Q Mô Òv PirSpB'ÓÐÒè§3 ż	PirS		5379732035	4		•		
17	Unused Disk Area	òÁ W PIRSEGAR	PIRS		5412446615	4		•		
18	Unused Disk Area	PIRSæ@ÐNÜs > B š'	PIRS		5447765504	4		•		
19	Unused Disk Area	PIRSD²zßýg¦Ÿö¦ ÙÒ	PIRS		5555080704	4		•		
20	Unused Disk Area	«• È€T,Iø PIRsé<ÿ)³ë(§°□‡i	PIRs		5570794762	4		•		
21	Unused Disk Area	PIRS ¦û¹žÐŠ£Í¨ ¼à€	PIRS		5658136064	4		•		
22	Unused Disk Area	PIRSŒ3ñ €é□f`-ËL	PIRS		5700406784	4		•		

FIGURE 7.14

The PIRS search hits on the post–system update drive. Note that the search hit count has changed and only includes 22 hits.

immediately revealed – it appears that the location, the physical sector of several of the PIRS files, was shifted with the update. EnCase was used to extract the data sets and linked them up for a comparative analysis. The change itself seems to be located within the first 9 to 10 files. When the comparative analysis is performed and the list of PIRS files are lined up against one another, the last 13 files of the list are located in the same location for both the pre– and post–system update files. The change is located in the first 9 to 10 files. In the pre–system update image file, there are 10 PIRS files before the 13 that are standard across the two images. In the post–system updated image, there are only nine of these files. The comparative list is listed here in Figures 7.15 and 7.16.

Examining the PIRS files, the 9 to 10 PIRS files that have been relocated provide some information that may be useful. As a result of the files not being recognized by any forensic utilities, I decided to examine the search hits more thoroughly. The first search hit from the pre–system update image had some plain text information located within it providing some insight into the purpose of the file itself. The text "C·o·m·m·u·n·i·t·y· ·G·a·m·e·s· ·P·l·a·y·e·r· ·P·a·c·k" is clearly visible. Figure 7.17 provides a screenshot of this information.

To furthermore examine this particular file, the first 2.4 MB of the file were carved out of the image and run through the Sysinternals Windows version of Strings. The default settings for the ASCII and UNICODE search hits were changed to 10 as the minimum string length. The information that was revealed provided more insight into the purpose of this particular file. Because of the information that was revealed through this process, it was decided to continue with

```
Preview File Offset (pre-system update)

PIRS'3N ƒS KRFFxÕÎ Uö-þ]¦ÒòÔÃ‡ôÛ ù ]GP Àì} Da… ³O Míe<˝ÝŽ î▯Wá CÛØ      4713160192
PIRSÀél°Ft+¬œaã&'u»'Î▯¼ ååT8°!j~u¶Ù†▯EÆ ëR½üø  TÕÊU„á¯Ö' o▯ê_ f%á¼      4731706880
PIRS z d•T"À !À; ´eJÐ.üã ®vè ▯ÊÄ–~ÿ>»£ "q¬˝ goi(Ýí cp,»¨-Ká<q}³E w      4733361664
PIRS°‡ µå?ã▯ÆÄ õò d¢Ù.³E%^=á-AW-%ÕÑÐ"ü®+J·I  :þâ Òw'®åñ<t   À Q !J     4747369984
PIRSO2\#%¬g ,l:¦}R6®oÀ/Be õ4@wà „ŸN€ÊÝÜÝ‰õ ,Ñî7¤üž•Põc  |ÄÜ²▯%C2 >     4763999744
PIRSÌÄ%4ÿ±Ï °¼£É64ÎE&E%®¡m‚‰ö kô3¥§Ü" Æ¦ ÙžÌ¢' '[îœ«`¦˝n¾Ä▯-«ˆ\ô¯"      4765097472
PIRSÐ( L7øfw˝Ê´,éRb«˚dKWÏÎ Ý_®ü$%Ž`‡pñ‰ ±á¬/ G-®¥¥ÿÍúîÏ U˚…~aC¥‚gÑ      4765179392
PIRSpój‚ú4_:¶‚^àÓÎ▯  EÄ¨Š®7ãµ5x+ÀÏ pÑ- !œžkÊ«z'æÐäŸÏ cA ▯1s$Tu† `\     4776402432
pirso³-á@ÖÆ·F ¦ öù³C Æ>E ÑÄ% ªL e˚& ¤ÿß ÕßÕF« !Vî, µ:Ïàª n-€ñm%  ¦     4948609832
PIRSÒ ÅB;ZxQ, Òu=,Ý¸ˆ:Ùo ÖÓ▯ÀÅy›î ý▯ Žì„…€%‹À¼xW•»¥¨PæŸ ´ÏŠD, 'ž †     5175922176
PIRS\j É&@µµæeUš JÚ`àõ Zü'™¨On1al˝æöæ‹Æíf–'„ì¾ \èÑ  òªg;xîÙí øNB˚Ä     5183835648
PIRSá▯£  m q.áGSÖ  ã™µÎRm;˚ÐáUÏ½~E Iße Š▯6ˆí 9Ñê tZ`ø¿®ZO–á{ $ãL\Y     5189062144
PIRS ?Ä&v ø¶¤ ëœÀxŽ[ g▯€b' R©8®èòå§s'▯iªèJíª \-™6k'žo® 'ÇÕEQ^(¿¡I§     5266312704
PIRS–—= ß__Õd Dy3žœmq%"k▯ š§▯, ˝lªò '  ô ^xtc ÏîBœ¢pÑ›r Å hT®  =ul     5324082688
pirs wD xü˚R▯C  0 Loyw‚$þž õŸ6OX °ØGÆ¡Ü ÆH®ä>Œ©®Öž² Œ š*ùÝMM"HZ CY     5330977243
PIRS¾y J¤lÄ‚å#¿gà¦' ³Ä  £ ÎîÏÌßêËÝÛw˜ Óc=   Due▯*Ì÷ØK=| j;æ÷ =UÜÕ=     5376052736
PirSpB'ÓÐÒè§3 a V œÖ°Z` kÿÆ▯ `Œ¡xëa8 âÏ™3‚Ûž»qüÄ t:▯*Ð¨Û¢z¡¼  ▯œ 6     5379732035
PIRSEGAR              Ò              K FEZÉL               p ,ð     5412446615
PIRSæ@ÐNÜs > B š'-¾ ""Ç ;%Ÿà*▯Åì~  G•"  Å¼;Æ™ŸÌ£ì¡Ü‰Ë¥}úëxv}Ž4 J†#     5447765504
PIRSD²zßýg¦Ÿö¦ ÙÒ«x-‰f+Ãrú:QÒÕÑÌ˚lª®v´h;▯ã©|gqŠKÜŸ-&&âý ÉšÇ F¢ÕÜ‹      5555080704
PIRsé<ÿ)³ë( §˚▯‡¡¡® Žôp±p BŠÐ  Ë#,TÅbsÀÿˆÊþ  z▯ : `•]C šfÒÇñ„[" LÄ%     5570794762
PIRS ¦Û'ŽÐŠ£Ï¨¾à€M í±4?oG`^t â³ y ö  m'> /±-^ÒÜëž*Ü ´u ò Ú;%þx0A '     5658136064
PIRSŒ3ñ €é▯f`-ËL l .V;šî²ñ!bSŒgûj9öóÊ}½p▯`  1Šä® ³,œÇzì,À÷' õ  é ×     5700406784
```

FIGURE 7.15

The pre–system update PIRS files consisting of 23 files; not all are PIRS file headers, this is simply the search hit list using EnCase.

```
Preview File Offset (post system update)


PIRS•-N(<sÀØ€CkëË òu.ÑÖþz [žóÜ;ô□ŠÏÔÒC'' +€ªš'÷,‹'õU,T(Ăx "¬}*0Ă8]      4713176576
PIRS ¨¯□îÇÙëqT {'¼äÀ'¡cdÝÂÈŽŒ$ÿ ÛK˝ßŽ×Ì·áI  Ő bËýÉ‰"é8ôE¡šæ¡$ã©E¢ª       4714831360
PIRSf!3¬É ¢' |Ã4  ¾ ÷ž™ JÂŒX´äûC¿V-œ  ~ôz "€{□Íïµ —'&Ð^üÜòmT ÷ 2 V     4731428352
PIRS 8‡£ÓőË  ôUäù¿·E±•ùã $ "ÝŸ n□ì÷K ´□õ*oâ¦"dN¦ó{<ñ·QÖ« □Þ %B¡W•Ë      4745436672
PIRS4¥æL !øëV□QBÌê□Ú/ªðF2tðñ. 'Æ±ùdø¼0·ïF ¼k9·X€(Ã^´æR□I1kü[D S'jâ     4746534400
PIRSZ ‹úVñƒ9FŽ÷}CÄ•LÊ¤<□®u=2¼ã£d  %T  Ä ‹¢Z«©ÝL□2% š"‹— `'Ô Ó □ÀÔ      4746616320
PIRSJöOË Ù4PVù€¥¼% ý«efì½ocarÿ™Âß5‡ ½ ó š7m M@$□ ´y£FÍæìS—…ú µ•Eöð      4757822976
PIRSÔ>rd ßrHþ¿GïØu3J¤ □Ëöªì¥ÕÙ›ýÈ8 ÷ "vx ÙùÏ^ Ër-Ýîž~€ □□oì·¡J •FT     4782579200
pirsoª-â@ÖÆ·F ¦ öù³C Æ>E ÑÃ% ªL e˚& ¤ÿß ÕßÕF« !Vì, µ:Íàª n—€ñm%  ¦     4948609832
PIRS\j É&@µµæeUš JÚ àõ Zü'™¨On1al˝æöæ‹Æíf—',,ì¼ \èÑ  òªg;xîÙí øNB˚Ă     5183835648
PIRSá□£  m q.áGSÖ  ã™µÎRm;˚ÐáUÌ½~E Ißе Š□6^í 9Ñê tZ`ø¿@ZO—á{ $ãL\Y      5189062144
PIRS ?Ã&v ø¶¤ ëœÂXŽ[ g□€b' R©8®èòå§s'□ìªèJíª \-™6k'žo® 'ÇõEQ^(¿¡I§     5266312704
PIRS—-= ß__Ôd Dy3žœmq%"k□ š§□, ˜lªò '  ô ^Xtc ÏîBœ¢pÑ›r Ă hT® ¯=ul     5324082688
pirS wD xü˚R□C  0 Loyw¸$þŽ õŸ6OX °ØGÆ¡ü ÆH@ä>ŒØ@0ž²`Œ š*ùÝMM"HZ CY     5330977243
PIRS¼y J¤lĂ¸â#¿gà¦' ªĂ  £ ÍïÏÌßêËÝÛw^ Óc=   Due□*Ì÷ØK=| j;æ÷ =UÜŐ=     5376052736
PirSpB'ÓÐÒè§3 a V œÖ°Z` kÿÆ□ `Œ¡xëa8 âÌ™3¸ûž»qüÄ t:□*Ð˝û¢z¡¼  □œ 6     5379732035
PIRSEGAR           `     Ô            K FEZÈL                p  ,ð      5412446615
PIRSæ@ÐNÜs > B š'-¼ ""Ç ;¾Ÿå*□Âì~  G•"  Ã¼;Æ™ÝÌ£ì¡ü‰Ë¥}úëxv}Ž4 J†#      5447765504
PIRSD²zßýg¦Ÿö¦ ÙÒ«x-‰f+Ărú:QÒőÑÌ˚lª®v´h;□ã©|gqŠKÜÝ-&&ây ÉšÇ F¢ÕÜ‹      5555080704
PIRSé<ÿ)ªë( §˚□‡¡¡® ŽôpÝp BŠÐ  Ë#,TÂbsÂÿ^Êþ  z□ :`•]C šfÒÇñ„[" LĂ¾    5570794762
PIRS ¦û'ŽÐŠ£Í¨¼à€M í±4?oG`^t âª y ö  m'> /±-^ÒÜëž*Ü ´u ò Ü;¾p×0Â '    5658136064
PIRSŒ3ñ €é□f`-ËL l .V;šîªñ!bsŒgûj9ÖóÊ}½p□`  1Šä® ª,œÇzì,À÷' ô  é ×     5700406784
```

FIGURE 7.16

The list of the PIRS files after the system update. Note that between the two lists, the last 13 files have not changed their location.

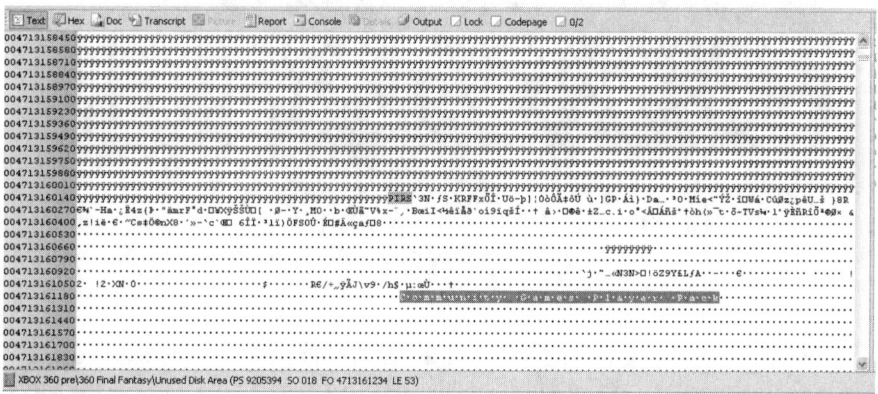

FIGURE 7.17

Screenshot of EnCase search hit on the pre–system update image, and this is the first PIRS file search hit.

the process with the other files. Figure 7.18 shows the results of running Strings against this 2.4 MB data portion of the first PIRS file.

In contrast, the first post–system update image PIRS file search hit has different plain text located within the file. Within this file, the plain text that is visible is "L·i·v·e· ·U·t·i·l·i·t·i·e·s· ·U·p·d·a·t·e." Again, a portion of the file was carved out of the image and run through Strings. This time, the size of the file was approximately 1.6

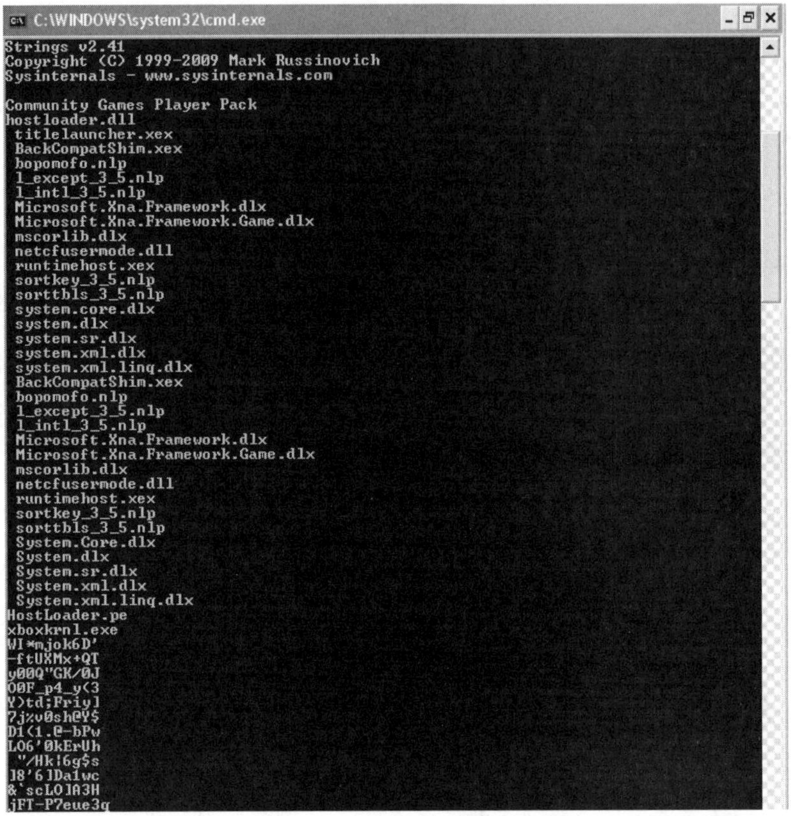

```
C:\WINDOWS\system32\cmd.exe
Strings v2.41
Copyright (C) 1999-2009 Mark Russinovich
Sysinternals - www.sysinternals.com

Community Games Player Pack
hostloader.dll
 titlelauncher.xex
 BackCompatShim.xex
 bopomofo.nlp
 l_except_3_5.nlp
 l_intl_3_5.nlp
 Microsoft.Xna.Framework.dlx
 Microsoft.Xna.Framework.Game.dlx
 mscorlib.dlx
 netcfusermode.dll
 runtimehost.xex
 sortkey_3_5.nlp
 sorttbls_3_5.nlp
 system.core.dlx
 system.dlx
 system.sr.dlx
 system.xml.dlx
 system.xml.linq.dlx
 BackCompatShim.xex
 bopomofo.nlp
 l_except_3_5.nlp
 l_intl_3_5.nlp
 Microsoft.Xna.Framework.dlx
 Microsoft.Xna.Framework.Game.dlx
 mscorlib.dlx
 netcfusermode.dll
 runtimehost.xex
 sortkey_3_5.nlp
 sorttbls_3_5.nlp
 System.Core.dlx
 System.dlx
 System.sr.dlx
 System.xml.dlx
 System.xml.linq.dlx
HostLoader.pe
xboxkrnl.exe
WI*mjok6D'
-ftUXMx+QT
y00Q"GK/0J
O0F_p4_y<3
Y>td;Friy]
7j%v0sh@Y$
D1<1.@-bPw
LO6'0kErUh
 "/Hk!6g$s
]8'6]Da1wc
&`scLO]A3H
jFT-P7eue3q
```

FIGURE 7.18

Strings results against the first PIRS file search hit on the pre–system update image file. Note the plain text hits such as Microsoft.XNA, BackCompatShim.xex, and System.

MB. Figure 7.19 provides a screenshot of the search hit depicting the plain text, and Figure 7.20 provides the Strings hits with the default string length set to 10 characters.

Running Strings with the default string length set to a value of 10 provided some very interesting results. Within this file, there are many plain text hits, hits that include the following:

- Macromedia Fireworks MX 2004
- Crown
- Avatar mini creator
- Marketplace
- xMsgr.xex

This is a short list because of the length of the search hits. The screenshot provides more information as to the file contents.

FIGURE 7.19

First PIRS search hit on the post–system updated drive. This search hit provides the plain text hit of "Live Utilities Update," which is in contrast to the pre–system update plain text hits.

```
Strings v2.41
Copyright (C) 1999-2009 Mark Russinovich
Sysinternals - www.sysinternals.com

Live Utilities Update
AvatarMiniCreator.xex
 crown1.png
 crown10.png
 crown2.png
 crown3.png
 crown4.png
 crown5.png
 crown6.png
 crown7.png
 crown8.png
 crown9.png
 Feedback.xex
 Friends.xex
 Marketplace.xex
 milestone1.png
 milestone2.png
 milestone3.png
 Party.xex
 Quickchat.xex
 StoresList.xml
 Voicemail.xex
 XMsgr.xex
avatarminicreator.dll
xboxkrnl.exe
NKYy3;z7=q*
Qk3N6q#<As1
JKx[Xkxm_o
<rs-2w^gxzs
```

FIGURE 7.20

Strings result against this first PIRS file on the post–system updated image.

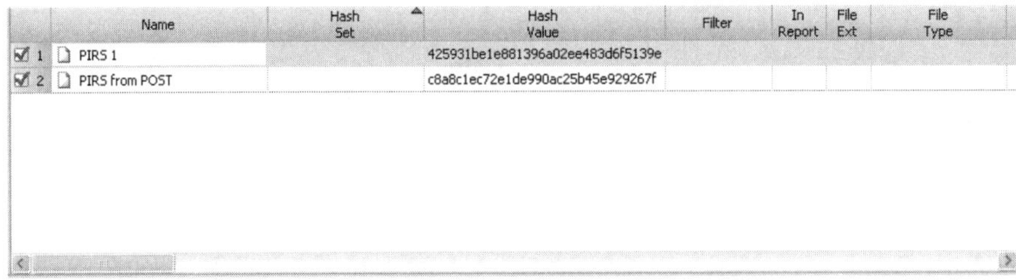

Name
Hash Set
Hash Value
Filter
In Report
File Ext
File Type
1 PIRS 1
425931be1e881396a02ee483d6f5139e
2 PIRS from POST
c8a8c1ec72e1de990ac25b45e929267f

FIGURE 7.21

PIRS hash value comparison.

Now that the process of examination of these files has been detailed, there is some value in proceeding with this process for each of these first 9 to 10 files in an attempt to determine the file that was lost. However, moving to the second PIRS file search hit on the pre–system update image file, it appears that this is a similar file to the first PIRS search hit on the post–system updated image. In order to confirm this information, the files were carved out of the image, run through Strings, and hashed to make a determination.

The files were extracted from both EnCase images and their file size was determined. Both files were 1,654,784 bytes in size. This seemed to be a good start, because there were some significant similarities. Once the files were exported from the image, they were imported into EnCase and the files were hashed, which revealed that the files were not the same. Figure 7.21 is the screenshot of the values as viewed in EnCase.

Now that we are fairly certain that these two files do not contain the same information, each file was run through Strings with the default string character length set to 10. The first several search hits appear to provide the same information. Table 7.1 provides the details of this comparison.

Moving forward with the comparison of the 9 to 10 files shows some plain text search hits that provide a comparison. The information was correlated and placed within Table 7.2 for easier comparison.

From the information listed within Table 7.2, it appears that the system itself was shipped with a system update file loaded on the drive; see PIRS file 10 on the pre–system update drive. Once there is a connection to the live servers, and the system update is executed, it appears to be deleted from the hard drive because there is no plain text entry in the post–system update drive.

CON AND LIVE FILE EXAMINATION

Along with the PIRS files, there are CON files, short for console, and LIVE files, files that are specific to the XBOX Live service. These two files use custom compression and contain information specific to console updates or to items that have been downloaded. The specifics of the files have been detailed in previous chapters, but similar to the PIRS files, there was a need to research these files between the system update to the console hard drive.

Table 7.1 List of the First Few Search Hits Running Strings Against the PIRS Live Utilities Update File Located within Each Image*

Pre–system Updated PIRS	Post–system Updated PIRS
Live Utilities Update	Live Utilities Update
AvatarMiniCreator.xex	AvatarMiniCreator.xex
crown1.png	crown1.png
crown10.png	crown10.png
crown2.png	crown2.png
crown3.png	crown3.png
crown4.png	crown4.png
crown5.png	crown5.png
crown6.png	crown6.png
crown7.png	crown7.png
crown8.png	crown8.png
crown9.png	crown9.png
Feedback.xex	Feedback.xex
Friends.xex	Friends.xex
Marketplace.xex	Marketplace.xex
milestone1.png	milestone1.png
milestone2.png	milestone2.png
milestone3.png	milestone3.png
Party.xex	Party.xex
Quickchat.xex	Quickchat.xex
StoresList.xml	StoresList.xml
Voicemail.xex	Voicemail.xex
XMsgr.xex	XMsgr.xex
avatarminicreator.dll	avatarminicreator.dll
XBOXkrnl.exe	XBOXkrnl.exe

**Although the files are not the same, as evidenced by the hash value, there are similarities within the Strings search hits*

Using the keyword "CON" provided many search hits that were not the CON files that are of interest, that is, the way in which the keywords were initially entered was not the way that should have been. This means that the CON file keyword needed to be listed a certain way with certain options selected to further narrow the search. However, what was found when reviewing the search hits from the mistake provided some interesting results. There were approximately 110,000 search hits using the term "CON." While reviewing these results, one of the first that grabbed my attention was the hit at number 74. This hit provided some interesting plain text information about network information, dates and times, ASP.net, and a wide variety of other information. The initial plain text may not render well with a screenshot, but one is provided here.

Table 7.2 An Overview of the Plain Text That Is Listed Near the Start of Each PIRS File Hit

PIRS File	PRE Image Text	POST Image Text
1	C·o·m·m·u·n·i·t·y· ·G·a·m·e·s· ·P·l·a·y·e·r· ·P·a·c·k	L·i·v·e· ·U·t·i·l·i·t·i·e·s· ·U·p·d·a·t·e
2	L·i·v·e· ·U·t·i·l·i·t·i·e·s· ·U·p·d·a·t·e	A·v·a·t·a·r· ·A·p·p· ·P·a·c·k·
3	A·v·a·t·a·r· ·A·s·s·e·t· ·P·a·c·k·a·g·e	A·v·a·t·a·r· ·A·s·s·e·t· ·P·a·c·k·a·g·e
4	A·v·a·t·a·r· ·A·p·p· ·P·a·c·k·	D·i·c·t·i·o·n·a·r·y· ·P·a·c·k
5	D·i·c·t·i·o·n·a·r·y· ·P·a·c·k	C·e·r·t·i·f·i·c·a·t·e· ·P·a·c·k
6	C·e·r·t·i·f·i·c·a·t·e· ·P·a·c·k	D·a·s·h· ·P·a·c·k·
7	D·a·s·h· ·P·a·c·k	M·i·g·r·a·t·i·o·n· ·P·a·c·k
8	M·i·g·r·a·t·i·o·n· ·P·a·c·k·	·C·o·m·m·u·n·i·t·y· ·G·a·m·e·s· ·P·l·a·y·e·r· ·P·a·c·k
9		
10	S·y·s·t·e·m· ·U·p·d·a·t·e·	F·u·s·i·o·n· ·T·i·t·l·e· ·U·p·d·a·t·e· ·v·1·.·9· ·5·8·2·9
11	F·u·s·i·o·n· ·T·i·t·l·e· ·U·p·d·a·t·e· ·v·1·.·9· ·5·8·2·9	F·o·r·z·a· ·M·o·t·o·r·s·p·o·r·t· ·3· ·C·u·s·t·o·m·i·z·a·t·i·o·n
12	·F·o·r·z·a· ·M·o·t·o·r·s·p·o·r·t· ·3· ·C·u·s·t·o·m·i·z·a·t·i·o·n	H·e·x·i·c· ·H·D
13	H·e·x·i·c· ·H·D	P·i·n·b·a·l·l· ·F·X
14	P·i·n·b·a·l·l· ·F·X·	
15		S·e·n·s·i·b·l·e· ·W·o·r·l·d· ·o·f· ·S·o·c·c·e·r
16	S·e·n·s·i·b·l·e· ·W·o·r·l·d· ·o·f· ·S·o·c·c·e·r	
17		W PIRSEGAR
18	W PIRSEGAR	P·e·g·g·l·e·
19	P·e·g·g·l·e·	G·a·l·a·g·a· ·L·e·g·i·o·n·s
20	G·a·l·a·g·a· ·L·e·g·i·o·n·s	
21		G·e·o·m·e·t·r·y· ·W·a·r·s· ·E·v·o·l·v·e·d·
22	G·e·o·m·e·t·r·y· ·W·a·r·s· ·E·v·o·l·v·e·d·	·W·e·l·c·o·m·e·V·i·d·e·o·
23	W·e·l·c·o·m·e·V·i·d·e·o	

To further examine this information, it was decided to stay with the process that worked on the PIRS files. Each file has a section carved out and was run through Strings. This was done in an effort to determine if any ASCII or UNICODE plain text was available that could provide more insight into the file itself. Figure 7.23 provides the results of the Strings search against this particular file.

This particular data seems to repeat itself throughout the search hits. It is unclear how the information is called upon through the executables, but it is seen again at several other locations on the drive. The date that is listed, August 2, 2010, is the date that the console was updated through the Live service. The other date that is present, the last modified date, is interesting and is something that was placed on or saved to the drive from the manufacturer. This research console was not even in possession in 2009.

Although the data sets that are detailed in Figures 7.22 and 7.23 are repeated throughout the storage drive, there are subtle differences. Within the plain text of the

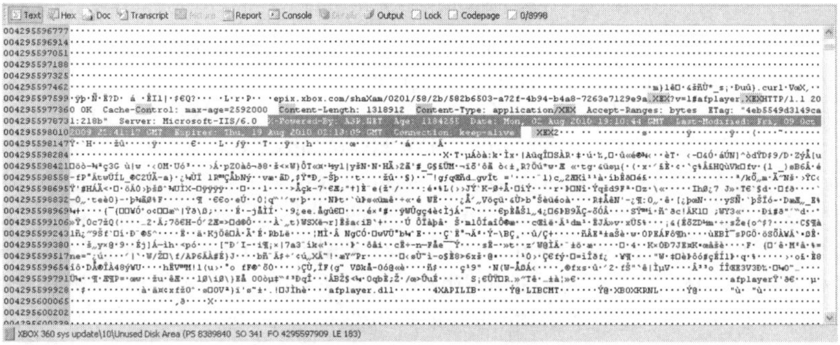

FIGURE 7.22

EnCase search hit on "CON" keyword.

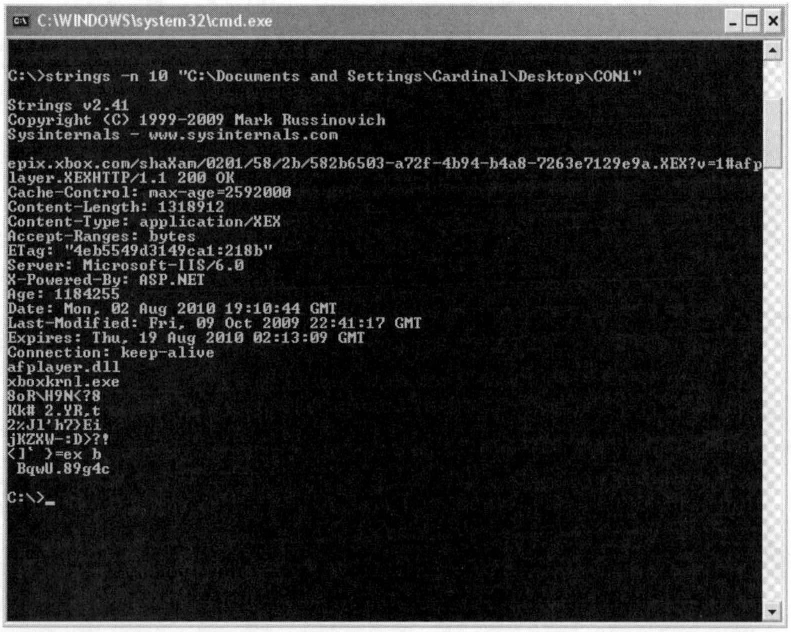

```
C:\>strings -n 10 "C:\Documents and Settings\Cardinal\Desktop\CON1"

Strings v2.41
Copyright (C) 1999-2009 Mark Russinovich
Sysinternals - www.sysinternals.com

epix.xbox.com/shaXam/0201/58/2b/582b6503-a72f-4b94-b4a8-7263e7129e9a.XEX?v=1#afp
layer.XEXHTTP/1.1 200 OK
Cache-Control: max-age=2592000
Content-Length: 1318912
Content-Type: application/XEX
Accept-Ranges: bytes
ETag: "4eb5549d3149ca1:218b"
Server: Microsoft-IIS/6.0
X-Powered-By: ASP.NET
Age: 1184255
Date: Mon, 02 Aug 2010 19:10:44 GMT
Last-Modified: Fri, 09 Oct 2009 22:41:17 GMT
Expires: Thu, 19 Aug 2010 02:13:09 GMT
Connection: keep-alive
afplayer.dll
xboxkrnl.exe
8oR\H9N<?8
Kk# 2.YR.t
2%J1'h7>Ei
jKZXW-:D>?!
<]` )=ex b
 BqwU.89g4c

C:\>_
```

FIGURE 7.23

The Strings results run against the particular CON file fragment. Note the date and time stamps.

first search hits, the XEX of an XBOX executable file is clearly visible. However, as the other instances of this data are discovered, the surrounding information is different. In one such case, there is header information for a JPEG file. Examples of this data are provided in Figures 7.24 and 7.25.

Continuing to review the search hits, another interesting data set presented itself at hit number 105. Viewing the associated plain text data that was in the first few bytes of the file indicated that it would be best to carve some of the data out and run Strings against it as well. Located within this file, there were references to a Web page, www.iec.ch, which turned out to be an international standards organization for electronics. A screenshot of the page, provided in Figure 7.26, might help provide more insight. In addition, Figure 7.27 provides a screenshot of the CON search with the associated URLs in plain text. Further results from this research are seen in Figure 7.28, which shows the Strings search results against a portion of the file.

The keyword list and the way in which the syntax and settings for "CON" were configured were reviewed, and it was noticed that there was one search hit that was in the proper format for the type of CON file we were interested in. That is, the CON in the file is the magic sequence, or file header, for the type of files that we were looking for. The text, the CON, that we are interested is preceded by the data string of ÿÿÿÿÿÿÿÿÿ. Thus, adding this string to the keyword list and searching for ÿÿÿÿÿÿÿÿÿCON presented some hits. This adjustment in the keyword string provided only two search hits. With this adjustment to the keyword and the associated two search hits, it was confirmed that this was the information that was being sought. The first hit had some plain text in close

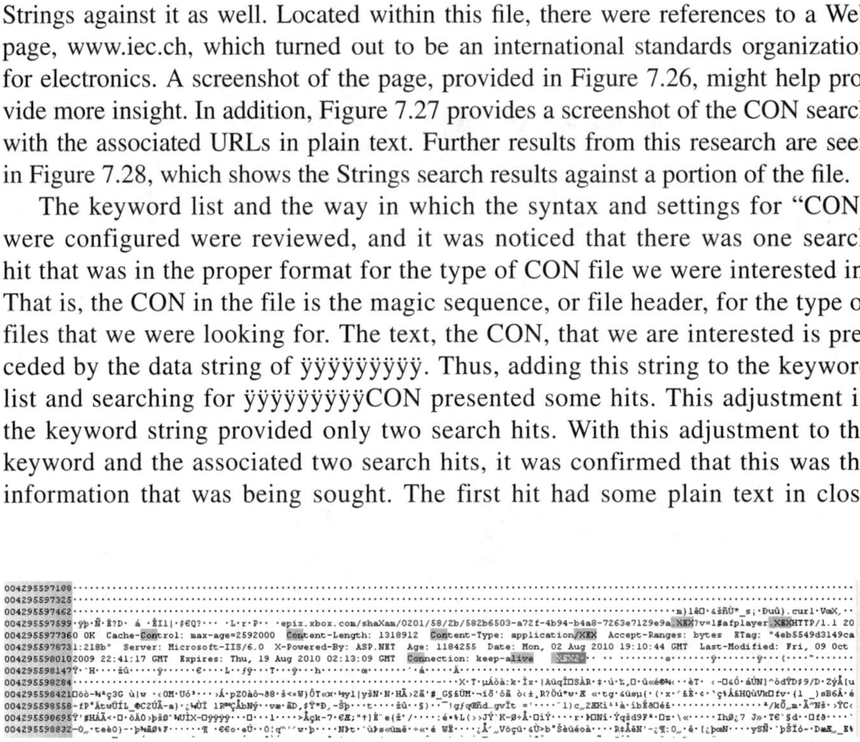

FIGURE 7.24

The XEX2 plain text associated to this CON file.

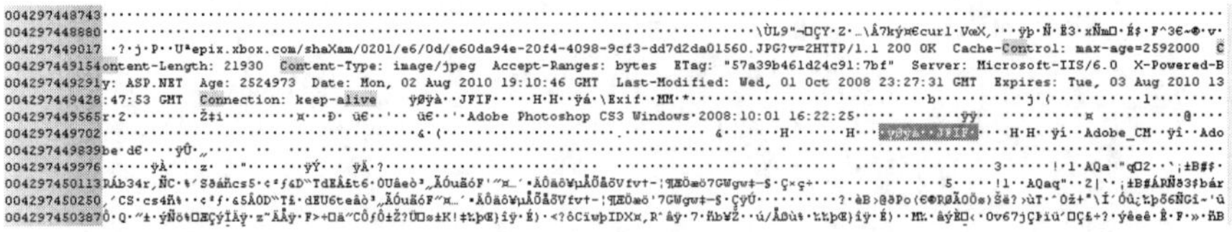

FIGURE 7.25

A similar CON search hit but with the JFIF header information that is indicative of a JPEG file.

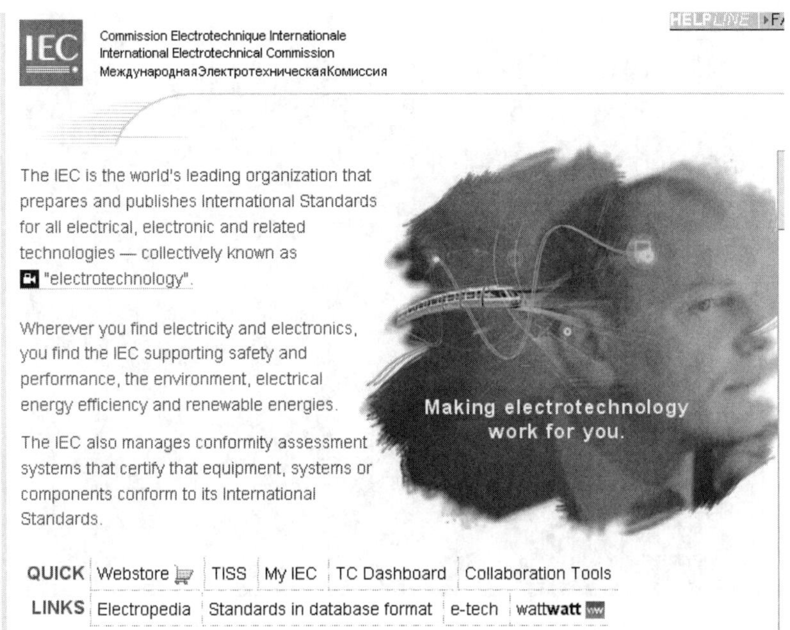

FIGURE 7.26

The home page of a site that is referenced within the CON search hits on the post–system update hard drive.

Last-Modified: Thu, 29 Jul 2010 22:59:14 GMT Expires: Tue, 31 Aug 2010 05:18:32 GMT Connection: keep-alive yØya··JFIF····d·d··yi··
Ducky·······2··ÿå·XICC_PROFILE······HLino····mntrRGB XYZ ·Î··· ···1··acspMSFT····IEC sRGB··············öÕ······Ó-HP
······························cprt···P···3desc···„···lwtpt···ð····bkpt········rXYZ········gXYZ···,····bXYZ···@····dmnd···T···pdmdd···Ä···ˆv
ued···L···†view···Ô···$lumi···ø····meas······$tech···0····rTRC···<····gTRC···<····bTRC···<····text····Copyright (c) 1998 Hewlett-Packard
Company··desc········sRGB IEC61966-2.1···········sRGB IEC61966-2.1··XYZ ······óQ······
XYZ ················XYZ ······o¢··8õ···XYZ ······b···_···ÚXYZ ······$ ···„··¶Îdesc········IEC http://www.iec.ch···········IEC http://
www.iec.ch···desc·······.IEC 61966-2.1 Default RGB colour space - sRGB···········.IEC 61966-2.
1 Default RGB colour space - sRGB···························desc·······,Reference Viewing Condition in IEC61966-2.1···········,Reference Viewi
ng Condition in IEC61966-2.1···························view······ ··_··Î···iÌ······\ž····XYZ ·····L V·P···W·çmeas·························
····sig ····CRT curv··············

FIGURE 7.27

EnCase screenshot of the CON search hit with Web reference in close proximity.

proximity to it that indicates that it is a XBOX 360 Dashboard file of some sort. Figure 7.29 provides a snapshot of the search hits with the associated physical sector locations.

Examination of the text found within the first search hit indicates that this file is somehow involved in the XBOX 360 Dashboard. In addition, the console security certificates can be clearly seen in the beginning of the file, indicated by the string of

```
C:\>strings -n 10 "C:\Documents and Settings\Cardinal\Desktop\105"

Strings v2.41
Copyright (C) 1999-2009 Mark Russinovich
Sysinternals - www.sysinternals.com

Condition in IEC61966-2.1
,Reference Viewing Condition in IEC61966-2.1
#<-27;@EJOTY^chmrw|
#""""#''''''''''
!! !!''''''''''''
S"VVUO7:<<
epix.xbox.com/shaXam/0201/27/4c/274c7e4f-6a43-4c6c-911d-1c0f0b1fb343.JPG?v=6HTTP
/1.1 200 OK
Cache-Control: max-age=2592000
Content-Length: 28100
Content-Type: image/jpeg
Accept-Ranges: bytes
ETag: "208e44407753ca1:218b"
Server: Microsoft-IIS/6.0
X-Powered-By: ASP.NET
Age: 1187673
Date: Mon, 02 Aug 2010 19:10:46 GMT
Last-Modified: Fri, 23 Oct 2009 00:24:57 GMT
Expires: Thu, 19 Aug 2010 01:16:13 GMT
Connection: keep-alive
YS2 "U<ff!
epix.xbox.com/shaXam/0201/fb/e2/fbe216c6-50c5-4866-96f5-e5c1e9296157.JPG?v=1HTTP
/1.1 200 OK
Cache-Control: max-age=2592000
Content-Length: 30096
Content-Type: image/jpeg
Accept-Ranges: bytes
ETag: "2ea0458c6f2ecb1:2bdd"
Server: Microsoft-IIS/6.0
X-Powered-By: ASP.NET
Age: 362214
Date: Mon, 02 Aug 2010 19:10:47 GMT
Last-Modified: Wed, 28 Jul 2010 16:11:33 GMT
Expires: Sat, 28 Aug 2010 14:33:53 GMT
Connection: keep-alive
```

FIGURE 7.28

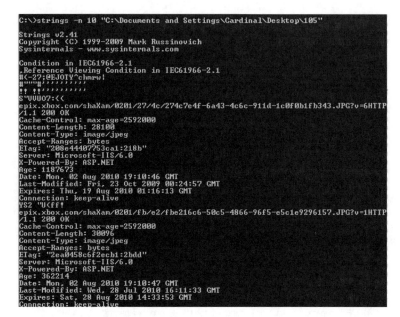

Strings run against a portion of the aforementioned file. Note the ASP.net references as well as Microsoft IIS text.

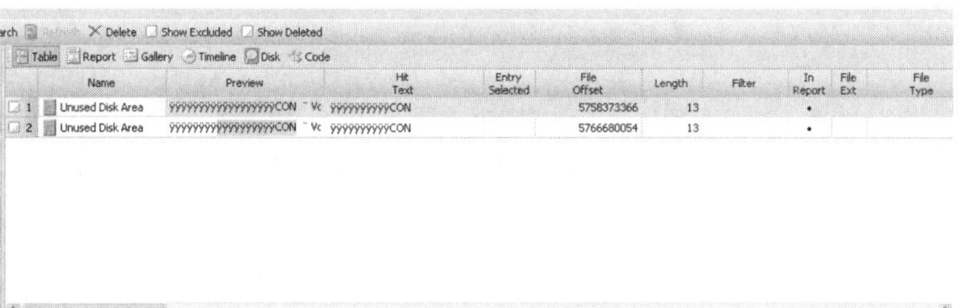

	Name	Preview	Hit Text	Entry Selected	File Offset	Length	Filter	In Report	File Ext	File Type
1	Unused Disk Area	ÿÿÿÿÿÿÿÿÿÿÿÿÿÿÿÿÿÿCON ¨ Vc	ÿÿÿÿÿÿÿÿÿÿCON		5758373366	13		•		
2	Unused Disk Area	ÿÿÿÿÿÿÿÿÿÿÿÿÿÿÿÿÿÿCON ¨ Vc	ÿÿÿÿÿÿÿÿÿÿCON		5766680054	13		•		

FIGURE 7.29

The search hits with the proper syntax for the CON files.

VœX, X852266-001. The next few figures, Figures 7.30 and 7.31, show the results of this examination and are screenshots of the data.

Running Strings against this file provided some other plain text hits. A listing of some of the information that is located within the file is as follows:

- X852266-001
- 902152BP2483S1XDWJLA
- E00000C1AE69C588
- XBOX 360 Dashboard

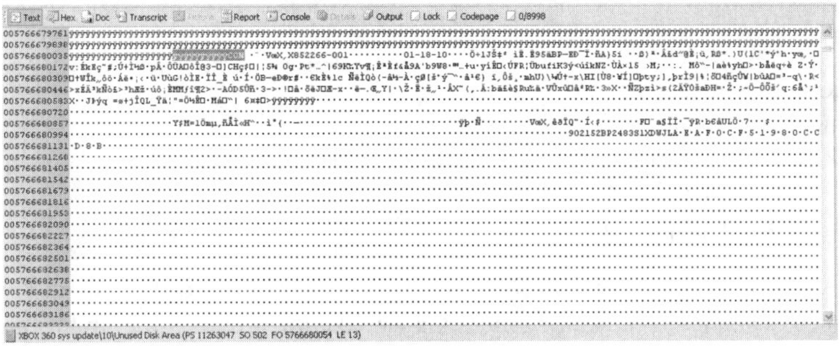

FIGURE 7.30

The CON file with the console security certificate.

FIGURE 7.31

Screenshot of EnCase showing the XBOX 360 Dashboard plain text within the CON file.

- tEXtSoftware
- Adobe ImageReadyq
- fxx[a_;.*+?;;
- dH[S74(OLLhee
- /17$!"5:Bb__jhh401rpq
- cpFFFE07D1.gpd
- h/tile_64.png
- h!tile_32.png
- h!584D07D1.gpd
- crAvatarAssets
- csFFFE07DE.gpd
- cpFFFE07D1.gpd
- tile_64.png
- h!tile_32.png
- h!584D07D1.gpd
- crAvatarAssets

- csFFFE07DE.gpd
- tEXtSoftware
- Adobe ImageReadyq
- Avatar Editor
- tEXtSoftware
- Adobe ImageReadyq
- XBOX 360 Dashboard

The second CON file that was identified through the keyword search did not provide an easy plain text indicator of its function like the previous file. In this case, the only option that was left was to run Strings to determine if there were any indicator keywords present. Figure 7.32 provides a detail of the text view of this beginning of this file and Figure 7.33 is a screenshot of the Strings result.

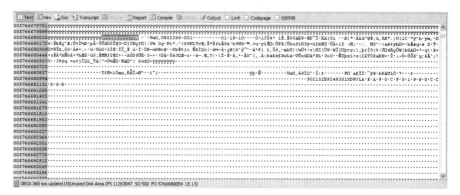

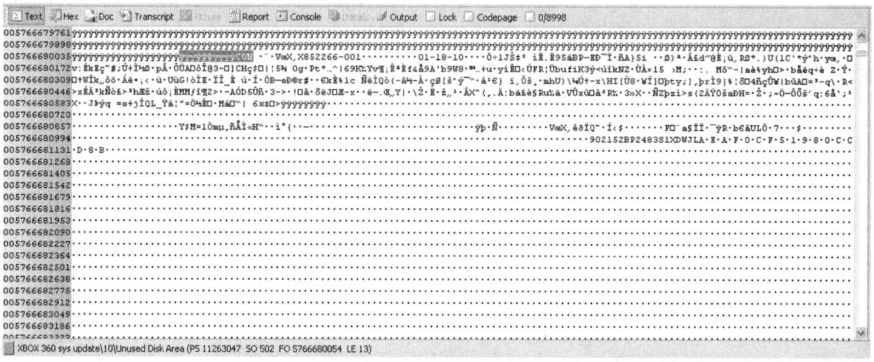

FIGURE 7.32

Screenshot of the text view of CON file.

FIGURE 7.33

Strings results run against a portion of the second CON file hit.

NEW IMAGES ADDED AFTER THE SYSTEM UPDATE

Another area that was thought important to address was the images that are created from the system update. In earlier chapters, we addressed the default images that are on the hard drive. During the course of the system update, more images are stored on the storage media.

The process used to identify the images was a rather straightforward forensic process. The disk image files were loaded into Access Data's Forensic Tool Kit v1.70.1 application. The program indexed and cataloged the case. Once completed, there were no files or images identified. Using the data carve feature within FTK, all image files that could be identified were carved for on the XBOX 360 hard drive image. FTK, like all the other mainstream forensic applications, does not recognize the FATX file system. Carving the image files from the image using FTK was rather simple. The drive image was loaded into FTK and all defaults were selected. Once loaded, like all other forensics applications, the application reported the entire drive as unallocated space. Navigating to the Tools menu and selecting the **Data Carve** option, the process of data carving was initiated. Once the Data Carve dialog box appeared, all the file types were selected and the process was run. Upon completion, FTK reported that it was able to carve 4427 image files from the drive image. Figures 7.34 and 7.35 provide screenshots of the data carve defaults, as well as the image container file results.

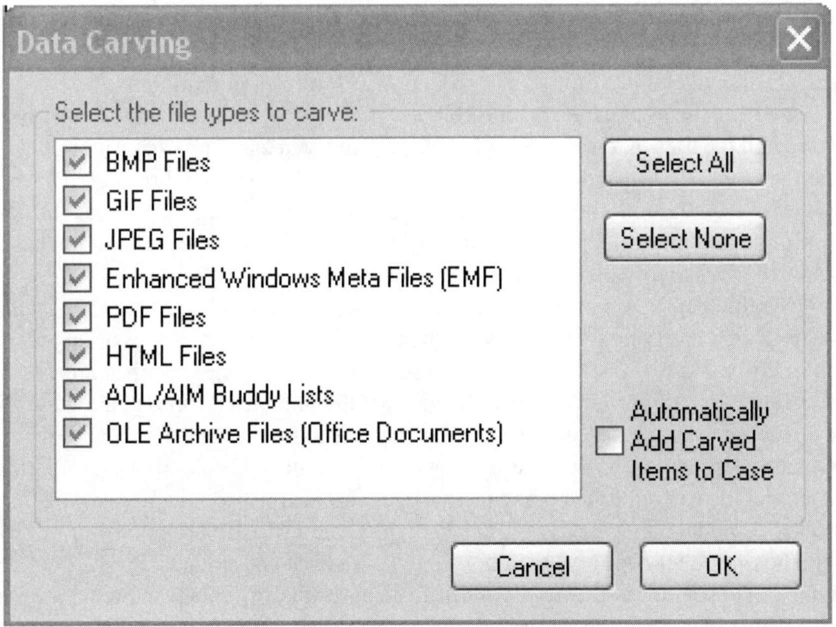

FIGURE 7.34

Default FTK data carve of the pre–system updated drive image.

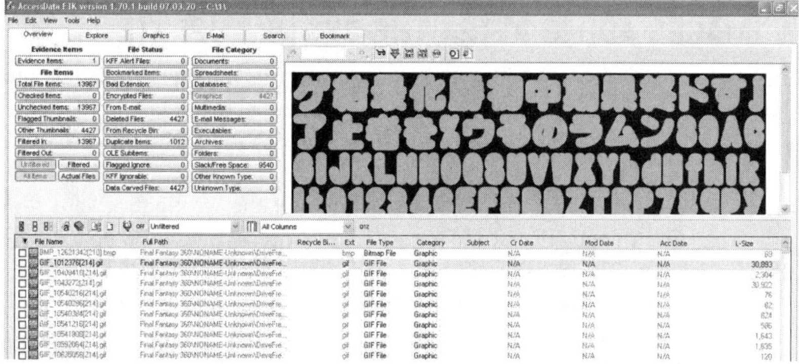

FIGURE 7.35

Screenshot of the results of the FTK data carve. Note the graphics report that is presented showing the end result of 4427 files.

The next steps were to repeat this process with the post–system updated hard drive image file. Navigating through the entire process once again and reviewing the end results from the data carve, there were some image files that had been added to the hard drive. Figure 7.36 provides a screenshot detailing the graphics report from FTK.

Taking the information from these two reports it appears as though there were some 125 new images added to the drive through the system update process. The next step was to identify these new images and make hash sets of both the pre– and post–system image files for comparison. Although this step is specific to this comparative analysis, it could be used for search reduction in future examinations.

Exporting the image files from FTK was straightforward, involving: simply highlighting all the files that were identified through the data carve process, right-clicking over the selected files, and choosing to export them to a specified directory. This process was repeated with the post–system updated drive, carving the images files and exporting them out of FTK. Now that there were two sets of images, it was possible to take the files and import them into EnCase.

Once the files were in EnCase, the images were reviewed to get an idea of where they might be used or called upon with the usage of the system. Many of the images appear to be from the start up of the console or from the games that are already preinstalled. In addition, there were images for the default Gamertags and icons for the game introductions. After conducting this manual review of the files, they were hashed and a custom hash set was created for further analysis. To create the hash set, all the files were hashed using the hash feature of EnCase. The items were "blue checked," and then they were right-clicked; the **Create Hash Set** option was selected from the right-click Option dialog box, and the hash set was named "PRE UPDATE." Figure 7.37 provides a screenshot of this the end result of this step, showing the hash set already created and the information within EnCase.

Once the hash set was created, the post–system image files were pulled into EnCase, and the Hash library was rebuilt to allow for the comparative analysis. This process revealed the 125 new image files that were added to the hard drive after the

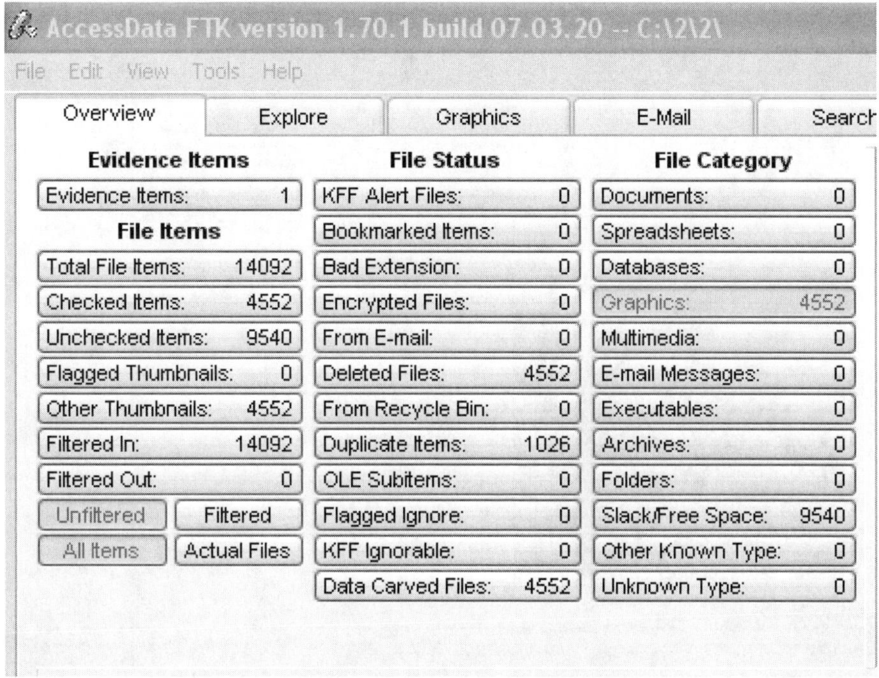

FIGURE 7.36

Post–system updated drive data carve for graphics. Note that this graphic number depicts an increase from the pre–system updated drive image.

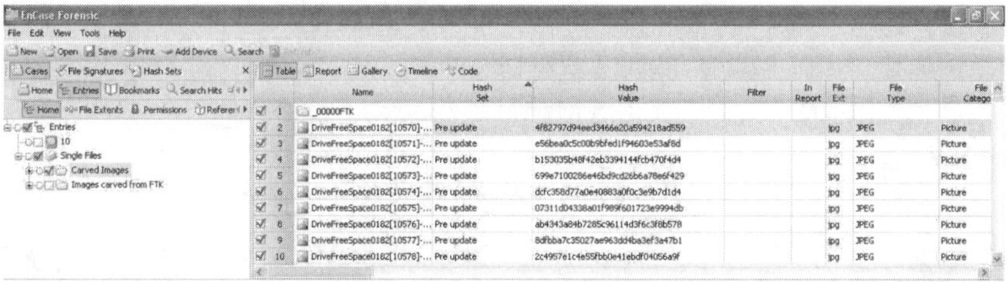

FIGURE 7.37

The hash set of pre–system update image files from EnCase.

system update. A manual review of these files was conducted and many of them appear to be advertisements for upcoming video games; Netflix, Facebook, and XBOX Live Gold account advertisements; summer arcade advertisements; marketplace deals; game expansion packs; and streaming audio. Many of the images were promotions for the upcoming sequels to the HALO series that is the flagship game series for the XBOX consoles. Figures 7.38 through 7.41 provide some snapshots of this data as it is represented in EnCase.

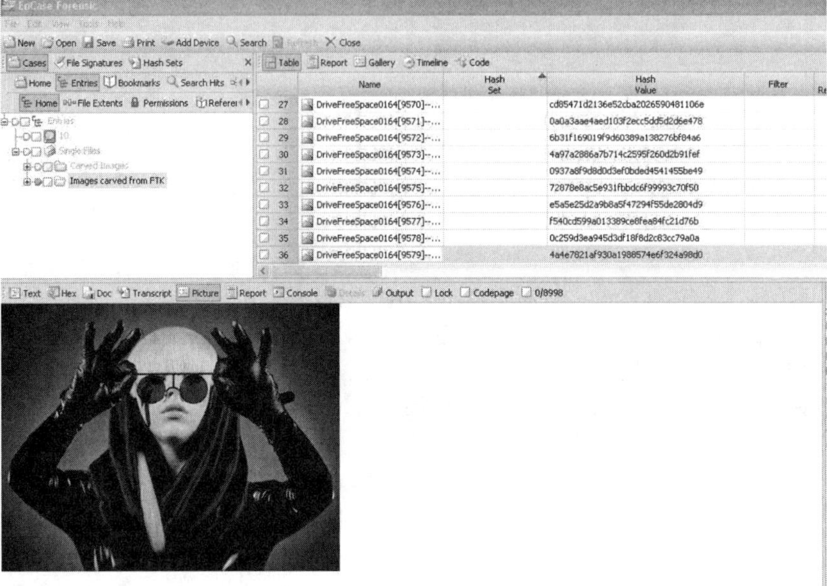

FIGURE 7.38

Sample image.

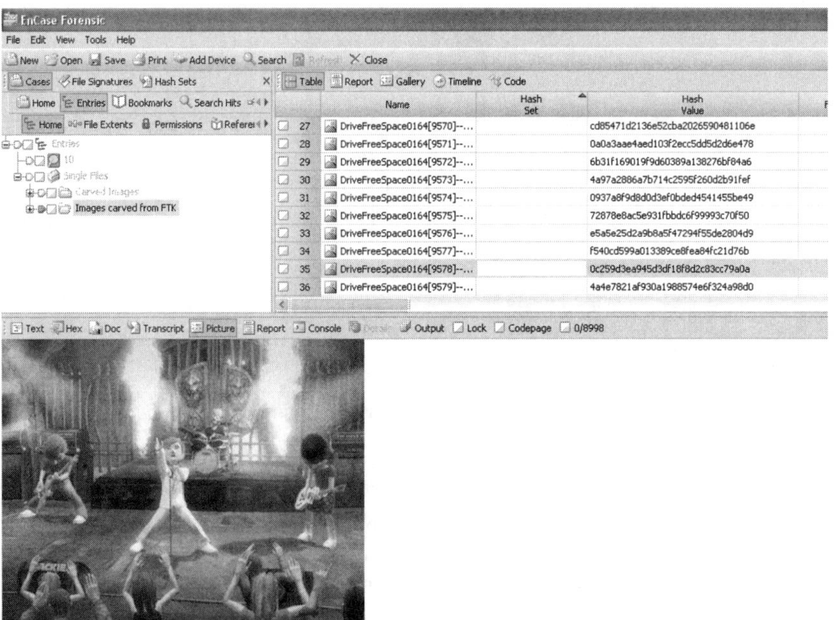

FIGURE 7.39

Sample image 2.

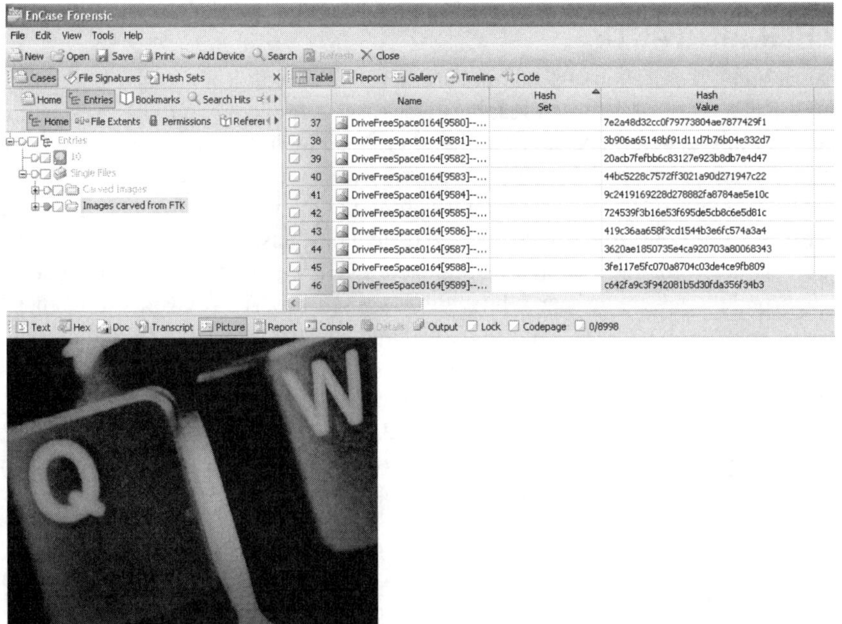

FIGURE 7.40

Sample image 3.

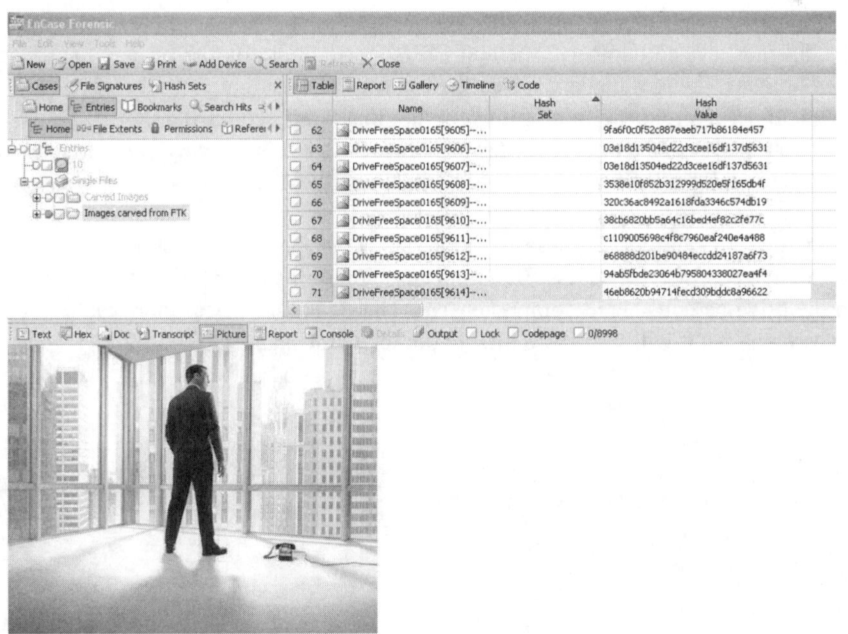

FIGURE 7.41

Sample image 4.

OTHER ARTIFACTS

In an attempt to ascertain other digital artifacts that could be of use in examining the hard drive, a range of keyword searches were used that were based on several items. The first thing to determine was whether the e-mail address that was used to configure the Live account was retained on the hard drive. A keyword search was run using a specific e-mail address, and nothing was found in the way of artifacts stored on the drive. The same holds true for the console ID and the console serial number; searches were conducted for these items, listing each as GREP, Unicode, and Unicode Big Endian, and there were no search hits with these settings. All keywords were entered into the keyword list of EnCase, as GREP, Unicode, and Unicode Big Endian.

The date of birth was also searched for, as this was required input at the time of configuration, but again, nothing was found in the way of digital artifacts.

Of course, this is not a definitive result as this is a science and an art. This research is continuing and perhaps the way that the keywords are being entered is off the mark and must be adjusted as further research is needed and is ongoing.

SUMMARY

Within this chapter, we discussed the changes that are made to the data that is stored on the storage media, once a system update is accepted and executed. This change is allowed by the end user once they accept the EULA of the XBOX Live service, while configuring the console for online game play and social interaction. Among the changes are the number of default PIRS files that are on the storage media and the number of images that are stored. One particular area that might be of interest to an examiner is the location of the Gamertag that was used during the online portal registration, the Live service. Research indicates that this information is tracked by Microsoft and that there is a record of the Gamertag log-ins to the Live service. This data can be preserved with the right court paperwork and the IP addresses that the Gamertag is using during these log-in sessions can be traced back to a subscriber for high-speed Internet access. By no means should this information on the changes to the drive be considered comprehensive. There is a great deal more that is being researched, but it will take more time to complete the analysis.

CHAPTER

Post–System Update Drive Artifacts

8

INFORMATION IN THIS CHAPTER

- Examining the XBOX 360 hard drive using Xplorer360
- Getting started
- Xplorer360 and the post–system update drive
- Cache folder
- Content folder
- Mindex folder

EXAMINING THE XBOX 360 HARD DRIVE USING XPLORER360

We have been examining the XBOX 360 hard drive through standard forensic applications such as EnCase, X-Ways, and the forensic tool kit. These applications provide a raw hex view of the data, but because they are not able to interpret the file system as of yet, they report the entire drive as unallocated space. There are a few applications that actually interpret the file system; one such application is Xplorer360. This application was designed by two individuals, Angerwound and Roofus (only their net handles were readily available). Their site, which hosted the download of the applications, was www.360gamesaves.com; however, recent searches for the site reveal that it may be down as of this writing. In any event, there are many alternative sites that also host this application for download. One such site is www.xbox-scene.com. The program itself is advertised as an application to assist in the "hacking" of gamer achievements and allows a user to unlock all the features or levels of a game. Xplorer360 gives the end user full read/write access to their drive. One drawback of these hacking methods is that the end user runs the risk of having Microsoft discover the hack, and then the console gets banned from the XBOX Live service. Microsoft is taking the hacking of their console very seriously.

In any event, there is a need to show the contents of the drive in a pre–system update configuration as well as a post–system update configuration, and that is what will be detailed within this chapter.

GETTING STARTED

In any event, an out-of-the-box 120 GB hard drive was used and extracted from the custom enclosure as previously described. Once removed, the drive was connected to the WiebeTech Ultra Dock and the examination machine. The Xplorer 360 application was then opened and pointed to the connected drive. The application presents a relatively sparse screen with no information readily available or displayed. The menu options that are present are similar in look and feel to all other Windows-based applications. Under the Drive menu, there are a few options:

- Open
- Close
- Backup image
- Restore image
- Exit

The **Open** option allows an end user to associate a FATX-formatted hard drive, memory card, or an image of one of these devices. Once a device that is formatted properly is opened within Xplorer360, the main screen is populated with the directory structure. Figure 8.1 provides a look at the application once a FATX-formatted drive has been loaded.

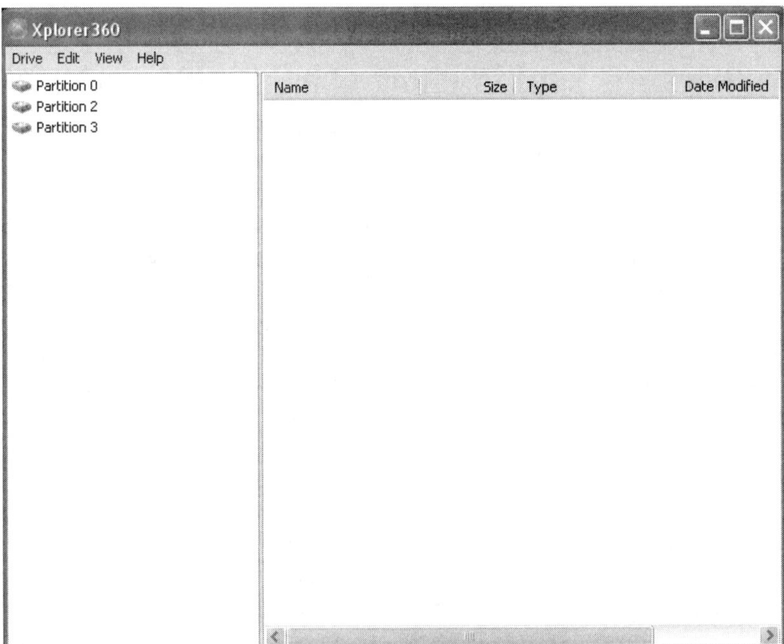

FIGURE 8.1

Initial load of a FATX-formatted drive into Xplorer360.

Once the drive has been loaded, it becomes clear that the application interprets the FATX file system well. However, we need to explore the folders and determine what information is present within them so that there is a better understanding of the files within each folder. Simply double-click on each folder to reveal the subfolders and the associated files. The first partition, Partition 0, is empty at this point; again this is the untouched drive, taken directly from the retail package. Figure 8.2 provides a screenshot of Partition 0 detailing that there are no subfolders.

You might notice that there is no Partition 1 displayed. This is one of the areas that is still under research. Remember from Chapter 7, "XBOX 360 Hard Drive: Documenting the Artifacts after the Initial System Update and Live Account Creation," that we discussed the five FATX search hits that were revealed using EnCase. There were two search hits that were suggested to be the location of secured storage from encrypted content. This is the working theory, but more research is needed and is ongoing.

Highlighting Partition 2 reveals many subfolders that we are going to examine to determine their relevance. Once the partition is highlighted, there is an immediate

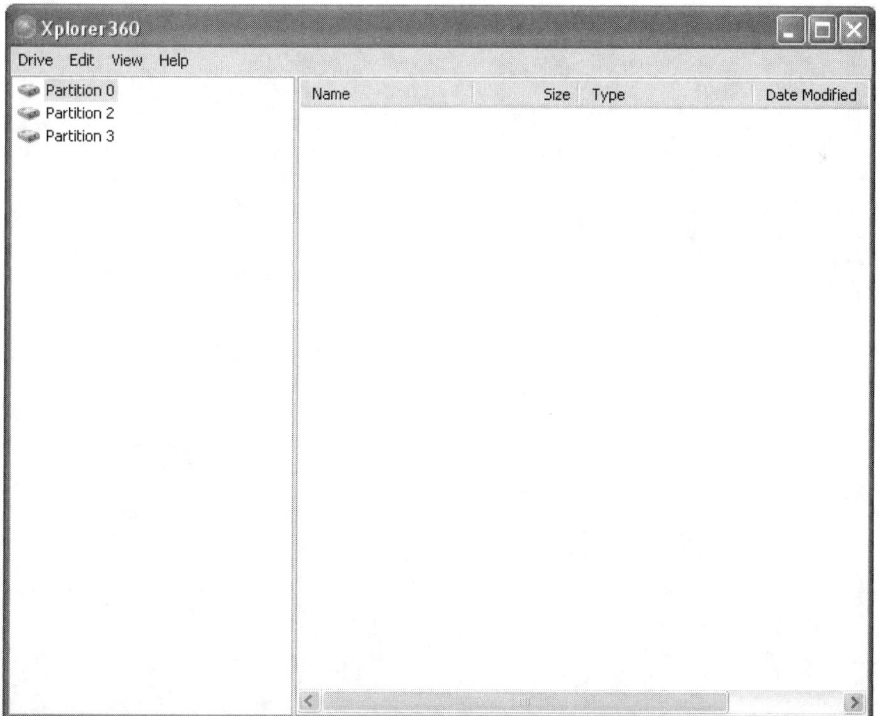

FIGURE 8.2

Partition 0 of a new retail drive showing that there is no further information located within the partition.

display of the subfolders in the right-hand pane. There are two subfolders that are displayed:

- Compatibility
- TDBX

In addition to the subfolders, a file named "index" is also revealed. Figure 8.3 details these folders and the file.

Each folder can be selected, and the subfolders or the files can be viewed. Xplorer360 allows the end user to extract files for examination. Although this is not the intended purpose, the end result is that this application is free and provides the ability to decipher the file system. Starting with the first file that was discovered, the index file, the user simply right-clicked on the file and selected **Extract** from the options. Since this file is being reported as a 10 KB file, the extraction of such a small file proceeded very quickly. There were several options now available. Two options were to import the file into EnCase or run Strings against it to find ASCII and UNICODE strings. The file itself was interesting once removed from the drive image. It was decided to run Strings against the file and open it as a WordPad file.

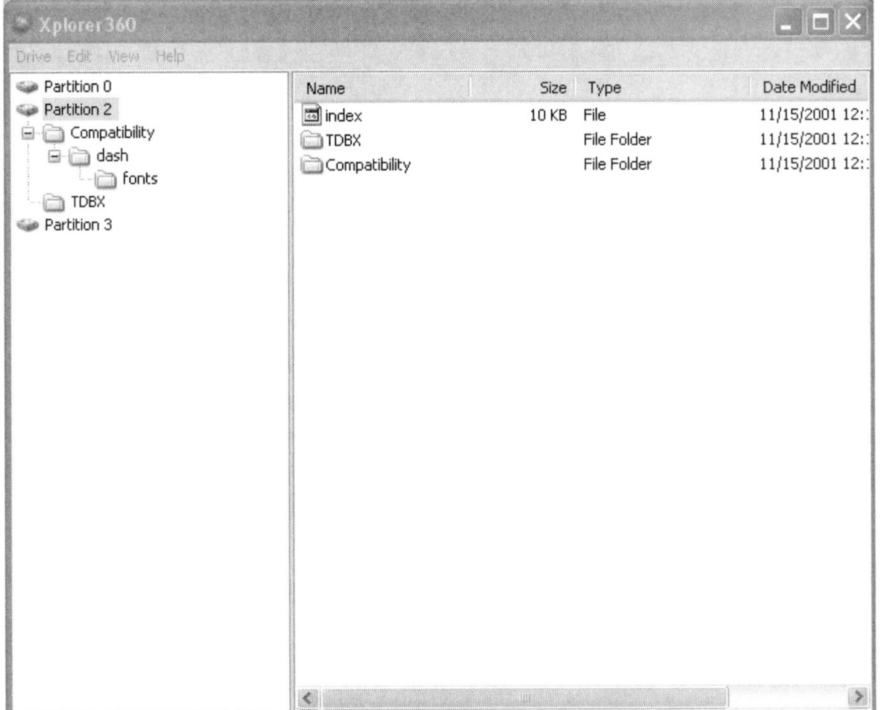

FIGURE 8.3

Details of the subfolders, compatibility, and TDBX as well as the file index.

Opening it with WordPad was a straightforward process: simply selecting the file, choosing open, and then selecting the application to open it with.

> **WARNING**
>
> Recall the earlier discussion of the limitations of WordPad and any files that are being examined in this manner should also be imported into a forensics application to ensure that all the data is viewed.

Once the file was opened, it revealed that this index file is an index of the files on the drive with their associated CRC hashes. Figure 8.4 shows a screenshot of this information.

> **TIP**
>
> The information within the index file changes as the console is used more by the end users. As information is downloaded and stored on the hard drive, this index file continues to populate.

Continuing on with the examination of the information, the Compatibility folder is expanded, and it reveals even more subfolders. The date that is posted for these files, if you look at Figure 8.3, is plainly visible as November 15, 2001, which is the release date of the original XBOX console. It is thought that this Compatibility folder


```
F14aBqHWqzLPO7XCjjdPuBKcDmbQKqnbiUSMcIUwmYnz9GS+k23cGW7iQftEDxkezCq+83MDjGbf3zux1qcDx/R+vTpOzWLAbd2SWV3QbuyopXRK4cPtSGLYiFDZHeft+1
[HEADER]
VERSION=1.0

[CONTENTS]
\Device\Harddisk0\Partition1\$SystemUpdate\su20076000_00000000 CRC:f2cd05f0
\Device\Harddisk0\Partition1\$TitleUpdate\FFFE07D2\tu20075c00_00000000 CRC:ba17a4cb
\Device\Harddisk0\Partition1\Cache
\Device\Harddisk0\Partition1\Content\0000000000000000\434387DC\00080000\D046F2C56A332C276B23B839DDE64BDF42F7C6C843 CRC:962217d3
\Device\Harddisk0\Partition1\Content\0000000000000000\485587DE\00080000\728497FA7B970606DA0D61BFF2C5FA5B2BFDCE8448 CRC:42ca1422
\Device\Harddisk0\Partition1\Content\0000000000000000\4C4187D3\00080000\292D38BCE52DF18213A77655F1A3F26E84A604B44C CRC:cda2c306
\Device\Harddisk0\Partition1\Content\0000000000000000\4D5307D5\00030000\0CEBF752A25CDA821FAA54CCEA54C30922AC257E4D CRC:9d67f749
\Device\Harddisk0\Partition1\Content\0000000000000000\4D5307E6\000C0000\12FDA3B04CA4FDEBC9E75711B4EAB79059E965B54D CRC:51386e55
\Device\Harddisk0\Partition1\Content\0000000000000000\4D5307E6\000C0000\34B37C46E0B4EDCC6312DC93A2DD70DA695578B84D CRC:bdc17284
\Device\Harddisk0\Partition1\Content\0000000000000000\4D5307E6\000C0000\80478667DECFA6BA1FBAA2ADE066840D3C42B8664D CRC:43023585
\Device\Harddisk0\Partition1\Content\0000000000000000\4D5307EA\000C0000\0DC9F7D52D72BB38FD70E98B3E92F31D59E926D14D CRC:1648513a
\Device\Harddisk0\Partition1\Content\0000000000000000\4D5307EA\000C0000\A815654DFD0CBA46F79052AE857BB0C7839DF4104D CRC:8856e9a1
\Device\Harddisk0\Partition1\Content\0000000000000000\4D530808\000C0000\5E56B920C4DEDACD9B639FD08AB2F8C6342237474D CRC:9fc1943c
\Device\Harddisk0\Partition1\Content\0000000000000000\584107D1\000D0000\584107D100000001 CRC:566cd787
\Device\Harddisk0\Partition1\Content\0000000000000000\584107D5\000D0000\E35E0B286F6225A6253B997406649E696784B57858 CRC:63619e14
\Device\Harddisk0\Partition1\Content\0000000000000000\584107D7\000D0000\FAFF44B4C6642F88B541801FD506FEEEF7208E8258 CRC:861735fe
\Device\Harddisk0\Partition1\Content\0000000000000000\584107E7\000D0000\DC1BD04E89B129F9B89F65AEA32462D3DBD0769958 CRC:cc4ae61f
\Device\Harddisk0\Partition1\Content\0000000000000000\584107ED\000D0000\3E0461FF3BCCA5E9DBAE5EBAC41BE8205BAE065958 CRC:0cc85684
\Device\Harddisk0\Partition1\Content\0000000000000000\584107EF\000D0000\90226B760A840A3AFC759094668DA3FBE4DF716D58 CRC:2d572998
\Device\Harddisk0\Partition1\Content\0000000000000000\584107F1\000D0000\8A47B623AC96F86F372A21A7ECC4B2752B82182958 CRC:d80538db
\Device\Harddisk0\Partition1\Content\0000000000000000\584107F3\000D0000\097C82E1F461E48F7E3AAF6CE9468140080BA0AF58 CRC:044e07c1
\Device\Harddisk0\Partition1\Content\0000000000000000\584107F4\000D0000\38AD647E68F9542F2F78C4EC1FEED0B5588D887558 CRC:c029293d
\Device\Harddisk0\Partition1\Content\0000000000000000\584107F8\000D0000\77CFA93BC58C32D13BC4E4CC7DB4BE7D1B7F98D658 CRC:368fffd9
\Device\Harddisk0\Partition1\Content\0000000000000000\584107FE\000D0000\E1081DE82E8223C43487C384ED1D3413F05C373B58 CRC:a2ef4141
\Device\Harddisk0\Partition1\Content\0000000000000000\58410810\000D0000\659F14A896AF32C6CFC3EDD9CAFB0101C21980FC58 CRC:4c16283c
\Device\Harddisk0\Partition1\Content\0000000000000000\58410811\000D0000\AE2EAEAF0A68E40EA6B04C46A1B5729B29068CDC58 CRC:e4f3dc7a
\Device\Harddisk0\Partition1\Content\0000000000000000\FFFE07C5\000C0000\BC0A9EBD0A7373 6818E4BDC604361FCAF520CB96FF CRC:38e10f97
\Device\Harddisk0\Partition1\Content\0000000000000000\FFFE07D1\00020000\FFFE07D11000.GamerPicture CRC:a5534d31
\Device\Harddisk0\Partition1\Content\0000000000000000\FFFE07D1\00020000\FFFE07D11001.GamerPicture CRC:e479169c
\Device\Harddisk0\Partition1\Content\0000000000000000\FFFE07D1\00020000\FFFE07D11002.GamerPicture CRC:101855de
\Device\Harddisk0\Partition1\Content\0000000000000000\FFFE07D1\00020000\FFFE07D11003.GamerPicture CRC:28dbd777
\Device\Harddisk0\Partition1\Content\0000000000000000\FFFE07D1\00020000\FFFE07D11004.GamerPicture CRC:53101527
\Device\Harddisk0\Partition1\Content\0000000000000000\FFFE07D1\00020000\FFFE07D11005.GamerPicture CRC:f7cc52e9
\Device\Harddisk0\Partition1\Content\0000000000000000\FFFE07D1\00020000\FFFE07D11006.GamerPicture CRC:b1f64922
\Device\Harddisk0\Partition1\Content\0000000000000000\FFFE07D1\00020000\FFFE07D11007.GamerPicture CRC:d063fe5f
```


FIGURE 8.4

Screenshot of the index file showing the contents of the drive and the associated CRC value.

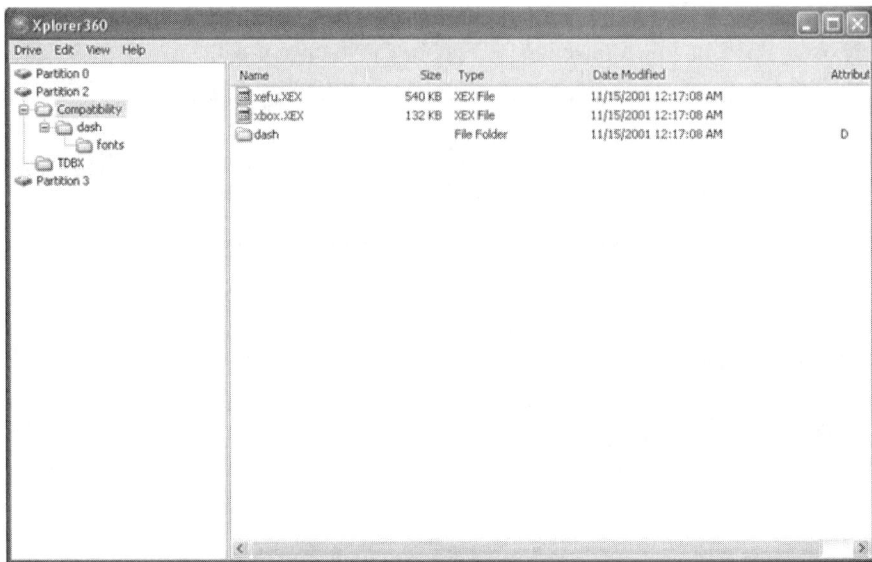

FIGURE 8.5

The contents of the Compatibility folder.

maintains the information that allows the XBOX 360 to be backward compatible with the original console games. This was one of the selling points of the new console that it could play the games from the first console. Figure 8.5 shows the details once the Compatibility folder is opened and the subfiles are revealed.

Note that there are two files that are the custom XBOX 360 executable extension of XEX and one folder, the Dash folder, which is no doubt a reference to the XBOX 360 dashboard. In order to examine this file, it was extracted using the extraction feature of Xplorer360. Once the file was copied from the image and placed into an external location, EnCase was launched, and the file was imported for examination. Viewing the file in EnCase provided some more information about the file. There were some more plain text indicators of the function of the file; chief among those indicators is the plain text phrase XBOXkernal.exe. Locating a .exe file on the drive was interesting because all research had, to this point, indicated that the executables on the console were in the proprietary format of XEX. There were several plain text hits within the file, such as

- @\Device\Harddisk0\SystemPartition\Compatibility\xefu.xex
- xb1krnl
- \@•XBOXKRNL•
- \@•LIBC
- \@•D3D9
- \@•PMCPB
- \••XGRAPHC
- \@•XAUD

Thus, the text is clearly a reference to the XBOX kernel and provides the path to the information that the console would need when launching a legacy application for the console itself, such as a video game from the original console. The LIBC entry could be an indicator to a library file of some sort for the backward compatibility. Speculation is that the XAUD is an XBOX audit file that could assist in the security of the console to ensure that there has not been any modification to the hardware. Remember that if there is a hardware modification and Microsoft becomes aware of it, then the console gets banned from the online XBOX Live portal. Figure 8.6 shows the file as it is rendered in EnCase.

Running Strings against the file provided no more useful information but provided the plain text in a more user-friendly format. Figure 8.7 shows the results from the Strings search.

It was decided that the file itself needed more examination, so returning to EnCase, the information that was displayed was reviewed. It appeared that there was some padding associated to the file, starting with the XEX2 text string at the beginning of the file. This information is reported as being 4116 bytes in length and may assist in the obfuscation of the code to make it harder to reverse engineer, but this is just speculation. Moving further through the file, the next ASCII string that is present is "xam.xex • xboxkrnl.exe," indicating that there is a call to an executable or an interpreter to convert between the XEX2 and the traditional .exe files. Or, this simply could be a statement that this is the location of the executable file for the console; not being a programmer, it is hard to say.

The last string that is identifiable starts with the header QK. Some research on this type of header, if indeed this is a file header, reveals that the QK file header is used in C and C++ programming. Several Web sites have provided information that may indicate its usage here. One site stated that this header must be used or included in all modules for a platform-independent public interface, which was not much help. However, there were other sites that suggested this was used in database calls, which would make sense particularly with the location on the drive this file resides.

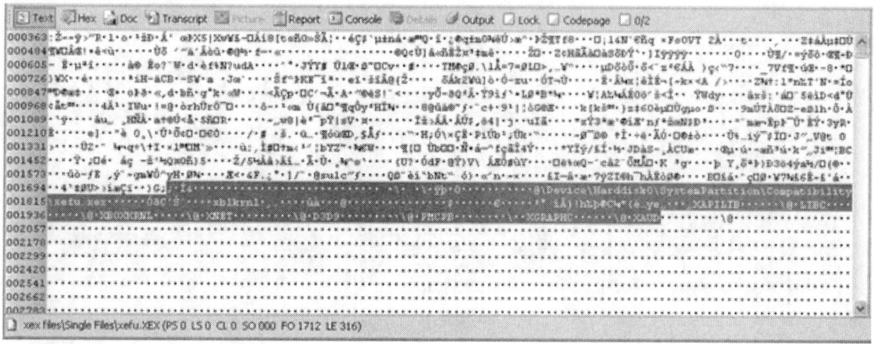

FIGURE 8.6

xefu.xex file as it is displayed within EnCase. Note the plain text that is present.

Because it is located within an area for backward compatibility and there is a file that must be downloaded in order to play the legacy games, it would make sense that this XEX2 application would need a database to call upon to allow for the legacy games to play. Perhaps, and this is speculation, this XEX2 file uses the C++ QK to call the database for the particular game that is being executed. Figures 8.8 to 8.10 provide screenshots of the information just addressed.

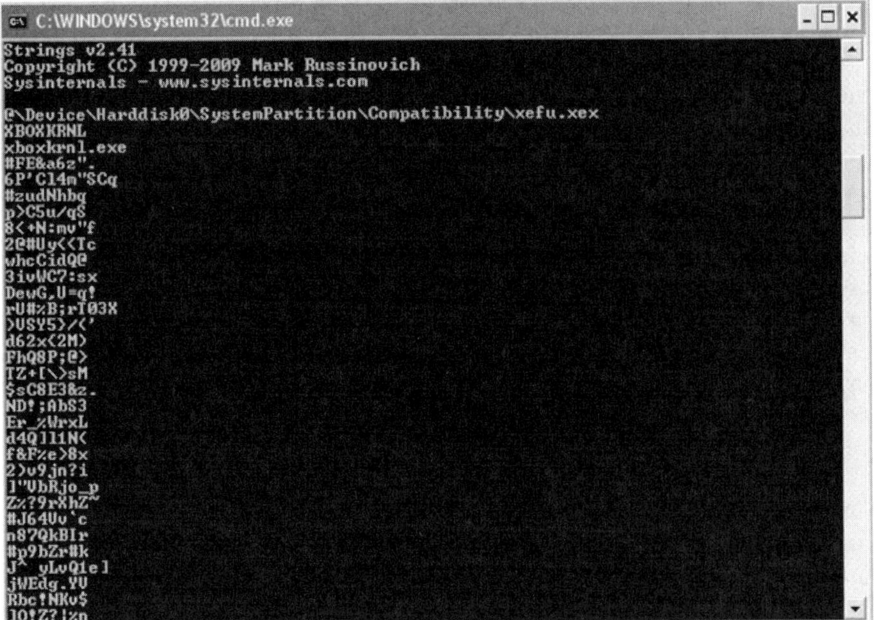

FIGURE 8.7

Strings run against the xefu.xex file.

FIGURE 8.8

XEX2 initial bytes of the file showing some plain text and perhaps padding of some sort.

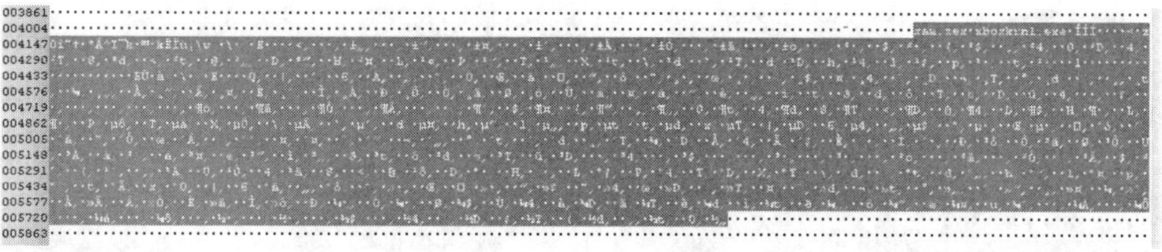

FIGURE 8.9

This screenshot shows how EnCase renders the "xam.xex • xboxkrnl.exe" section of the XEFU file.

FIGURE 8.10

EnCase screenshot of the "header" QK. If this is indeed a file header, then this could be a c++ database management executable.

```
Strings v2.41
Copyright (C) 1999-2009 Mark Russinovich
Sysinternals - www.sysinternals.com

@\Device\Harddisk0\SystemPartition\Compatibility\xbox.xex
xboxkrnl.exe
s0]sp>s?Tl
5D%.SC5$(e=
```

FIGURE 8.11

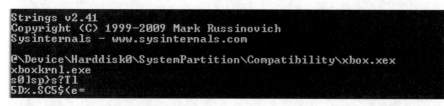

Strings results against the xbox.xex file with the Strings value set to 10.

The next file within the Compatibility folder is the xbox.xex file. This file is used to load an emulator to allow the end user to play legacy XBOX games. The file may contain the emulation software as well as the pointers to other resources that are needed, akin to the DLLs commonly found in Windows operating systems. Again, a copy of this file was extracted from the drive for examination. The file was imported into EnCase and Strings were run against it, as with the previous file. The information that was provided through Strings searches failed to provide anything of groundbreaking importance, but there were some strings that were present. Figure 8.11 provides a screenshot of the information that was revealed through the Strings search. Figure 8.12 provides string results with the default string length set to seven.

Importing the file into EnCase provides more information for examination. The file, expectedly, appeared to have similar artifacts as the first XEX file that was examined. In fact, the same XEX2 string was located along with the other ASCII

FIGURE 8.12

Strings results against the xbox.xex file with the default string length set to seven characters.

FIGURE 8.13

EnCase interpretation of the data located within the xbox.xex file. Note the plain text entries.

entries such as xboxkrnl. Figure 8.13 provides a snapshot of the EnCase entry for this file with the plain text highlighted. Some researchers in this arena also believe that the XBOX backward compatibility list for the XBE files (the original XBOX game profiles) reside in the xbox.xex file, telling the console which original games it has emulation for [1].

Continuing to research this particular file provided some interesting results from the researchers at www.free60.org. As they endeavor to run Linux on the console,

XEX Header

Total length: 24 bytes.

Byte ordering: Big Endian.

Offset	Length	Type	Information
0x0	0x4	ascii string	"XEX2" magic
0x4	0x8	module flags (see below)	Flags
0x8	0xC	unsigned int	PE data offset
0xC	0x10	unsigned int	Reserved
0x10	0x14	unsigned int	Security Info Offset
0x14	0x18	unsigned int	Optional Header Count

FIGURE 8.14

Details of the XEX file header found at www.free60.org/XEX.

Optional Headers

Following the XEX header is a list of the optional headers within the file. Use the Optional Header Count field to determine how many there are.

Each Optional Header is composed of the following:

Offset	Length	Type	Information
0x0	0x4	unsigned int	Header ID (see below)
0x4	0x8	unsigned int	Header Data / Offset to data (see below)

To handle the data you would first check to see what its size is, to do this you need to AND the Header ID by 0xFF.

If ID & 0xFF == 0x01 then the Header Data field is used to store the headers data, otherwise it's used to store the data's offset.
if ID & 0xFF == 0xFF then the Header's data will contain its size
if ID & 0xFF == (Anything else) the value of this is the size of the entry in number of DWORDS (times by 4 to get real size)

FIGURE 8.15

Detail of the optional headers provided by free60.org. This information could be used to establish a linkage between a suspect and a victim. If an executable was necessary to engage in online game play, this is the format that the examiner would need to dissect.

they have done a very good job of dissecting the files that they have located. The dissection of the XEX files is detailed here in Figures 8.14 and 8.15. Figure 8.14 provides the details of the XEX file header, and the Figure 8.15 provides a sample of the identified header IDs. This information can be located www.free60.org/XEX.

Continuing to explore the drive with the Xplorer360 application reveals that under the Dash folder, there is a subfolder called Fonts. Opening this directory to explore its contents reveals that there are two files that need to be examined. The information is represented in Xplorer360 as depicted here in Figure 8.16. The files are as follows:

- xbox.xtf
- xboxbook.xtf

Research indicates that these files are used to provide the fonts for the console and the associated dashboard fonts that must be rendered to the end user. Examining the information by importing the files into EnCase provides little in the way

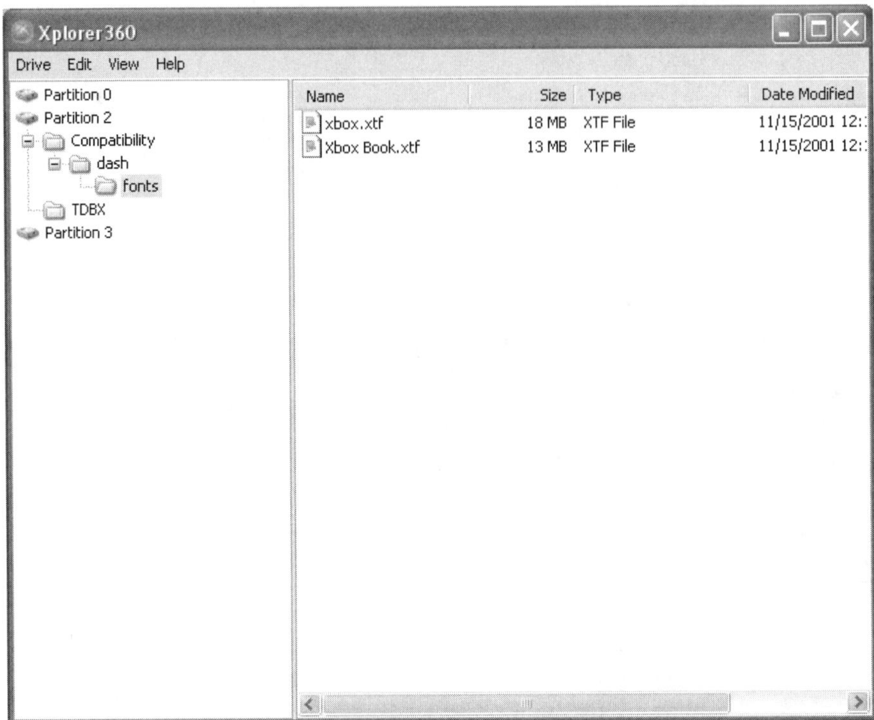

FIGURE 8.16

The two files located in the fonts subfolder within the second partition on the drive.

of indicators as to confirm or deny the speculation. Figures 8.17 and 8.18 provide screenshots of these two files as viewed with EnCase.

The last file located within Partition 2 is called TDBX.db. As a result of the endianess of the drive, it is an easy assumption that this file is rendered in Big Endian; therefore it would be XBDT, which translates to this XBOX data table. This folder contains one file that is reported with the application to be 156 MB in size. Online research on this particular file found a lot of confusing information. It appears that there was some debate among the modification community as to what information was stored in this database. Some believe it was the emulation software for the legacy games and still others believe it is the storage location for the supported titles, providing a table of the backwards compatible game titles that have been stored on the drive or storage media. One of the authors of the Xplorer360 application posted this entry on http://forums.ps3scene.com/lofiversion/index.php/.../t478570-50.html, explaining his understanding of the structure and function.

Once imported into EnCase, the TDBX.db file is reported as a "Paradox database," which is something that is unfamiliar. Research into this type of file revealed that it has been around for some time. The information that was located detailed that,

FIGURE 8.17

Screenshot of EnCase and XBOX book.xtf file.

FIGURE 8.18

xbox.xtf file as seen in EnCase.

if this file is a database, then it is a relational database management system, which makes sense because speculation is that it holds the list of backward compatible titles and perhaps pointers as mentioned earlier during the discussion of the xbox.xex file. The Paradox database was the predecessor to Microsoft Access, and it would make sense if the company used off-the-shelf code and altered it a bit. Figure 8.19 provides some discussion from the creator of Xplorer360 regarding the structure of the HDD, and Figure 8.20 provides a view of the TDBX.db file as depicted in EnCase.

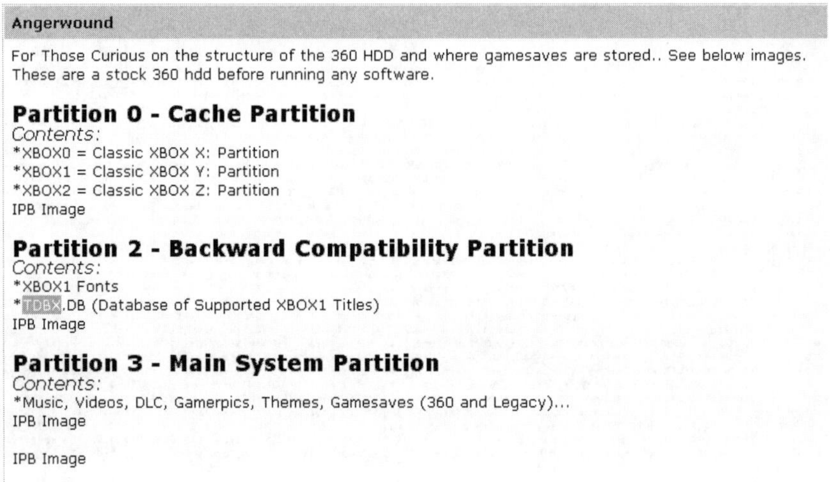

Angerwound

For Those Curious on the structure of the 360 HDD and where gamesaves are stored.. See below images.
These are a stock 360 hdd before running any software.

Partition 0 - Cache Partition
Contents:
*XBOX0 = Classic XBOX X: Partition
*XBOX1 = Classic XBOX Y: Partition
*XBOX2 = Classic XBOX Z: Partition
IPB Image

Partition 2 - Backward Compatibility Partition
Contents:
*XBOX1 Fonts
*TDBX.DB (Database of Supported XBOX1 Titles)
IPB Image

Partition 3 - Main System Partition
Contents:
*Music, Videos, DLC, Gamerpics, Themes, Gamesaves (360 and Legacy)...
IPB Image

IPB Image

FIGURE 8.19

TDBX information suggesting that the TDBX file is a database of supported legacy titles.

FIGURE 8.20

EnCase rendering of the TDBX.db file. Interpretation of the data within is problematic.

This ends the examination of the XBOX 360 hard drive using the Xplorer360 application. The information that is resident on the drive was intentionally shipped for a variety of reasons, one being the support for the flagship game Halo.

XPLORER360 AND THE POST–SYSTEM UPDATE DRIVE

Now that we have covered the information that is resident on the drive, we need to view and examine the information that is pushed to the drive once the system update is completed. One of the first things that is immediately noticeable is that Partition 3

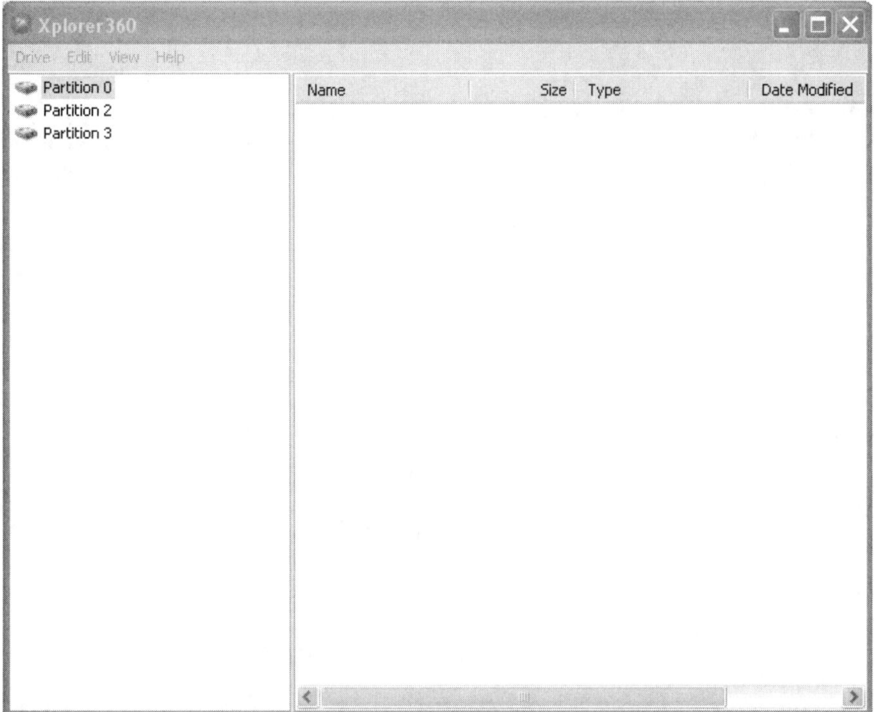

FIGURE 8.21

Provides a screenshot showing the empty partition.

is no longer empty, it is full of information that has been pushed down through the Microsoft system update that is required for an end user to interact through the XBOX Live portal. This partition is now full of data that needs to be examined and documented. However, before examining this data, we need to step through the other folders and the subfolders to determine what information is there and if it has changed.

Partition 0 remains empty as viewed through the Xplorer360 application. Perhaps this area is reserved for future storage of specific data types or for a specific application or feature that is run on the console. Figure 8.21 shows Partition 0 remaining empty.

Continuing through the folder structure to Partition 2, we find that the folders and subfolders appear to be the same. Immediately noticeable is the date change, shifting from 11/15/2001 to 11/22/2005. This new date corresponds to the release date of the XBOX 360 console in the United States and Canada. Figure 8.22 provides a snapshot of the Xplorer360 application and the rendering of the information.

Opening the Compatibility folder reveals that there is a new file that has been pushed to the system from the system update as well as the two files from the previous image, the XEFU and xbox.xex files. These files were extracted, and a hash analysis was conducted with the earlier versions to determine if a change had been made to these files. The results revealed that the hash values were the same, indicating that the data within had remained untouched by the process of the system update.

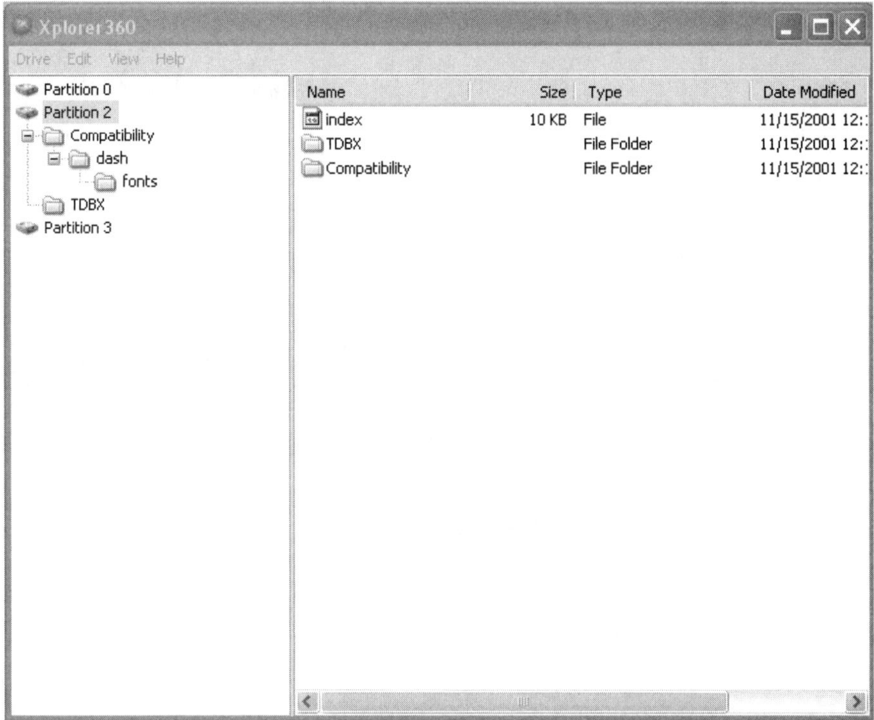

FIGURE 8.22

Xplorer360 with the new post–system update drive showing Partition 2. The "D" in the attribute column appears to denote these two folders as directories.

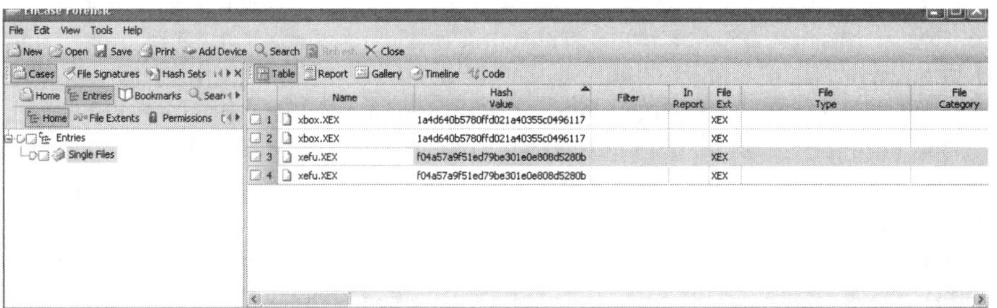

FIGURE 8.23

Detail of the hash analysis using EnCase to compare the hash values of the xbox.xex and xefu.xex, both before and after the system update. The values remain the same.

Because these files were proven to have been unchanged through the process, further examination was not warranted at this time. Figure 8.23 shows that the hash value of these files has not changed.

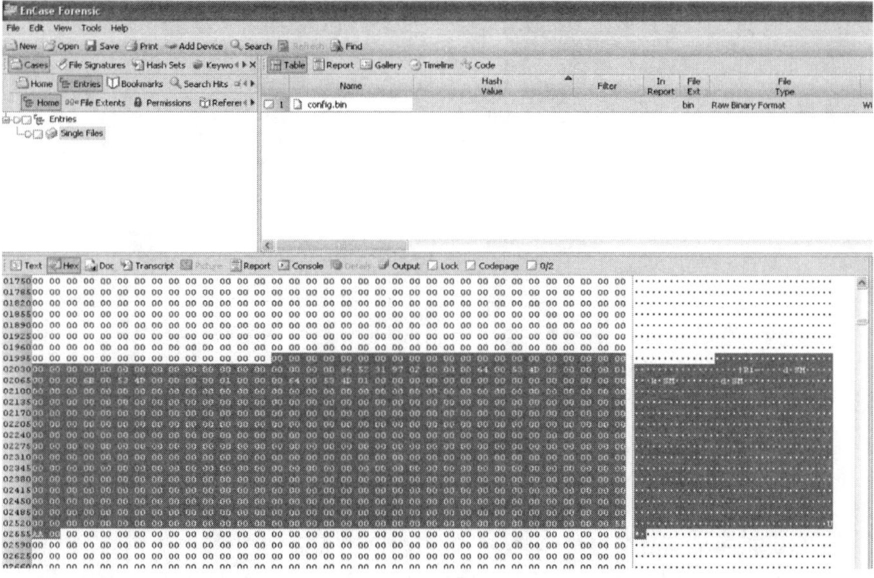

FIGURE 8.24

EnCase rendering of the config.bin file. The highlighted portion is the data within this file in its entirety.

There was a new file that was revealed once the image was explored using Xplorer360. This new file, config.vlc, was extracted for further examination with forensic tools. Initially, the file was copied from the drive image and imported into EnCase. The file is reported as a 16 KB binary file. When pulled into EnCase, the data appears to be somewhat limited in its contents. Although the file reports that it is 16 KB in size, the data within it is extremely sparse; see Figure 8.24 for a screenshot.

Research on this file indicates that it has something to do with the NAND chip that is on the motherboard. This chip is the onboard Flash memory, and the more research that was conducted on the config.bin file, the more the hits kept coming back to this chip. It appears that this file is used in the configuration of the onboard flash memory of the console, the NAND chip.

Under the Dash directory, there were some changes because of the system update. When examining the original drive, before the system update, there was only one folder under this directory—the Fonts folder, which contained two files. Examining this directory after the system update now reveals that there are two folders, including one new folder, and one new file. Figure 8.25 provides the details of this change.

Examination of this file in EnCase proved to be less than thrilling. The file itself was 880 bytes, which is not very large at all. Once imported into EnCase and viewed through the text pane, there was not very much data contained within it. Clearly, this file is associated with the dashboard of the console, the GUI that the end user interfaces with. While navigating through the GUI during the initial assessment of

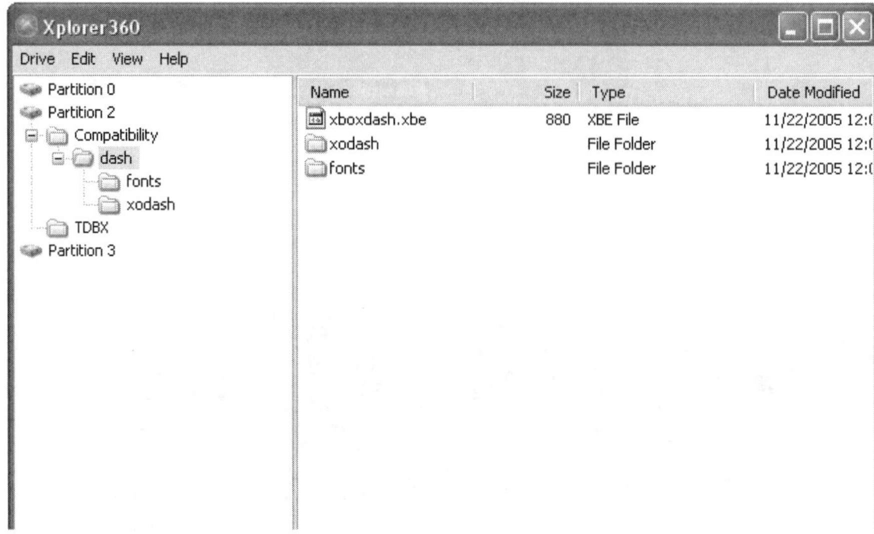

FIGURE 8.25

The new XODASH and XBOXdash.xbe file that was added after the system update.

the console, the dashboard was presented differently depending on whether or not the drive was connected. Reviewing these files provided some insight into this observation. It is assumed that there are additional files for the online dashboard as well, because the GUI is different as well. Researching this information and the known security measures for the console, it is feasible that this file is a pointer to the Flash NAND chip for the full code to execute. A decompiler for the .XBE files was sought, but research indicated that the modifications to these .XBE files were being done through hex editors. Figure 8.26 provides a snapshot of the data as it is represented in EnCase.

Opening the XODASH folder revealed that there was another file, titled xonlinedash.xbe, within. The file reported as being 880 bytes in size and was extracted from the drive image and examined as the other files were. The presence of this file also provides some circumstantial evidence that there are at least two versions of the dashboard, an online and an offline; both were experienced when navigating the console and now the location of the files has been revealed. Visually inspecting each file indicated that the files contained the same data. Acting on this hunch, the files were hashed and a comparison was conducted. The hash values were the same. Figure 8.27 provides a snapshot of this data. This revelation then sparks more questions: does this then mean that there are pointers somewhere so that the console loads the appropriate dashboard depending on the presence of a FATX-formatted storage device?

Moving on through the directory structure in Xplorer360, the next folder for review is the Fonts folder. Within this folder are the two files that were earlier identified in the pre–system updated drive, the xbox.xtf and XBOX book.xtf files.

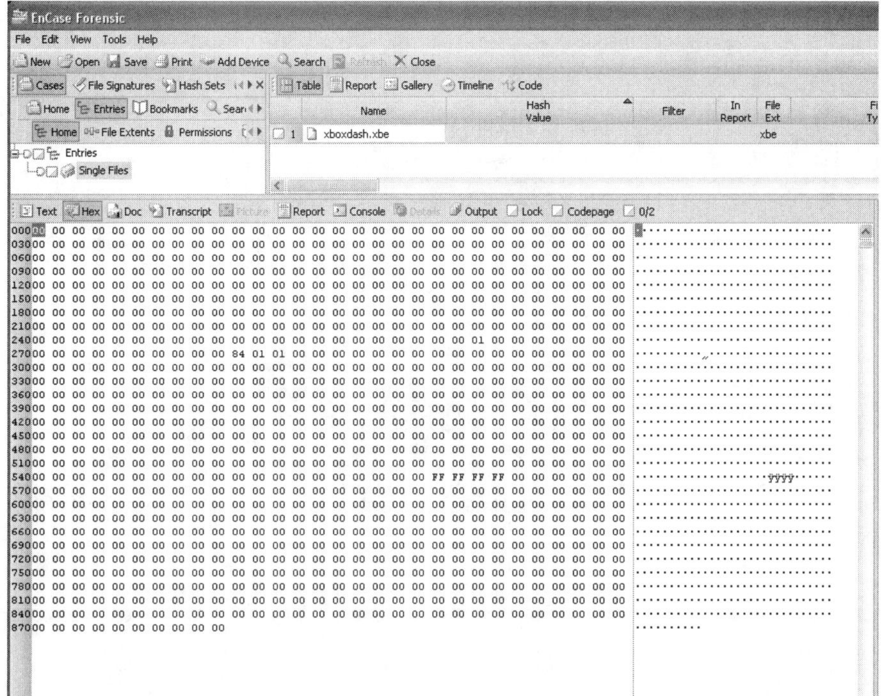

FIGURE 8.26

Screenshot of the xboxdash.xbe file viewed with EnCase.

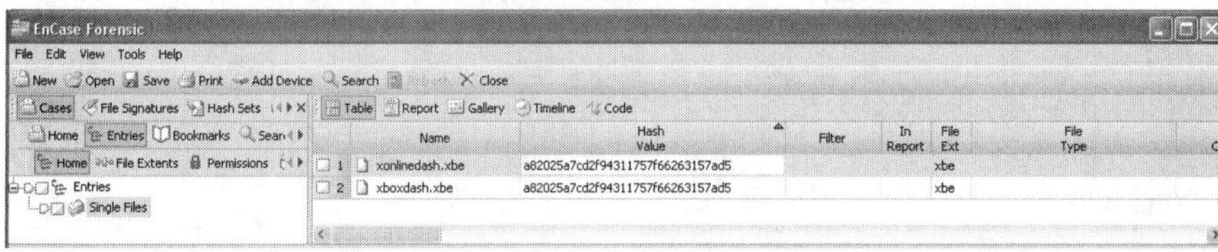

FIGURE 8.27

Hash comparative analysis of the two XBOX Dashboard files, indicating that the files are the same.

It seemed that the system update did not change files that were already present, but added files to the drive; it was decided to import the files into EnCase and hash them for comparison. Once again, the hash values matched, so at this time, further examination of the files was not warranted. Figure 8.28 provides the snapshot of the hash analysis.

The next folder and subsequent file to be examined was the TDBX.db file located within the TDBX folder. Copying the file from the drive and importing it into EnCase for hash analysis was prudent because the other files that were resident prior to the

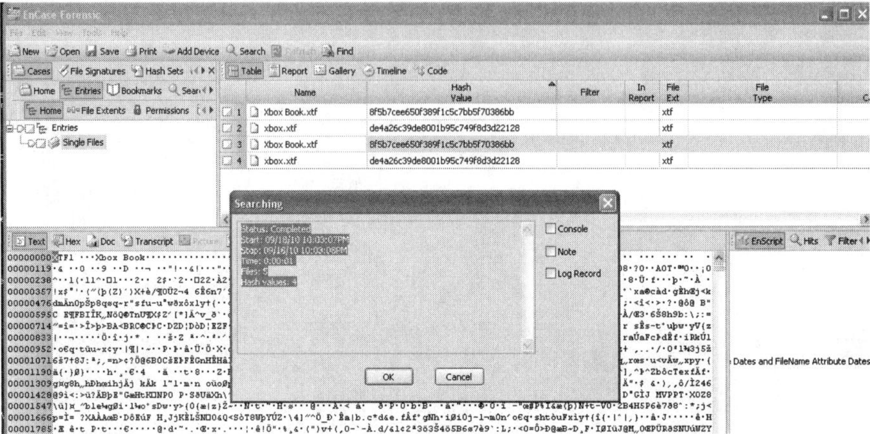

FIGURE 8.28

Hash analysis of the two files contained within the fonts folder, the xbox.xtf and the XBOX book.xtf.

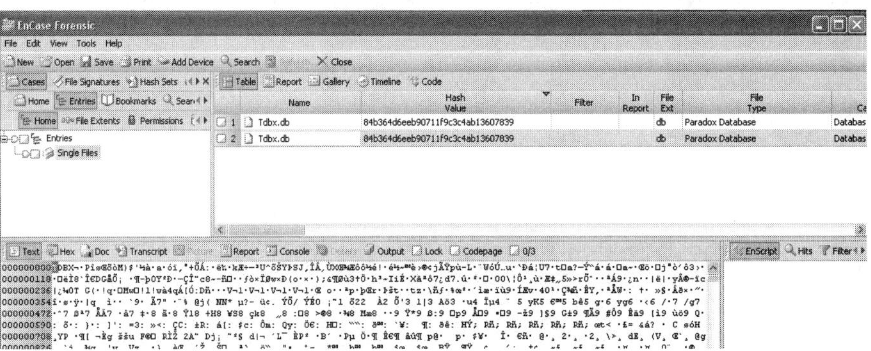

FIGURE 8.29

Hash analysis of the TDBX.db file showing that the file was not changed after the system update.

system update were not altered. Again, a hash analysis was conducted and there was no change in the hash value. Figure 8.29 shows the results of this analysis.

To this point in the analysis, it does not appear that there have been any significant changes made to the drive through this system update. However, a look at Partition 3 provides indicators that there were some significant files pushed to the system and stored on the attached storage device. Figure 8.30 shows the directories, as noted by the "D" in the attribute column, which are now available in Partition 3. Note that before the system update, Partition 3 was empty.

Opening the Partition 3 folder to view the contents reveals that there are several new folders to examine. An initial review of the reported information shows that there are some dates that need researching. The first folder that is reported in the

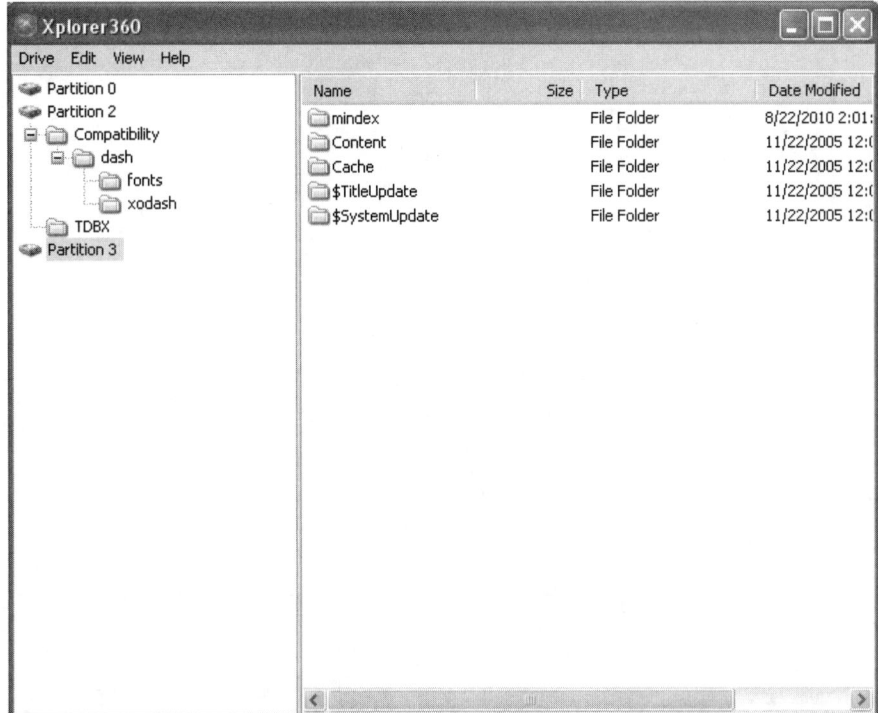

FIGURE 8.30

New directories that are in Partition 3.

right-hand window is the Mindex folder, which reports the date that corresponds to the date that the system update was performed. The remainder of the dates correspond to the release of the XBOX 360 as mentioned earlier.

By opening the folder for Partition 3 using the Xplorer360 application, an unusual thing happens that is not a forensic issue that I am aware of, but is curious nonetheless. When double-clicking on the folder, the subfolders open in the left-hand pane, but they are in reverse order from how they are reported in the right-hand pane. The same folders and files are present, but because few examiners out there will have an XBOX drive to walk through this process, it was worth mentioning. Figure 8.31 shows this flipped order of the files.

Navigation from this point forward for examination was through the listing of the files within the right-hand pane. So the first folder to review is the $System Update folder. Opening this folder reveals that there is an associated file entitled "su20076000_00000000." Extracting this file from the drive image and importing it into EnCase provide some plain text hits that clearly showed this is the system update file that was downloaded to the console drive. Reviewing the information provides some interesting data, including some plain text information that indicates the items

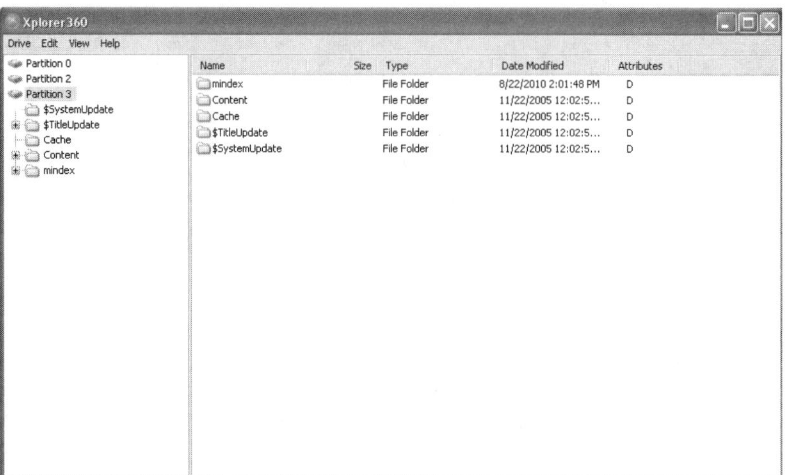

FIGURE 8.31

Depiction of the files within Partition 3.

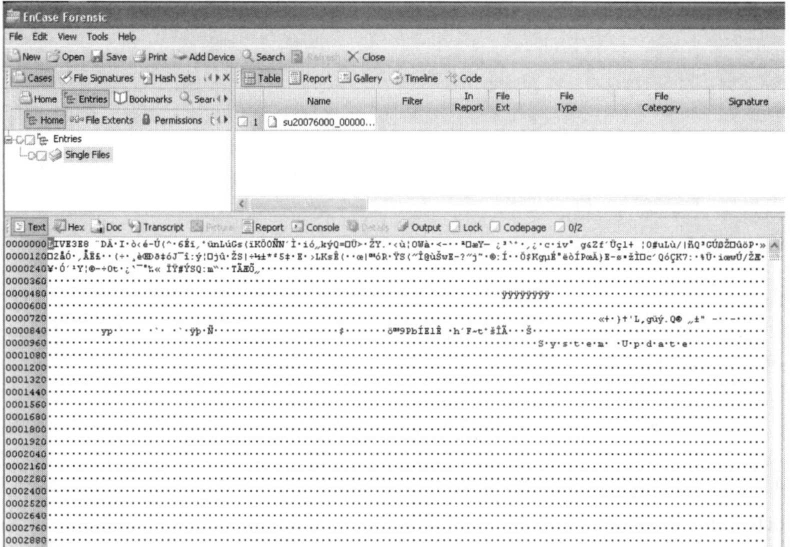

FIGURE 8.32

EnCase view of the SU, or system update file that is pushed to the XBOX 360's attached storage.

that are updated when the file is downloaded and executed on the console. Figure 8.32 shows the leading data that is located in the file as it is viewed through EnCase.

In addition to the plain text of "SystemUpdate," this file is a LIVE file as discussed in earlier chapters; it is the special compressed format file that is pushed from Microsoft and complies with the format that was detailed earlier. Examining this file

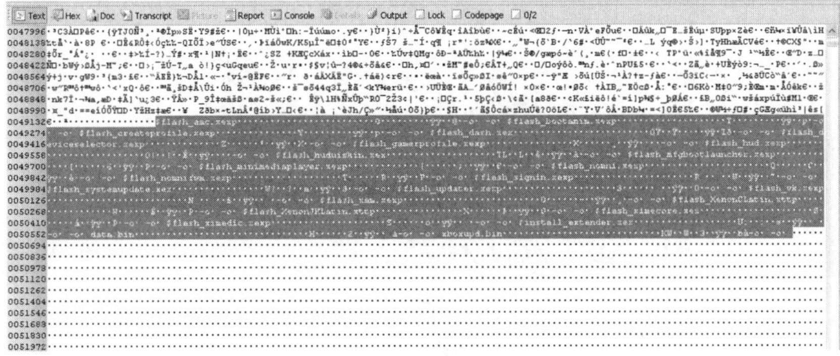

FIGURE 8.33

EnCase view of the Flash references found within the SU file.

and the associated plain text information that is located within it was an interesting endeavor. Starting at file offset 49152, information that specifically addressed Flash was listed with several names that indicated that this is the alteration of the NAND Flash chip; this is the flashing of the firmware. These plain text calls to the Flash continue until file offset 50634. Figure 8.33 provides the information in graphic form.

Running Strings against this file provided a more user-friendly result that clearly details the information for the flashing of the NAND chip. Within this listing, there appear to be calls to change the boot animation, the profile, the heads up display, and several other files with names that are of interest. Figure 8.34 provides a snapshot of the Strings results.

Reading through this list, the $flash_mfgbootlauncher.xexp immediately caught my eye. One of the methods that is being discussed within the modification community to hack the console is to alter the files that are stored on the NAND chip to initiate the booting from removable media or other injected code. However, there is some discussion that the information stored within the NAND chip has AES asymmetric encryption as a security measure and Microsoft's private key has not been shared. Research into this file specifically, and some of the other plain text that is listed here, provided some more information. It appears that the mfgbootlauncher and all other files that are stored on the Flash chip have what is called by one researcher a "restricted pathname." What this does is that it only allows code to be executed if the file name matches the file name that is stored on the chip. When reviewing some of the other files in this list, there is a reference to the processor; this is indicated by the following two entries:

- $flash_XenonCLatin.xttp
- $flash_XenonJKLatin.xttp

There is a method to decompile an XEX program using an IDA pro and an XEX tool that are both available at little or no cost. The references to this process and a step-by-step walkthrough will be covered in Chapter 9, "XBOX Live Redemption Code and Facebook," so as to dissect an XBOX 360 executable file.

```
Strings v2.41
Copyright (C) 1999-2009 Mark Russinovich
Sysinternals - www.sysinternals.com

System Update
$flash_aac.xexp
 $flash_bootanim.xexp
 $flash_createprofile.xexp
 $flash_dash.xex
 $flash_deviceselector.xexp
 $flash_gamerprofile.xexp
 $flash_hud.xexp
 $flash_huduiskin.xex
 $flash_mfgbootlauncher.xexp
 $flash_minimediaplayer.xexp
 $flash_nomni.xexp
 $flash_nomnifwm.xexp
 $flash_signin.xexp
 $flash_systemupdate.xex
 $flash_updater.xexp
 $flash_vk.xexp
 $flash_xam.xexp
 $flash_XenonCLatin.xttp
 $flash_XenonJKLatin.xttp
 $flash_ximecore.xex
 $flash_ximedic.xexp
 $install_extender.xex
 xboxupd.bin
q()=g5$,/#i'^
```

FIGURE 8.34

Strings results run against the SU file showing the calls to Flash the onboard NAND chip.

The next plain text Strings hits are as follows:

- A=dashuisk
- $:dashcomm
- \Device\Flash\dash.xex
- xboxkrnl.exe
- xboxkrnl.exe

These results show some calls being made to alter or update the code to the xboxkrnl and the dashboard. This could have been the upgrade to the dashboard moving from the older style to the new NXE dashboard interface. It is hard to tell what the specific purpose of these entries is without having access to the onboard NAND chip. There are several other Strings located within the SU file that appear to be directory listings or calls to .dlls and executables, such as the following:

- \Device\Flash\huduiskin.xex
- $\Device\Flash\systemupdate.xex
- systemupdatefc.exe
- xboxkrnl.exe
- \Device\Flash\XIMECORE.xex

- XIMECORE.dll
- xboxkrnl.exe
- installsuc.dll
- xboxkrnl.exe

Continuing to navigate through the directory structure, the next file in the list is located under the $TitleUpdate folder. Highlighting this folder reveals a subfolder that appears to be an address in hexadecimal value. Opening this subfolder reveals a file that is in a similar format as the earlier discussed SU file. The date of this file also reflects the original release date of the XBOX 360. The TU file, or title update, was extracted for further examination using EnCase and Strings. Figure 8.35 provides a screen shot of the new folders and subfolder.

Initial examination of the TU file using EnCase shows that this is a PIRS file, conforming to the earlier-mentioned format of the PIRS files. The header is clearly listed as PIRS and reading further down into the data the plain text of "fusion system update" is visible. Figure 8.36 shows this information.

Running the file through Strings provides some plain text search hits that are of interest. The default search string length was again set to 10 characters in order to reduce the large hit count that was typical when examining these files. There are several strings that follow the format of #xefu#.xex. Research into these xefu# files indicates that they are associated with the emulation of legacy game titles. Further evidence of this emulation linkage is located a little further in the Strings results. There is another search hit that provides a directory path back to the Compatibility folder. Figures 8.37 and 8.38 provide screenshots of this information.

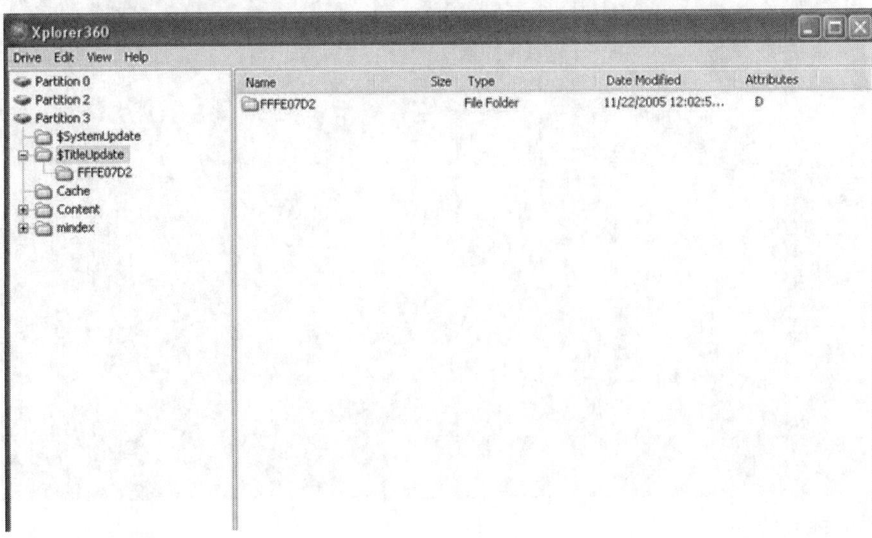

FIGURE 8.35

Title Update folder and subfolder.

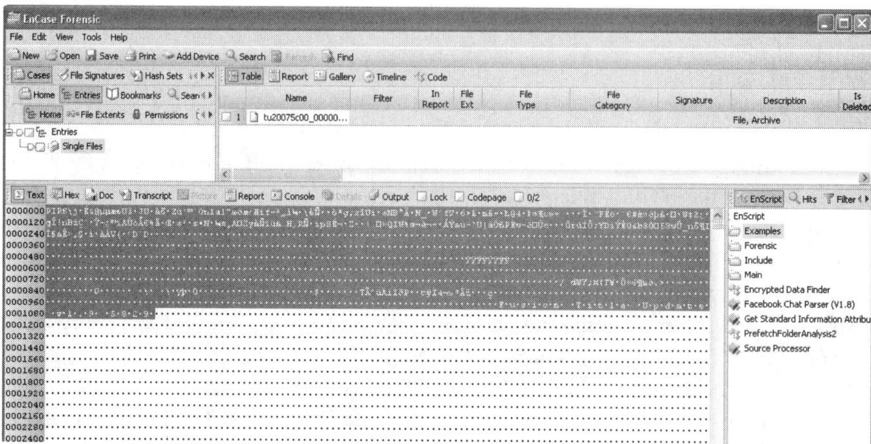

FIGURE 8.36

Title Update PIRS file with fusion title update and version in plain text.

```
C:\WINDOWS\system32\cmd.exe

Strings v2.41
Copyright (C) 1999-2009 Mark Russinovich
Sysinternals - www.sysinternals.com

Fusion Title Update v1.9 5829
.xefu1_1.xex
1xefu2.xex
1xefu3.xex
1xefu5.xex
1xefu6.xex
1xefu7.xex
1xefu7b.xex
1xefutitle5.xex
1xefutitle6.xex
1xefutitle7.xex
1xefutitle7b.xex
19%FZUo>B$
X^)1gQL3F!
we'3zaC;>z
4Ldpf^#;x}
Y@d&NfzJ5J!
1pH siH'O Gj
Azg,{#e5>$
xk">9qboN`
Ab2tm0s"`t^
.5x@D>>4!I
piJn\%!I/yk
{!Yi41iWJk
X">sqstgc;
```

FIGURE 8.37

Strings results run against TU, or title update, file.

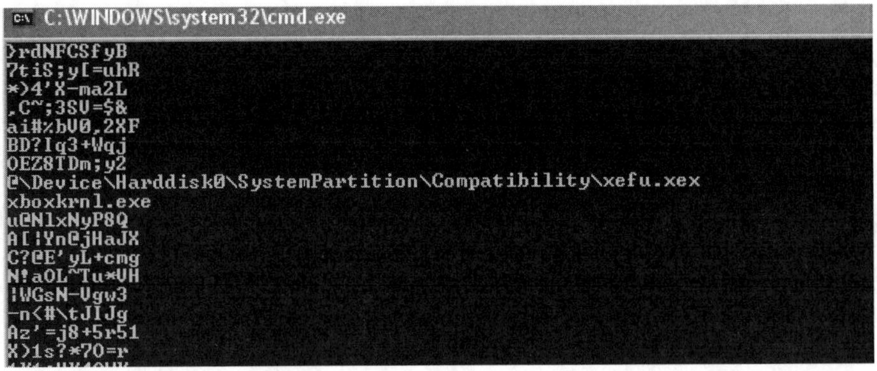

```
C:\WINDOWS\system32\cmd.exe
>rdNFCSfyB
7tiS;y[=uhR
*)4'X-ma2L
,C~;3SU=$&
ai#%bU0,2XF
BD?Iq3+Wqj
OEZ8TDm;y2
@\Device\Harddisk0\SystemPartition\Compatibility\xefu.xex
xboxkrnl.exe
u@NlxNyP8Q
A[!Yn@jHaJX
C?@E'yL+cmg
N!aOL^Tu*UH
!WGsN-Ugw3
-n<#\tJIJg
Az'=j8+5r51
X>1s?*70=r
```

FIGURE 8.38

String search against the TU file showing the path to the Compatibility folder.

CACHE FOLDER

Continuing our examination of the folder structure, the next in line is the Cache folder. Double-clicking the folder reveals the list of files that are stored within this folder. There are 13 of these files in total, and each has the associated date of the system configuration that was performed. Even though the system update was performed once and the drive has not been reconnected as of yet, there are a few files that have their time stamps out of the range of the rest of the files. Figure 8.39 shows these files as they appear in the Xplorer360 application.

The examination process for each one of these files follows the process that has been used to this point. The files were extracted from the drive image, stored in a defined location, and one by one imported into EnCase. X-Ways and Strings were run against them to determine if there were any plain text ASCII or UNICODE test strings that could provide indicators or clues as to the function of each file.

The first file in the list is a file that starts with the letters " VC." Importing the file into EnCase provided little in the way of information, with the exception of the console security certificate at the beginning of the file. Running the file through Strings again only revealed the text string for the console security certificate. Research into the Cache folder provided information that the folder stores code or pointers to code in order to enhance performance, just like the function of most other Cache folders. If this is indeed a verification of the console to the XBOX Live service, then it would be in a location that would enable the information to be passed quickly to verify that the console was not on a banned list to the service. Figure 8.40 provides a view of the file in EnCase.

The next file in the list belongs to a set of files starting with the letters "TK," possibly a token file of some sort. Each one of these files has a unique numerical string to finish the file name. Upon examination of these files within EnCase, they all start

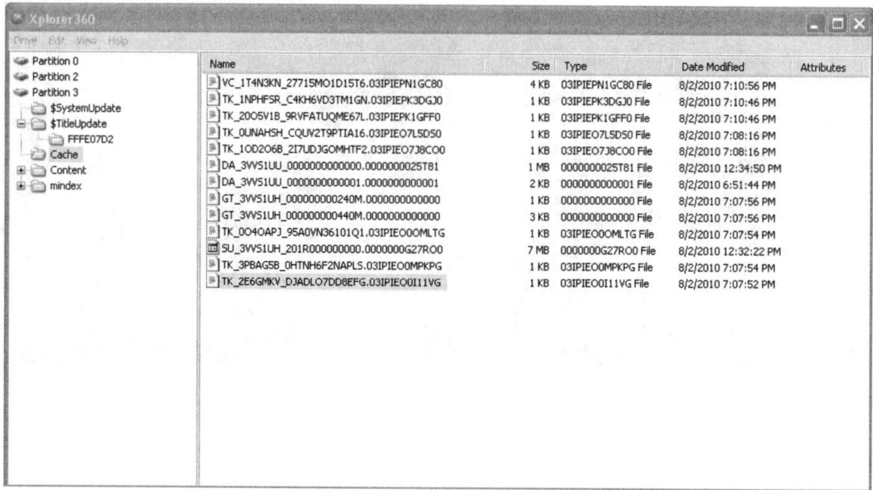

FIGURE 8.39

Files stored under the Cache folder.

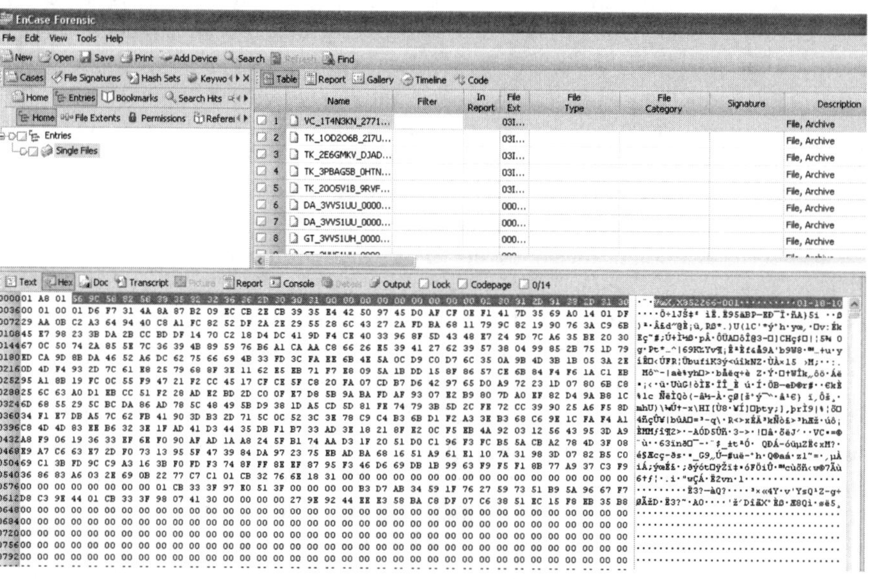

FIGURE 8.40

EnCase view of the VC file with the console security certificate highlighted.

with the text PROD, perhaps an indicator to a "product." The remainder of the data appears to be encrypted; there is no sign of a security certificate, as was the case with the VC file. Speculation is that these files are the updates to the games that are already installed on the hard drive of the console. Figure 8.41 provides an image of the TK file being reviewed within EnCase.

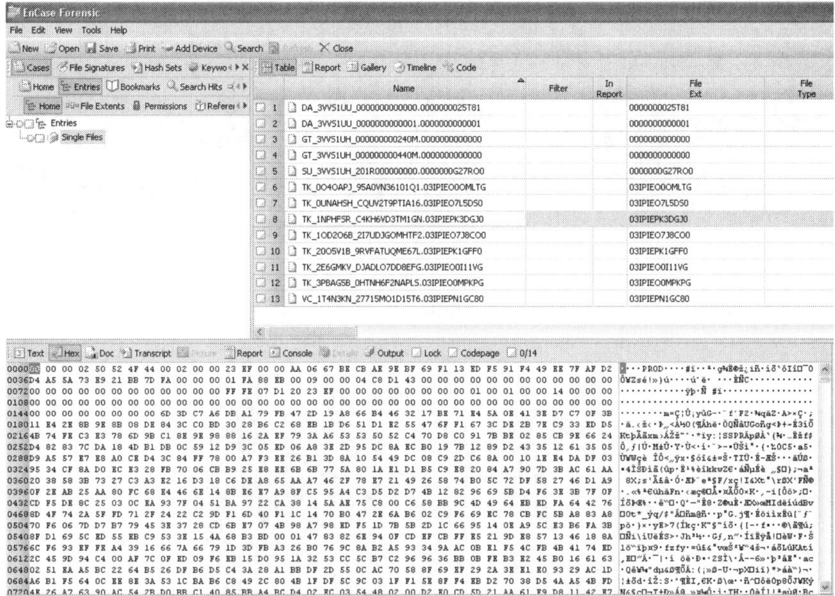

FIGURE 8.41

EnCase view of one of the TK files that are located within the Cache folder. Each of these files starts with the PROD text string.

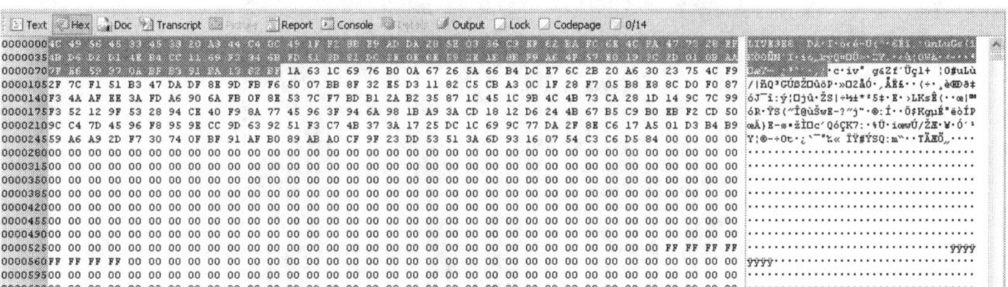

FIGURE 8.42

Snapshot detailing the SU file header showing the LIVE "magic" signature.

Located within this Cache folder is another SU file, and again the examination reveals the clear text of "system update." The file header here is a LIVE file, which is indicative of a file that is signed by Microsoft and downloaded via the XBOX Live service. In examining the file further, it appears that the data is identical to the data located within the other system update file. There were several plain text search hits that listed the same Flash updates as well as similar directory paths. Research indicates that these may be pointers to libraries, such as DLLS. Figures 8.42 and 8.43 show the Live magic signature and the system update information in the hex view of EnCase. Figure 8.44 provides a sample of the Strings hit against this file as well.

FIGURE 8.43

Plain text search string showing the "system update" string.

```
System Update
$flash_aac.xexp
 $flash_bootanim.xexp
 $flash_createprofile.xexp
 $flash_dash.xex
 $flash_deviceselector.xexp
 $flash_gamerprofile.xexp
 $flash_hud.xexp
 $flash_huduiskin.xex
 $flash_mfgbootlauncher.xexp
 $flash_minimediaplayer.xexp
 $flash_nomni.xexp
 $flash_nomnifwm.xexp
 $flash_signin.xexp
 $flash_systemupdate.xex
 $flash_updater.xexp
 $flash_vk.xexp
 $flash_xam.xexp
 $flash_XenonCLatin.xttp
 $flash_XenonJKLatin.xttp
 $flash_ximecore.xex
 $flash_ximedic.xexp
 $install_extender.xex
 xboxupd.bin
g<>=g5$,/#i'^
\Device\Flash\dash.xex
xboxkrnl.exe
xboxkrnl.exe
```

FIGURE 8.44

Strings search hits showing the plain text flash updates and the directory paths.

Continuing to examine and document the files located within the Cache folder, there are two more files that have similar names. Both of these files start with the letters GT but have different ending numerical values. It is believed that these two files are the associated files to the two Gamertags that exist on the console. The file with larger numerical digits, 440M, correlates to the Gamertag that has the XBOX Live Gold account associated to it. These file names are listed here as follows:

- GT_3VVS1UH_000000000440M
- GT_3VVS1UH_000000000240M

The first file ending in 440M was imported into EnCase for examination. The header of the file included the console security certificate that was previously discussed and detailed. When navigating more through the file, the header for a PNG file is clearly visible, so it was decided to carve the PNG file from the file and determine if there was anything there that was of relevance. Figures 8.45 and 8.46 show the file and the associated plain text that was discussed.

Carving out the data was a simple task accomplished by identifying the header and signature and saving the file as a PNG file. Once saved, the file was then opened

FIGURE 8.45

Header of the GT file showing the console security certificate signature.

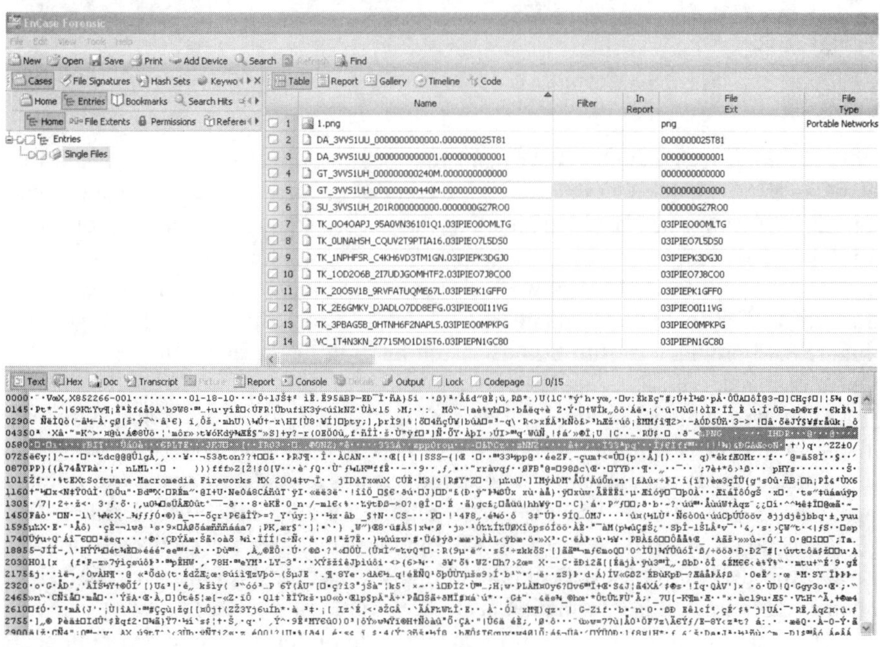

FIGURE 8.46

Details of the PNG file header embedded within the GT file.

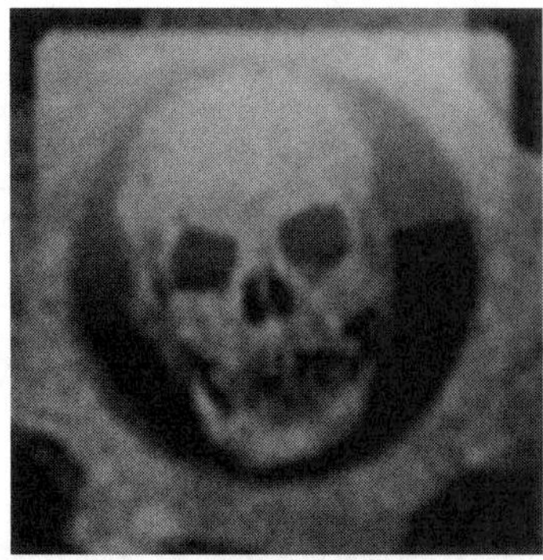

FIGURE 8.47

Graphic carved from the GT file ending in 440M.

```
C:\>strings -n 7 "C:\Documents and Settings\Cardinal\Desktop\XBOX after sys Xplo
rer360 extractions\CACHE\GT_3VVS1UH_000000000440M.0000000000000"

Strings v2.41
Copyright (C) 1999-2009 Mark Russinovich
Sysinternals - www.sysinternals.com

X852266-001
01-18-10
*.>U<1C'*
9A'b9W8
%tEXtSoftware
Macromedia Fireworks MX 2004
```

FIGURE 8.48

Strings results against the GT 440M file.

with the Microsoft Picture Viewer and revealed a graphic that is associated to a popular game. Figure 8.47 provides a snapshot of the graphic from the game Gears of War which was the Gamertag icon that was chosen for the account that connected to XBOX Live.

To cover all bases, Strings was run against the file as well, and there were a few references including a plain text hit for Macromedia Fireworks MX 2004. Figure 8.48 provides the full Strings search hit with the default string length set to seven characters.

There was another GT file, this one ending in 240M, that was examined in much the same manner as the above GT file. The console security certificate string was present, and the PNG image that was carved out was a similar image. The difference was in the size of the file. The first GT file reported as 2.87 KB and 4096 KB on disk. This second GT file reported as 1.29 KB and the same 4096 KB on disk, which was to be expected. Both files were imported into EnCase for a comparative analysis of their relative sizes; this information is presented in Figure 8.49.

There are two files that remain for analysis within this Cache folder; both begin with the letters "DA." It is unclear what these letters indicate; this is something that continued research will reveal. The first DA file is rather small, roughly 3 KB in size.

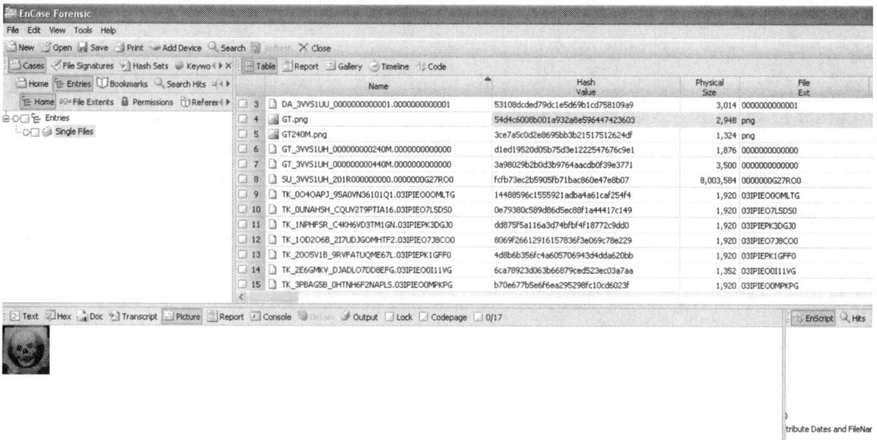

FIGURE 8.49

Comparison of the two GT files, their size and hash values, showing different hash values.

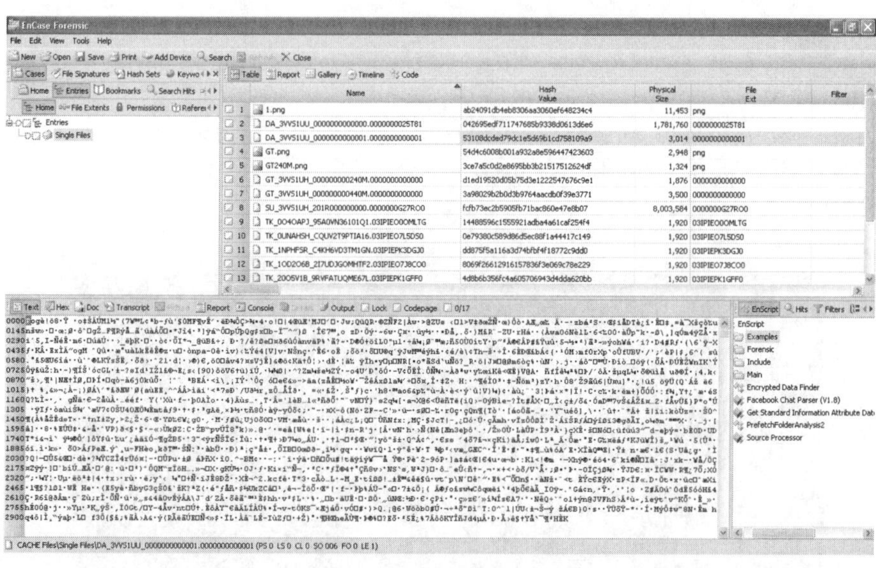

FIGURE 8.50

First DA file showing the data contained within.

It is full of data that appears to be encoded or encrypted. There are no strings that can be extracted that are meaningful, and research is ongoing to determine this file's purpose. Figure 8.50 provides a view of this file within EnCase to detail how the information is represented.

The second DA file is much larger in size and has some interesting data contained within it. The first thing that was noticed was the considerable size difference between this file and the other DA file. This file is being reported as 1740 KB in size. Extraction of the file from the disk image and importation of the file into EnCase for review provided some information about the file, as shown in Figure 8.51. Initial manual review of the data revealed that the file header is an XEX file, meaning that it is an executable for the XBOX 360. Navigating through the data, there are some plain text entries that reveal this file has something to do with the XBOX Live setup. The Strings searches that were run against this file are presented in Figure 8.52.

These artifacts indicate that this file is involved in the XBOX Live signup process. Further examination of the file is warranted to determine if there are any specific

FIGURE 8.51

This is an EnCase view of the DA file. The file header is marked as XEX and toward the end of the highlighted data the plain text data reveal "LiveSignup.exe," indicating that the file is associated with this function.

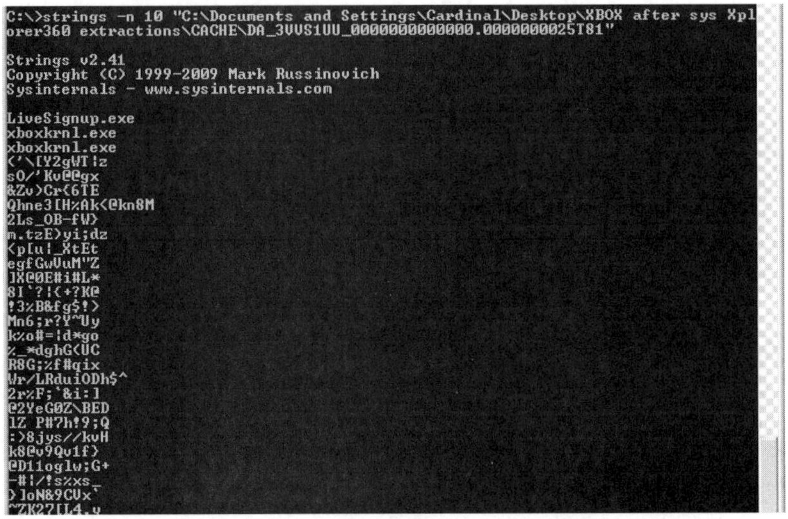

FIGURE 8.52

Strings run against the larger DA file revealing more plain text indicators of function.

artifacts, such as the email address that was used during configuration or the network settings. This examination would involve the decompiling of the executable, which will be addressed in Chapter 9, "XBOX Live Redemption Code and Facebook."

CONTENT FOLDER

Continuing the examination of Partition 4, the next folder in the directory structure is the Content folder, which contains several subfolders that in turn contain files for examination. There are four directories that contain subfolders, and within each subfolder, there is a file that will be examined. An initial observation is that there are two dates being presented with these directories, folders, subfolders, and files. The dates vary from the release date of the XBOX 360 console (November 15, 2005) and the date that the research console was connected to the XBOX Live service and accepted the EULA (August 2, 2010). Figure 8.53 shows this data.

Opening the first subfolder, the one with the name that is all zeros, reveals that there are many subfolders stacked underneath. Each folder has a naming convention that is similar to what has been observed previously, meaning that it appears to be a base address in hexadecimal, as shown in Figure 8.54.

Continuing on with the examination, the first folder, 4d53084D, was opened, and there is a file that was revealed and that was extracted for further examination using EnCase, X-Ways, and Strings (Figures 8.55 to 8.57.) Navigating through the folders and subfolders, we come to a file with an extremely long file name beginning with the numbers "56A," which for convenience will be the name that we use to reference

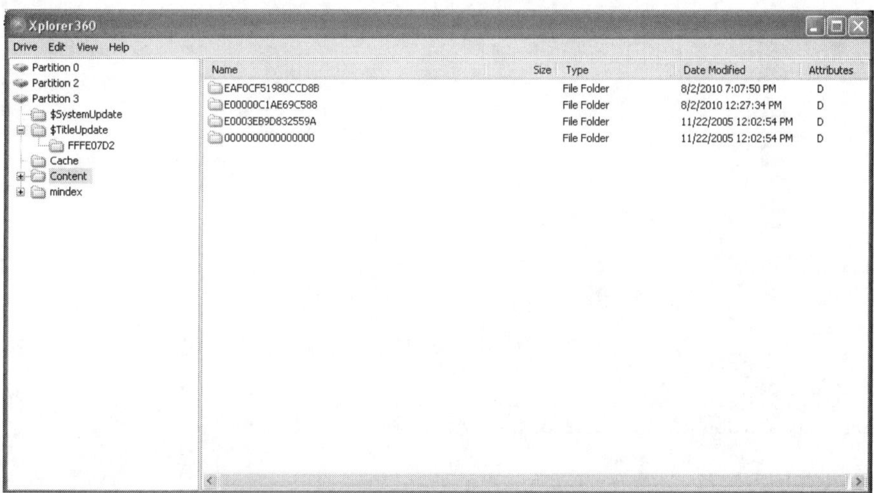

FIGURE 8.53

View of the Content folder with the four subfolders. Note the date of the subfolders on the right hand side.

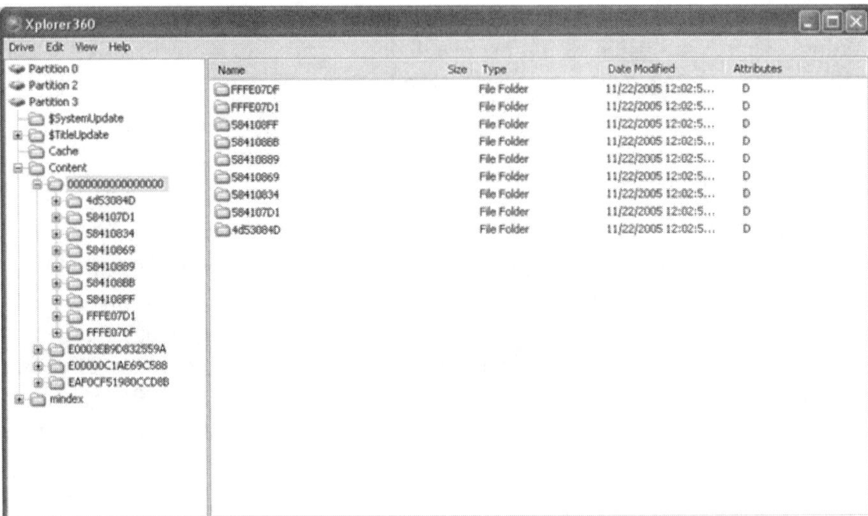

FIGURE 8.54

The subfolders under the main directory named with all zeros and their hexadecimal naming convention.

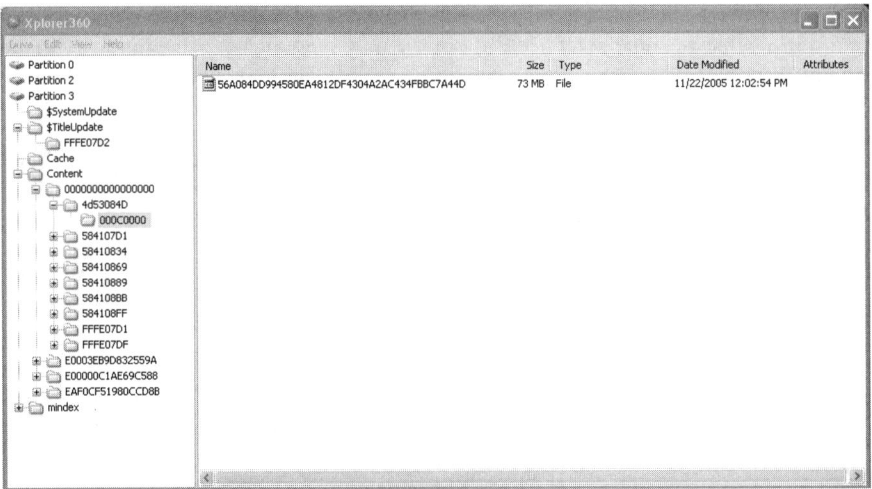

FIGURE 8.55

Directory structure of the folders located within the Content folder.

the file. The file is not that large, reporting as 73.6 MB. Initial review of the file once loaded into EnCase reveals that the file has a PIRS header, indicating that it is a Microsoft signed file that is delivered through means other than the Live service [2].

The file also contains more plain text information that indicates it is a customization for one of the Microsoft game titles that is included on the console. The game

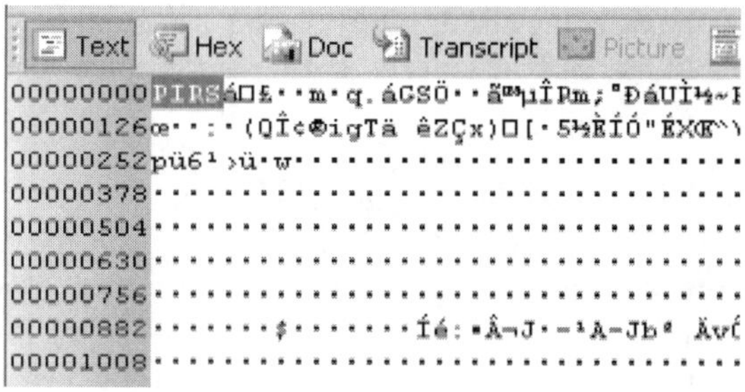

```
Text  Hex  Doc  Transcript  Picture
00000000PIRSáП£··m·q.áGSö··ã"µÎRm;"ÐáUÌ¼~I
00000126œ··:·(QÎ¢®igTä êZÇx)□[·5¼ÈÍÓ"ÉXŒ"\
00000252püé¹›ü·w·······························
00000378·································
00000504·································
00000630·································
00000756·································
00000882·······$·······Íé:•Â¬J·-¹A-Jbª Äví
00001008·································
```

FIGURE 8.56

PIRS file header from the 56A file.

```
Strings v2.41
Copyright (C) 1999-2009 Mark Russinovich
Sysinternals - www.sysinternals.com

Forza Motorsport 3 Customization
Microsoft Game Studios
Forza Motorsport 3
\?JC6=DCK
\?JC6=DCK
default.wmv
$Windows Media Audio 10 Professional
0384 kbps, 48 kHz, 5.1 channel 16 bit 1-pass CBR
DeviceConformanceTemplate
WM/WMADRCPeakReference
WM/WMADRCPeakTarget
WM/WMADRCAverageReference
WM/WMADRCAverageTarget
AspectRatioX
AspectRatioY
WMFSDKVersion
11.0.5721.5251
WMFSDKNeeded
0.0.0.0000
(ASFLeakyBucketPairs
y292<8@0<
} 0=JH3U@I
\+|/ANC9_
888888888;
PPPPPPPPPP_
FUUUUUUUT
```

FIGURE 8.57

Strings results from analysis of the 56A file that was extracted.

title is Forza Motorsport 3. The best way to visually represent this information is through the Strings search hits that were acquired during the examination.

There are many other ASCII strings that are cause for further examination, such as the following:

- \?JC6=DCK
- The network information that is displayed
- WM/WMADRCPEAK files
- ASKLEAKYBUCKETPAIRS

Speculation on the meaning of this information is that it all pertains to the game, and these are files for further customization that are enabled for the XBOX Live online game play.

Each of the other subfolders within the Content folder follows an identical pattern. There is a folder, then a subfolder, and then finally a file. Examination of the resultant files followed the same pattern in an attempt to identify the information within and determine the functionality of the file on the console. The results are displayed over the next few pages showing the Strings and EnCase images along with a graphic of the folders and files showing the information and how it relates. The file is associated with Hexic HD game that is preinstalled and illustrated in Figures 8.58 and 8.59. Figure 8.60 shows the Strings results run against this file.

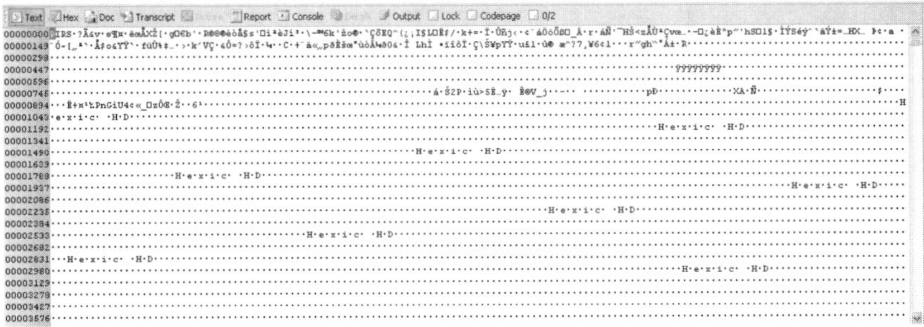

FIGURE 8.58

Details of the 584107D100000001 file as represented in EnCase.

584107D100000001

Offset	0	1	2	3	4	5	6	7	8	9	A	B	C	D	E	F	
00000000	50	49	52	53	04	3F	C3	26	76	15	F8	B6	A4	14	EB	9C	PIRS ?Ã&v ø¶¤ ë▮
00000010	C5	58	8E	5B	1C	67	90	80	62	27	0F	52	A9	38	AE	E8	ÅX▮[g▮▮b' R©8®è
00000020	F2	E5	A7	73	27	81	EC	AA	E8	4A	ED	B3	14	5C	96	99	òå§s'▮ìªèJí³ \▮▮
00000030	36	6B	27	9E	6F	AE	1A	91	C7	F5	45	51	5E	28	BF	A1	6k'▮o® ´ÇõEQ^(¿¡
00000040	49	A7	4C	8D	CB	24	2F	1E	6B	2B	3D	18	CF	17	DB	F1	I§L▮Ë$/ k+= Ï Ûñ
00000050	6A	8B	1D	A2	A8	E1	D6	F6	D5	DF	81	5F	C4	16	72	1A	j▮ ¢¨áÖöÕß▮_Ä r
00000060	E1	D1	27	AF	48	8A	3C	7A	C5	D9	AA	C7	76	9C	85	13	áÑ'¯H▮<zÅÙªÇv▮▮
00000070	96	8F	BF	E8	C8	22	70	94	27	68	53	9D	6C	A7	11	CC	▮▮¿èÈ"p▮'hS▮l§ Ì
00000080	DD	53	E9	FD	88	91	E4	DD	B1	3D	85	48	58	85	0A	DE	ÝSéý▮´äÝ±=▮HX▮ Þ
00000090	A2	11	61	0D	1D	A8	D3	7E	5B	84	AA	91	0C	C5	24	6F	¢ a ¨Ó~[▮ª´ Å$o
000000A0	26	59	9F	91	01	66	FC	D9	25	87	85	0C	9B	1C	6B	92	&Y▮´ füÙ%▮▮ ▮ k´
000000B0	56	C7	13	26	D4	3D	3F	9B	F4	CF	0B	BC	18	15	43	00	VÇ &Ô=?▮ôÏ ¼ C
000000C0	2B	A8	E4	AB	84	70	F0	C8	9A	9C	B0	F9	F2	C2	BC	F0	+¨ä«▮pðÈ▮▮°ùòÂ¼ð
000000D0	30	26	08	CE	A0	4C	68	CC	09	95	EF	EE	F4	CF	1F	C7	0& Î LhÌ ▮ïîôÏ Ç
000000E0	5C	8A	A5	70	59	9F	11	75	A3	31	1A	FB	AE	0A	E6	5E	\▮¥pY▮ u£1 û® æ^
000000F0	3F	37	B8	A5	36	A2	31	17	01	15	72	94	67	68	93	B0	?7¸¥6¢1 r▮gh▮°
00000100	C1	B1	0E	52	00	00	00	00	00	00	00	00	00	00	00	00	Á± R
00000110	00	00	00	00	00	00	00	00	00	00	00	00	00	00	00	00	
00000120	00	00	00	00	00	00	00	00	00	00	00	00	00	00	00	00	
00000130	00	00	00	00	00	00	00	00	00	00	00	00	00	00	00	00	
00000140	00	00	00	00	00	00	00	00	00	00	00	00	00	00	00	00	

FIGURE 8.59

584107D100000001 file using X-Ways.

```
>.>.>.>.>.>.>%
; This file specifies where files get binplaced during the build
; Content files
HexicHD.xlast              apps\Arcade\HexicHD
HexicHD_mp.png             apps\Arcade\HexicHD
HexicHD.png                apps\Arcade\HexicHD\Package
HexicDeluxe.swf            apps\Arcade\HexicHD\Package
HexicHDLoading.swf         apps\Arcade\HexicHD\Package
KeyMap_HXIC.xml            apps\Arcade\HexicHD\Package
g.xml                      apps\Arcade\HexicHD\Package
de_g.xml                   apps\Arcade\HexicHD\Package
es_g.xml                   apps\Arcade\HexicHD\Package
fr_g.xml                   apps\Arcade\HexicHD\Package
it_g.xml                   apps\Arcade\HexicHD\Package
ja_g.xml                   apps\Arcade\HexicHD\Package
ko_g.xml                   apps\Arcade\HexicHD\Package
pt_g.xml                   apps\Arcade\HexicHD\Package
zh_g.xml                   apps\Arcade\HexicHD\Package
ConvectionUI.ttf           apps\Arcade\HexicHD\Package
Gothic.ttf                 apps\Arcade\HexicHD\Package
SdGD_M.ttf                 apps\Arcade\HexicHD\Package
XArialUni.ttf              apps\Arcade\HexicHD\Package
ArcadeInfo.xml             apps\Arcade\HexicHD\Package
Achievement01.png          apps\Arcade\HexicHD\Package
Achievement02.png          apps\Arcade\HexicHD\Package
Achievement03.png          apps\Arcade\HexicHD\Package
```

FIGURE 8.60

Strings run against the 584107D100000001 file.

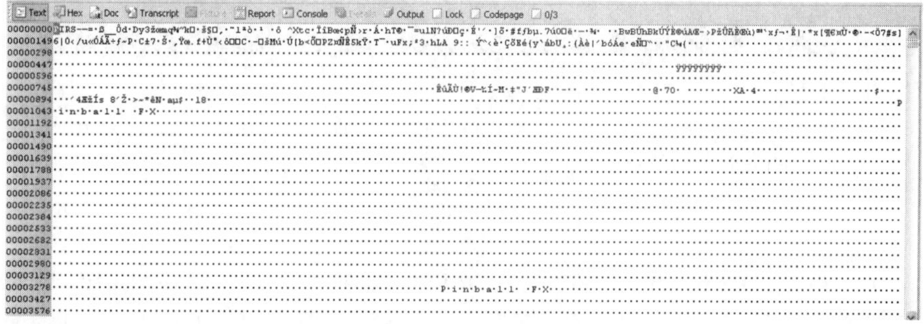

FIGURE 8.61

File header again showing the PIRS file header.

The next file is named 584107D100000001 and is reporting as 55 MB in size.

The next file has a rather lengthy name, CAFBC3D921AE569789CD7E4D-1D87224AB4C6D04658. Examining the data within the file provides details that the file is associated to the Pinball game that is resident on the drive. There are several PNGs that can be carved out, and it also keeps with the standard that this is a PIRS file. Figure 8.61 shows the file header PIRS, and Figure 8.62 provides the Strings results.

```
C:\>strings -n 10 "C:\Documents and Settings\Cardinal\Desktop\content\CAFBC3D921
AE569789CD7E4D1D87224AB4C6D04658"

Strings v2.41
Copyright (C) 1999-2009 Mark Russinovich
Sysinternals - www.sysinternals.com

Pinball FX
Pinball FX
Pinball FX
OiCCPPhotoshop ICC profile
OiCCPPhotoshop ICC profile
agents.pxp
 ArcadeInfo.xml
 common.pxp
 default.xex
 external_files
 extreme.pxp
 speedmachine.pxp
 achievement_alien_technology.png
 achievement_angel.png
 achievement_cloned.png
 achievement_emerald_flasher.png
 achievement_first_aid_kit.png
 achievement_mr_hawk.png
 achievement_on_the_top.png
 achievement_platina_cylinders.png
 achievement_professional.png
 achievement_speed_machine.png
 achievement_survivor_type.png
 achievement_swat_membership.png
 CERO_A.png
 ESRB_E.png
 gamelogo.png
 KMRB_A.png
 OFLC_AU_A.png
 PEGI_3P.png
 PEGI_4P.png
 USK_6.png
dotmatrix/1.dmv
dotmatrix/2.dmv
dotmatrix/3.dmv
dotmatrix/4.dmv%P
dotmatrix/5.dmv
dotmatrix/6.dmv
dotmatrix/7.dmv
dotmatrix/Font16x16_agent.dft
dotmatrix/Font32x32_agent.dft
```

FIGURE 8.62

Strings results run against the CAFBC showing the PNG file listing and other file names located within this PIRS file.

The fourth file is named 057AC5DDAE9956CAD5D5AEB05A5ABCE0F5F1-3F3258 and is located within the fourth subfolder reports as 68 MB in size and, as with the first four files, reports a date of 11/22/2005. The data within the file is listed below and indicates that this is the associated file to the Sensible World of Soccer, SWOS, game. The plain text is shown as viewed in EnCase in Figure 8.63, and the Strings results are provided in Figure 8.64.

The fifth file in the listings is located under the 58410889 folder and is named 87D0A5D366F24C8FF8BEE120E5F72D78F100E18958. The file is reported as 102 MB in size and has an 11/15/2005 date listed. The plain text strings that were located indicate this file is associated to the Peggle game title. Again, the file is listed as a PIRS file as shown in Figure 8.65, and the Strings results are provided in Figure 8.66.

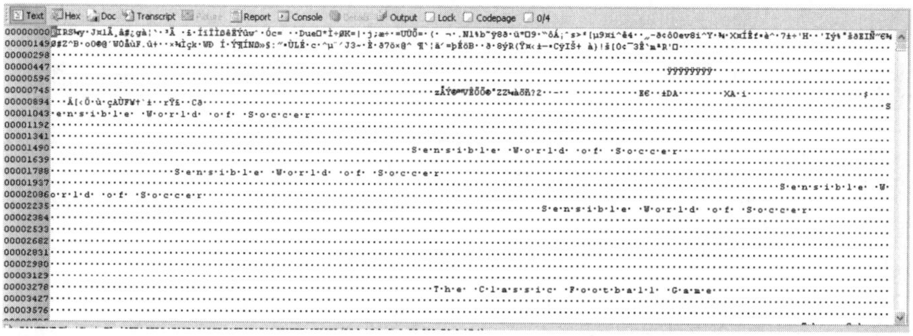

FIGURE 8.63

EnCase view of the 057AC5DDAE9956CAD5D5AEB05A5ABCE0F5F13F3258 file showing the Sensible World of Soccer game title.

```
Strings v2.41
Copyright (C) 1999-2009 Mark Russinovich
Sysinternals - www.sysinternals.com

Sensible World of Soccer
Sensible World of Soccer
Sensible World of Soccer
Sensible World of Soccer
Sensible World of Soccer
The Classic Football Game
The Classic Football Game
The Classic Football Game
The Classic Football Game
The Classic Football Game
Sensible World of Soccer
tEXtSoftware
Adobe ImageReadyq
)wvvvjG>l2
tEXtSoftware
Adobe ImageReadyq
)wvvvjG>l2
ArcadeInfo.xml
 Champs.png
 default.xex
 DemonicPossession.png
 DeusExSocca.png
 FlyingHeaderHero.png
 GentlemanlyConduct.png
 GoalScoringSuperstarHero.png
 HighTension.png
 ItIsNow.png
 MarketplaceBanner.png
 OverTheMoon.png
 Rating_CERO_A.png
 Rating_ESRB_E.png
 Rating_KMRB_A.png
```

FIGURE 8.64

Sample of the Strings results run against the 057AC5DDAE9956CAD5D5AEB05A5AB-CE0F5F13F3258 file. There are several files listed within the Strings results.

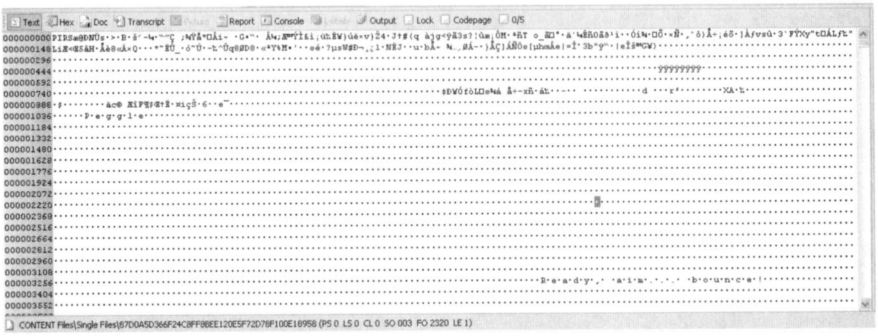

FIGURE 8.65

EnCase view of the Peggle file detailing the PIRs file header.

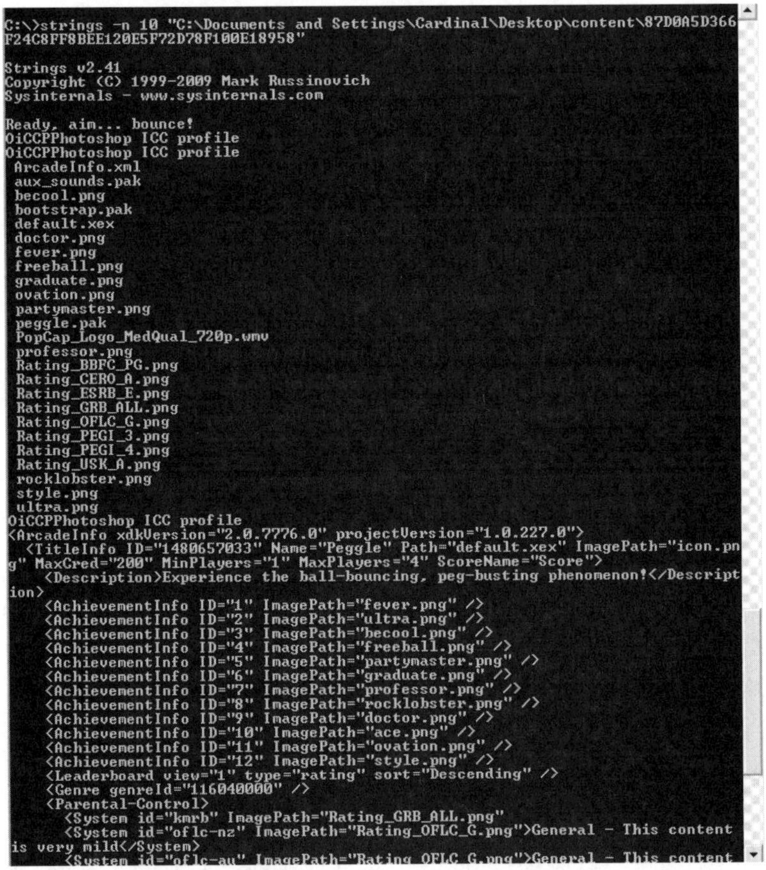

```
C:\>strings -n 10 "C:\Documents and Settings\Cardinal\Desktop\content\87D0A5D366
F24C8FF8BEE120E5F72D78F100E18958"

Strings v2.41
Copyright (C) 1999-2009 Mark Russinovich
Sysinternals - www.sysinternals.com

Ready, aim... bounce!
0iCCPPhotoshop ICC profile
0iCCPPhotoshop ICC profile
 ArcadeInfo.xml
 aux_sounds.pak
 becool.png
 bootstrap.pak
 default.xex
 doctor.png
 fever.png
 freeball.png
 graduate.png
 ovation.png
 partymaster.png
 peggle.pak
 PopCap_Logo_MedQual_720p.wmv
 professor.png
 Rating_BBFC_PG.png
 Rating_CERO_A.png
 Rating_ESRB_E.png
 Rating_GRB_ALL.png
 Rating_OFLC_G.png
 Rating_PEGI_3.png
 Rating_PEGI_4.png
 Rating_USK_A.png
 rocklobster.png
 style.png
 ultra.png
0iCCPPhotoshop ICC profile
<ArcadeInfo xdkVersion="2.0.7776.0" projectVersion="1.0.227.0">
  <TitleInfo ID="1480657033" Name="Peggle" Path="default.xex" ImagePath="icon.pn
g" MaxCred="200" MinPlayers="1" MaxPlayers="4" ScoreName="Score">
    <Description>Experience the ball-bouncing, peg-busting phenomenon!</Descript
ion>
    <AchievementInfo ID="1" ImagePath="fever.png" />
    <AchievementInfo ID="2" ImagePath="ultra.png" />
    <AchievementInfo ID="3" ImagePath="becool.png" />
    <AchievementInfo ID="4" ImagePath="freeball.png" />
    <AchievementInfo ID="5" ImagePath="partymaster.png" />
    <AchievementInfo ID="6" ImagePath="graduate.png" />
    <AchievementInfo ID="7" ImagePath="professor.png" />
    <AchievementInfo ID="8" ImagePath="rocklobster.png" />
    <AchievementInfo ID="9" ImagePath="doctor.png" />
    <AchievementInfo ID="10" ImagePath="ace.png" />
    <AchievementInfo ID="11" ImagePath="ovation.png" />
    <AchievementInfo ID="12" ImagePath="style.png" />
    <Leaderboard view="1" type="rating" sort="Descending" />
    <Genre genreId="116040000" />
    <Parental-Control>
      <System id="kmrb" ImagePath="Rating_GRB_ALL.png"
      <System id="oflc-nz" ImagePath="Rating_OFLC_G.png">General - This content
is very mild</System>
      <System id="oflc-au" ImagePath="Rating_OFLC_G.png">General - This content
```

FIGURE 8.66

This is a portion of the Strings results against the 87D0A5D366F24C8FF8BEE120E5F72D-78F100E18958 file.

Next, the file named CED63B0E9958E30F4D3E506624A04135DBB08B3B58 is 98 MB in size and has a date of 11/22/2005. Data within the file is associated to the Galaga Legions game title. In addition, the file header is again the PIRS "magic" string, as depicted in Figure 8.67, with the Strings results in Figure 8.68.

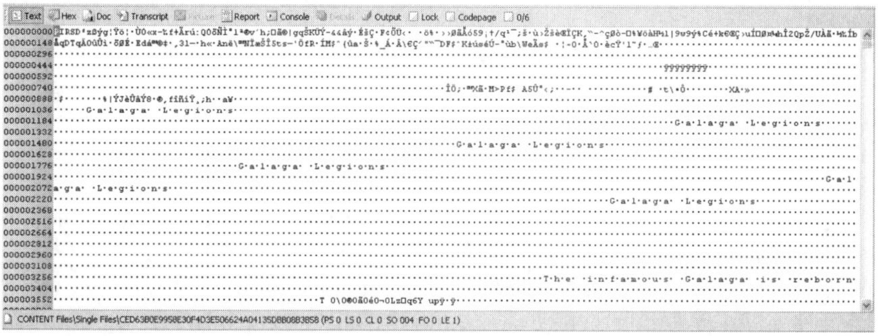

FIGURE 8.67

PIRs file header showing the text string of Galaga Legions.

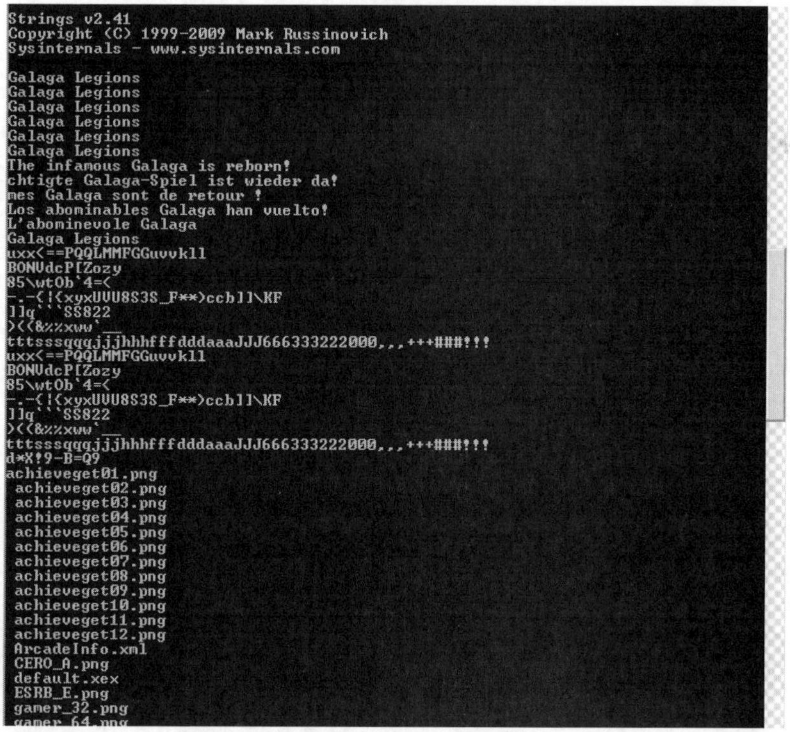

```
Strings v2.41
Copyright (C) 1999-2009 Mark Russinovich
Sysinternals - www.sysinternals.com

Galaga Legions
Galaga Legions
Galaga Legions
Galaga Legions
Galaga Legions
Galaga Legions
The infamous Galaga is reborn!
chtigte Galaga-Spiel ist wieder da!
mes Galaga sont de retour !
Los abominables Galaga han vuelto!
L'abominevole Galaga
Galaga Legions
uxx<==PQQLMMFGGuvvkll
BONUdcP[Zozy
85\wtOb`4=<
-.-{!{xyxUUU8S3S_F**>ccb]]\KF
]]q``SS822
><<&%%xww`__
tttsssqqqjjjhhhfffdddaaaJJJ666333222000,,,+++###!!!
uxx<==PQQLMMFGGuvvkll
BONUdcP[Zozy
85\wtOb`4=<
-.-{!{xyxUUU8S3S_F**>ccb]]\KF
]]q``SS822
><<&%%xww`__
tttsssqqqjjjhhhfffdddaaaJJJ666333222000,,,+++###!!!
d*X!9-B=Q9
achieveget01.png
 achieveget02.png
 achieveget03.png
 achieveget04.png
 achieveget05.png
 achieveget06.png
 achieveget07.png
 achieveget08.png
 achieveget09.png
 achieveget10.png
 achieveget11.png
 achieveget12.png
 ArcadeInfo.xml
 CERO_A.png
 default.xex
 ESRB_E.png
 gamer_32.png
 gamer_64.png
```

FIGURE 8.68

Strings results run against the CED63B0E9958E30F4D3E506624A04135DBB08B3B58 file. Note the PNG files to display achievements and the multiple language support.

Under the folder labeled 584108FF, another file is located, titled 834312072 F4985F9D33D0B9549FFAA32C505FDAD58. This file reports as 40 MB in size and has the 11/22/2005 date associated to it. Again the PIRS "magic" file header is present, shown in Figure 8.69. The plain text located in this file indicates that the file is associated to the Geometry Wars game title; String results are provided in Figure 8.70.

Continuing to navigate through the directories, the next file is located under the FFFEO7D1 folder. The file is titled "Welcome Video" and is reported as 55 MB in size, and has the 11/22/2005 date. The file header is the PIRS entry once again and the information is depicted in Figure 8.71, with the Strings results shown in Figure 8.72.

The last file under the folder with all zeros is located under a subfolder titled FFFE07DF and is titled "Bookmarks.dat." It reports as 72 KB in size and has the 11/22/2005 date. This is the only file located within this subfolder that has a CON file header. In addition to this change in the file header, the console security certificate is present, as shown in Figure 8.73. Running Strings against the file provided the plain text search results of XBOX Dashboard and video bookmark data; Figure 8.74 shows this information.

The next folder in the list has no associated data file within it. This is not to say that with more usage of the console that the folder will not be populated, but at the time of this writing, the usage of the console was limited because of certain factors. The empty folder is presented in Figure 8.75.

Under the next folder, E00000C1AE69C588, and the associated subfolders FFFE07D1 and 00010000, there is a file named E00000C1AE69C588. The information within this indicates that it is a 128 KB file and the associated date to the file is the date of the system update, 08/02/2010. Examining the file provides that there are several PNG files located within that can be carved out of the file. The file has the CON header, shown in Figure 8.76. At file offset 49600, there is a reference to the dashboard preferences, which is an indicator that is the storage

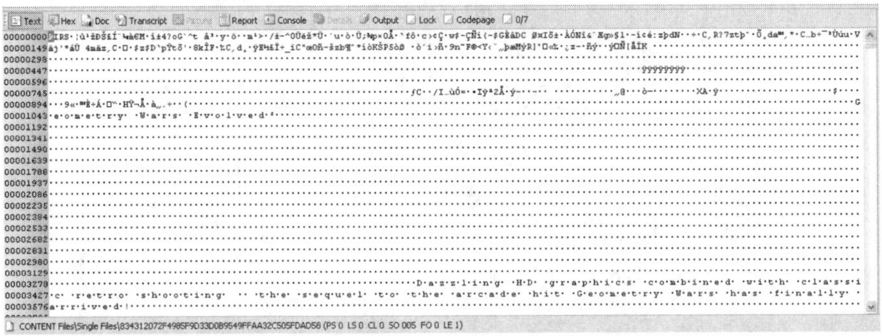

FIGURE 8.69

PIRS header of the 834312072F4985F9D33D0B9549FFAA32C505FDAD58 file and associated plain text for Geometry Wars.

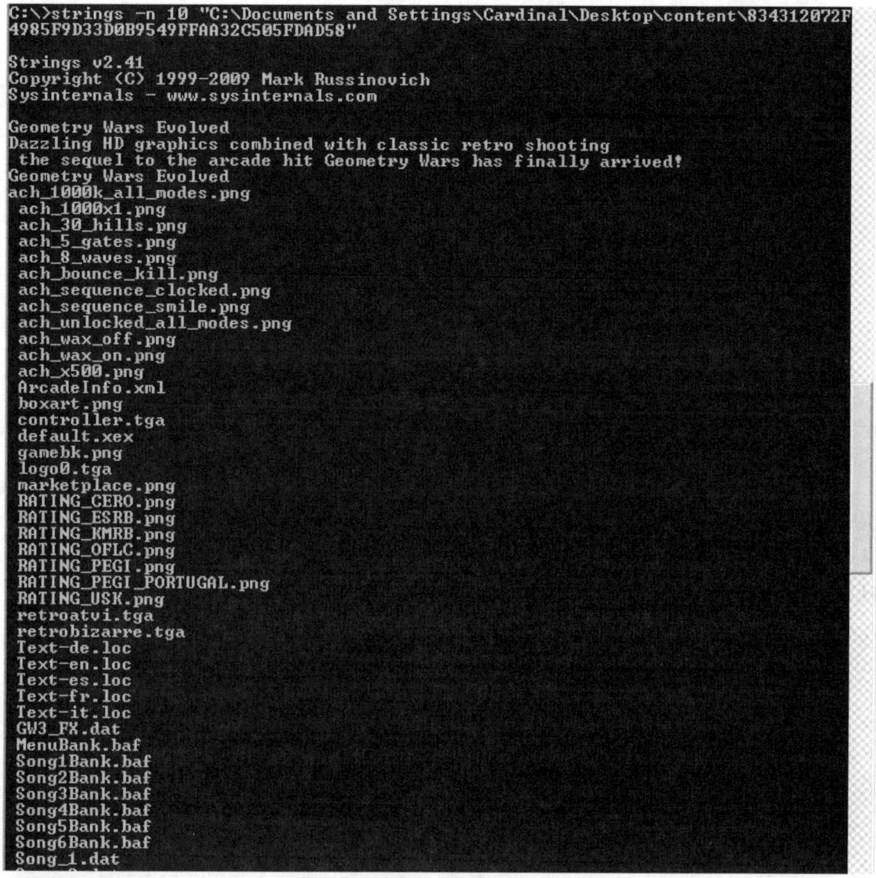

```
C:\>strings -n 10 "C:\Documents and Settings\Cardinal\Desktop\content\834312072F
4985F9D33D0B9549FFAA32C505FDAD58"

Strings v2.41
Copyright (C) 1999-2009 Mark Russinovich
Sysinternals - www.sysinternals.com

Geometry Wars Evolved
Dazzling HD graphics combined with classic retro shooting
 the sequel to the arcade hit Geometry Wars has finally arrived!
Geometry Wars Evolved
ach_1000k_all_modes.png
 ach_1000x1.png
 ach_30_hills.png
 ach_5_gates.png
 ach_8_waves.png
 ach_bounce_kill.png
 ach_sequence_clocked.png
 ach_sequence_smile.png
 ach_unlocked_all_modes.png
 ach_wax_off.png
 ach_wax_on.png
 ach_x500.png
 ArcadeInfo.xml
 boxart.png
 controller.tga
 default.xex
 gamebk.png
 logo0.tga
 marketplace.png
 RATING_CERO.png
 RATING_ESRB.png
 RATING_KMRB.png
 RATING_OFLC.png
 RATING_PEGI.png
 RATING_PEGI_PORTUGAL.png
 RATING_USK.png
 retroatvi.tga
 retrobizarre.tga
 Text-de.loc
 Text-en.loc
 Text-es.loc
 Text-fr.loc
 Text-it.loc
 GW3_FX.dat
 MenuBank.baf
 Song1Bank.baf
 Song2Bank.baf
 Song3Bank.baf
 Song4Bank.baf
 Song5Bank.baf
 Song6Bank.baf
 Song_1.dat
```

FIGURE 8.70

Sample of the Strings hits against the Geometry Wars file. There is a great deal of information within this file including text files, multi language support, and PNG files.

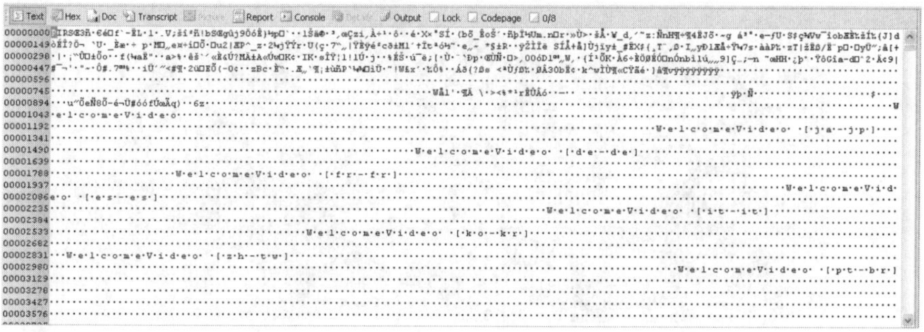

FIGURE 8.71

PIRS file header to the welcome video.

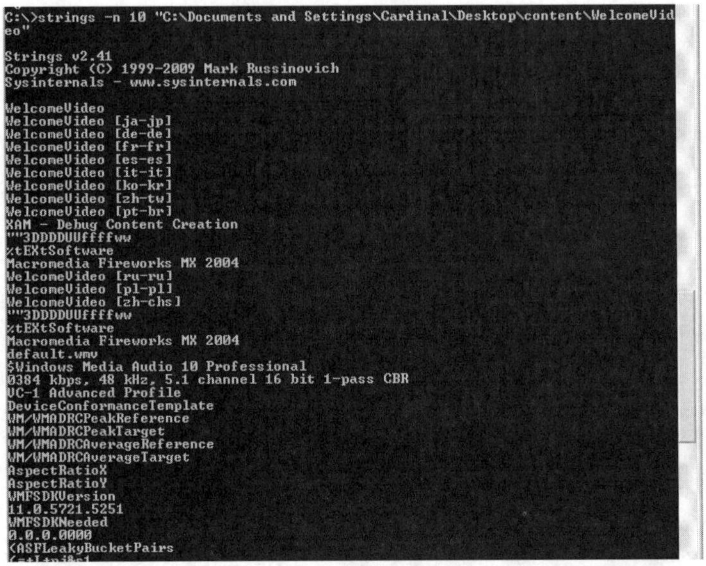
C:\>strings -n 10 "C:\Documents and Settings\Cardinal\Desktop\content\WelcomeVideo"
Strings v2.41
Copyright (C) 1999-2009 Mark Russinovich
Sysinternals - www.sysinternals.com
WelcomeVideo
WelcomeVideo [ja-jp]
WelcomeVideo [de-de]
WelcomeVideo [fr-fr]
WelcomeVideo [es-es]
WelcomeVideo [it-it]
WelcomeVideo [ko-kr]
WelcomeVideo [zh-tw]
WelcomeVideo [pt-br]
XAM - Debug Content Creation
""3DDDDUUffffww
xtEXtSoftware
Macromedia Fireworks MX 2004
WelcomeVideo [ru-ru]
WelcomeVideo [pl-pl]
WelcomeVideo [zh-chs]
""3DDDDUUffffww
xtEXtSoftware
Macromedia Fireworks MX 2004
default.wmv
$Windows Media Audio 10 Professional
0384 kbps, 48 kHz, 5.1 channel 16 bit 1-pass CBR
VC-1 Advanced Profile
DeviceConformanceTemplate
WM/WMADRCPeakReference
WM/WMADRCPeakTarget
WM/WMADRCAverageReference
WM/WMADRCAverageTarget
AspectRatioX
AspectRatioY
WMFSDKVersion
11.0.5721.5251
WMFSDKNeeded
0.0.0.0000
<ASFLeakyBucketPairs

FIGURE 8.72

A portion of the Strings output from the welcome video once again showing the language support.

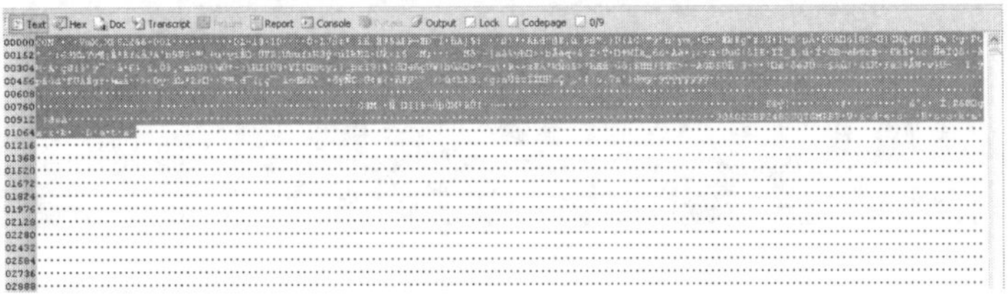
Text
Hex
Doc
Transcript
Report
Console
Output
Lock
Codepage

FIGURE 8.73

CON file header for the bookmark.dat file.

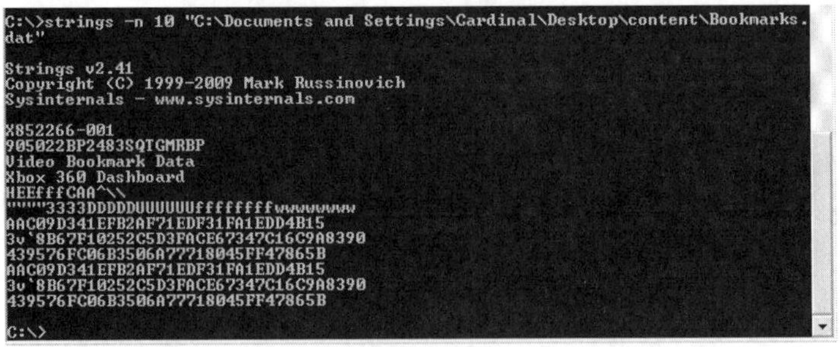
C:\>strings -n 10 "C:\Documents and Settings\Cardinal\Desktop\content\Bookmarks.dat"
Strings v2.41
Copyright (C) 1999-2009 Mark Russinovich
Sysinternals - www.sysinternals.com
X852266-001
905022BP2483SQTGMRBP
Video Bookmark Data
Xbox 360 Dashboard
HEEfffCAA^\\
""""3333DDDDUUUUUUffffffffwwwwwww
AAC09D341EFB2AF71EDF31FA1EDD4B15
3v`8B67F10252C5D3FACE67347C16C9A8390
439576FC06B3506A77718045FF47865B
AAC09D341EFB2AF71EDF31FA1EDD4B15
3v`8B67F10252C5D3FACE67347C16C9A8390
439576FC06B3506A77718045FF47865B
C:\>

FIGURE 8.74

Strings hits against the bookmark.dat file. Note the console security certificate and the reference to Dashboard.

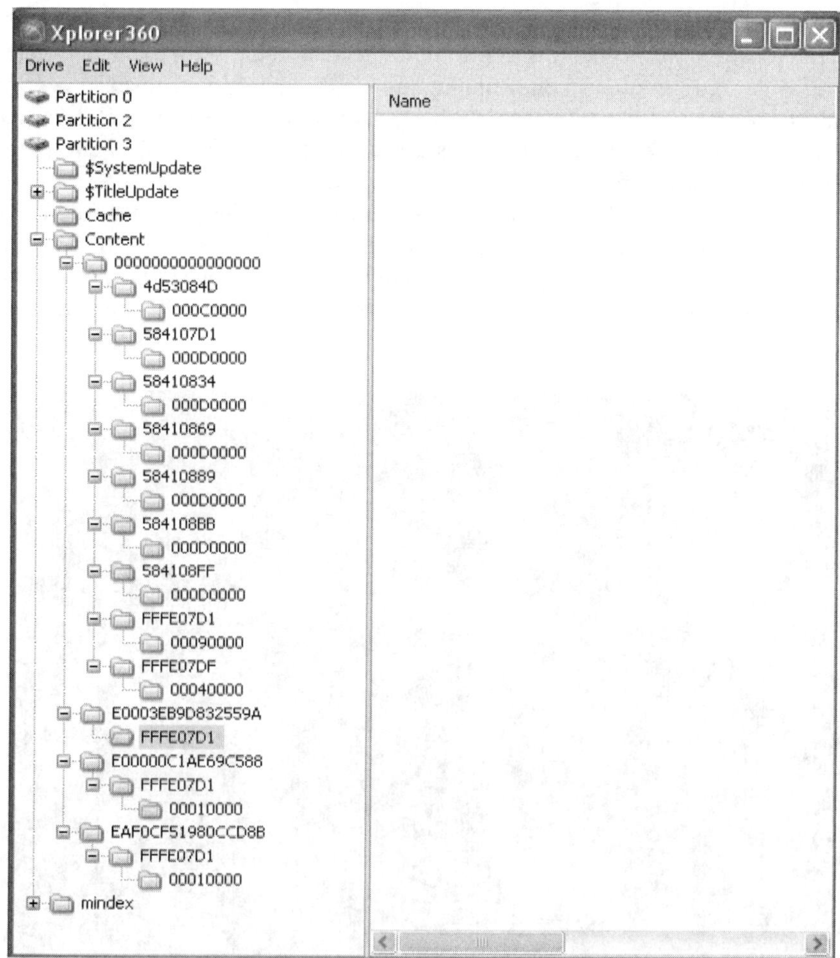

FIGURE 8.75

Empty folder.

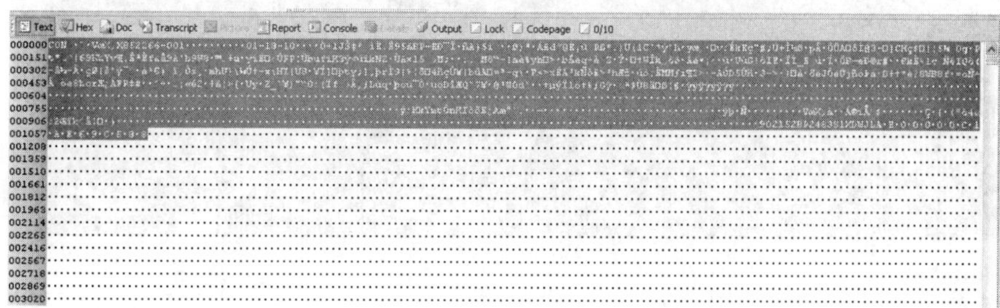

FIGURE 8.76

CON header of the E00000C1AE69C588 file.

area for the customization of the dashboard settings. At file offset 57344, there are references to the account, which could indicate account settings such as game zone, avatar settings, and so on. Running the file through Strings revealed a great deal of information regarding the applications and software manufacturers that are working with the XBOX 360 and its associated games. Figure 8.77 shows the Strings results of this file.

There were eight PNG files that could be extracted from this particular file. There are three versions of image 1, shown in Figure 8.78, and five versions of image 2, shown in Figure 8.79. The image file shown in Figure 8.78 is one of the profile ions for the two profiles that were created for this research. Figure 8.79 is a "ghosted"

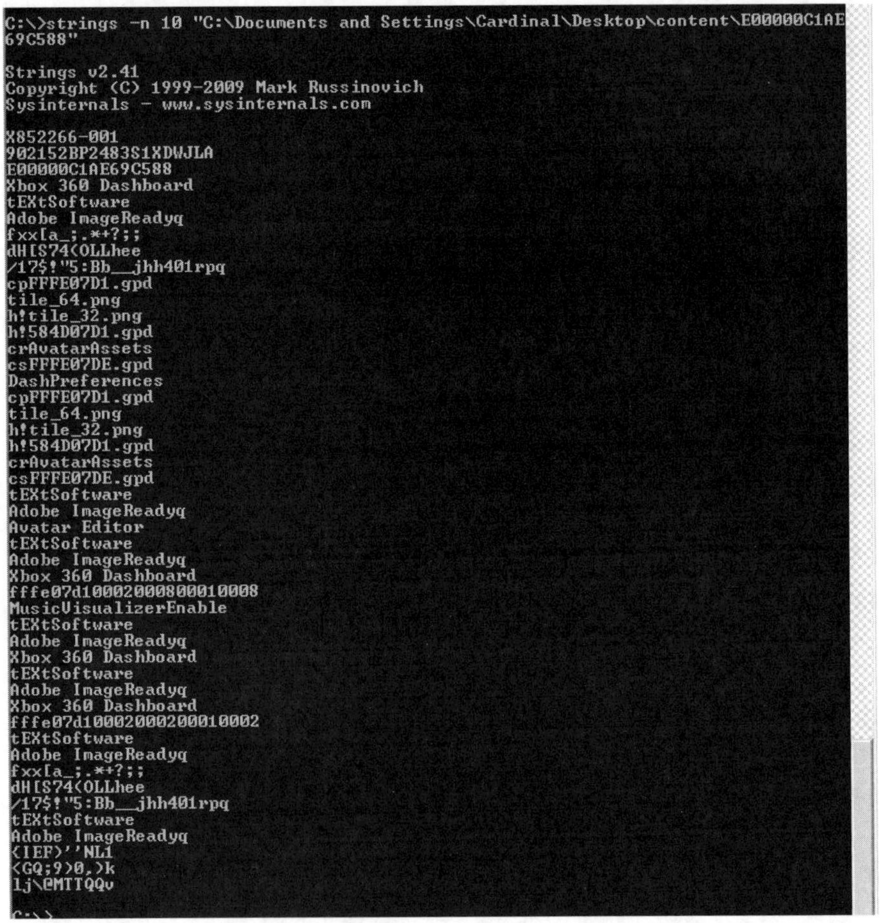

```
C:\>strings -n 10 "C:\Documents and Settings\Cardinal\Desktop\content\E00000C1AE
69C588"

Strings v2.41
Copyright (C) 1999-2009 Mark Russinovich
Sysinternals - www.sysinternals.com

X852266-001
902152BP2483S1XDWJLA
E00000C1AE69C588
Xbox 360 Dashboard
tEXtSoftware
Adobe ImageReadyq
fxx[a_;.*+?;;
dH[S74<OLLhee
/17$!"5:Bb__jhh401rpq
cpFFFE07D1.gpd
tile_64.png
h!tile_32.png
h!584D07D1.gpd
crAvatarAssets
csFFFE07DE.gpd
DashPreferences
cpFFFE07D1.gpd
tile_64.png
h!tile_32.png
h!584D07D1.gpd
crAvatarAssets
csFFFE07DE.gpd
tEXtSoftware
Adobe ImageReadyq
Avatar Editor
tEXtSoftware
Adobe ImageReadyq
Xbox 360 Dashboard
fffe07d10002000800010008
MusicVisualizerEnable
tEXtSoftware
Adobe ImageReadyq
Xbox 360 Dashboard
tEXtSoftware
Adobe ImageReadyq
Xbox 360 Dashboard
fffe07d10002000200010002
tEXtSoftware
Adobe ImageReadyq
fxx[a_;.*+?;;
dH[S74<OLLhee
/17$!"5:Bb__jhh401rpq
tEXtSoftware
Adobe ImageReadyq
<IEF>''NL1
<GQ;9>0,>k
1j\@MTTQQv

C:\>
```

FIGURE 8.77

Strings results from the E00000C1AE69C588 file. Note the references to Adobe, XBOX 360 Dashboard, and text software.

FIGURE 8.78

Three versions of this image file are located within this "dashboard" file.

FIGURE 8.79

There are five versions of this particular file located within the "dashboard" file.

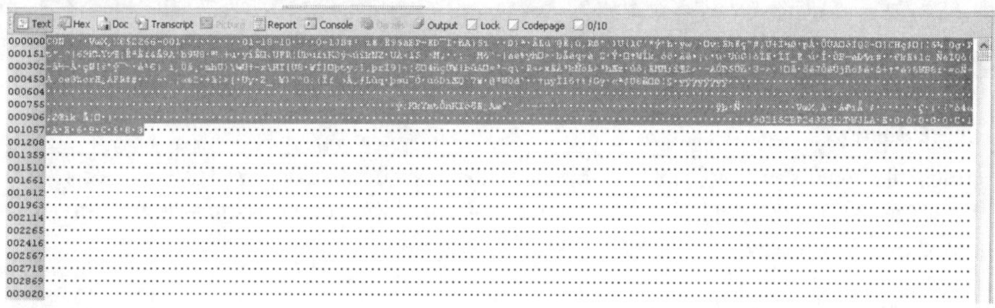

FIGURE 8.80

CON magic file header.

icon of the XBOX 360 console, which is a dominant theme when the console is being used. This icon is displayed when the user signs into certain features.

The last file that is located within this list of folders has the system configuration date of 08/02/2010 and is 192 KB in size. The file information reports that it is a CON file header and there is the console security certificate present, as shown in Figure 8.80. The Strings results are shown in Figure 8.81, detailing the plain text that was located.

```
C:\>strings -n 10 "C:\Documents and Settings\Cardinal\Desktop\content\EAF0CF5198
0CCD8B"

Strings v2.41
Copyright (C) 1999-2009 Mark Russinovich
Sysinternals - www.sysinternals.com

X852266-001
902152BP2483S1XDWJLA
EAF0CF51980CCD8B
%tEXtSoftware
Macromedia Fireworks MX 2004
FFFE07D1.gpd
UFFFE07DE.gpd
tile_64.png
tile_32.png
avtr_64.png
avtr_32.png
584D07D1.gpd
AvatarAssets
FFFE07D1.gpd
SFFFE07DE.gpd
tile_64.png
tile_32.png
avtr_64.png
avtr_32.png
584D07D1.gpd
AvatarAssets
fffe07d10002101600011016
tEXtSoftware
Adobe ImageReadyq
Xbox 360 Dashboard
tEXtSoftware
Adobe ImageReadyq
4sx6ch6mp6e
tEXtSoftware
Adobe ImageReadyq
Xbox 360 Dashboard
X852266-001
tEXtSoftware
Adobe ImageReadyq
IDATHXUUw\S
%tEXtSoftware
Macromedia Fireworks MX 2004
%tEXtSoftware
Macromedia Fireworks MX 2004
tEXtSoftware
Adobe ImageReadyq
Avatar Editor
fffe07d10002101600011016

C:\>
```

FIGURE 8.81

Strings hits against this file. Note the Macromedia search hits along with the avatar assets. This file could be associated with the gamer avatar and the accomplishments that are earned over game play.

MINDEX FOLDER

The last folder within Partition 3 is the Mindex folder. The file reports as 6 KB in size and has a file extension of .xmi. Figure 8.82 provides a view of these files through Xplorer360. Research into this file extension provided several possible file formats that could provide the legitimate use on the console. It is hard to determine with certainty, but there were two formats that stood out as contenders.

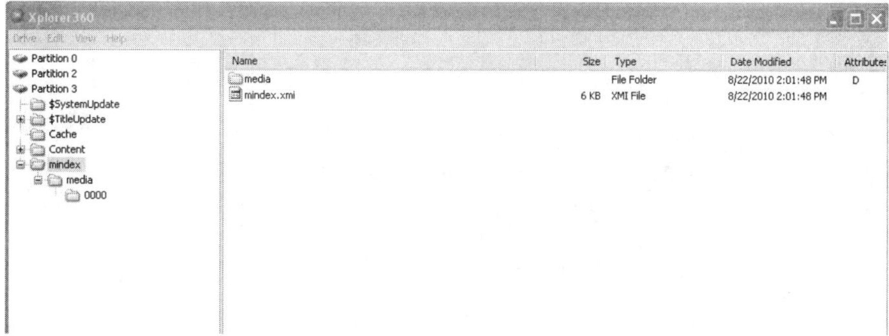

FIGURE 8.82

Folder structure for the last file in Partition 3.

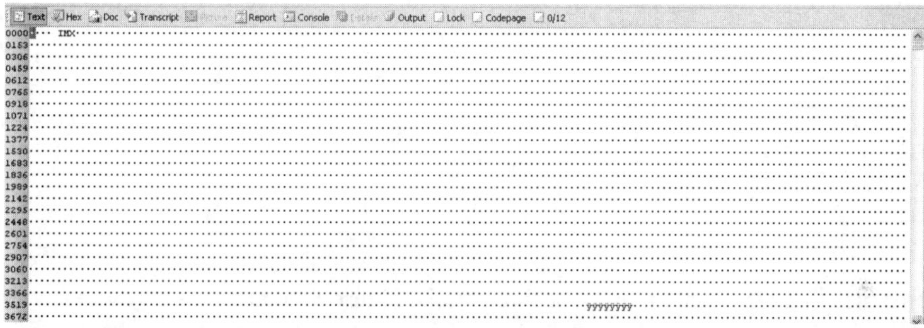

FIGURE 8.83

EnCase view of the mindex.xmi file. Speculation is that this file would track user settings as the console gets used.

- XML Metadata Interchange Format
- Extended MIDI File

Figure 8.83 provides a view of the mindiex.xmi file as seen using EnCase.

SUMMARY

A great deal of information was been presented in this chapter. There are many new files, folders, and partitions that are created when the console system update is performed. The subfiles under the Content folder provide a great deal of information about the game titles that are present, bookmarks, and the welcome video. There are

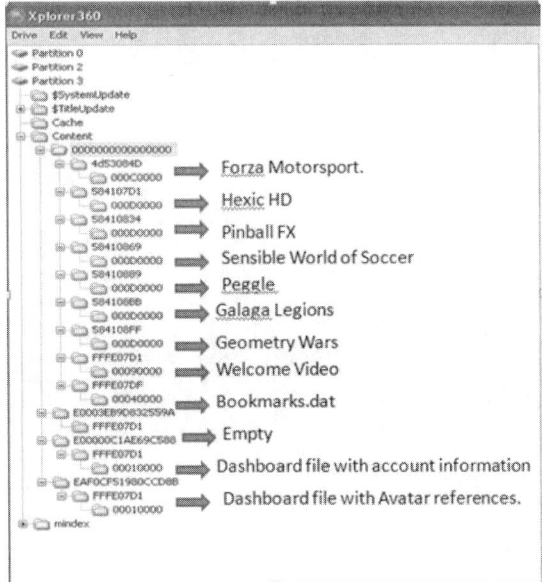

FIGURE 8.84

Summary of the folder information.

two files that may contain user-specific details. Figure 8.84 provides an overview of the information that was discussed, presenting a table of sorts that shows the associated information presented to the end user.

References

[1] XBOX Hacker. "Modifying Tdbx.db?" http://www.xboxhacker.org/index.php?topic=14312.0;wap2 (accessed September 23, 2010).

[2] XBOX Hacker. "MfgBootLauncher." http://www.xboxhacker.net/index.php?topic=7274.0 (accessed September 22, 2010).

CHAPTER

XBOX Live Redemption Code and Facebook

9

INFORMATION IN THIS CHAPTER

- XBOX Live
- Redeeming the prepaid card
- Facebook
- XBOX Live Facebook artifacts
- Xplorer360 and Facebook

XBOX LIVE

Once an account has been created and the console is ready to be used by the end user, there is one additional step that can be taken. This is the final step to connect to the network portal or XBOX Live and enjoy the full functionality of the console. It is this network functionality that provides the need for the forensic examiner to be concerned with the console. Configuring the XBOX Live account and creating a Gamertag are not enough to connect to the full functionality. The full feature online portal is a paid-for service that has varying price points depending on the length of months that the user is willing to pay for. A prepaid XBOX Live 12-month Gold membership was purchased, providing all the needed functionality for the research. There is a code on the card that has to be entered, and this links the Gamertag to the account subscription. Once the XBOX Live account is active, then the end user can sign into the Live service and access the many features that are discussed.

This chapter discusses the process of the XBOX Live account code entry, as well as the steps that are necessary to connect to the Facebook portal that is available. Along the way, there will be artifact analysis and an attempt to link that information from the redemption of the Gold subscription prepaid card and the artifacts that may be linked through interaction in Facebook.

REDEEMING THE PREPAID CARD

There are a few ways in which an end user can pay for his or her account and get his or her console connected to the XBOX Live service. The first way is to pay for the service through a credit card like any other online purchase. The card number will be saved at Microsoft, and the user will be charged the amount he or she agreed upon for the service he or she wants. The second method is to purchase a Microsoft XBOX Live prepaid card specific to the Live service. Microsoft keeps a record of the Gamertag and the credit card number that was used to activate the membership. To redeem the card, a user simply has to log into their account and navigate to his or her "My XBOX" pane. Once there, the user selects the page and is presented with some options. Within those options is a selection called "Manage My Account"; it is under this selection that a code can be entered to be redeemed, which then activates the account to the Live service.

Once the Live service configuration was completed, the process continued with a few more configuration steps that were required, specifically, configuration of the Facebook interface for the XBOX Live service was completed before disconnecting the drive for imaging.

The drive had been connected to the custom interface and placed back within the internal housing so that it would firmly connect to the console itself. With this setup, the drive was able to securely connect to the console so that it was recognized when the machine was turned on. The external housing was not replaced for this process because of the almost immediate need to extract the drive from the custom case for imaging. The drive was removed in the same fashion as mentioned earlier. It was disconnected from the console and then disconnected from the custom interface. Once the drive was disconnected from this interface, it was a matter of sliding it out from the custom internal housing. Once the drive was isolated, it was connected to the WiebeTech UltraDock and then to the forensic research system for importation and examination using EnCase. It was expected from previous research that some artifacts pertaining to the connection and linkage to the XBOX Live account would be located on the drive. These actions were taken in an effort to determine if there were any remnants of this configuration activity that are stored locally on the hard drive or within the onboard storage that has, as of yet, not been able to be accessed or if the information is simply transmitted and linked to the XBOX Live account.

The image of the hard drive after the redemption of the XBOX Live Gold account was loaded into EnCase for examination. The code that was used to activate this account was added as a keyword within EnCase, selecting GREP, ANSI Latin, and Unicode Big Endian for search parameters. The first 10 characters of the code were entered as the keyword, and the EnCase keyword search was initiated. Figure 9.1 provides an image of these settings.

The importance of locating this code is that it may provide a link between the gamer that redeems it and the purchase location, which means that it could be tracked back to a credit card, or in some cases, retail stores take video of every purchase

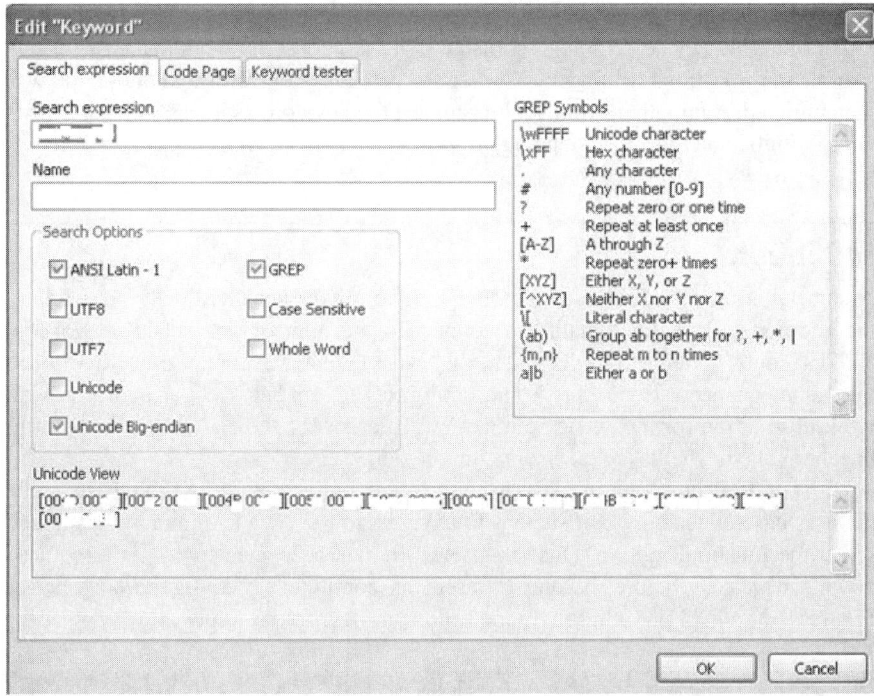

FIGURE 9.1

Keyword configuration of the "redemption code" for the XBOX Live Gold account. The information has been obstructed for security reasons.

with RFID inventory tracking. A possible scenario would play out like this. A suspect, in the process of grooming a victim, provided the victim with a prepaid Microsoft Points card as an enticement, or simply sent the victim the card code through chat or e-mail. The card could get redeemed, and the victim could then have access to the online Live service allowing for more covert communication between the parties. Of course, this is not unique to this scenario. The communication aspect of the Live service and the gaming console can be used in this manner because these communication features are not well known to certain communities. If this was a child, the parents may not even know that the child has received a code and is online chatting with strangers. Remember that a majority of U.S. households have gaming consoles, and parents have not, for the most part, been educated as to the functions of such consoles and think that they simply play games. A great effort has been pushed by such organizations as the National Center for Missing and Exploited Children to educate parents on the ramifications of network communication, but the game consoles may not be viewed by the parents as an issue. They are completely unaware of the networking functions of the console.

The way in which the code was entered into the keyword list through EnCase did not provide any search hits. To ensure that the widest net would be cast for this search, all the options within EnCase were selected for keywords and the search was then initiated. Again, there were no hits against the keyword as it was entered. This is not a definitive on the code not being present; crafting keywords is an art and science.

FACEBOOK

A somewhat recent addition to the XBOX Live NXE (New XBOX Experience) is the addition of the functionality to connect to the number one social networking site, Facebook. The need to document the artifacts that are stored on the drive once the gamer connects to Facebook and configures his or her account could provide vital information for a case or examination. In order for the end user to connect to Facebook, he or she has to take some initial steps.

First, a user must sign into his or her account and connect to XBOX Live. Once the user has connected, he or she has to navigate to the "My Community" page and select the **facebook** option. Once this selection has been made, there is a required download, just as before, before the user can continue the configuration process. Figures 9.2 and 9.3 provide some screenshots of these initial screens.

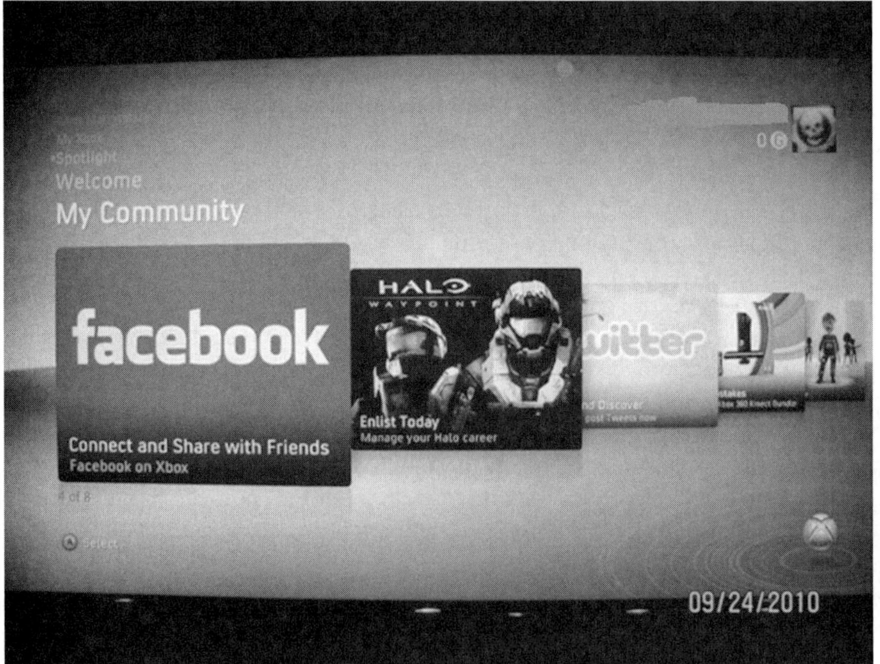

FIGURE 9.2

"My Community" page to begin the Facebook configuration.

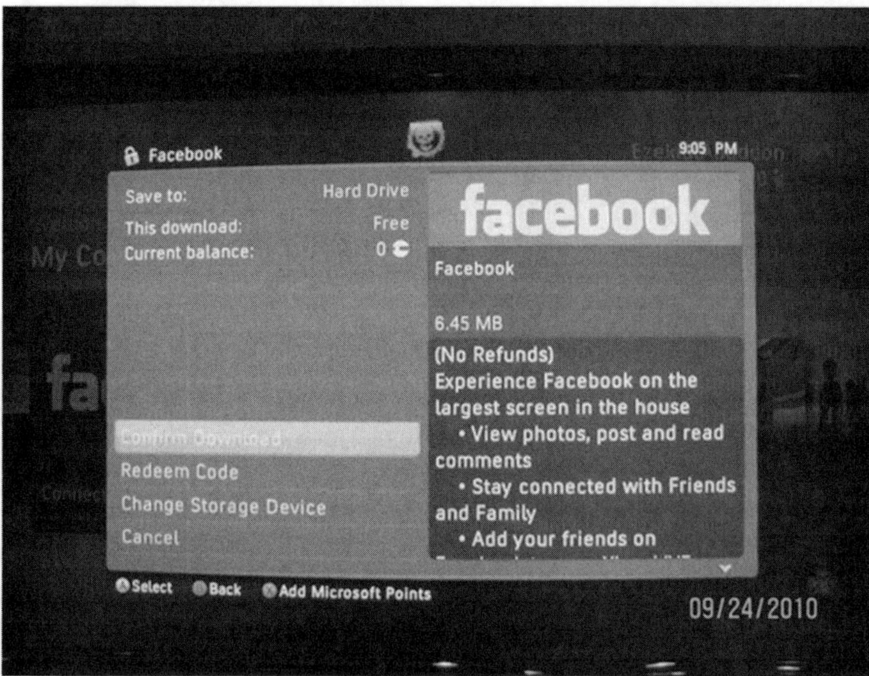

FIGURE 9.3

This is the screenshot of the page the end user is presented with once they select the Facebook application. A download is required for the end user to use this feature.

Once the download has been accepted, a download window appears notifying the end user of the progress of the download. The storage location for this file is documented later; there are no options available to the end user to specify the location with only one storage media connected. Under the **Change Storage Device** option, shown in Figure 9.3, the end user can choose to store the download on another associated FATX-formatted drive. Once the download is completed, the console is rebooted and the end user is presented with the gamer sign in. Because the console is a multiuser platform, there are options for signing in that allow the selection of which user to be signed in, detailed in Figure 9.4.

Once signed in, after the download and installation have been completed, the end user is prompted to enter his or her e-mail address and password that are associated with his or her Facebook account, as shown in Figure 9.5. This information will be searched for using EnCase later, but the terms that are being entered during this configuration will build the keyword list that will be used later.

Another screen is presented to the end user once they have entered their Facebook account information. Because this is the connection of two social networking mediums, there is a request presented to the user to display their information regarding their XBOX Live Gamertag on their Facebook account. This is another

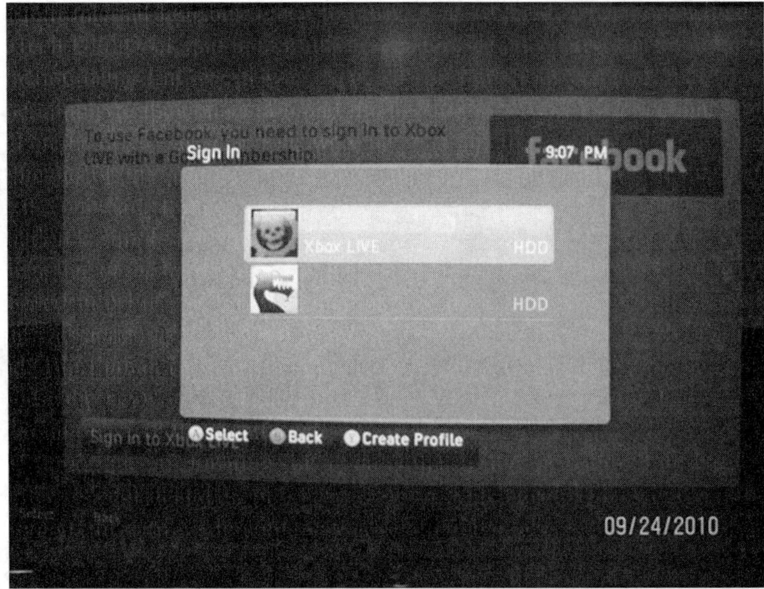

FIGURE 9.4

Screenshot of the multiuser, multiGamertag, sign-in screen.

FIGURE 9.5

This is a screenshot of what the user is presented with once they are ready to configure their console to connect to Facebook.

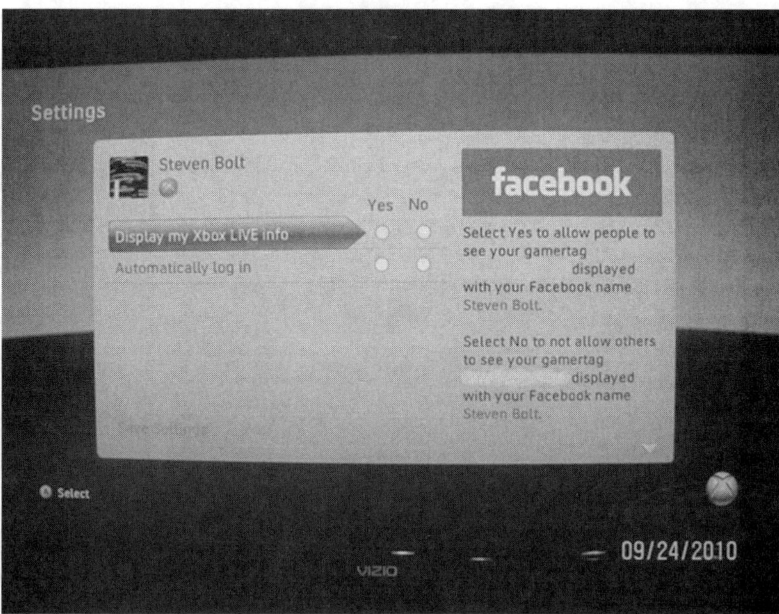

FIGURE 9.6

Screenshot of the window that is displayed to the end user for linking their Facebook and XBOX Live information, advertising their Gamertag on their Facebook page.

potential linkage of information that an examiner or an investigator must contend with. Figure 9.6 provides the final configuration screen that is presented to the user before they are able to navigate Facebook over the XBOX Live service. Once logged in, the user is presented with their friends list and a list of their friends who are on Facebook and XBOX Live. Selections at this point are driven by the user. Once a user makes their friend selection, there are more options that are presented to them. Figures 9.7 and 9.8 show some of the information as it is presented to the end user during this process.

While navigating through these screens, several subpages were presented. Some of these were mundane; others provided some information that provided more insight into the navigation and functionality of this Facebook portal. This is a stripped-down version of the main Facebook Web site, but some of the same functionality is presented to the end user. Because chat logs can be an integral part of any forensic examination, it was decided to explore the options that are presented for chatting (see Figure 9.9).

Another option that is available to a user is the ability to sign up for Windows Live Messenger. Reviewing all the folders and options, it becomes more and more clear that the console's Live features are pushing the social networking capabilities to link everyone. Figures 9.10 and 9.11 show the XBOX Live screens that are presented once Facebook has been configured.

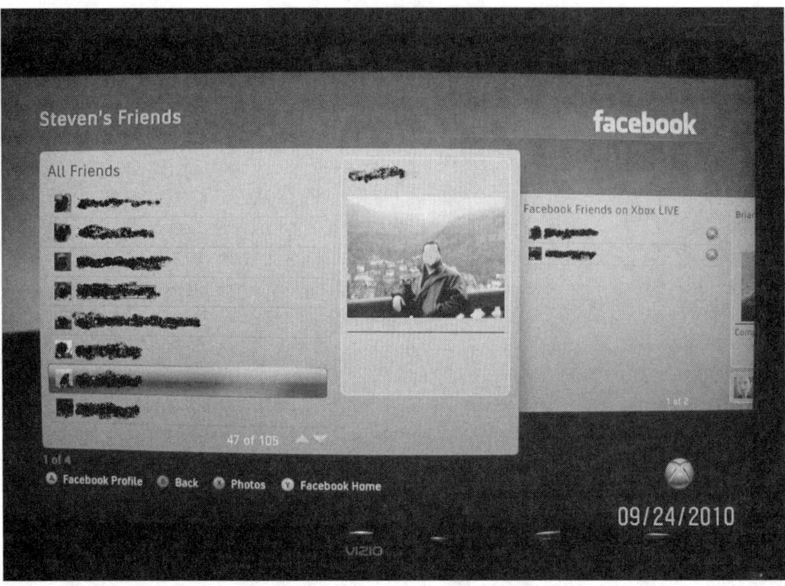

FIGURE 9.7

Initial login page to the Facebook portal on XBOX Live.

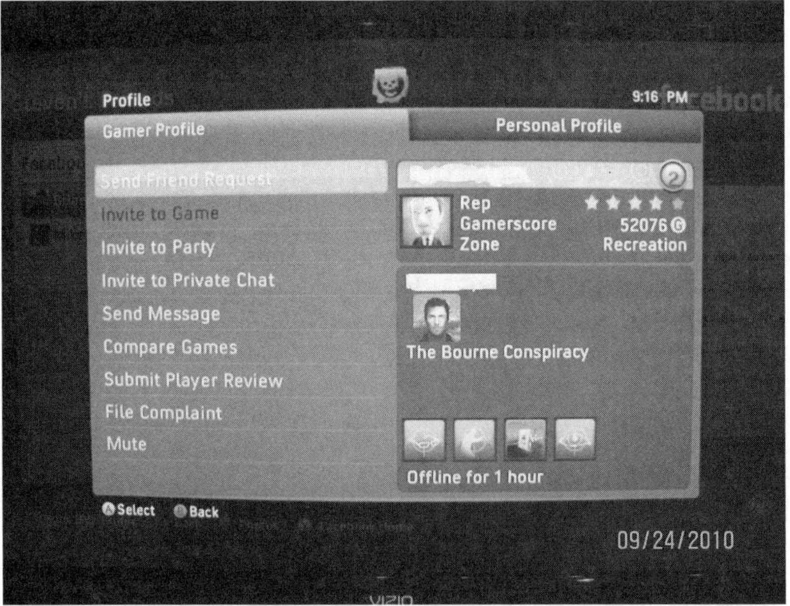

FIGURE 9.8

This screenshot provides an image of the information that is presented to an end user when they have selected one of their Facebook friends.

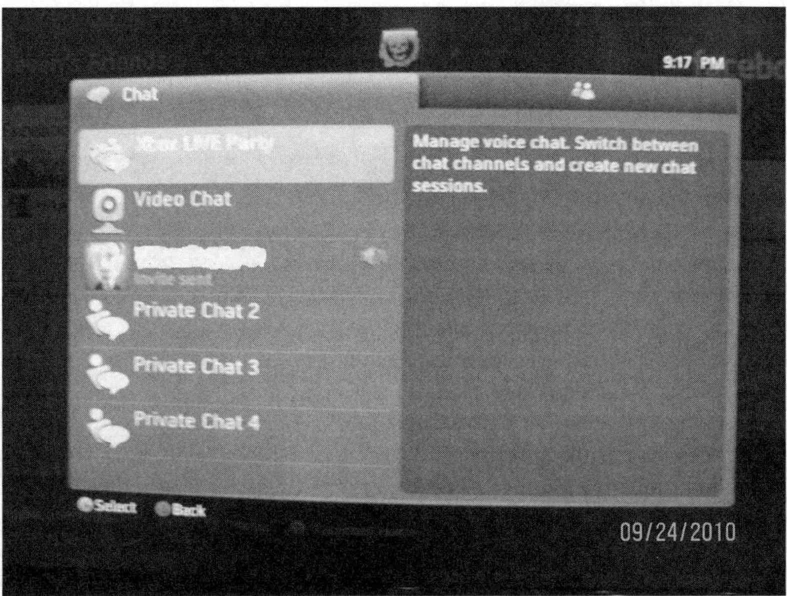

FIGURE 9.9

This is a screenshot of the chatting options that are available once an end user selects a Facebook friend.

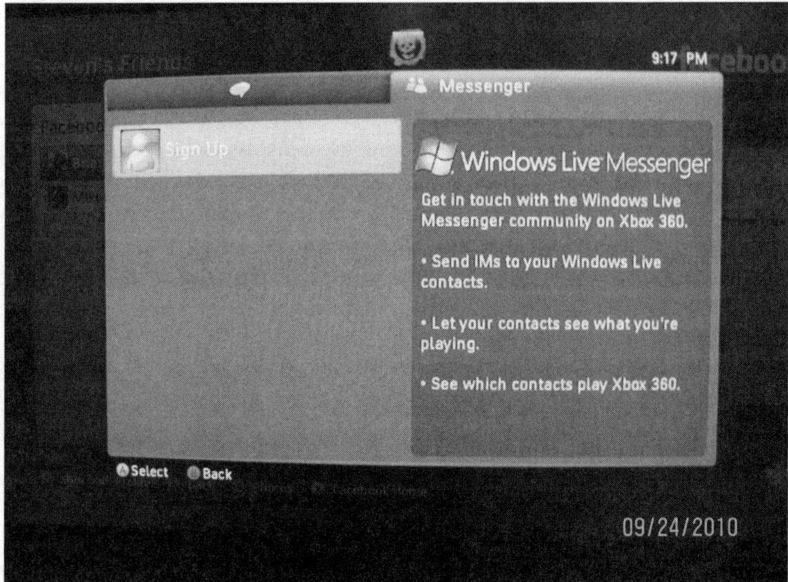

FIGURE 9.10

Windows Live Messenger initial screen.

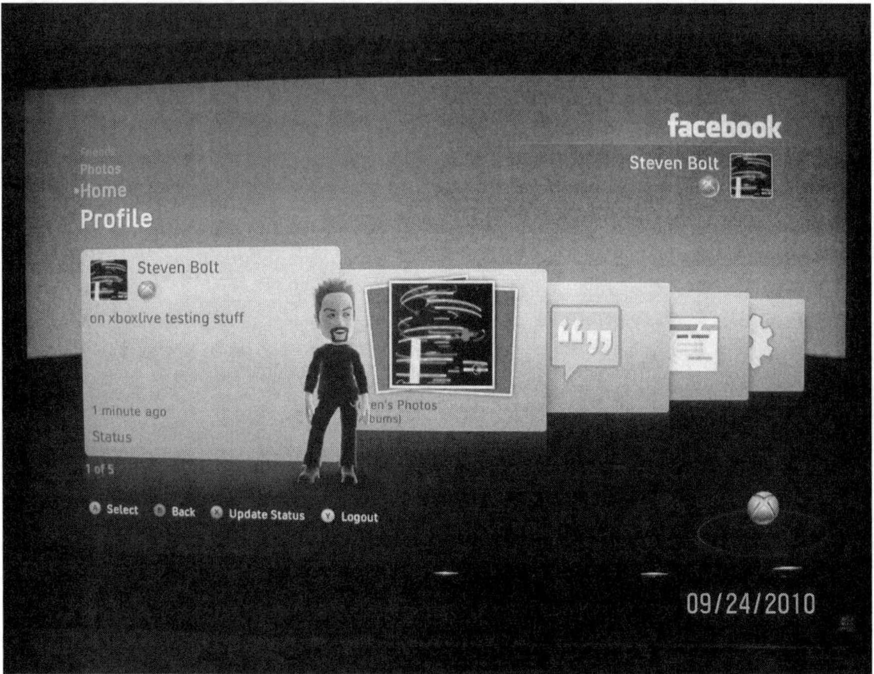

FIGURE 9.11

Profile tab for the Facebook portal showing the status message that is displayed on Facebook. In this case, the phrase "on XBOXlive testing stuff" was entered as a status message.

There is a great deal of functionality with the portal that could be explored, showing all the steps, screens, and subscreens to navigate through the Facebook portal. If time permits, each function would be explored and then the drive would be imaged. The process would be quite time consuming as one action would have to be taken, then the drive would have to be pulled and imaged, and this process would need to be repeated for each and every function that is provided, with a generation of keyword lists based on the actions taken. The artifacts that were generated because of the actions taken while logged in are documented in the following section.

XBOX LIVE FACEBOOK ARTIFACTS

Walking through the process of installing Facebook on the XBOX 360 console provided information to determine the artifacts that may be resident on the attached drive. The research process began with the installation of the Facebook application as described above. Once completed, the drive was removed from the custom case, connected through a WiebeTech UltraDock Write Blocker and imaged using EnCase. In addition, the drive was opened with Xplorer360, while still connected to the write blocker.

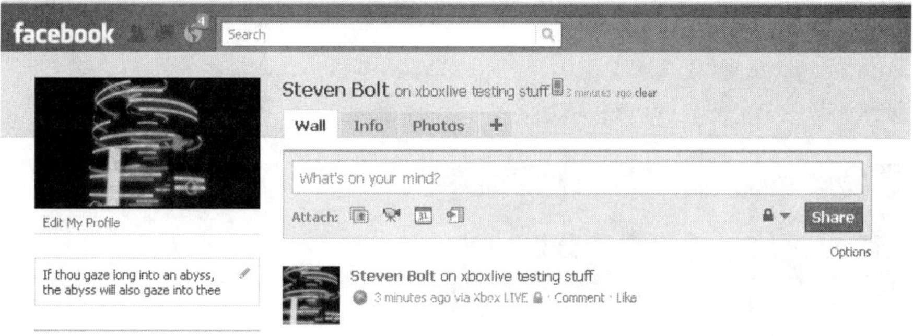

FIGURE 9.12

Screenshot of the Facebook account with the status message displayed and propagated to the Facebook Web portal.

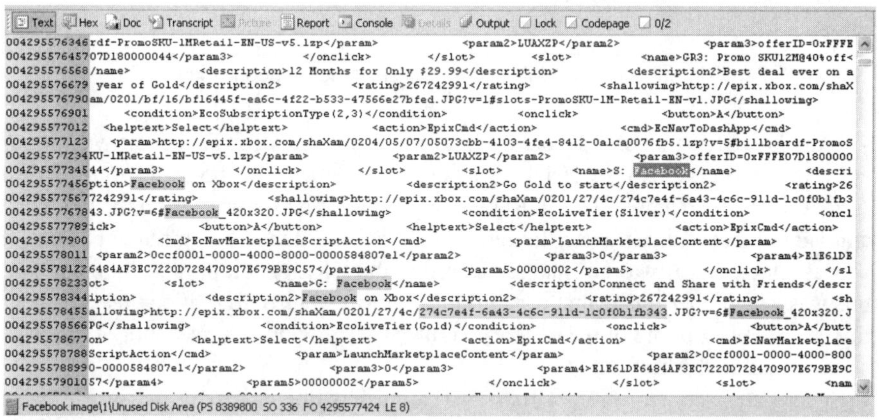

FIGURE 9.13

Search hit for Facebook as a keyword. This search hit is surrounded by a lot of other information, including what appears to be a URL [1].

Viewing the drive in EnCase, the keyword list was constructed based on the parameters and navigation that was completed in the last section. The first search term that was used was "Facebook," which returned 31 hits. Several of these hits are duplicates, simply shifting by one byte with the addition of the Unicode dot on the left or right of the search term.

As mentioned in Figure 9.12, several of these search hits include URL addresses. A review of the data shows that a majority of the information appears to be the advertisement for the Facebook portal over XBOX Live, displayed in Figure 9.13. I copied the URL and entered it into my Web browser to determine how the Web address would be rendered. The results of this are displayed in Figure 9.14.

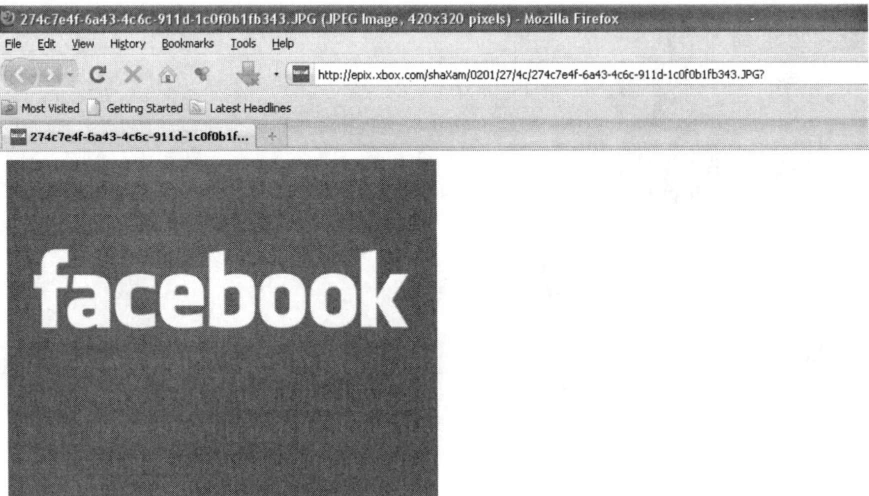

FIGURE 9.14

Display of the URL that is located within the search hits for Facebook [1].

Another URL that was located within the search hits for Facebook was http://epix.xbox.com/shaXam/0201/bf/16/bf16445f-ea6c-4f22-b533-47566e27bfed.JPG?v=1#slots-PromoSKU-1M-Retail-EN-v1.jpg. It was copied from the hex view and again placed in a browser to determine what the image being rendered was. It was assumed that it was an image, given that the URL ended in .jpg. Sure enough, this was yet another image that was presented during the configuration that was mentioned at the beginning of the chapter. Figure 9.15 provides a screenshot of the page as displayed in the browser.

There were several more URLs that could have been carved out of the drive image that were resident in close proximity to the Facebook search hits. This is a process that can be duplicated several times over in an attempt to document all of the artifacts. Many of the images that are displayed to the end user over the console can be replicated through a normal browser window so long as the URL can be identified and extracted. One area that may concern an investigator or an examiner, one who is not a gamer, is where the images came from. This will have to be explored in great depth. There are so many game titles available for the console, this would be a book unto itself. The final page that can be extracted is a link to Twitter, yet another social networking page. The URL, http://epix.xbox.com/shaXam/0201/13/c6/13c6425a-4c66-4958-a4e1-38268e5e3f61.JPG?v=3#Twitter_s_v1.jpg, was extracted, and the rendered page is displayed in Figure 9.16.

Continuing to move through the data that is presented with the search hits, there are four hits that all have a PNG file associated to them. Each PNG was carved out of the image file, saving the files for later examination. Once the images were extracted, they were imported into EnCase for hash analysis. All four files were the same image,

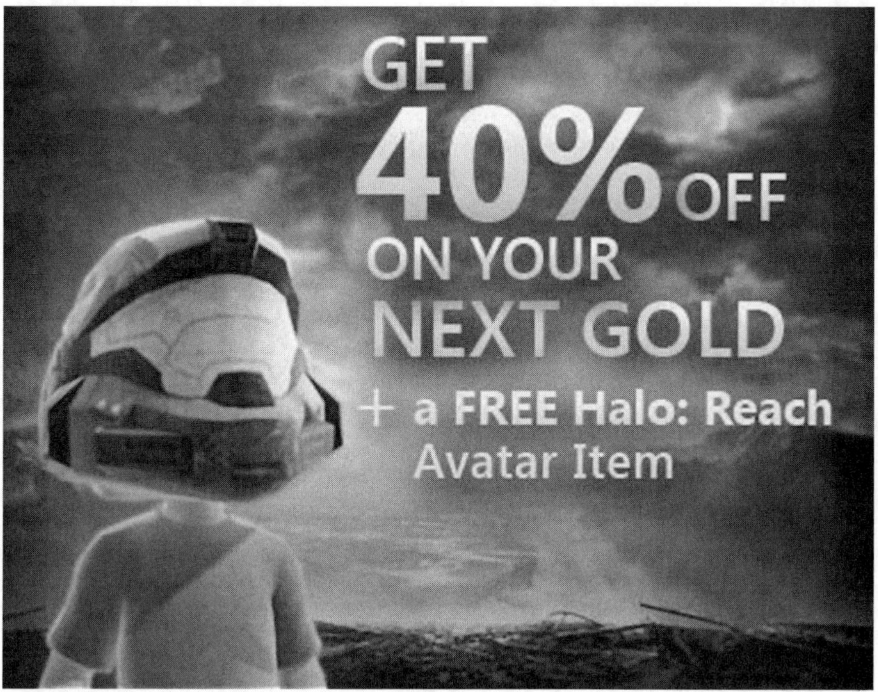

FIGURE 9.15

Another URL extracted from the Facebook search hits. This image was displayed during the configuration of Facebook on the XBOX 360 console.

FIGURE 9.16

Twitter image pulled from the URL extracted in Facebook search hits.

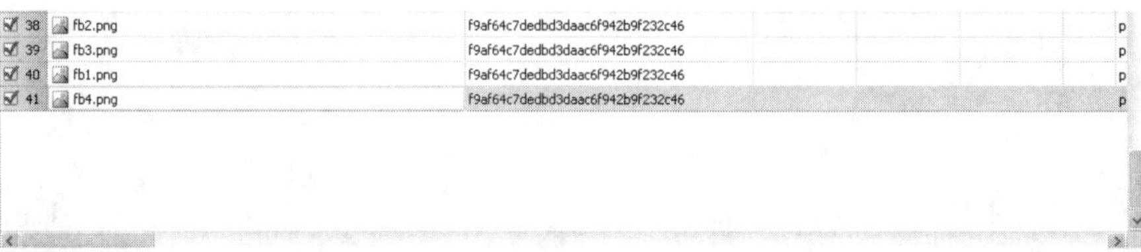

FIGURE 9.17

Hash analysis of the four PNG files that were extracted from the Facebook search hits.

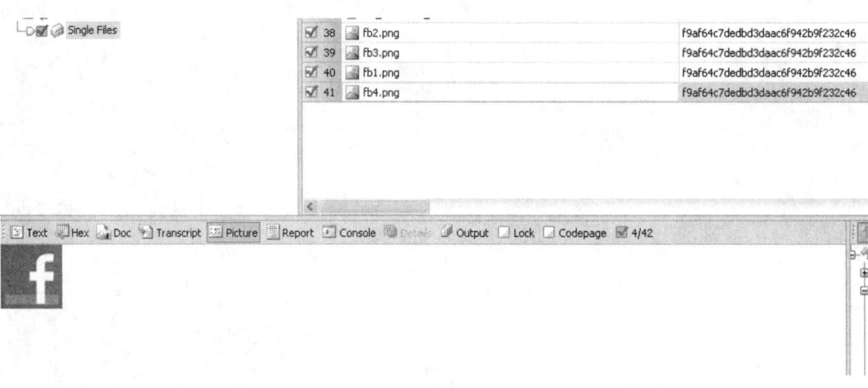

FIGURE 9.18

Hashed PNG files with the resultant image. This image is one of the Facebook icons that is displayed.

and the hash values confirmed that they were all the same image. Figures 9.17 and 9.18 provide screenshots of this information.

The next search term keyword result in the list was number 23. Reviewing this data reveals that it has the "magic" header of LIVE. So this is a file that is signed by Microsoft and delivered over the XBOX Live service. The researchers at www.Free60.org have provided more information on the deconstruction of these types of files. Figures 9.19 and 9.20 provide information from www.free60.org that is a representation of the data contained within these LIVE files.

As mentioned earlier, search result number 23 from the search string provided a LIVE file pertaining to Facebook. This information is displayed here in Figure 9.21. The file can be dissected using the information from www.free60.org, which provides the hex offsets.

Moving through the data in the search hits window, the next hit that provided more information of relevance was hit number 27. Within this data field, the plain text string of facebook.exe is clearly present. Speculation is that this is an entry in the data table, similar to an $MFT record, providing the pointer to the file itself. Examining this entry and the surrounding data, it appears that there is a similar format to the data—there is a string of crypting code previous to the actual entry. This could be a hash value or some other entry that points to the file or a hash of the

XContent Header

Offset	Length	Type	Information
0x0	0x4	unsigned int	Signature Type

The signature type can be one of the following:

Signature Type	Information
"CON "	Signed by a console. Found on many files such as cache files, profiles, saved games.
PIRS	Signed by Microsoft. Found on files delivered by Microsoft through non-Xbox Live means such as system updates.
LIVE	Signed by Microsoft. Found on files delivered over Xbox Live such as items from the Marketplace like themes.

For console signed ("CON ") packages, the Console Security Certificate is used.

For remotely signed (LIVE/PIRS) packages, the following format is used:

Offset	Length	Type	Information
0x4	0x100	bytes	Package Signature
0x104	0x128	bytes	Padding

The Package Signature is generated using the value at 0x32C (Content ID/Header SHA1).

FIGURE 9.19

XContent header information.

XContent Metadata

Offset	Length	Type	Information
0x22C	0x100	license entries (see below)	Licensing Data (used to check package owner)
0x32C	0x14	bytes	Content ID / Header SHA1 Hash
0x340	0x4	unsigned int	Entry ID
0x344	0x4	signed int	Content Type (see below)
0x348	0x4	signed int	Metadata Version (see below)
0x34C	0x8	signed long	Content Size
0x354	0x4	unsigned int	Media ID
0x358	0x4	signed int	Version (system/title updates)
0x35C	0x4	signed int	Base Version (system/title updates)
0x360	0x4	unsigned int	Title ID
0x364	0x1	byte	Platform (xbox/gfwl?)
0x365	0x1	byte	Executable Type
0x366	0x1	byte	Disc Number
0x367	0x1	byte	Disc In Set
0x368	0x4	unsigned int	Save Game ID
0x36C	0x5	bytes	Console ID
0x371	0x8	bytes	Profile ID
0x379	0x1	byte	Volume Descriptor Structure Size (usually 0x24)

FIGURE 9.20

Information pertaining to the metadata that is located within each of these types of files.

file. Figure 9.22 provides a view of EnCase as it interprets the data associated to the facebook.exe plain text.

The last file within the search hits for "Facebook" has another LIVE "magic" header, yet the plain text that was hit upon is "F·a·c·e·b·o·o·k· ·T·i·t·l·e· ·U·p·d·a·t·e· ·#·3." The question was immediately asked, Where were title updates 1 and 2? No search hits returned title updates other than number 3. The drive was again searched for this new keyword, but it was unsuccessful in locating any other title updates. Perhaps this is a version number for the Facebook application, or the tracking of title updates, meaning that this is title update 3, independent of the application that

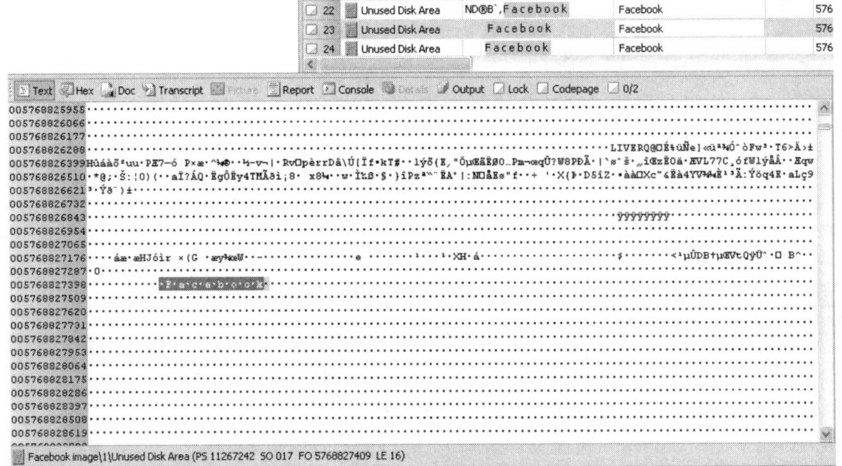

FIGURE 9.21

Encase text representation of search hit 23 showing the LIVE file that was downloaded during the configuration of Facebook on the console.

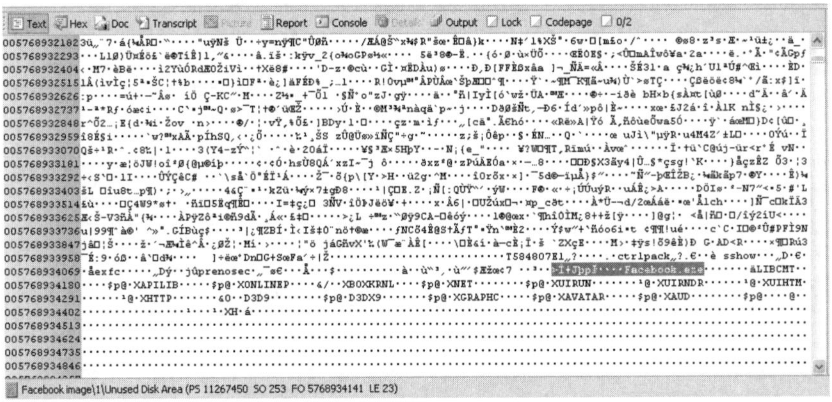

FIGURE 9.22

Facebook executable entry with what appears to be a specific format similar to data table entries for tracking.

was being updated. A portion of the data was copied from the image and run through Strings to determine if there was any other information. The results from the Strings search did not reveal any more relevant data. Figure 9.23 provides a screenshot of the data.

In reviewing the information located with the examination of Facebook artifacts, it was noticed that one of the search hits had an associated date timestamp with it. The format and the date were displayed here: "Date: Sat, 25 Sep 2010 00:58:55 GMT." Examining the data that was physically located around this entry provided another URL

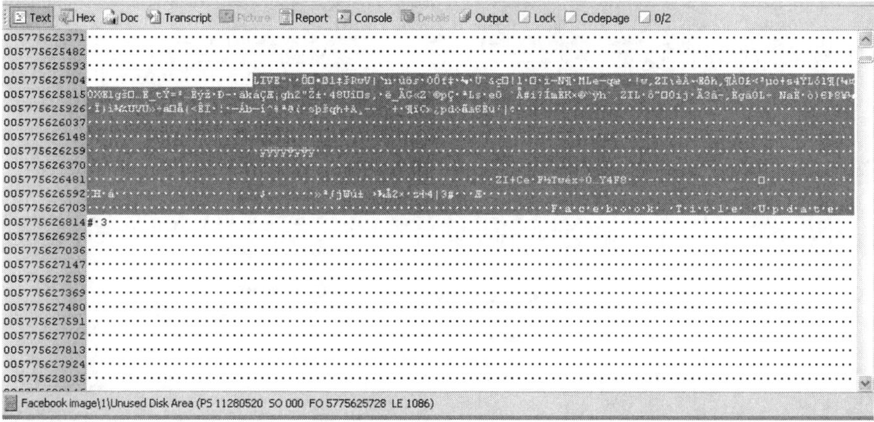

FIGURE 9.23

Facebook title update 3 entry from the search hits.

that was input into the browser to determine the information presented. The URL was http://epix.xbox.com/shaXam/0201/58/2b/582b6503-a72f-4b94-b4a8-7263e7129e9a.XEX?v=1#afplayer.xex. Entering this URL into a browser immediately started a download. It is known that the executables that are on the XBOX consoles have the .xex extension. The file was downloaded and run through Strings as an initial preview of what may be contained within. The Strings search showed that the file had some plain text that was typical of other XEX files that have been presented. Figures 9.24 and 9.25 provide snapshots of the file properties, as well as the Strings results.

Further examination of this file is required, but the file needs to be decompiled. This is a subject of ongoing research. Research has been able to successfully use two applications to decompile XEX files; one is called XexTool, which is a free download, and the other is IDA Pro v5.5. IDA Pro supports most game console files, and the XexTool is used to create a specific file that is required for IDA Pro.

XPLORER360 AND FACEBOOK

Knowing the Xplorer360 is able to interpret the folder structure of the FATX format, it was prudent to upload the drive image into Xplorer360 and determine the changes that were made with the Facebook update that was performed. In order to accomplish this task, the files that were identified in Chapter 8, "Post–System Update Drive Artifacts," would have to be compared with the files that are present on the drive once the Facebook update was performed.

Xplorer360 reveals that there is still no data present in Partition 0. This is perhaps a holding location for reserved space that has been the hallmark of other Microsoft operating systems. Figure 9.26 provides a screenshot showing that Partition 0 remains empty.

It also appears that Partition 2 has not received any changes through the Facebook system update. The files are still reporting the dates as they were documented in

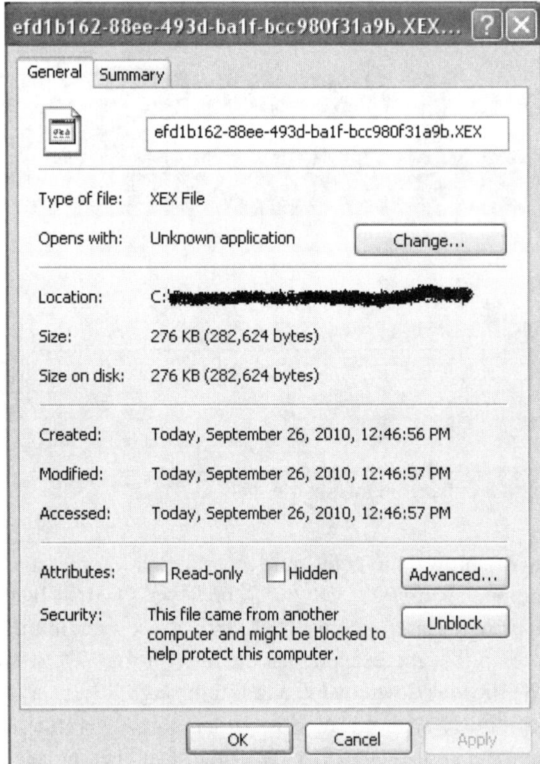

FIGURE 9.24

Properties of the XEX file that was downloaded over the embedded URL.

```
Strings v2.41
Copyright (C) 1999-2009 Mark Russinovich
Sysinternals - www.sysinternals.com

rtp~w!
Is:Ddsa
programg
Primetime.dll
4LIBCMT
XBOXKRNL
XAPILIB
dash.xex
xboxkrnl.exe
xam.xex
xam.xex
bGm[*c
eY+qJ
{@xP3]
wmb\]
[w47.
=Sq/U
```

FIGURE 9.25

Strings results run against the XEX download.

FIGURE 9.26

An empty Partition 0 after the Facebook system update.

Table | Report | Gallery | Timeline | Code

	Name	Hash Value	Hash Set	Hash Category	Entry Modified
1	xbox.XEX	1a4d640b5780ffd021a40355c0496117	Pre FB update	Known	09/18/10 08:29:42PM
2	xbox.XEX	1a4d640b5780ffd021a40355c0496117	Pre FB update	Known	09/26/10 03:14:55PM
3	config.bin	643d1aeadd8bffdcbea887b5ce8cfec0	Pre FB update	Known	09/18/10 08:51:05PM
4	config.bin	643d1aeadd8bffdcbea887b5ce8cfec0	Pre FB update	Known	09/26/10 03:14:55PM
5	Tdbx.db	84b364d6eeb90711f9c3c4ab13607839			09/18/10 10:15:56PM
6	Tdbx.db	84b364d6eeb90711f9c3c4ab13607839			09/26/10 03:16:07PM
7	Xbox Book.xtf	8f5b7cee650f389f1c5c7bb5f70386bb	Pre FB update	Known	09/18/10 10:01:51PM
8	Xbox Book.xtf	8f5b7cee650f389f1c5c7bb5f70386bb	Pre FB update	Known	09/26/10 03:15:21PM
9	xboxdash.xbe	a82025a7cd2f94311757f66263157ad5	Pre FB update	Known	09/18/10 09:32:15PM
10	xboxdash.xbe	a82025a7cd2f94311757f66263157ad5	Pre FB update	Known	09/26/10 03:15:06PM
11	xonlinedash.xbe	a82025a7cd2f94311757f66263157ad5	Pre FB update	Known	09/18/10 09:52:01PM
12	xonlinedash.xbe	a82025a7cd2f94311757f66263157ad5	Pre FB update	Known	09/26/10 03:15:36PM
13	xbox.xtf	de4a26c39de8001b95c749f8d3d22128	Pre FB update	Known	09/18/10 10:01:51PM
14	xbox.xtf	de4a26c39de8001b95c749f8d3d22128	Pre FB update	Known	09/26/10 03:15:21PM
15	xefu.XEX	f04a57a9f51ed79be301e0e808d5280b	Pre FB update	Known	09/18/10 08:29:32PM
16	xefu.XEX	f04a57a9f51ed79be301e0e808d5280b	Pre FB update	Known	09/26/10 03:14:55PM

FIGURE 9.27

Results of the comparative hash analysis of the files located within Partition 2. The TDBX.db files were not included in the hash set; therefore, the Category was not set. The dates show the two dates, pre and post Facebook system updates.

Chapter 8, "Post–System Update Drive Artifacts." To verify that the files did not change, they were extracted using the same process as discussed earlier and imported into EnCase for a comparative hash analysis. The files that were previously extracted from Partition 2 were imported into EnCase and hashed. Next, a hash set was created with these files for comparative analysis (see Figure 9.27). An error in the hash creation was that the TDBX.db file was not imported before making the hash set. The set could have been rebuilt including this file, but it was decided to show that there are mistakes that can and do happen and they can be explained away. In any event, the TDBX.db file from before the Facebook update and after the Facebook update was imported into EnCase and the comparison was completed. All of the files reported the same hash value indicating that the files had not changed due to this system update for Facebook. Figure 9.28 shows the results of the comparative hash analysis.

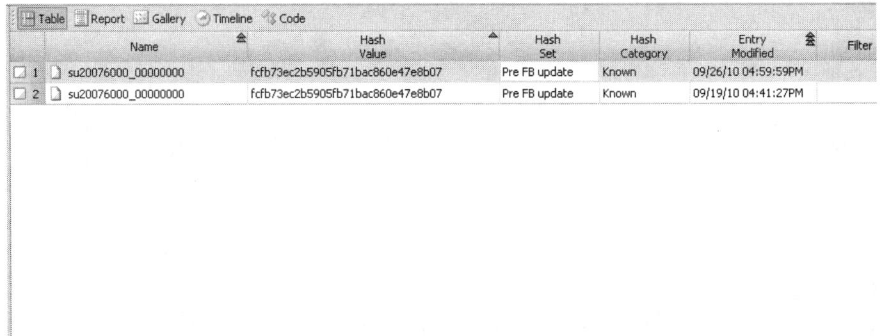

	Name	Hash Value	Hash Set	Hash Category	Entry Modified	Filter
1	su20076000_00000000	fcfb73ec2b5905fb71bac860e47e8b07	Pre FB update	Known	09/26/10 04:59:59PM	
2	su20076000_00000000	fcfb73ec2b5905fb71bac860e47e8b07	Pre FB update	Known	09/19/10 04:41:27PM	

FIGURE 9.28

Comparison of the pre– and post–system update files, note there is no change in the hash value.

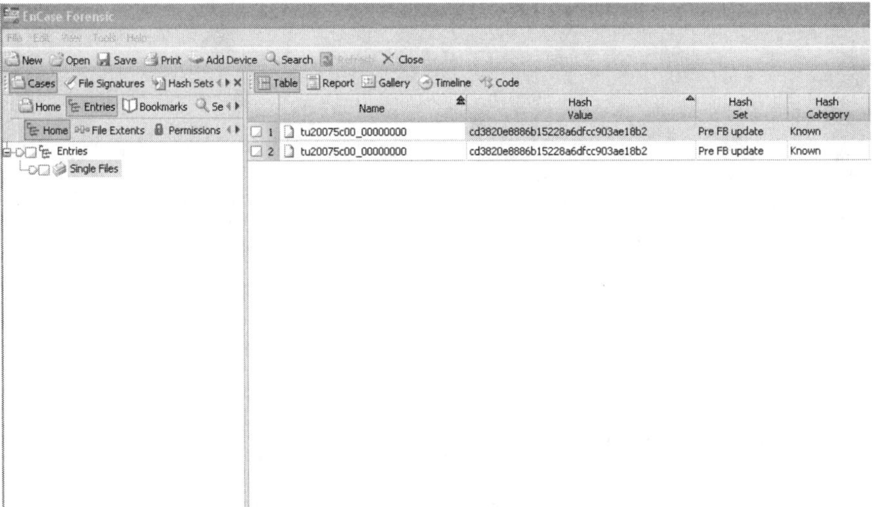

	Name	Hash Value	Hash Set	Hash Category
1	tu20075c00_00000000	cd3820e8886b15228a6dfcc903ae18b2	Pre FB update	Known
2	tu20075c00_00000000	cd3820e8886b15228a6dfcc903ae18b2	Pre FB update	Known

FIGURE 9.29

Comparison of the title update file pre and post Facebook update, note there is no change in the hash value.

The next sets of files for comparison were the system update files and the title update files. Again, these files reported the same dates as previously documented. Again, they were imported into EnCase for hash comparison, and again, there was no change in the hash value, as shown in Figures 9.28 and 9.29.

In addition to the system update and title update files, there is also the mindex file located within Partition 3. Once again, this file showed the original date documented in Chapter 8, "Post–System Update Drive Artifacts," so it was extracted from the image, imported into EnCase, and a hash analysis was conducted. The hashes matched, so the Facebook update did not alter this file, as depicted in Figure 9.30.

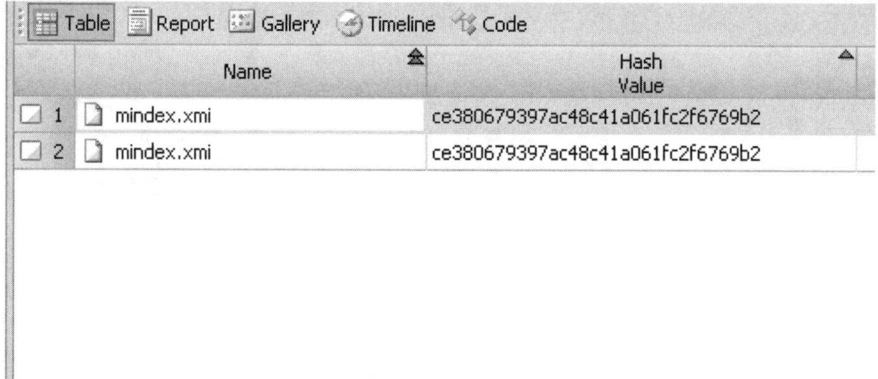

FIGURE 9.30

Hash analysis of the mindex.Xmi file showing that there was no change made to this file because of the Facebook update.

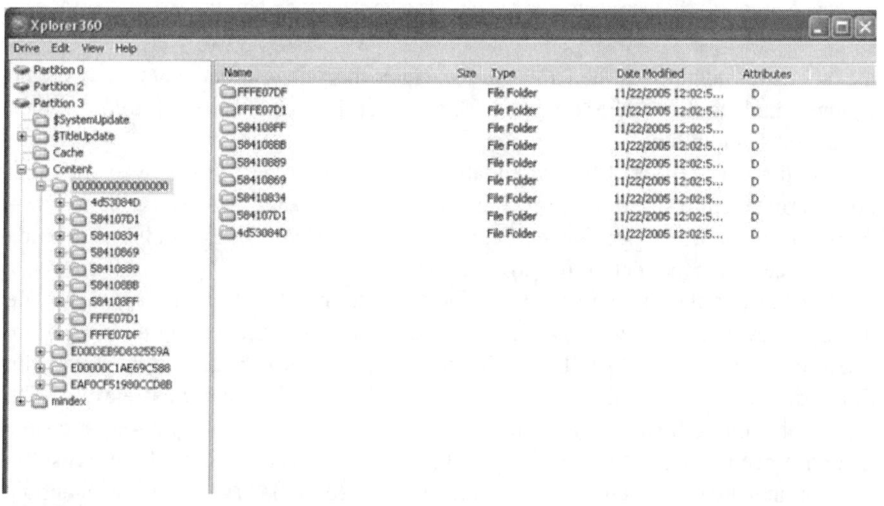

FIGURE 9.31

Content folder with the first subfolder containing nine files.

There were two folders that contained the most number of files for examination: the Cache folder and the Content folder. A manual review of each of these files reveals that the Cache folder holds the highest number of additional files since the Facebook update. Because the Cache folder contains the most information, it will be examined last. The Content folder only has one change that was made to it that needs to be reviewed.

The first subfolder under the main Content folder was originally populated by nine folders, as displayed in Figure 9.31. However, after the Facebook system update, there are 10 folders that now populate the Content folder, as in Figure 9.32. All of

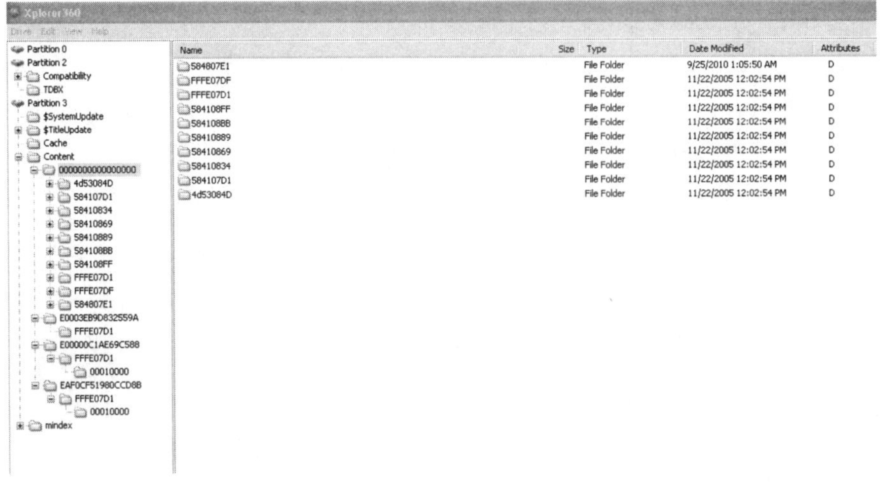

FIGURE 9.32

Content folder with the newly created file after the Facebook system update.

the other subfolders contained a single file. Hash analysis revealed that there were no changes made to these other nine files. The only addition was the tenth folder, which contained a single file.

The file was extracted for examination as with the other files. However, it was noticed that the file size of this new file was roughly the same size as the file that was reported for the download for the Facebook update. Figures 9.33 and 9.34 provide some screenshots that detail this observation.

The file was then imported into EnCase for examination. Upon review, this file had been reviewed earlier as part of the search hits using Facebook as a search term. The file has the "magic" LIVE header, but now the file size is known, so it was run through Strings to determine if there was any information that was relevant. The results of running Strings against this file provided some of the same search results that have been seen in other files. Figure 9.35 provides a screenshot of these results.

The final area in which there were new files added to the hard drive was under the Cache folder. This is probably the area that has the most individual additions through the Facebook configuration. The number of files that are present in this folder now has increased considerably. To determine the new files from the files that were resident previous to the Facebook download, the files were extracted, imported into EnCase, and a hash analysis was once again conducted. The pre-Facebook update Cache file contained 13 files in total. Once the Facebook download was performed and the Cache folder reviewed, there were a total of 24 files, so nine new files were created. The original 13 files are shown in Figure 9.36, and the additions are shown in Figure 9.37.

Creating the hash set for comparison revealed that only four of the files remained the same after the update. The four files that remained the same included both GT, or Gamertag files, the SU, or system update file, and one of the DA files, perhaps identity files for the user and console. The changes that were made were to operational files.

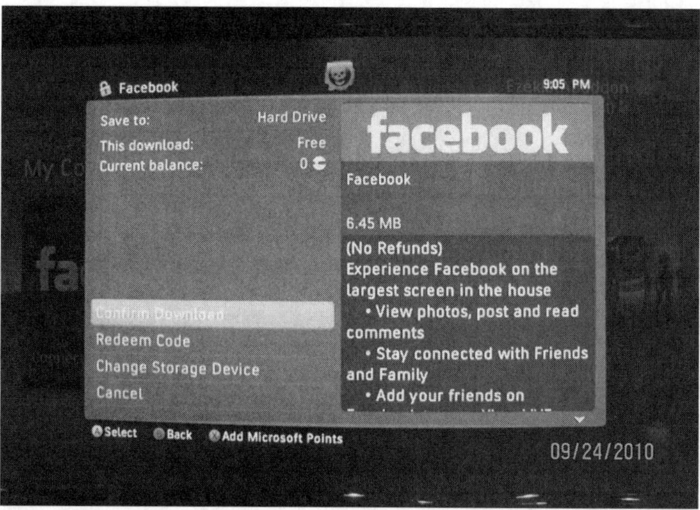

FIGURE 9.33

The download confirmation for the Facebook application.

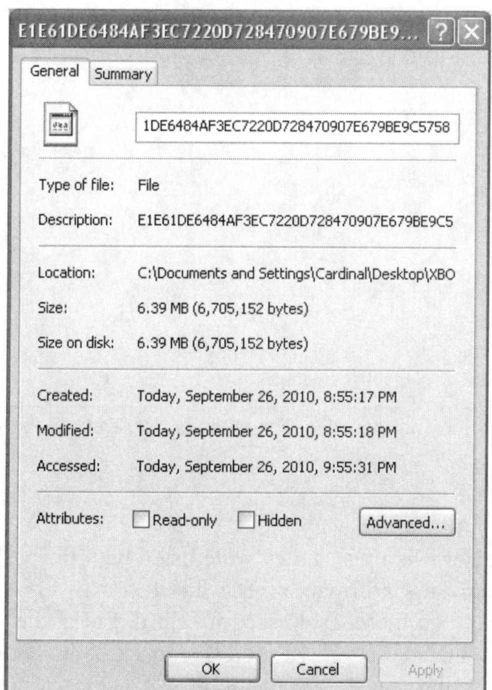

FIGURE 9.34

File properties as they are reported using Windows. Note the file size and compare it with the file size in Figure 9.32.

```
Strings v2.41
Copyright (C) 1999-2009 Mark Russinovich
Sysinternals - www.sysinternals.com

LIVERQ@
Facebook
Microsoft
Facebook
tEXtSoftware
Adobe ImageReadyq
tEXtSoftware
Adobe ImageReadyq
=k(;y^u
default.xex
T584807E1
ctrlpack
prenosec
Facebook.exe
XAPILIB
XONLINEP
XBOXKRNL
XUIRNDR
XGRAPHC
XAVATAR
xam.xex
xboxkrnl.exe
xam.xex
Hw.=\v,7
3b",v^-x
9>(%\qI-
FzzK:K:9
```

FIGURE 9.35

Strings results against the Facebook file. Note the plain text results at the beginning of the list and the .xex and .exe file names.

Beginning to review the files as they were listed with the hash analysis, several files contained interesting information. The first file, AT_1B5A1UK_0000000000002.0000000000000, had the console security certificate at the start of the file. In addition, the file contained a PNG within it. Figures 9.38 and 9.39 show this information. This icon appears on the Facebook profile of one of the "friends" whose Facebook profile was reviewed during this process.

The next file was again labeled with the AT_ format, and it had a PNG file embedded. The image file was carved, and it is presented in Figure 9.40.

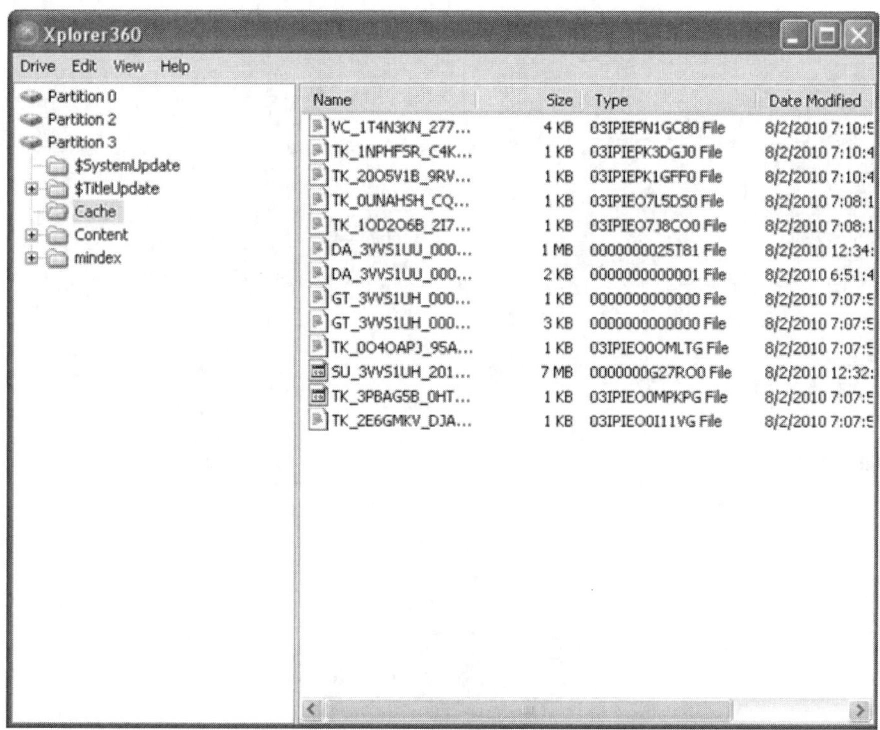

FIGURE 9.36

Pre-Facebook Cache folder showing the original 13 files.

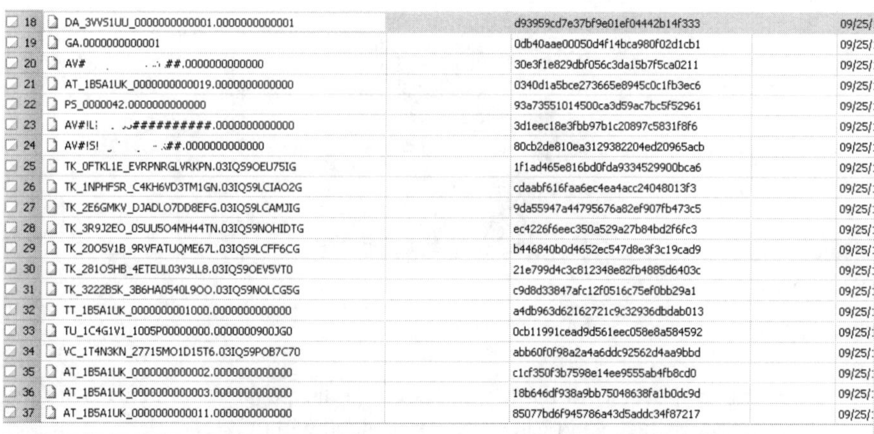

FIGURE 9.37

Cache files that are not part of the original file set are displayed within this folder. The AV files indicate Gamertag files, so the individual Gamertags have been sanitized.

FIGURE 9.38

Depiction of the AT file with the console security certificate.

FIGURE 9.39

Image carved from the AT_1B5A1UK_0000000000002.0000000000000 file.

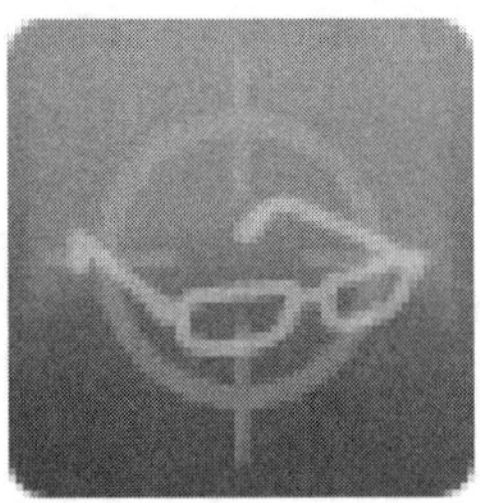

FIGURE 9.40

Image carved from the second AT_ file.

Continuing to move down the list, the next file once again was signed with the console security certificate and had a PNG embedded within it.

Continuing to review the files, it became clear that there were many files associated to the "friend" on the Facebook portal whose page was reviewed on the console's Facebook portal. The AT, or attribute, files were small images that were displayed on the profile page, as shown in Figures 9.42 and 9.43.

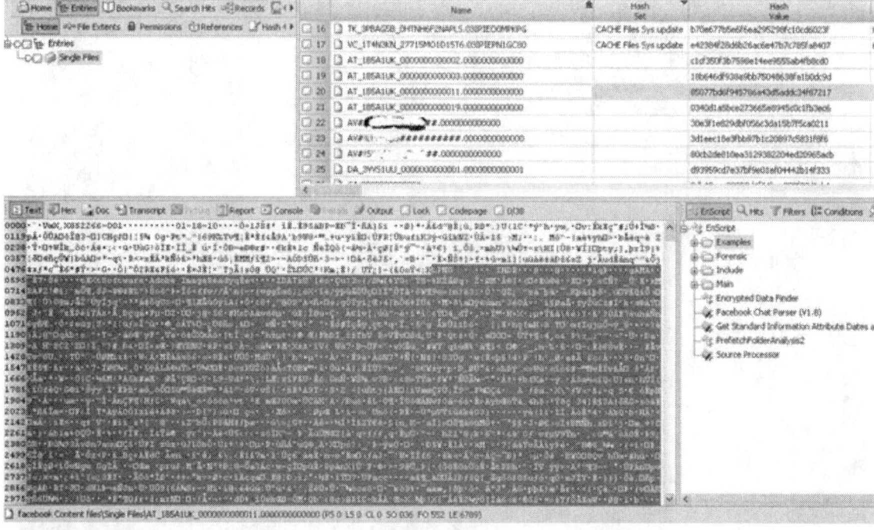

FIGURE 9.41

EnCase image of the AT_ file. Again the blank areas are sanitized because of specific Gamertags being listed in plain text.

FIGURE 9.42

PNG carved from the AT file detailed in Figure 9.41.

The files with the preceding letters of AV# are the Facebook gamer profiles that are displayed. In this case, there were a few that were listed that were clearly some of the friends who were connected through Facebook over the console. Each one of these files has the console security certificate associated to it.

Deciphering the information within these files is a matter of ongoing research. However, a general sense of the files is listed below:

- **AT files:** Associated to Facebook profiles that have been viewed over the console, perhaps "attribute" files.
- **AV files:** Facebook and Gamertag names listed in plain text.
- **DA:** Unsure of the nature of this file, Strings provided no hits and research continues.

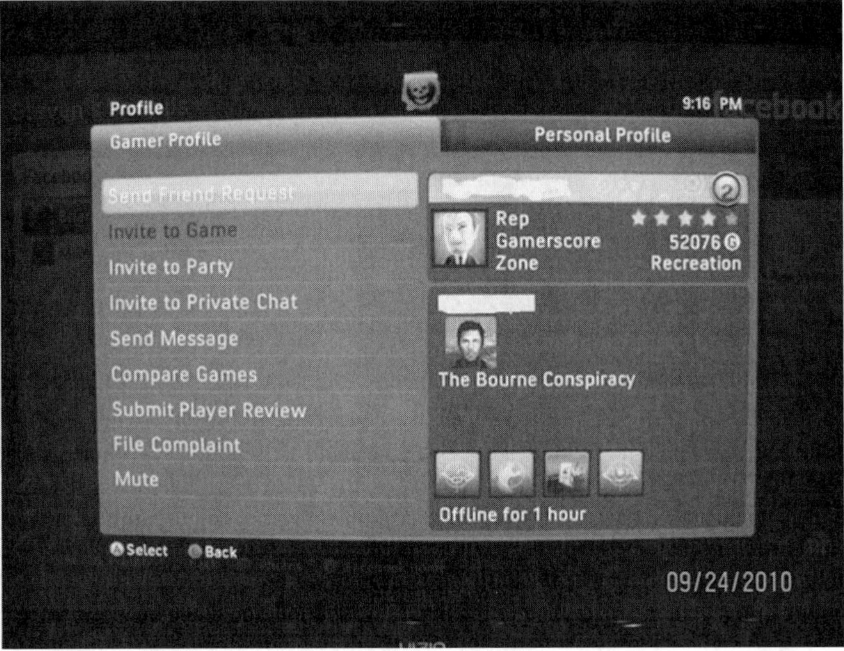

FIGURE 9.43

The images in the lower right-hand corner are the PNGs that were carved and detailed in the preceding figures.

- **GA:** Gamer/Facebook profile name is listed at the end of this file. It could be the Gamertag information regarding rating (gamer accomplishments).
- **PS file:** Unknown, the file provides little in the way of data. Below is all the data:
  - "K–□É÷Sˆ·Æ¤Òéýd·×CBYKh·ôÎ6ÌX/AíÅù¯_|·a®©Uÿ²Á}&·–·¿I§+@R]DV-ªôà%·Š¡ô□Þk·çC€òV?…µË·ûá ø(yîdÿœD"¥"
- **TK files:** Again, unsure what these files are at this point. However, each file starts with the "magic" header of PROD, which be a reference to product; perhaps these are security token files.
- **TT file:** This file has an embedded PNG file that is once again associated to the Gamertag/Facebook profile that has navigated over the portal.
- **VC file:** Unclear as to the purpose of this file.

Many of these new files are specific to the Facebook profile that was navigated when exploring the portal. More research and perhaps some reverse engineering might be required in order to make more sense of these files. Some of these files provide plain text indicators of their function, others do not. In any event, there are some clues here that will assist an examiner when presented with a console for examination. Knowing the format in which the Facebook profiles are stored on the XBOX 360 console may assist in the link analysis that is sure to be performed.

SUMMARY

A great deal of information has been covered within this chapter. Game consoles have evolved to the point where on a network they are indistinguishable from personal computers. The functionality mirrors the functions that are available to an end user on any other network device, with Web surfing and social networking available at the touch of a few buttons. In order for these features to be taken advantage of the XBOX 360, a user must pay for their subscription, which can be accomplished through a prepaid card or by entering a credit card number. This number or code does not appear to be resident on the digital storage media that is required for a user to be networked over the console. Once the user is connected with the Live service with a Gold account, they can connect to their friends through a stripped version of the number one social networking site, Facebook. To connect to Facebook, the user must accept a download that populates the drive with many artifacts. As the end user navigates through the Facebook portal over the console, several artifacts get populated to the digital storage media. The format of these files appears to be a standard format and provides a potential list of the Facebook friends that may have been connected while the console was in use.

Reference

[1] http://epix.xbox.com/shaXam/0201/27/4c/274c7e4f-6a43-4c6c-911d-1c0f0b1fb343.jpg

CHAPTER

Game Play

10

INFORMATION IN THIS CHAPTER

- Gaming
- Game artifacts
- Xplorer360 and game artifacts
- Cache folder analysis
- XBOX Live friends
- Other cache files
- Content folder changes

GAMING

This research began back in 2006 from a case that was referred to a previous employer that involved a suspect who had reportedly made initial contact with his victim while playing an online game using the XBOX Live service. The XBOX Live service provides a portal for communication that goes beyond simple game play. From the social networking features that were discussed earlier to the online gaming portal, this console is designed to connect people to chat, stream video, play games, and simply connect to one another. The games of today are a far cry from the Atari 2600 and Coleco Vision consoles that were staples of the first generation gamers. Modern games have the ability to stream audio and video to each networked player for a much more enhanced gaming experience.

Turning to the gaming functionality of the console brought several challenges that had to be overcome. First, there was a need to learn the functionality of the modern games, how to connect to the network, how to engage other gamers, how to send friend requests, and many other features. The features on the console have changed with the integration and updating of the dashboard for the NXE. To play a game, an end user simply inserts the game CD and logs into his or her profile or Live account. If there is a Live account, the user logs into that account and is then able to play the game as a standalone game, or if the feature is supported by the game, they are able to connect and play online against or with other players. To play with or against other online players, a required download is pushed to the system. These downloads could be a variety of things, but generally they include what is called a system update, consisting of map packs, weapons, characters, and so on. If a gamer plays a game with another player, in which for some reason a connection was made, a friend request can be sent which will link the two players, notifying one another if they are online, how long they have been offline, what game they played last, and a host of other information.

Part of this online gaming experience includes what is called true skill matching by Microsoft. This is an attempt to match players against one another who have roughly the same skill set so as to ensure that the gaming experience is something that will get the end users coming back for more as opposed to being totally outclassed. This is similar to the way in which sports teams, during try outs, attempt to match players of similar skill to a team. These true skill attributes are tracked and linked to the Gamertag, in part, through accomplishments that have been earned during the local game play by the end user. Most modern games include games that are action, adventure, shooters, or racing games. Throughout each of these games, as a user progresses, he or she achieves goals and unlocks other features of each game. These new features could include new cars, weapons, levels, and a wide variety of other items or maps. It is these accomplishments that are linked to the Gamertag and are used in the calculation of the true skill level.

So, you might be asking yourself why the lengthy descriptions of modern game play on the XBOX Live service. Well, the truth of the matter is that almost all of these games, either networked or local, leave artifacts on the storage media, including some of the descriptors and narratives that are presented within the game play, such as text that would be displayed to the gamer. The need to distinguish what is the information from the game manufacturer and what is the information that may be pushed to a console by a suspect is vital. An examiner could be reading what looks like a manifesto, and when more research is conducted, it turns out to be text located within the game.

The need to play a game, save the game at different check points, and experience the gaming environment was required in order to determine the artifacts that would be left on the hard drive by these actions. In order to progress, a game was inserted into the console and game play commenced. The game itself was from Bethesda Softworks and is called Fallout 3. While playing the game, there were three different locations within the game that were save points. The console was logged in through the XBOX Live gamer profile, and the game was started.

Along with gaming and the save points, a friend request was sent to a Facebook friend who also has an XBOX Live account, and a video that is associated with the Fallout 3 game was downloaded. All these steps were taken to generate artifacts to determine what changes were being made to the hard drive. A review of the drive after these steps is what follows.

The image was loaded into EnCase and several searches were conducted. One of the first keywords was the name of the game that had been played, Fallout 3. It is necessary to mention that the reason the research progressed as it did was that no forensic application would interpret the file structure. Every tool, EnCase, X-Ways, and FTK, interpreted the data as unallocated space, forcing keyword searches and data carving. In the future, perhaps, Microsoft will release a hash set for a Gold Build for the XBOX 360. The character name that was input into the game created another keyword; the name was "templar." There were three save points that were created, and there was a video trailer downloaded that pertained to the game as well.

GAME ARTIFACTS

The disk was imaged and a new case was started within EnCase. The keywords mentioned above were entered and a search was conducted. Reviewing the results showed that there were more than 2700 hits for the Fallout game. Most of these hits were directly related to text that was located as direction or narrative within the game. The game itself is a role playing game that includes many memos, bulletins, and directions that are displayed to the gamer throughout the game play. Figure 10.1 provides a screenshot depicting some of the text.

Continuing to review the search hit, there were several locations that showed paths to some audio files. Keep in mind that these games are full of multimedia files, including video and audio that is called on at different times throughout the game play. Research into the game files that are associated with Fallout 3 revealed a Web site that lists the information. The Web site www.file-extensions.org/fallout-3-file-extensions actually lists the file extensions that are used with this particular video game. Figure 10.2 shows a screenshot of the list that is provided on the file extensions Web site. Figure 10.3 shows the EnCase screenshot of the associated file.

Continuing to explore the Web site for more information about this file type revealed that there was an associated application that claims to be able to open a wide variety of files that are associated with the file specified in the data path. Navigation

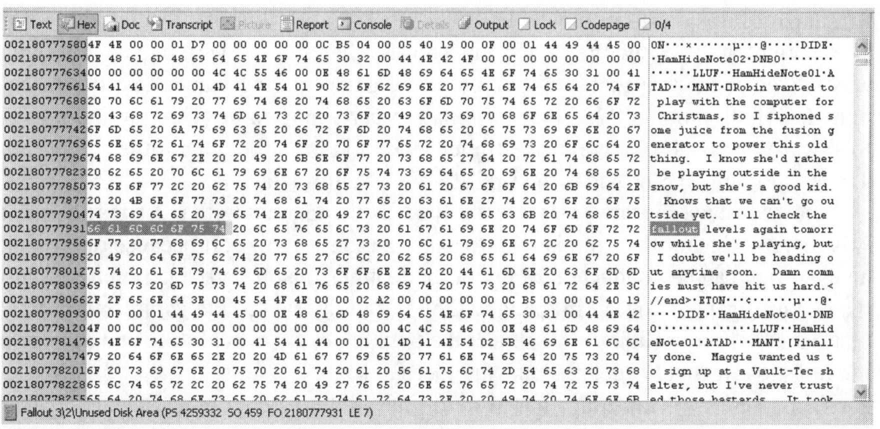

FIGURE 10.1

EnCase "Fallout" search term hit. Note the plain text on the right-hand side, which is specific to the game itself.

FIGURE 10.2

URL showing the files that are associated with the Fallout 3 video game.

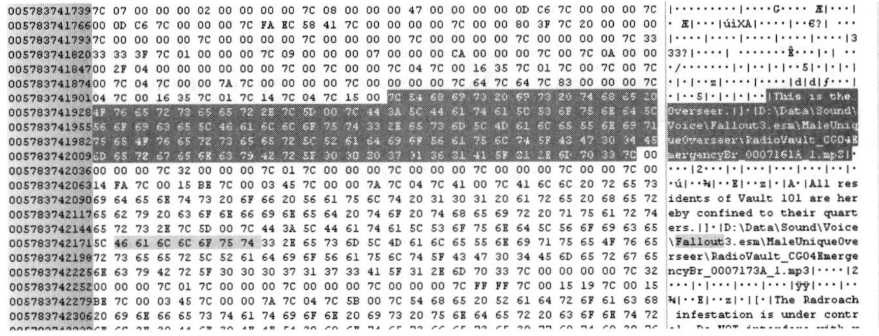

FIGURE 10.3

Path to the media file that is associated to game play audio.

to this application download link is provided through a few subpages, but is located at www.file-extensions.org/esm-file-extension. The name of the application is XnView and is available through an external Web site at www.xnview.com/en/index.html. There is a long list of files that XnView claims to be able to interpret and open; this list, in part, is displayed in Figure 10.4.

Continuing to review the search hits showed that almost every one of these hits was related to the text that is displayed to the gamer during game play. It was not until search hit number 2728 that information pertaining to the video trailer download was located. The name of the trailer video file is "Fallout 3 Mother Ship Zeta Trailer"; Figure 10.5 provides the EnCase view of this data.

Another keyword that was searched for was the Gamertag that a friend request was sent to. This information is vital to examinations of this sort because of the link analysis that can be conducted. Many of the features that are provided innocently to the end user gamers to stay in touch with their online friends and game could easily be turned to more malicious intent, and the tracking could provide one end user with the tools to effectively "cyber stalk" another gamer.

There were two Gamertags that were displayed during the online interaction over the console. These Gamertags were entered into the search terms, and a keyword search was conducted. Remember that these Gamertags can be tracked if the appropriate documents are submitted to Microsoft. In any event, the Gamertags were hit upon through the

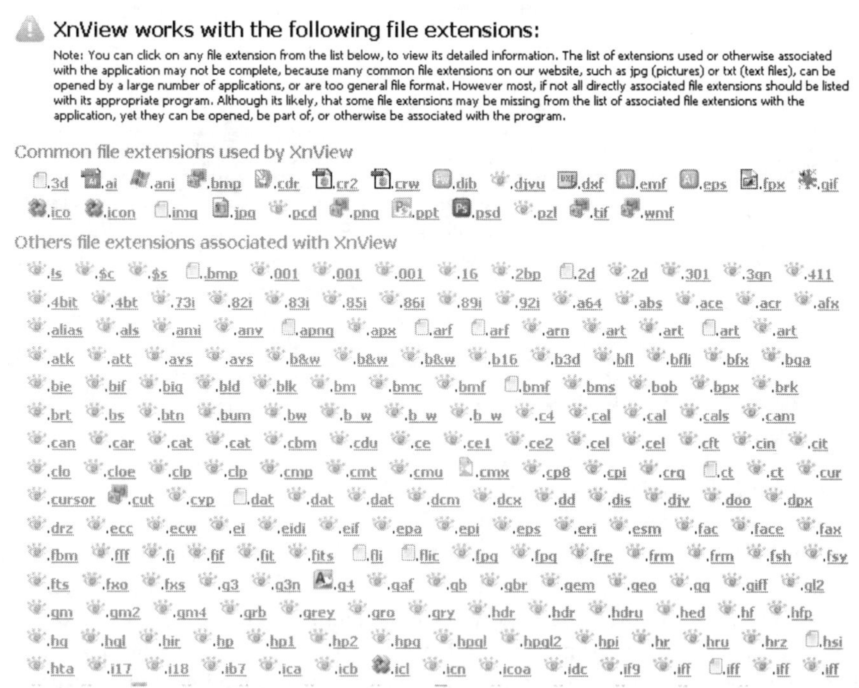

FIGURE 10.4

Partial list of files that XnView claims to be able to interpret.

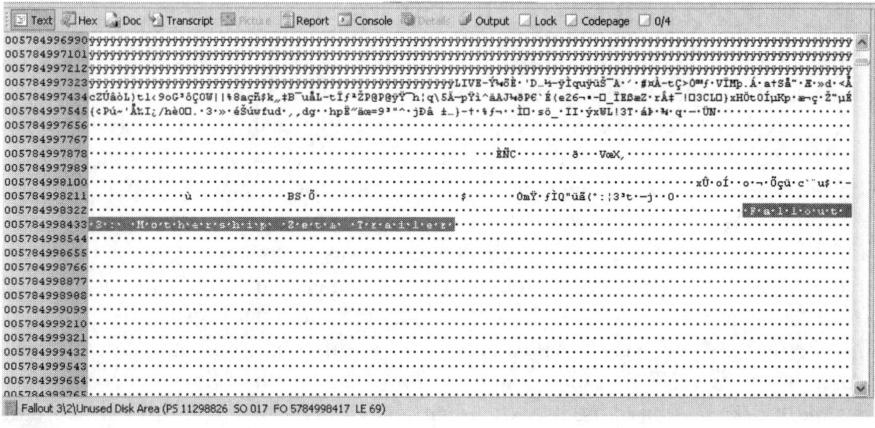

FIGURE 10.5

Video trailer artifact.

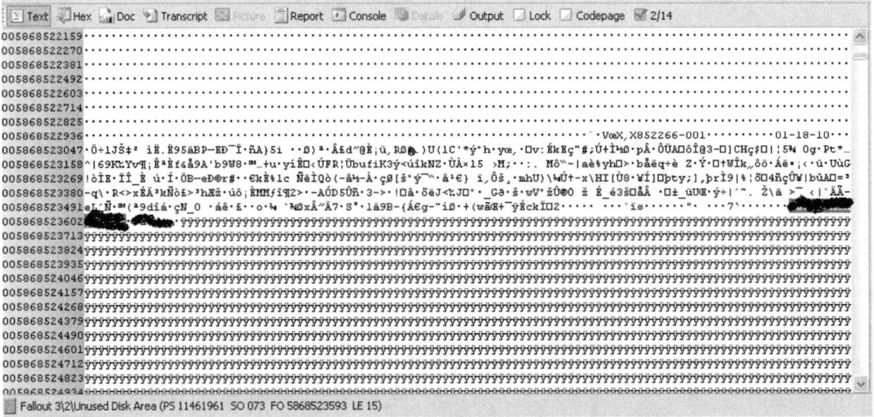

FIGURE 10.6

Gamertag search hit location. Note that the header is the console security certificate.

keyword search. This appears to be the area of the drive that is reserved for the gamers' friends as the information gets populated. The results are displayed in Figure 10.6.

Without knowing the specific keywords pertaining to the game of choice or a particular download, an examiner may have a difficult time parsing through all the data. The keywords can come from a variety of sources, including game boxes that are stored at a victim or suspect's house, similar to the software boxes that can be located around a suspect's computer system. Additional sources could include names of games or Gamertags that are provided through various means such as other investigators, social networking, and so on.

XPLORER360 AND GAME ARTIFACTS

Turning back to the Xplorer360 application to determine if changes have been made to the drive provided some interesting information. Once again, Partition 0 remained empty. Figure 10.7 provides a screenshot documenting that the partition is still empty.

Moving through the directory structure displayed with Xplorer360 shows that there were no date changes to the file or directories that are displayed under Partition 2. The index file was extracted and imported back into EnCase for hash analysis as detailed in the previous chapter; there was no change to the file. It is speculation, but there is good research that supports that each hard drive that is released from the manufacturer, Microsoft, will have an index file that lists the default items that are on the drive. Recall that each release has different information, or "extras," stored on the drive. This could be an indicator of the length of time that console has been in the possession of the user or perhaps assist in narrowing down a time frame for purchasing. The files that are associated to Partition 2 were all extracted as previously detailed and a hash analysis was conducted, and these files did not change through the course of game play. Figure 10.8 provides a snapshot of this information.

The next two files to be examined to determine if there was any change resulting from this game play were the system update and title update. Each was extracted and pulled into EnCase for hash analysis. Once again, there was no change to either of these file's hash values, indicating that there was no change to the files because of this game play. Figure 10.9 provides a screenshot of the hash values.

The next file that was examined was the mindex.xmi file under the Mindex folder. Once again, the process of extraction and comparison was conducted and the results

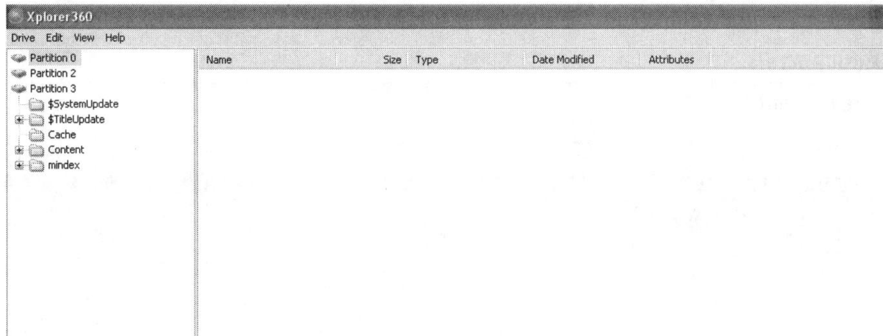

FIGURE 10.7

Yet again, an empty partition 0.

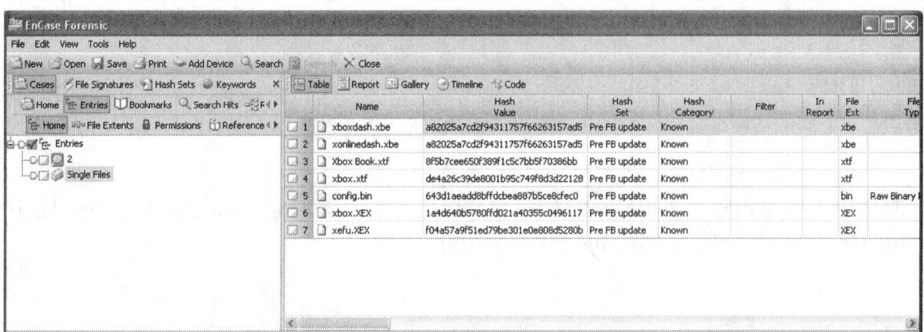

FIGURE 10.8

Hash analysis of partition 2 files detailing that game play does not change these files.

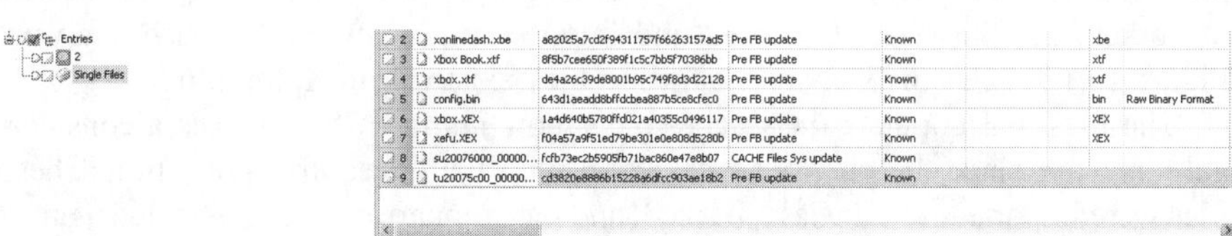

FIGURE 10.9

Hash analysis of the system update and title update files showing they were not altered due to game play.

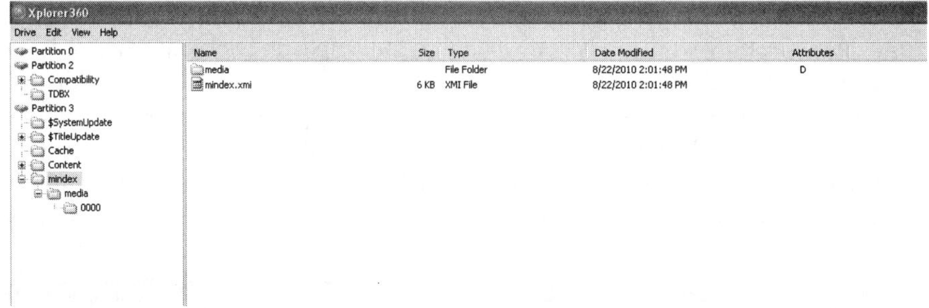

FIGURE 10.10

Directory structure showing the mindex.xmi file.

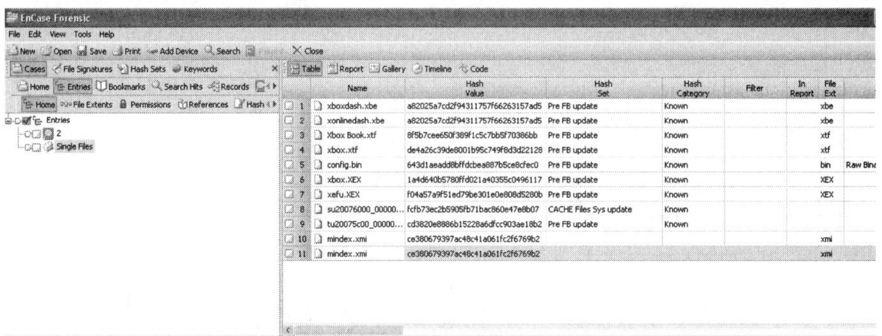

FIGURE 10.11

Hash analysis showing that the mindex.xmi file was not altered by the gaming process.

again showed that the file was not altered by the gaming process. Figures 10.10 and 10.11 provide views of this information.

CACHE FOLDER ANALYSIS

The Cache folder had what appear to be significant changes made to it by the game play. The file dates had changed and as such, sticking with the process that showed it worked, the files were extracted and imported into EnCase for hash analysis. Figure 10.12 shows the view of the files as they exist within Xplorer360.

The files that populate the Cache folder now number 75, which is a considerable increase since the previous interaction with the Facebook application. These files were imported into EnCase, hashed, and the comparison was conducted against the hash set that was created after the Facebook update was added to the system. The files themselves retained the naming convention that was observed in previous examinations of this folder and the resultant files. However, the more the files were examined, the more the information began to make sense. For instance, the files that

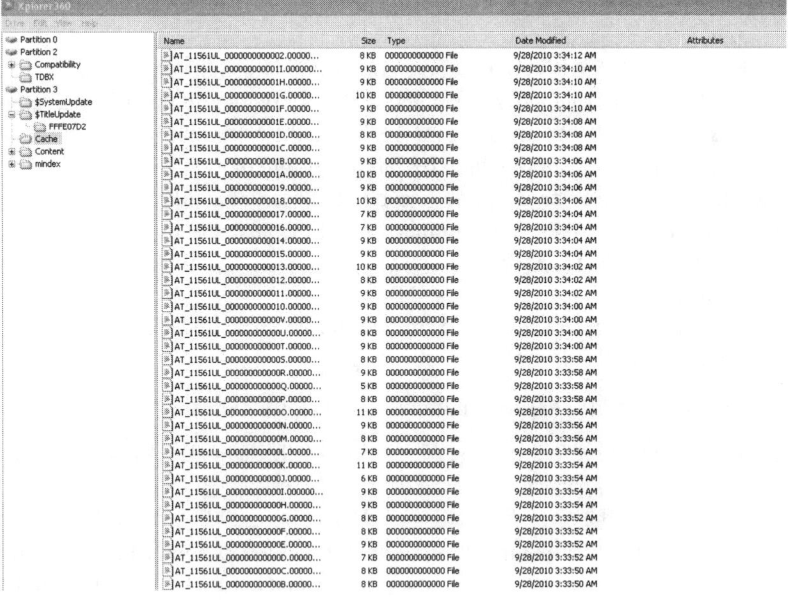

FIGURE 10.12

Depiction of the new files within the Cache folder after game play.

began with the header AV#!L! appeared to be the file format for the Gamertags of other users. Recall that these are unique identifiers that have records associated to them and the records can be retrieved similar to requesting e-mail information from Microsoft. Because of the limited number of "friends" (other XBOX Live gamers) that this sample represents, more research is required to definitively state that the AV#!L! is the header for Gamertags. So the syntax of these files is as follows:

- AV#!L! [*Gamertag*]

This information can be used to subpoena records from Microsoft and gain knowledge of the account activity. Because the Gamertag is a unique identifier, its presence may show direct participation in an event and could be grounds for obtaining a warrant. This information is akin to using an e-mail address or IP address as the basis for a warrant. However, because the XBOX console is a multiuser device, placing the fingers on the controller, or keyboard, is a challenge that is currently faced by investigators. It is incumbent on the high-tech investigator to abide by their policies and procedures and when in doubt, ask the controlling legal authority the best way in which to proceed. Some information that can be retrieved includes log-on IP addresses and dates and times. Several home burglaries in which XBOX 360 consoles have been stolen have been solved by tech savvy investigators obtaining the Gamertag sign in records from Microsoft and tracking the information to an ISP, then obtaining the records from the ISP based on the information from Microsoft and leading finally to the home of the perpetrator.

Figure 10.13 shows the files as they are depicted in EnCase with their associated hash values.

Of the new files that populated the Cache folder for the limited game play that occurred, 72 of the files had a hash value that did not belong to the hash set, identifying them as part of the pregame play image. Thus, the examination of these files was prudent, and that is the way in which research continued.

The files that were to be examined needed to be organized in some way to bring order and make it easier for an examiner to sort through the information. The best method for this organization was through the file names, specifically through the first few letters of each file.

The first file classification to be examined started with the letters AT. The naming convention of these files follows the following syntax:

- AT_11561UL_000000000000(numbers).000000000000

However, there were other files that started with the same AT, but the naming convention included other values.

Examination of the first file, AT_11561UL_00000000000A.000000000000, showed that the file once again was signed with the console security certificate and included a PNG file that was carved out of the file. This PNG file was found to be an icon that was displayed during game play, so the relevance of the file information

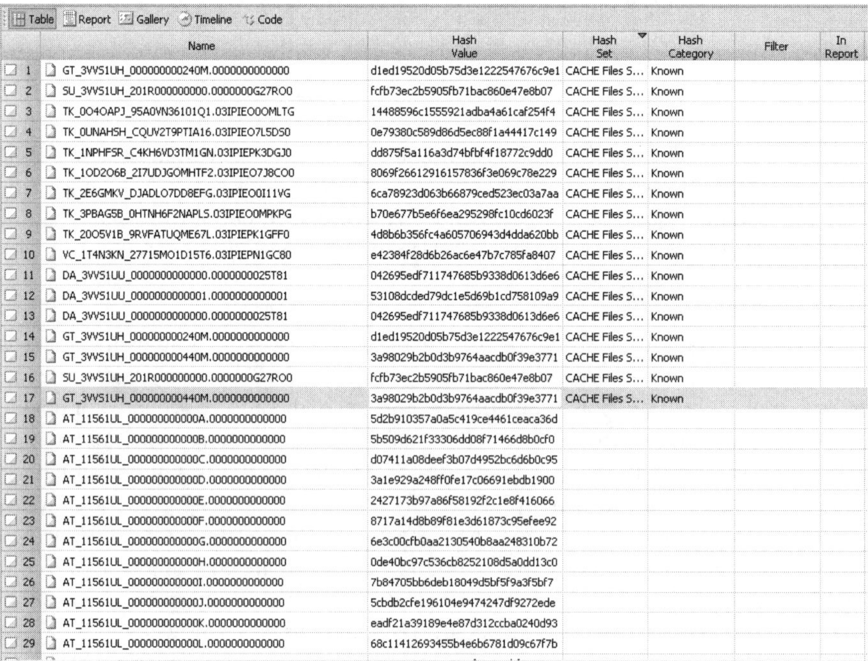
Table Report Gallery Timeline Code

	Name	Hash Value	Hash Set	Hash Category	Filter	In Report
1	GT_3VVS1UH_00000000240M.000000000000	d1ed19520d05b75d3e1222547676c9e1	CACHE Files S...	Known		
2	SU_3VVS1UH_201R00000000.0000000G27RO0	fcfb73ec2b5905fb71bac860e47e8b07	CACHE Files S...	Known		
3	TK_0O4OAPJ_95A0VN36101Q1.03IPIEO0OMLTG	14488596c1555921adba4a61caf254f4	CACHE Files S...	Known		
4	TK_0UNAHSH_CQUV2T9PTIA16.03IPIEO7L5DS0	0e79380c589d86d5ec88f1a44417c149	CACHE Files S...	Known		
5	TK_1NPHFSR_C4KH6VD3TM1GN.03IPIEPK3DGJ0	dd875f5a116a3d74bfbf4f18772c9dd0	CACHE Files S...	Known		
6	TK_1OD2O6B_2I7UDJGOMHTF2.03IPIEO7J8CO0	8069f26612916157836f3e069c78e229	CACHE Files S...	Known		
7	TK_2E6GMKV_DJADLO7DD8EFG.03IPIEO0I11VG	6ca78923d063b66879ced523ec03a7aa	CACHE Files S...	Known		
8	TK_3PBAG5B_0HTNH6F2NAPLS.03IPIEO0MPKPG	b70e677b5e6f6ea295298fc10cd6023f	CACHE Files S...	Known		
9	TK_2O05V1B_9RVFATUQME67L.03IPIEPK1GFF0	4d8b6b356fc4a605706943d4dda620bb	CACHE Files S...	Known		
10	VC_1T4N3KN_27715MO1D15T6.03IPIEPN1GC80	e42384f28d6b26ac6e47b7c785fa8407	CACHE Files S...	Known		
11	DA_3VVS1UU_000000000000.000000025T81	042695edf711747685b9338d0613d6e6	CACHE Files S...	Known		
12	DA_3VVS1UU_000000000001.000000000001	53108dcded79dc1e5d69b1cd758109a9	CACHE Files S...	Known		
13	DA_3VVS1UU_000000000000.000000025T81	042695edf711747685b9338d0613d6e6	CACHE Files S...	Known		
14	GT_3VVS1UH_00000000240M.000000000000	d1ed19520d05b75d3e1222547676c9e1	CACHE Files S...	Known		
15	GT_3VVS1UH_00000000440M.000000000000	3a98029b2b0d3b9764aacdb0f39e3771	CACHE Files S...	Known		
16	SU_3VVS1UH_201R00000000.0000000G27RO0	fcfb73ec2b5905fb71bac860e47e8b07	CACHE Files S...	Known		
17	GT_3VVS1UH_00000000440M.000000000000	3a98029b2b0d3b9764aacdb0f39e3771	CACHE Files S...	Known		
18	AT_11561UL_00000000000A.000000000000	5d2b910357a0a5c419ce4461ceaca36d				
19	AT_11561UL_00000000000B.000000000000	5b509d621f33306dd08f71466d8b0cf0				
20	AT_11561UL_00000000000C.000000000000	d07411a08deef3b07d4952bc6d6b0c95				
21	AT_11561UL_00000000000D.000000000000	3a1e929a248ff0fe17c06691ebdb1900				
22	AT_11561UL_00000000000E.000000000000	2427173b97a86f58192f2c1e8f416066				
23	AT_11561UL_00000000000F.000000000000	8717a14d8b89f81e3d61873c95efee92				
24	AT_11561UL_00000000000G.000000000000	6e3c00cfb0aa2130540b8aa248310b72				
25	AT_11561UL_00000000000H.000000000000	0de40bc97c536cb8252108d5a0dd13c0				
26	AT_11561UL_00000000000I.000000000000	7b84705bb6deb18049d5bf5f9a3f5bf7				
27	AT_11561UL_00000000000J.000000000000	5cbdb2cfe196104e9474247df9272ede				
28	AT_11561UL_00000000000K.000000000000	eadf21a39189e4e87d312ccba0240d93				
29	AT_11561UL_00000000000L.000000000000	68c11412693455b4e6b6781d09c67f7b				

FIGURE 10.13

EnCase view of the hash analysis of the files in the Cache folder.

could include an artifact that a game was played, which may be an issue in dispute in cases that involve an XBOX 360 console. Examination of the information at the beginning of the file was problematic. Speculation is that the information may be a reference to the game achievements or simply a tracking mechanism for the progress that a gamer has made in the game. The information on the files is depicted in Figures 10.14 and 10.15.

This process of examination of each of the AT{hex value}UL files continued in the same manner as described above. Each file in turn contained similar information: the console security certificate along with an associated PNG file. The header of the first two files was examined to determine what differences were present. It appears

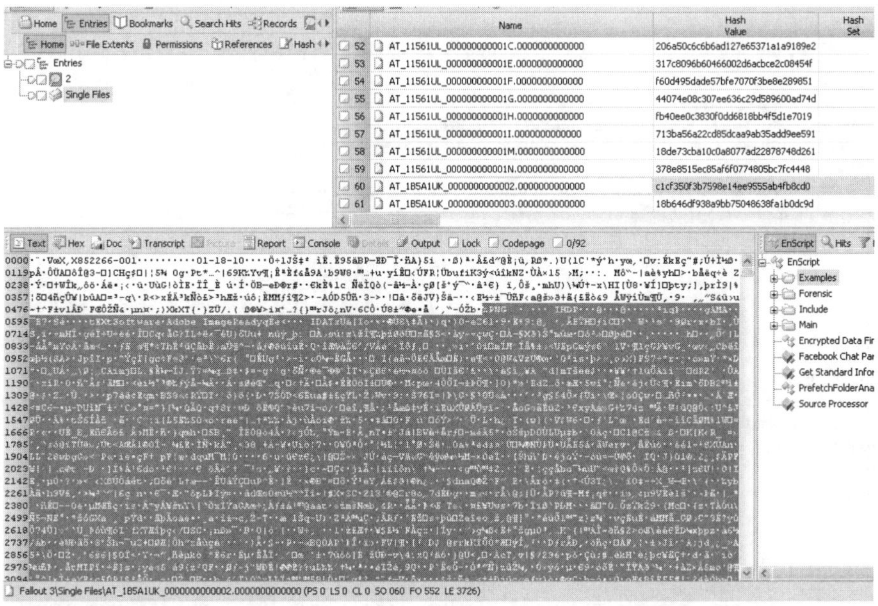

FIGURE 10.14

File AT_1B5A1UK_0000000000002.0000000000000 as viewed within EnCase. There is a PNG file that encompasses the majority of the file and the header is the console security certificate.

FIGURE 10.15

Icon carved from the file shown in Figure 10.14. This icon appears to be an accomplishment icon.

that the differences in the code reside in the last few lines of each header. The header is defined here as the information that is present before the start of the PNG file. The results, at least for these first two files, are represented in Figure 10.16. In addition, several files following this format were viewed and the associated PNG files were carved out; some are depicted in Figures 10.17 through 10.20.

Review and examination of these AT files provides evidence that each of these files is an icon file that is linked to the particular game. Data within the header of each file may have a serial number or developer number that uniquely identifies the game title, and therefore, the console's operating system and file system can load the appropriate information. A total count of files that conformed to this naming convention numbered 48 for approximately 2.5 hours of game play.

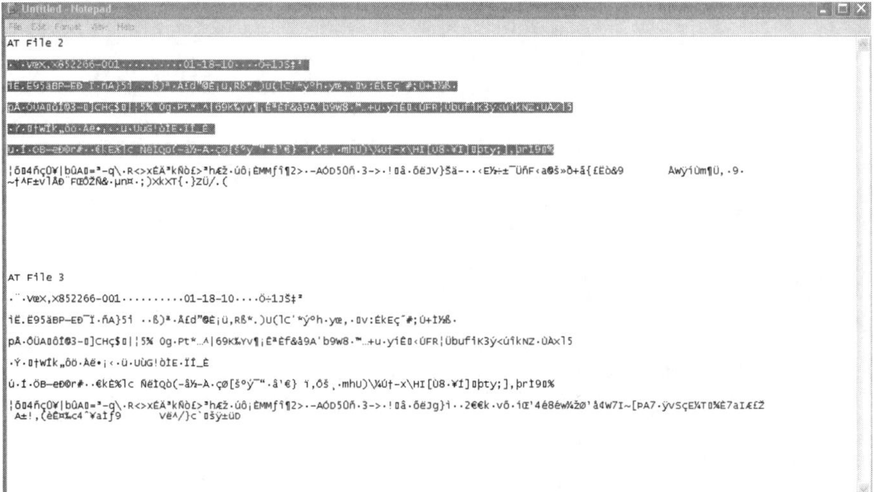

FIGURE 10.16

This is a list of the information found in the header of the first two AT files. Each section of data has been carved from the associated files before the start of the embedded PNG files. The highlighted area appears to be common to both files.

FIGURE 10.17

Icon from AT file B, the naming contained hex values; icon is from the Fallout 3 game.

FIGURE 10.18

Carved PNG file that appears to be a game icon; icon is from the Fallout 3 game.

FIGURE 10.19

Another carved game icon; icon is from the Fallout 3 game.

FIGURE 10.20

Yet another carved game icon; icon is from the Fallout 3 game.

The next file name naming convention was similar, but the numbers and letters used in the hex value were altered a bit, indicating a different purpose. There were only four of these files that had a slightly altered naming convention. The file names are as follows:

- AT_1B5A1UK_0000000000002.0000000000000
- AT_1B5A1UK_0000000000003.0000000000000
- AT_1B5A1UK_0000000000011.0000000000000
- AT_1B5A1UK_0000000000019.0000000000000

Examination of these files progressed in much the same manner as identified earlier. However, the files that are named with the UL in the file name, such as

AT_11561UL_000000000000A.0000000000000, appear to be related directly to game content. The files mentioned earlier that conform to the naming convention, such as AT_1B5A1UK_0000000000002.0000000000000, appear to be accomplishment icons for progress that the gamer has made during the course of game play and that are displayed on the gamers' Gamertag information page. However, these accomplishment icons are not for the gaming that occurred on the test machine, whereas they are the icons that were displayed from the Facebook friend that a friend request was sent to. These icon accomplishments are for an entirely different game. Speculation is that within the header information there is a link, perhaps, encrypted that ties these accomplishments to the game as well as the Gamertag. The icons for each of the associated files are displayed in Figures 10.21 through 10.24.

The files that are present in the Cache folder that conform to the naming convention in Figures 10.21 through 10.24 were present after the connection to the Facebook application. Another hash analysis was conducted, this time with the cache files that were populated to the drive after the Facebook update. The

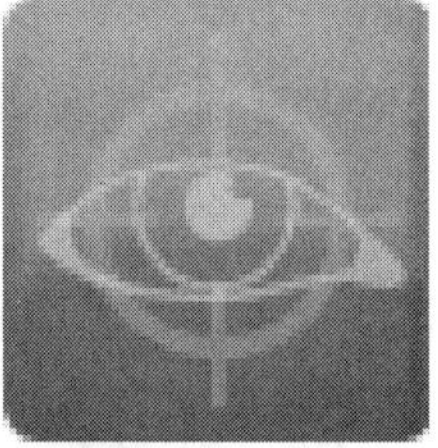

FIGURE 10.21

Game accomplishment icon, file AT_1B5A1 UK_0000000000002.0000000000000.

FIGURE 10.22

Game accomplishment icon, file AT_1B5A1 UK_0000000000003.0000000000000.

FIGURE 10.23

Game accomplishment icon, file AT_1B5A1 UK_0000000000011.0000000000000.

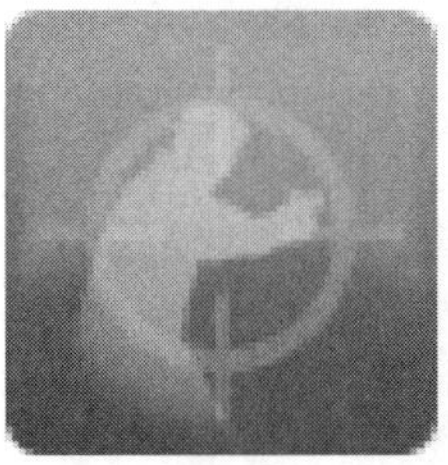

FIGURE 10.24

Game accomplishment icon, file AT_1B5A1UK_0000000000019.0000000000000.

results showed that there were some 100 files in total, and 59 of those files did not have a hash value that matched the files located in the Cache folder immediately following the Facebook update and navigation. Most of these files, 48 of them, were the icon-type files mentioned in Figures 10.18 through 10.20. The other files still needed examination.

XBOX LIVE FRIENDS

The next file in the list is named FM_00280002CHKA3.0000008000000. Earlier research into this file indicates that the FM at the beginning of the file stands for "friend manager." In short, this file is used to manage the XBOX Live friends of the gamer. This is a list that investigators will most certainly want to examine as it will be full of Gamertags that have been associated to the resident Gamertag for the console under examination. Because of the lack of extensive game play on this console, the FM file only has a few entries, but over time, this list has the potential to include hundreds of entries. It also appears that the simple act of searching for Facebook friends that have XBOX Live accounts populates this file. The Gamertags of the friends are located at the end of the file and are listed in plain text. The header of the file is once again the console security certificate. The friend manager file naming convention is as follows:

- FM_00280002CHKA3.0000008000000

Examination of the contents of the file itself reveals that the header information is once again the console certificate. The remainder of the information is speculated to be pointers that are utilized in notification through the Microsoft XBOX Live servers about friends, information that could include games played, the current game being played, accomplishments, and so on.

Figure 10.25 provides an EnCase screenshot showing the files that are left for examination, along with the FM file. The file itself is somewhat lacking in data, which is more than likely because of the lack of extensive game play and associated friend requests. The text of the file is relatively short and is displayed here in Figure 10.26.

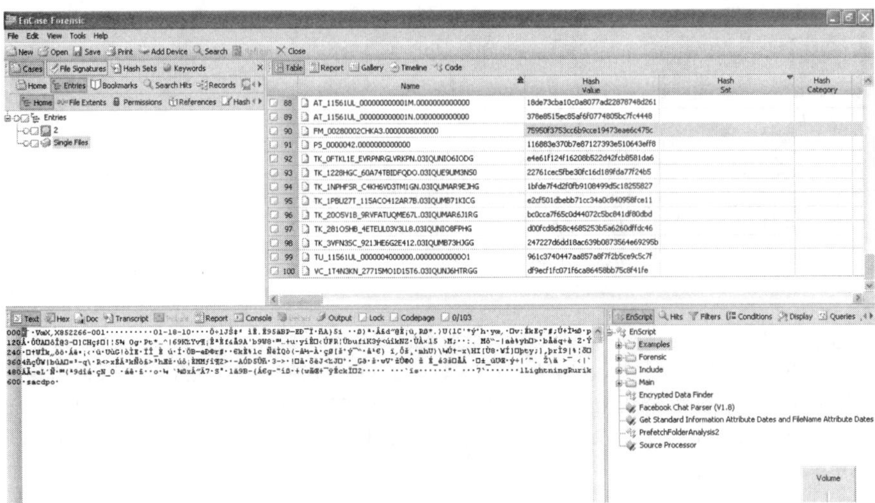

FIGURE 10.25

EnCase view of the remaining files for examination, including the FM file.

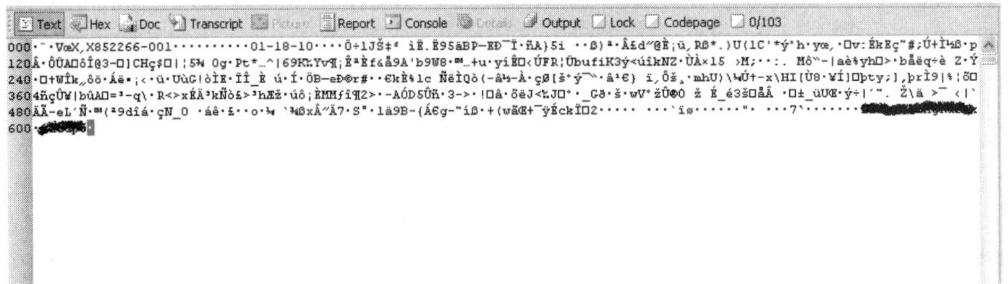

FIGURE 10.26

Text of the FM file. The two areas that have been “sanitized” are the plain text entries of the Gamertags of the identified friends.

OTHER CACHE FILES

There is only a short list of files from the Cache folder left that need to be examined. There are approximately 10 more files remaining:

- PS_0000042.0000000000000
- TK_0FTKL1E_EVRPNRGLVRKPN.03IQUNIO6IODG
- TK_1228HGC_60A74TBIDFQDO.03IQUE9UM3NS0
- TK_1NPHFSR_C4KH6VD3TM1GN.03IQUMAR9EJHG
- TK_1PBU27T_115ACO412AR7B.03IQUMB71KICG
- TK_20O5V1B_9RVFATUQME67L.03IQUMAR6J1RG
- TK_281OSHB_4ETEUL03V3LL8.03IQUNIO8FPHG

- TK_3VFN3SC_921JHE6G2E412.03IQUMB73HJGG
- TU_11561UL_0000004000000.00000000000O1
- VC_1T4N3KN_27715MO1D15T6.03IQUNJ6HTRGG

Examining the first file in the list, the PS file, there were not a lot of indicators as to the function of this file. As mentioned earlier, there are several items that need more investigation and examination. This file clearly has something to do with the game play that occurred, but the actual functionality remains unknown.

The next groups of files are the files with the naming convention starting with TK. Speculation is that these are a security token for the network authentication to XBOX Live and the particular online game. Each file starts with the "PROD" magic header, and the information in the remainder of the file could be a security token of some kind. Figure 10.27 provides a screenshot of the data within this file.

Continuing down the list of files for examination, the next file in the list is the TU file, or the title update file. This file is the title update for the game that was being played. At the onset of the gaming experience, there was a required download in order to play the game. This title update file appears to be the file that was the required download. This could once again be an area of contention during an investigation. It appears that every game title that has network game play functionality that requires a download of this nature. If there is a dispute over whether a game was played online, this file will provide evidence of an affirmative action on the part of the end user that he or she had to accept this download in order to play the particular online game. Figure 10.28 shows a sample of the data that is in this file; the data contains the plain text entry for the game title.

The last file that was new to the Cache folder was the VC file. This file, along with the PS file, seems to have some encrypted data within it. There is no identifying strings data within the file that provides an indication of the files purpose. The file does begin with the console security certificate, but that is the only identifying information within the file. Figures 10.29 and 10.30 provide screenshots of this information.

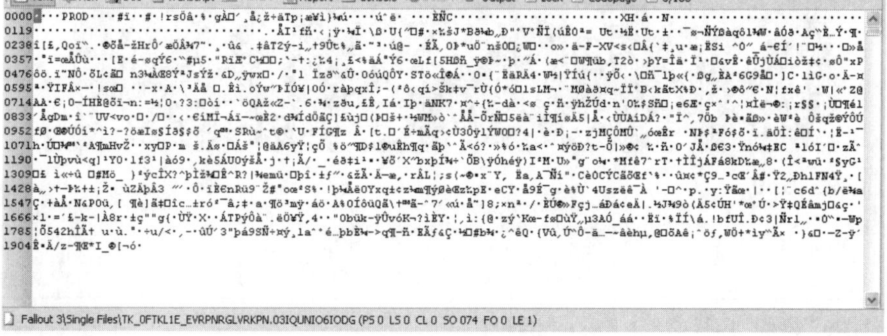
Text
Hex
Doc
Transcript
Report
Console
Output
Lock
Codepage
0/103
Fallout 3\Single Files\TK_0FTKL1E_EVRPNRGLVRKPN.03IQUNIO6IODG (PS 0 LS 0 CL 0 SO 074 FO 0 LE 1)

FIGURE 10.27

Example of a TK file showing the PROD magic header.

FIGURE 10.28

Title update file showing the plain text of the game the update is for.

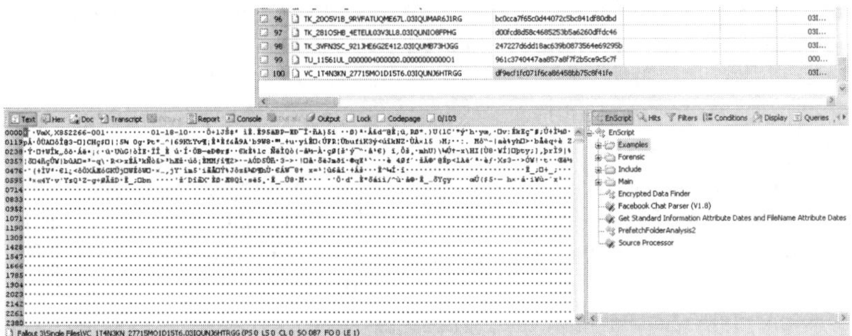

FIGURE 10.29

EnCase view of the VC file showing the console security certificate.

```
Strings v2.41
Copyright (C) 1999-2009 Mark Russinovich
Sysinternals - www.sysinternals.com

X852266-001
01-18-10
*.)U<1C'*
^!69K
9A'b9W8
bufiK3
mhU)\
x\HI[
ty;],
v'YsQ

C:\>

C:\>_
```

FIGURE 10.30

Strings results showing the console security X852266-001.

CONTENT FOLDER CHANGES

Continuing to move through the directory structure that was displayed by Xplorer360, the next folder in line that needed examination was the Content folder. There are many folders and subfolders throughout this top-level directory. The best way to proceed was to determine which folders contained files that had been altered by the game play. The only way to do this was to navigate through each folder and determine the changes, if any, which had occurred.

Viewing the information that is located within the Content folder revealed that there are four immediate subfolders. Each of these subfolders contains an additional layer of subfolders that may or may not contain associated files. Each of the folders had to be expanded and examined to determine any changes made. The initial review detailed that the second folder did not contain any files; therefore, further review was not needed. Figures 10.31 and 10.32 detail this information.

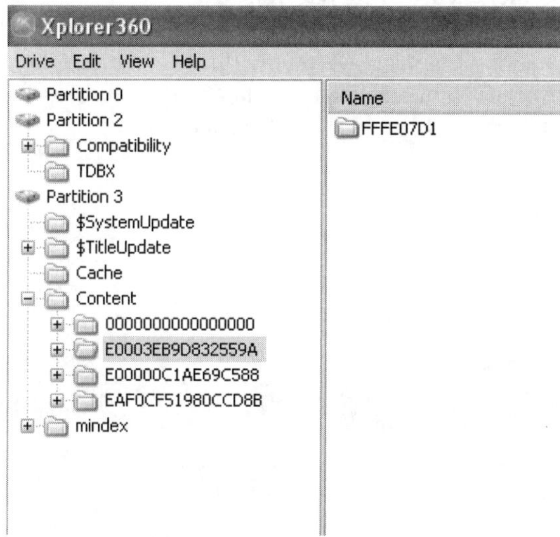

FIGURE 10.31

Screenshot showing the four subfolders within the Content folder.

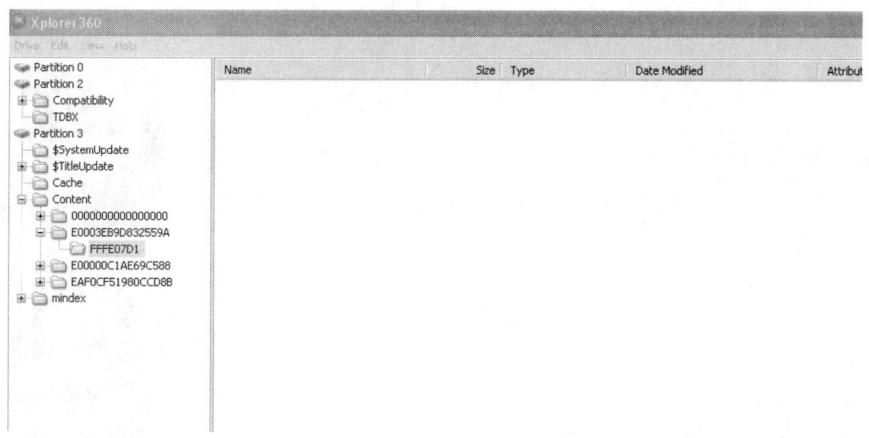

FIGURE 10.32

Detail of the second subfolder showing that there was no additional file in this folder.

The third folder located under the Content folder contained one file for examination. This file was exported from the drive image using the features of Xplorer360, and then the file was imported into EnCase for examination. Reviewing the file revealed that it was a CON file, conforming to the format detailed in earlier chapters. The console security certificate was present, as to be expected with a CON file. Reviewing the data within the file revealed some interesting information. One of the first data entries that was of interest had a plain text entry referring to account information. It appeared as though there were calls to 32-bit and 64-bit entries for PNG files. The entire file was reviewed, and there were several PNG files that were located within the file; each was carved from the file and saved. There were references to an account, and there appeared to be two calls to 32-bit and 64-bit PNG files. Continued examination of the data within the file revealed that there were two PNG files that were one of the Gamertag icons created for the console—a 32-bit and 64-bit image. Figures 10.33 through 10.35 show this data.

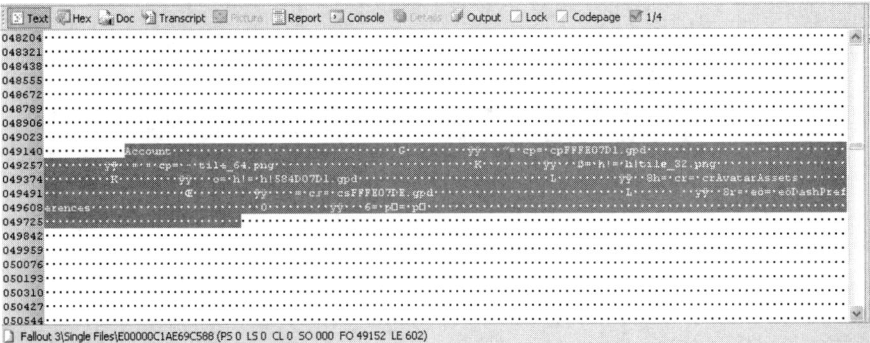

FIGURE 10.33

Detail from the third subfolder showing the references to "account" and the 32-bit and 64-bit PNG entries.

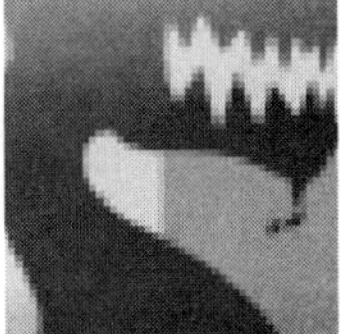

FIGURE 10.34

Icon for the Gamertag, possible icon being referenced in the data of figure 10.33.

FIGURE 10.35

This is 32-bit version of the same file, possibly the 32-bit file referenced in the data in figure 10.33.

Continued examination of this file revealed more plain text information, which appeared to be configuration information for the gamer's dashboard and other information. In short, this file appears to be a configuration file for the specific gamer, similar to a customized desktop of a multiuser PC. Figures 10.36 through 10.39 provide some screenshots of the data.

The fourth subfolder within the Content folder has two folders within it. Each folder contains files that need to be examined. The first folder contained a file that was not altered during the course of the game play. Figure 10.40 provides a screenshot.

FIGURE 10.36

One of the embedded PNG files, note the plain text "Avatar Editor."

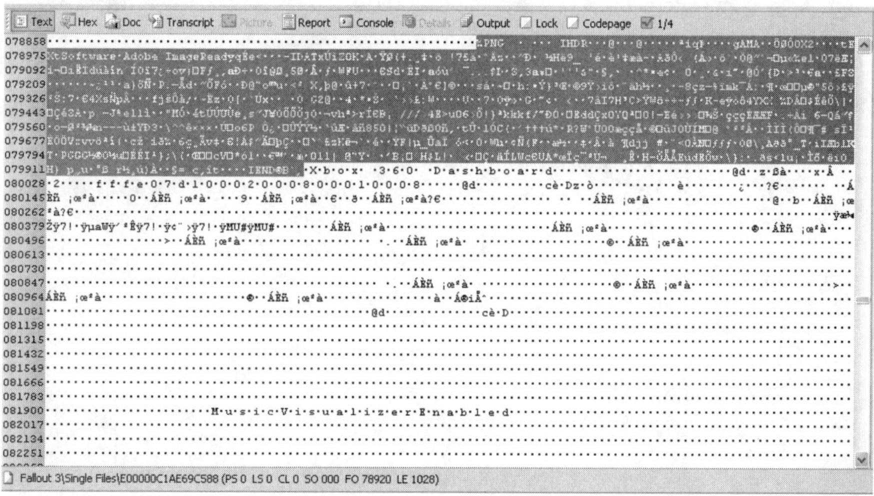

FIGURE 10.37

Another embedded PNG file, note the plain text of "XBOX 360 Dashboard" and "Music Visualization Enabled."

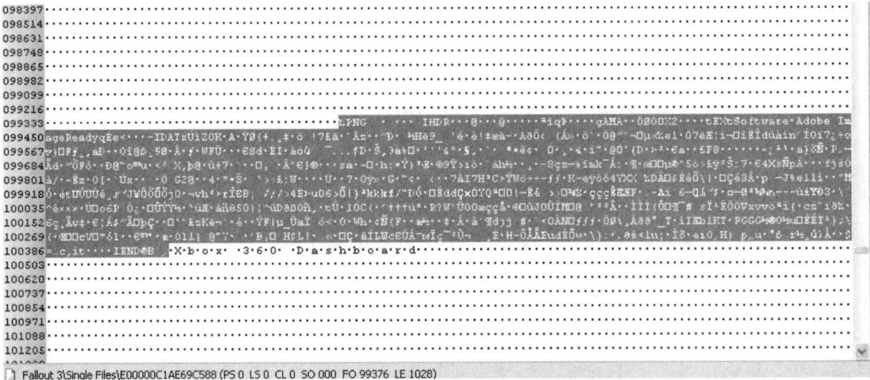

FIGURE 10.38

Another embedded PNG file, note the plain text of "XBOX 360 Dashboard."

FIGURE 10.39

This PNG file was located five times within this particular file. The icon is used during game interaction.

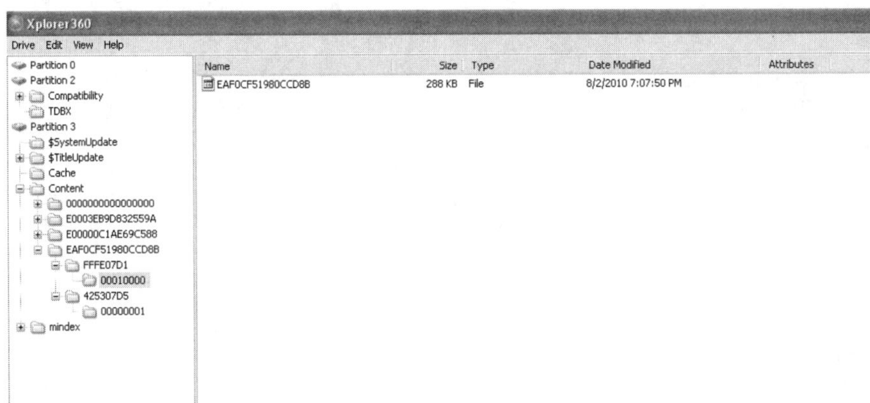

FIGURE 10.40

Screenshot of the Content folder's subfolders showing one of the files that was not changed due to game play. This file was previously examined.

The second subfolder here, the one titled "425307D5," contained several files that needed to be examined. Although the file names provide some indication of the file's purpose, an examination still needs to be conducted. The files within this subfolder are the save game points that were generated during game play. Figure 10.41 shows the files as they represented in Xplorer360.

The files listed in Figure 10.41 were extracted from the drive image and imported into EnCase. The first of these files that was examined was the autosave.fxs file. This file contained several embedded PNGs that were icons used within the game to indicated game progression. Figure 10.42 provides a sample one of these icon files.

The details of the autosave file header show that the file is a CON file with the console security certificate. Additional information that is listed in plain text is the name of the character that was used, which was "templar," along with the stage within the game that the game was saved. Figure 10.43 shows the EnCase view of this data. Each of the save game files follows this format.

The final section of the Content folder that requires examination is the very first subfolder, titled with all zeros. This folder contains several subfolders, each of which has a file within it. Initially, there were only nine folders located within this directory. Over the course of the game play, two additional folders were added. The first nine folders that were present are listed here in Figure 10.44, and the new folders are listed in Figure 10.45.

Xplorer360

Drive Edit View Help

Partition 0
Partition 2
Compatibility
TDBX
Partition 3
$SystemUpdate
$TitleUpdate
Cache
Content
0000000000000000
E0003EB9D832559A
E00000C1AE69C588
EAF0CF51980CCD8B
FFFE07D1
00010000
425307D5
00000001
mindex

Name	Size	Type	Date Modified	Attributes
Save 3 - templar Vault 101 Entrance .fxs	1 MB	FXS File	9/28/2010 2:59:20 AM	
Save 2 - templar Vault 101 Atrium 0.fxs	1 MB	FXS File	9/28/2010 2:34:38 AM	
Save 1 - templar Vault 101 00.33.39.fxs	1 MB	FXS File	9/27/2010 7:21:48 PM	
autosave.fxs	1 MB	FXS File	9/28/2010 3:01:28 AM	

FIGURE 10.41

The save game files.

FIGURE 10.42

Icon file representing game progression; icon is from the Fallout 3 game.

FIGURE 10.43

Details of the autosave file showing the character name, "templar," the CON header and the location indicated for game progression, in this case "The Capital Wasteland."

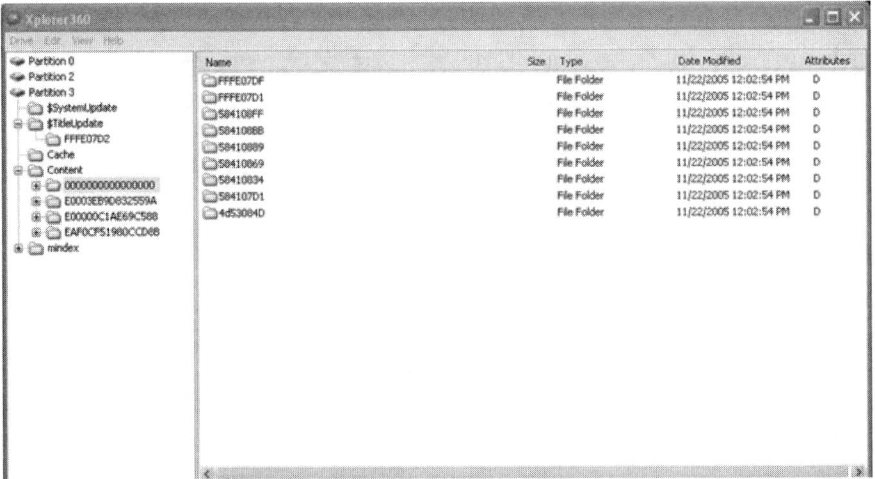

FIGURE 10.44

These are the original nine folders that were listed under the first folder in the content file.

A review of the folders and the subsequent files revealed that two new folders were created and that one of the folders had an additional file added to it. The first folder that showed a change was labeled "FFFE07DF." Within this folder, there were two files; one had a date that correlated to the game play. This new file was titled "InGameAccessTimes." This file continues to comply with the format in other files

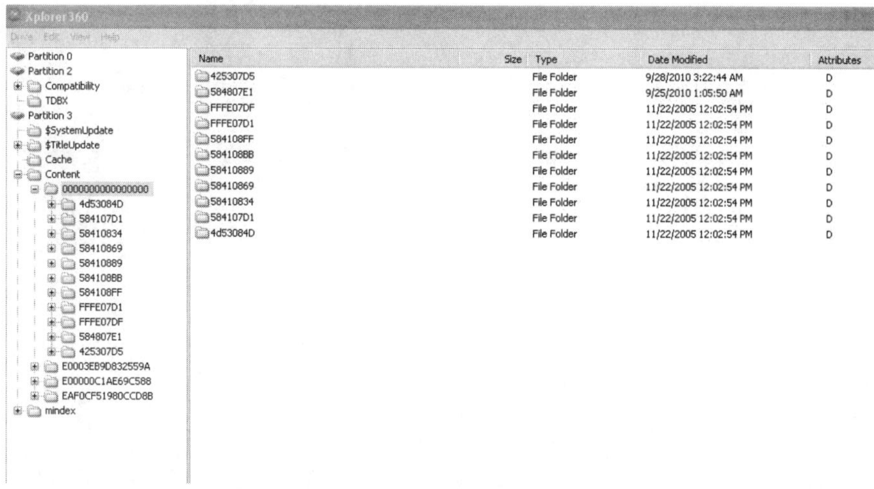

FIGURE 10.45

The new folders that populate the parent folder.

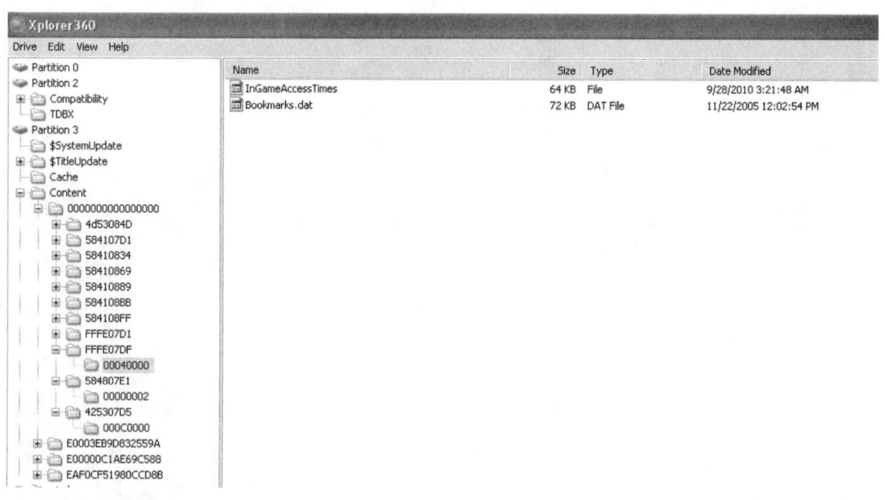

FIGURE 10.46

Directory structure showing the InGameAccessTime file.

that have been examined and is a CON file. The header of the file is the magic byte "CON" and the console security certificate is utilized once again. There were two embedded PNG files that were carved out. Figure 10.46 provides a snapshot of the files, Figure 10.47 provides a snapshot of the file header, and Figures 10.48 and 10.49 are the carved PNGs.

The last file for examination is located within the folder named "425307D5." The file is reported as being 79 MB in size. The file was extracted from the image,

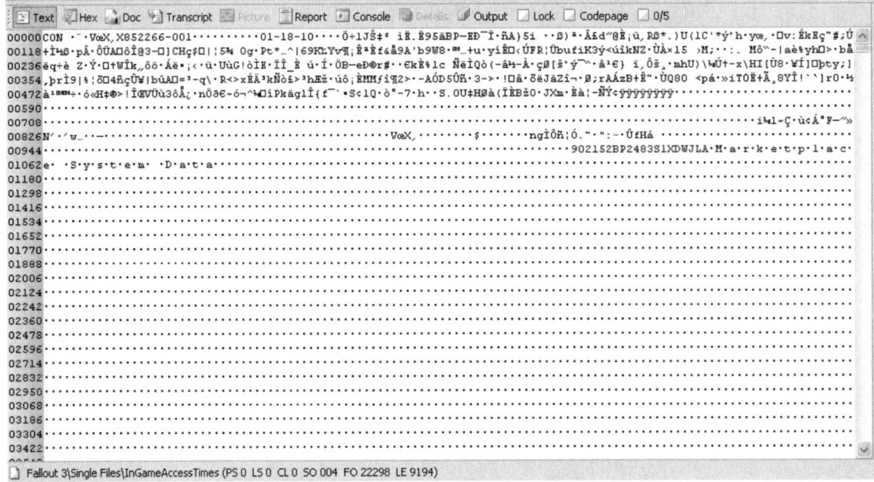

FIGURE 10.47

Header information for the InGameAccessTime file.

FIGURE 10.48

First embedded icon file; icon is from the Fallout 3 game.

FIGURE 10.49

Second embedded icon file specific to the Fallout 3 game.

imported into EnCase, and examined. Examination of this file revealed that it is the video trailer that was downloaded through the XBOX Live service that was available. Reviewing the information in EnCase provided many plain text strings that verify that this is a video file. The file header on this file reveals that it has the "magic" header of LIVE, so it would follow the details laid out in Chapter 6, "XBOX 360–Specific File Types." Figure 10.50 shows the details revealed in hex view.

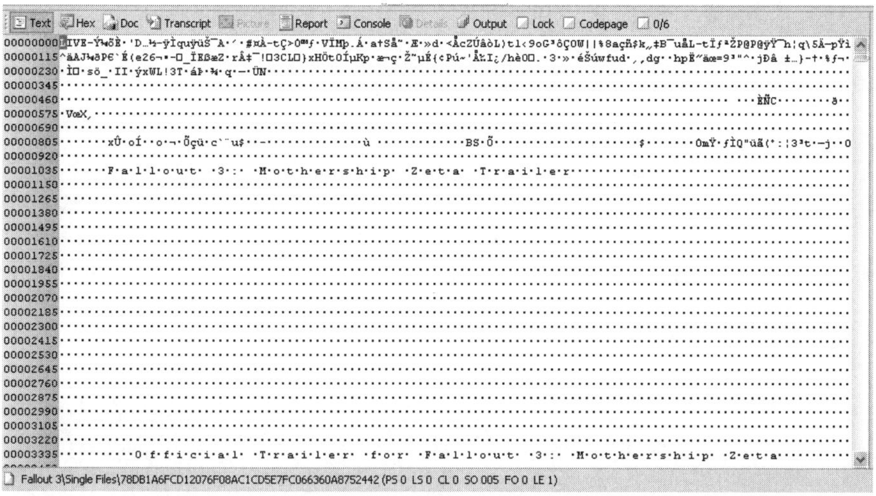

FIGURE 10.50

Hex view of the trailer file. The plain text information shows that this is indeed the trailer for "Fallout 3 Mothership Zeta." The file was extracted, but was not able to be opened with Media Player.

SUMMARY

This chapter addressed the issues and changes that are made to a drive when the console connects to XBOX Live service for online game play. There are many changes that are made that leave several artifacts on the digital media. From downloads to friend lists and other game artifacts, once the console is connected to the Live service, the digital storage media begins to be populated with all sorts of artifacts. These artifacts can be game specific, Gamertag specific, or can be specific to an action taken by the end user. These artifacts can assist investigators in establishing the vector of communication between two parties, or even refute claims that online gaming did or did not take place.

CHAPTER

11 Additional Files and Research Techniques

INFORMATION IN THIS CHAPTER

- Introduction
- Additional files "player_configuration_cache.dat" and "preferences.dat"
- Network traffic examination
- Network capture box
- Decompiling XEX files
- Additional tools available for analysis

INTRODUCTION

There are a few areas that still need to be reviewed that have not been touched upon yet. Some of these topics have not been addressed in other chapters, and since this is ongoing research, the knowledge base continues to grow. This chapter will explore other areas, such as associated files for online game play, decompiling XEX files, network traffic analysis, online investigative capture boxes, and some of the tools that are on the horizon that can be utilized by the community for examination and online investigations.

As a user of this console indulges in its full functionality, the digital storage media will be populated with far more artifacts than can be created and documented here. The information that is provided within this book will provide some needed documentation of the baseline information, as close to a Gold Build as can be created, to assist high-tech crime investigators and forensic examiners. This information is one piece of a larger puzzle, and if it assists one investigator, then the effort has been worth it.

ADDITIONAL FILES "PLAYER_CONFIGURATION_CACHE.DAT" AND "PREFERENCES.DAT"

Files that are found on the storage media of the console can be grouped into many different general classifications. These classifications are umbrella categories and include console files, game files, gamer files, videos, and social networking–related files.

With all the video games and user data that can be stored on the drive, it would be difficult to identify each and every type of file that can be placed on the console; this would be like trying to determine every application that was placed on a Windows PC that has had years of use. In the future, perhaps Microsoft or some other organization will have enough time and money to create a hash set similar to the National Software Reference Library (NSRL) hash sets that are a mainstay of forensic examinations. These hash sets allow an examiner to reduce the number of files to review/examine by removing the known files.

The list of files that were examined and discussed in earlier chapters was a sampling of files that can be on the drive because of several factors. A forensic examiner that receives an XBOX 360 console for examination will have far more files to examine than what was displayed in the screenshots provided, and the files that were examined in the preceding chapters. The usage of the research console was not in line with a console that would exist in normal life; specifically, this was the case so that a baseline of information could be used for comparison to a machine that is collected as part of an investigation. The file examination revealed that games, once played, require a download and leave artifacts that are specific, which may include either a serial number or vendor code of some sort in order to assist in identification. The files themselves have unique names that can quickly be triaged to determine their association to a specific video game.

Other files exist that are specific to other gamers that have been connected through online game play, Facebook connections, or other interaction over the XBOX Live service. Many of these interactions leave artifacts that have these Gamertags listed in plain text. A Gamertag can be correlated to an e-mail address, providing login Internet protocol addresses, dates, times, and the length of network connection. Each Gamertag is unique, and there are some artifacts that can be logged and maintained by Microsoft that would be useful to an investigator. Research indicates that the information supplied during account creation is maintained by Microsoft, including the initial Internet protocol address.

One location that failed to provide any artifacts during the research for this project was the area that was identified as Partition 0 through Xplorer360. However, during earlier research, this partition was populated with some data that could be relevant to an investigation. This partition had several files in it that appeared to be specific to online game play. It is prudent to point out that these files and folders that were populated to the drive were from the initial research more than 4 years ago. With the system updates that have been made to the console and the associated XBOX Live features and functionality, these files may not exist or may exist in a different location.

After more online game play, Partition 0 was populated with three new folders: XBOX0, XBOX1, and XBOX2. XBOX0 contained files that were associated with online game play. The files were map files and game saves that occurred during the course of game play. Figure 11.1 provides a screenshot of the files as they are reported in EnCase.

In the XBOX2 folder, there are two files that would be important to any investigation that involves one of these consoles. The first of these files is titled "player_configuration_cache.dat," and the second is titled "preferences.dat." Together, these files provide more information about online game play and game play options. At the time of this research, the game that was being played was one of the XBOX console's flagship game titles, Halo 2 (from Bungie Software). Examination of the

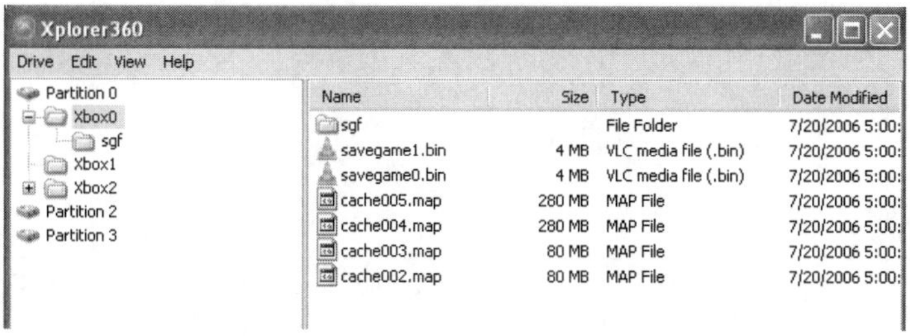

FIGURE 11.1

XBOX0 new files.

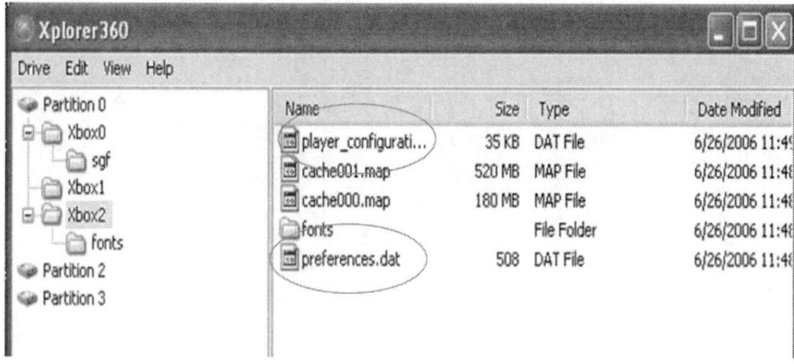

FIGURE 11.2

New entries into partition 0 from the older research. This partition appears to populate after more online game play.

"preferences.dat" file provides details of the type of online game play for Halo 2. It should be noted that with many of these games, there are different online game options available to the gamer. Some games have capture-the-flag options, others have cooperative play, and others still have sort of an everyone for themselves aspect. In the case of the game play with Halo 2, there are options for game play that have two teams pitted against one another. One option is called "slayer," and this is clearly visible in the preferences.dat file.

The next file within Partition 0 that is of investigative interest is the "player_configuration_cache.dat." This file contains a list of what appears to be all the Gamertags that the end user has come in contact with over the course of their online game play. Consider this a log file that tracks all the gamers that the end user, the owner of the console, has interacted with online. More than likely this information is used by the servers and services at XBOX Live for tracking, notification, and friend linkage. There is a format to the Gamertags and how they are listed. Each Gamertag is preceded by a few different data sets: the majority start with "$q," some start with "mq," and there are some that have other symbols in their data string. Recall that the gamers that the end user has played with online can fall into a few categories, such as a friend or a gaming clan member. One entry, "Skilful tree," was a Gamertag that was associated as a friend. There

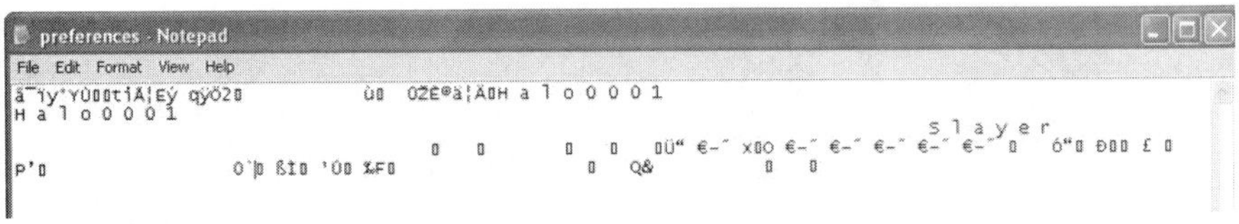

FIGURE 11.3

The data that is located within the preferences.dat file. The plain text "Halo 0001" was a profile that was created on the console and the text "slayer" indicates the type of online game that was played.

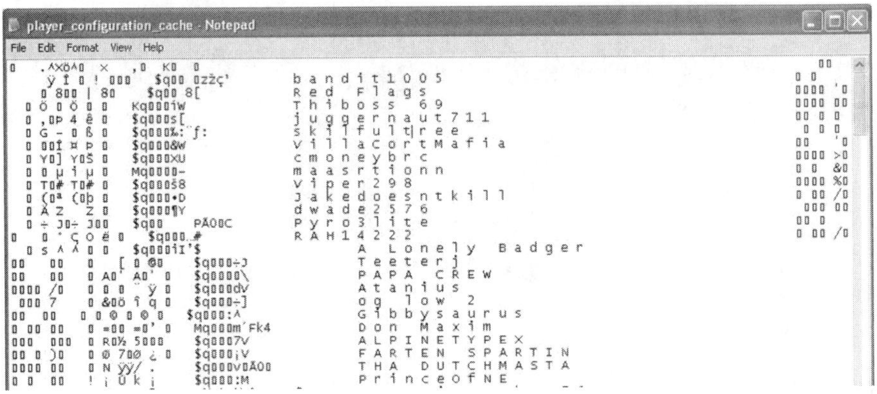

FIGURE 11.4

The data and plain text found within the "player_configuration_cache.dat" file. This data has been formatted in Notepad to organize it better, but the Gamertags are clearly listed with the preceding data, which may provide an indicator of the closeness each of these Gamertags has to the end user of the console.

is a cursive lower case "f" in the leading data for this gamer entry; perhaps this is an indicator of the friend linkage. Figures 11.2 through 11.4 provide screenshots of this data.

NETWORK TRAFFIC EXAMINATION

The XBOX 360 gaming console is designed to connect through a network for a variety of reasons. Examining the network traffic and some of the artifacts that are pushed to the console storage media provides some indication of how the network functions. The research that was conducted for this book afforded a few different network functions that were examined. There are a few ways in which the console can function over a network that were examined—by no means is this comprehensive, but it at least provides a look at the network traffic.

Network gaming with the console occurs in a couple of ways. It has already been discussed that the gamers either play against one another or with one another, but there is more to the way in which the network connections are established. Microsoft appears to be there to negotiate the connections, acting as a middleman, letting the gamers connect to one another. Once the connections have been made, the XBOX Live servers remove themselves from the equation. Once a gamer decides to play a particular game, they are placed into something akin to a bull pen. They connect to the Microsoft Live servers, which in turn search for other gamers who want to play the same game and have a similar true skill level. Then the gamers are placed into the bull pen area—another analogy could be a green room—and once the appropriate number of gamers is connected and ready to play, the games begin. The first gamer into the staging area is generally the host for the network play. Each additional gamer connects to this gamer and all network traffic passes to the host. This information is represented in Figures 11.5 and 11.6.

It has already been discussed that there are three general classifications of files that are downloaded to the console: the PIRS, CON, and LIVE files. Revisiting the information that is provided by the researchers at www.free60.org regarding these file types, it appears that each of these files comes from roughly the same source, and it is a matter of which file type needs to be downloaded. It appears that the network traffic for these files is akin to a single sign on to a network, meaning that the end user connects to the Live service, and depending on the requested file, the user is directed to that alternate server or resource. Figure 11.7 provides the information that is discussed. Figure 11.8 revisits the PIRS, CON, and LIVE container files.

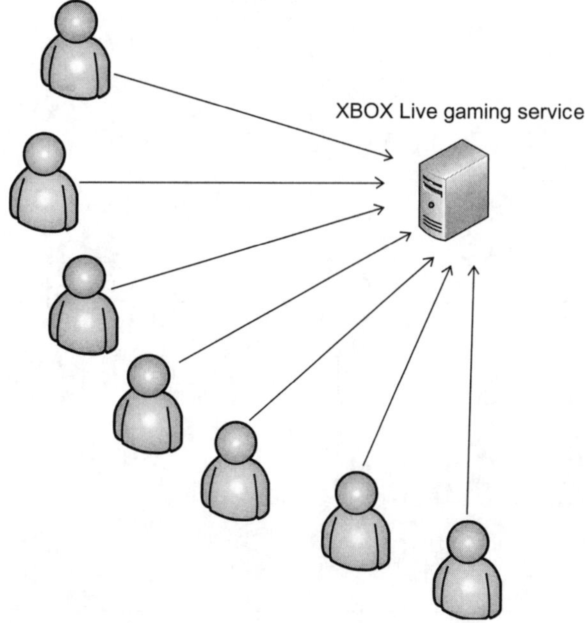

FIGURE 11.5

Representation of the network game process.

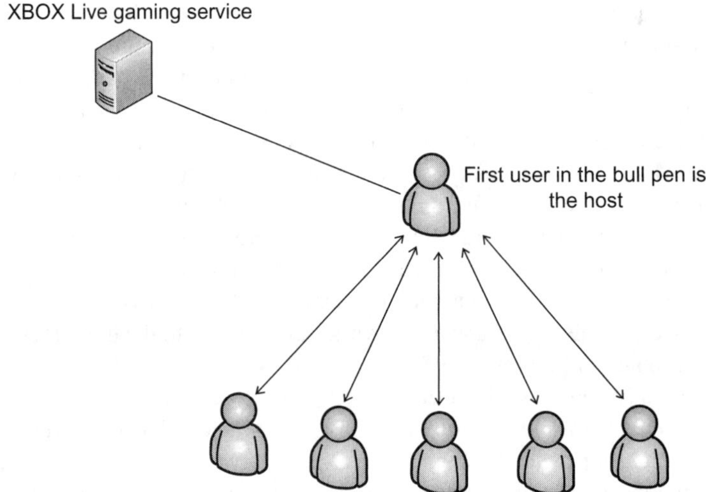

FIGURE 11.6

Once the appropriate number of gamers is ready to play, the live servers remove themselves and allow the first gamer in the staging area to host the network game play.

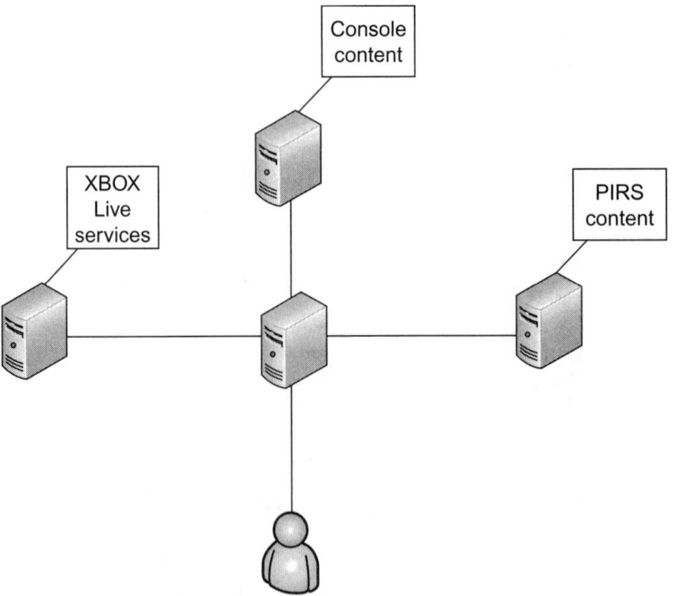

FIGURE 11.7

Signing into live is similar to a single sign-on technology in a business network environment, similar to kerberos authentication. Once signed in, the end user is routed to the resource that is needed or requested during the network session.

Signature Type	Information
"CON "	Signed by a console. Found on many files such as cache files, profiles, saved games.
PIRS	Signed by Microsoft. Found on files delivered by Microsoft through non-Xbox Live means such as system updates.
LIVE	Signed by Microsoft. Found on files delivered over Xbox Live such as items from the Marketplace like themes.

FIGURE 11.8

From www.free60.org, the descriptions of the three broad classifications of files.

Network traffic analysis of the online game play provided some interesting information pertaining to the ports and protocols that are utilized during network negotiation and game play. Examination shows that the vast majority of the traffic is user datagram protocol, UDP, traffic, which is to be expected. UDP is a connectionless-oriented protocol that is used with communication in which the loss of a packet or two is not critical. Because the traffic with the XBOX 360 console and the associated game play is pushing a tremendous amount of video and audio, the loss of the occasional packet of information would more than likely to go unnoticed. UDP traffic tends to be faster, resulting from the lack of the overhead that is required for connection-oriented traffic. The network captures that were collected for this research were not for a lengthy period of time; they were designed simply to grab network data flow and determine what information could be captured.

Examination of the data provided that the vast majority of the UDP traffic was being pushed over port 3074. Researching this information confirmed that Microsoft Live uses this port and a few others for network communication. Along with the UDP ports, Live apparently uses a few other TCP and UDP ports. The information was located on the support page for XBOX Live and appears to be designed to help end users configure their console to connect. Figures 11.9 and 11.10 provide a few more details.

The traffic was reviewed using Wireshark, and there were some interesting port names and addresses that were not viewed in the JPCAP. One paring of destination and source ports that were labeled in an unsuspected convention were XBOX and Blackjack. Researching these port addresses was interesting and revealed that the XBOX port was the UDP 3074 port that was identified in the JPCAP traffic analysis. The Blackjack port assignment appears to be a Microsoft standard network assignment to port 1025. A little deeper look into this port and the potential information that is running over it provides that this is potentially DCOM traffic:

> *DCOM (Distributed Component Object Model) is a set of Microsoft concepts and program interfaces in which client program objects can request services from server program objects on other computers in a network. DCOM is based on the Component Object Model (COM), which provides a set of interfaces allowing clients and servers to communicate within the same computer (that is running Windows 95 or a later version).*
>
> *For example, you can create a page for a Web site that contains a script or program that can be processed (before being sent to a requesting user) not on the Web site server but on another, more specialized server in the network. Using DCOM interfaces, the Web server site program (now acting as a client object) can*

SUMMARY

If you have a firewall or network hardware, such as a router, you might need to make a configuration change in order for your Xbox 360 console to communicate with Xbox LIVE. This configuration change is sometimes called "opening ports" or "port forwarding."

Xbox LIVE requires the following ports to be open:

- TCP 80
- UDP 88
- UDP 3074
- TCP 3074
- UDP 53
- TCP 53

If you're connected to a network through your workplace or school, ask the network administrator to open the ports used by Xbox LIVE.

FIGURE 11.9

Ports and protocol list for XBOX Live, extracted from http://support.xbox.com/support/en/us/nxe/kb.aspx?category=xboxlive&ID=908874&lcid=1033.

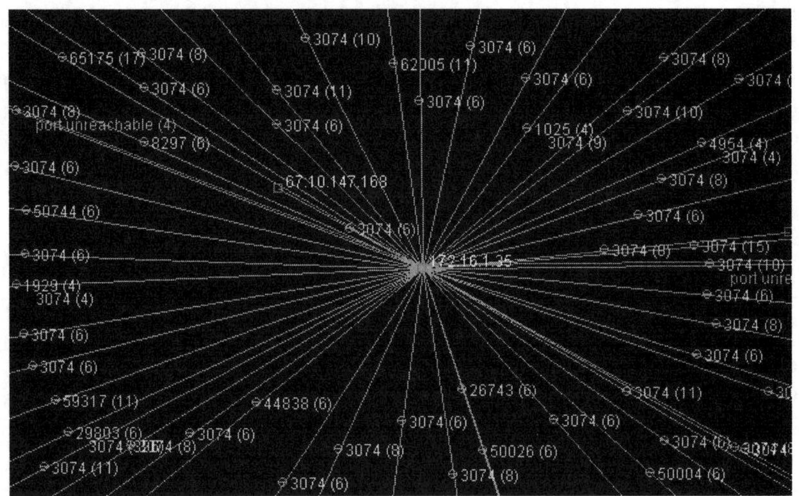

FIGURE 11.10

This is a view of the PCAP file from XBOX Live network traffic, showing the UDP traffic and associated ports. The program used to show the visual representation of the traffic is a free program called JPCAP.

forward a Remote Procedure Call (RPC) to the specialized server object, which provides the necessary processing and returns the result to the Web server site. It passes the result on to the Web page viewer [1].

Examining the network traffic in Wireshark, in particular the Blackjack entries, clearly details the information showing the destination and source information.

The IP addresses are translated, and the Microsoft IP addresses for this session are provided in clear text. Research in the network traffic is ongoing. Of particular interest is the initial connection and the required download to login to XBOX Live. It is speculated that there is a hash value taken of some aspect of the console at the time of this initial login to the Live service. This hash value is then used in subsequent network sessions to verify that the console has not been modified to run rogue code. If such a console is located by the security measures of Microsoft, then the console is banned from the Live service on a violation of terms of use.

As with other online investigations, there is generally a need to determine the endpoints of the communication. Investigations that involve peer-to-peer networks or child sexual exploitation cases routinely attempt to identify all the endpoints of a network communication. These endpoints could expand the investigation greatly or they could be used to determine if the scope of the investigation remains within the jurisdiction of the investigator. In the case of an XBOX Live investigation, because the majority of the traffic in a network game is a peer network, the ability to capture and view the network addresses could provide more evidence of the connection and may verify other investigative artifacts. In order to view the endpoints of the communication in Wireshark, simply load the capture file into Wireshark, navigate to the Statistics menu and select the **Endpoints** option. Figure 11.11 provides a screenshot of the information for one of the network captures.

This information seems to fall in line with what is known about the network traffic and the way in which information is pushed and pulled over the network. With the specialized server concept that was outlined above and ad hoc networks being created for

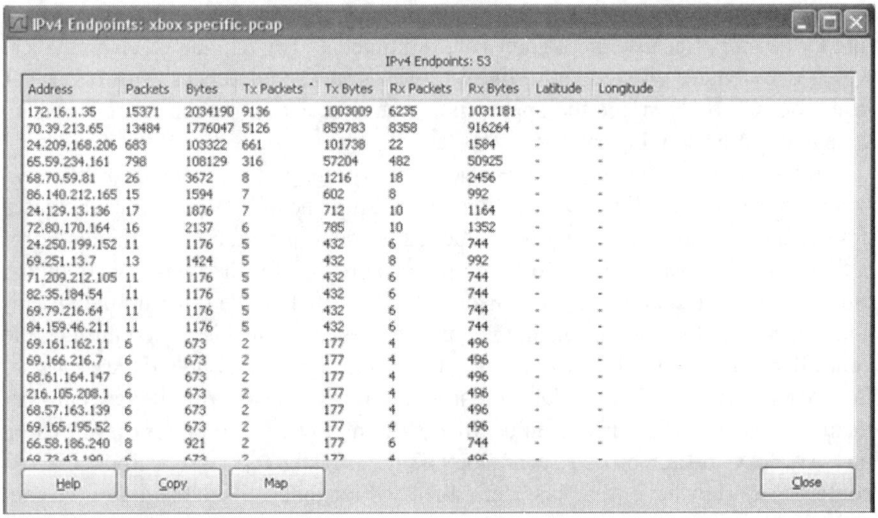

IPv4 Endpoints: xbox specific.pcap

IPv4 Endpoints: 53

Address	Packets	Bytes	Tx Packets	Tx Bytes	Rx Packets	Rx Bytes	Latitude	Longitude
172.16.1.35	15371	2034190	9136	1003009	6235	1031181	-	-
70.39.213.65	13484	1776047	5126	859783	8358	916264	-	-
24.209.168.206	683	103322	661	101738	22	1584	-	-
65.59.234.161	798	108129	316	57204	482	50925	-	-
68.70.59.81	26	3672	8	1216	18	2456	-	-
86.140.212.165	15	1594	7	602	8	992	-	-
24.129.13.136	17	1876	7	712	10	1164	-	-
72.80.170.164	16	2137	6	785	10	1352	-	-
24.250.199.152	11	1176	5	432	6	744	-	-
69.251.13.7	13	1424	5	432	8	992	-	-
71.209.212.105	11	1176	5	432	6	744	-	-
82.35.184.54	11	1176	5	432	6	744	-	-
69.79.216.64	11	1176	5	432	6	744	-	-
84.159.46.211	11	1176	5	432	6	744	-	-
69.161.162.11	6	673	2	177	4	496	-	-
69.166.216.7	6	673	2	177	4	496	-	-
68.61.164.147	6	673	2	177	4	496	-	-
216.105.208.1	6	673	2	177	4	496	-	-
68.57.163.139	6	673	2	177	4	496	-	-
69.165.195.52	6	673	2	177	4	496	-	-
66.58.186.240	8	921	2	177	6	744	-	-

Help Copy Map Close

FIGURE 11.11

The information provided in this screenshot shows how Wireshark presents the endpoints of the network traffic, complete with the number of packets that are sent. There is also a column that can provide GeoTag information if enabled.

game play, the information provides more insight into the way in which the network game play progresses. Investigators may be faced with conducting investigations using the game console and as such, need to be aware of all the investigative aspects that are the standard operating procedures for this type of case. In addition, they need to ensure that they have the required legal authority to capture the traffic and remain in compliance with their organization's standard operating procedures, or SOPs. Areas of consideration for this type of investigation could include the following:

- Capture box configuration
- Court authority
- Gamer etiquette
- Chat, voice, IM, and other means of communication
- Microphone, on or off
- Gamertag creation or assumption

NETWORK CAPTURE BOX

Online investigations that involve the XBOX 360 console will become more prevalent once the knowledge becomes common that these consoles are potentially a large source of data. In addition, the consoles, with certain games, can be considered the poor man's military or terrorist simulator. Some games are designed specifically to mimic military and law enforcement weapons and tactics, which could be used as rudimentary virtual reality simulator for the use of such items and tactics.

The need to capture an online game play session presents some issues for investigators. The first, and probably the most concerning, is the legal authority to capture the session. Because these games are multimedia, they include video and voice, which may require wiretap authority. An investigator should check with his or her legal counsel to determine the appropriate course of action if such a need were to arise to capture a gaming session.

With the market share that the console currently enjoys, the potential for an investigator to launch an online investigation while using one of these consoles increases dramatically. From taking over the Gamertag account of a victim to launching proactive investigations, the need to develop a capture box for the two-way audio and video is essential to preserve the session. Currently, and unlike other online investigative measures that can be taken, the console's voice channel is ported through the controller, which makes it somewhat problematic to capture one side of the conversation. Microsoft may have a solution that it is willing to share with the law enforcement community. There is a team of Microsoft employees who present information on the XBOX 360 at the High Technology Crime Investigators Association (HTCIA) conferences. They have what has been called a "Frankenbox," the facilitates the capturing of the two-way voice communication.

Barring the "Frankenbox" solution, other methods using off-the-shelf solutions have been researched that provide the ability to capture the entire session, including all audio and video. The two areas of concern with creating such a setup are the voice capture and the video capture, while still being able to interact in the game.

The solutions that have been created to capture the video all involved "Y" splitters being used for the component audio/visual cables. One set of cables went to the video screen while the other set went to the computer system that had software to capture the video. There was an off-the-shelf device called a Dazzle, available from most major electronic stores, which was used with the included video software to record the session. Older TIVO and DVR systems could also be used to capture the video.

Capturing the audio was accomplished through the use of a four-channel mixing board and a standard microphone. The microphone was placed next to the online investigator and the session was initiated. Although a little low tech, the end result is a complete recording of the online gaming session that could be used as evidence and that shows both sides of a game session.

It should be noted that Microsoft states that it will assist investigators when cases of this nature present themselves. There are several contact numbers available for the law enforcement community to contact the corporation and seek what assistance is available.

DECOMPILING XEX FILES

One area of interest in the forensics and network security field is the issue of reverse engineering. This technique allows examiners to reverse the code that is located and provides them with a deeper understanding of the way that the executable works. The XEX files that have been detailed in the earlier chapters can be decompiled and reviewed with a few tools; one is commercial and the other is a free download. The information on how to decompile XBOX 360 executable files was discovered while researching the file types for the XBOX 360 console. It is of interest, and the prevailing theory is that the information might be useful to an examiner so it is included here.

There are two software tools that are required in order to decompile or reverse code located on the XBOX 360 console. The first is a commercial product called IDA Pro, which is available from www.hex-rays.com/idapro/. The second application that is needed is called XexTool, version 5.2 and is available at www.xbox-scene.com/xbox1data/sep/EkpFVyEAFEvBQMAXMf.php. To provide an idea of what XexTool is designed for, the readme file provides some details, and a portion is provided here in Figure 11.12.

The instructions on how to use these tools in order to decompile an XBOX 360 XEX file can be found at www.se7ensins.com/forums/topic286460-how-to-decompile-an-xex-in-ida/. However, it is always good to have a reference detailing all the steps.

The first step in the process is to obtain the two applications that were mentioned earlier. In addition, the examiner must have an XEX file that they wish to decompile and know the location of the file, so this could be one of the extractions mentioned earlier using either Xplorer360 or wxPIRS. Once purchased, downloaded and installed, the user needs to open a command shell and navigate to the location of the XexTool. In the case of this research the folder containing the subsequent files for XexTool was uncompressed into the root of C. The first step in the process is to determine the "base file" that is described in the readme file. XexTool allows the

```
XexTool - xorloser


:: Overview

This is a tool to extract information on an xex file. It will print out
xex information to the console, alter xex attributes, extract executable code
and other basefiles and create idc scripts files to help with disassembling
the extracted executable code.

Note: any altered or created retail xex files will not be correctly signed.


:: Xex Format Basics

An xex file consists of a basefile that the xex is built around and headers
which contain various attributes to be used with the basefile.

Usually the basefile is an executable file, however it can also be data file,
as seen with ximedic.xex from the xbox360 flash. When the basefile is an
executable file it is either an exe or dll, however it is not stored in its
normal exe or dll format but instead as a binary file.

Some of the xex header attributes are required, and others are optional. Some
of these attributes are things such as the regions the xex is made for and the
media the xex is allowed to boot from.

The basefile can be optionally encrypted using aes encryption. All contents
of the basefile are hashed and then rsa signed. Microsoft is the only one with
access to the private key required to sign xexs in order to allow them to boot
on a retail xbox360. A different key is used to sign xex files in order to
allow them to boot on a development xbox360.
```

FIGURE 11.12

XexTool readme file excerpt.

examiner to determine information that is required to properly load the XEX file into IDA Pro. In addition, XexTool also creates an associated file to the XEX file that is an IDA Pro scripting language file, which is required to properly interpret the data. The IDA Pro scripting files have the .idc extension.

In keeping with a file that was already identified, the AvatarMiniCreator.xex file that was extracted using wxPIRS will be used. The file was copied from the extraction location and placed into the XexTool directory. Thus, within the XexTool directory should be the readme file, the XexTool executable and the AvatarMiniCreator.xex file. Open a command prompt and navigate to the XexTool directory. Once there, the syntax for the extraction of the base file information and the creation of the .idc file are as follows:

> Xextool.exe –b (name of the .xex file but with an exe extension) –i (name of the .xex file with the .idc extension) name of the .xex file.

Figure 11.13 shows the information as it was input into the system for this research. The total results that are reported back to the end user are represented in Figure 11.14. The results shown in Figure 11.14 inform the examiner that the processor type is the Power PC, which was known, and inform them of the load and entry point addresses. This information will be used once the file is loaded into IDA Pro. In addition to providing this information, two new files were created, the AvatarMiniCreator.exe

```
C:\XexTool_v5.2>XexTool.exe -b AvatarMiniCreator.exe -i AvatarMiniCreator.idc Av
atarMiniCreator.xex
XexTool v5.2  -  xorloser 2006-2008
Successfully dumped basefile idc to AvatarMiniCreator.idc
Successfully dumped basefile to AvatarMiniCreator.exe
```

FIGURE 11.13

Syntax of the XexTool and the report that the information is being dumped.

```
C:\XexTool_v5.2>XexTool.exe -b AvatarMiniCreator.exe -i AvatarMiniCreator.idc Av
atarMiniCreator.xex
XexTool v5.2  -  xorloser 2006-2008
Successfully dumped basefile idc to AvatarMiniCreator.idc
Successfully dumped basefile to AvatarMiniCreator.exe

Load basefile into IDA with the following details
DO NOT load as a PE or EXE file as the format is not valid
File Type:        Binary file
Processor Type:   PowerPC: ppc
Load Address:     0x90100000
Entry Point:      0x90104878

C:\XexTool_v5.2>_
```

FIGURE 11.14

Results of the XexTool base file extraction.

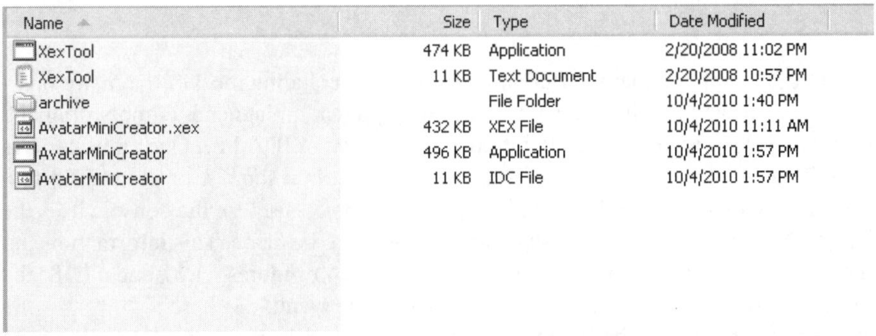

Name	Size	Type	Date Modified
XexTool	474 KB	Application	2/20/2008 11:02 PM
XexTool	11 KB	Text Document	2/20/2008 10:57 PM
archive		File Folder	10/4/2010 1:40 PM
AvatarMiniCreator.xex	432 KB	XEX File	10/4/2010 11:11 AM
AvatarMiniCreator	496 KB	Application	10/4/2010 1:57 PM
AvatarMiniCreator	11 KB	IDC File	10/4/2010 1:57 PM

FIGURE 11.15

Root of XexTool directory showing all the files that are present and the newly created files. It should be noted that the archive folder contains several other attempts and is not standard; it was user created to store other attempts. There is one file that is missing that is essential to the next steps with IDA Pro; that file is titled x360 Imports and is actually located in the user-created archive folder. It was later placed back at the root of the XexTool folder.

and AvatarMiniCreator.idc files, which were both created into the directory where the application was executed from. So the root directory of the XexTool is now populated with several files. Figure 11.15 provides a screenshot of the information.

The next step in the process is to start IDA Pro. Once started, an initial splash screen is displayed. This screen presents the end user with several options on what they wish to work on. There are artifacts present in this splash screen from the research that has been conducted to this point; these artifacts are listed in the window space in this initial splash screen. Select **Go** to "work on your own" and to decompile code, depicted in Figure 11.16.

FIGURE 11.16

Initial IDA Pro splash screen. Note the artifacts in the window space showing previous attempts to decompile XEX code.

IDA Pro supports many different types of data, including most of the major operating systems and gaming consoles. Once the application launches, simply drag and drop the newly created XEX file into the work space of IDA Pro. Once this step has been completed, a dialog box will appear that requires some user input. The first information that must be defined is the processor type. Because the console uses the Power PC processor, that is the selection that needs to be made. This information and the associated drop-down menu are presented here in Figures 11.17 and 11.18; the Power PC would be listed under the Processor Type menu.

Once the binary file has been selected and the processor type has been set, select **OK**. Immediately following this selection, IDA Pro will provide another dialog box that notifies the end user that the processor type has been changed and asks if this selection is OK, as shown in Figure 11.19. Select **Yes** to proceed.

The next dialog box that appears is the disassembler memory organization dialog box, which once again requires input. The initial defaults must be changed in order for the information to correctly load into the application. Recall the information that was gathered using the XexTool; it will be required during this step. The ROM size and loading size fields should be set to "0x00F00000," the information provided from XexTool, specifically the load address. Figure 11.20 shows the default settings, and Figure 11.21 shows the dialog box with the appropriate addresses entered.

Once loaded into IDA Pro, the information is somewhat cryptic, and the process is not yet complete. The initial load is somewhat chaotic as the information is presented to the end user, as shown in Figure 11.22. The .idc file that was created using the XexTool will be used in order to make more sense of the data.

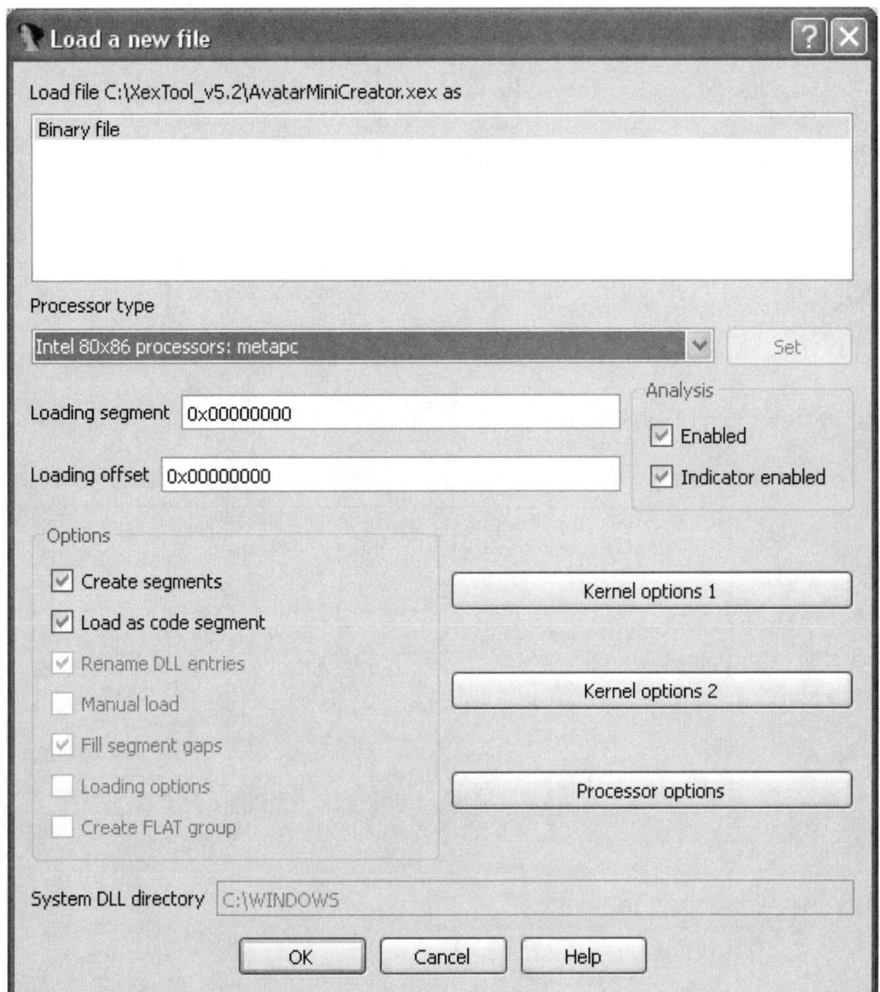

FIGURE 11.17

IDA Pro initial drag and drop of the XEX file into the application requires some user input.

In order to link the .idc file that was created, the end user must click on the Hex Viewer in the tab selections. Once the hex view is displayed, the user must select an area within the Hex Viewer in order to verify the selection and ensure that their navigation is now within that working space. The next step is to navigate to the File menu and select the IDC file option. The application should, by default, orient the user to the directory where the XexTool and XEX files were loaded from. Once the dialog box appears, select the associated .idc file and the select **Open**. Another dialog box will appear prompting the end user to select to analyze the file as code; select **Yes** and allow the data to load.

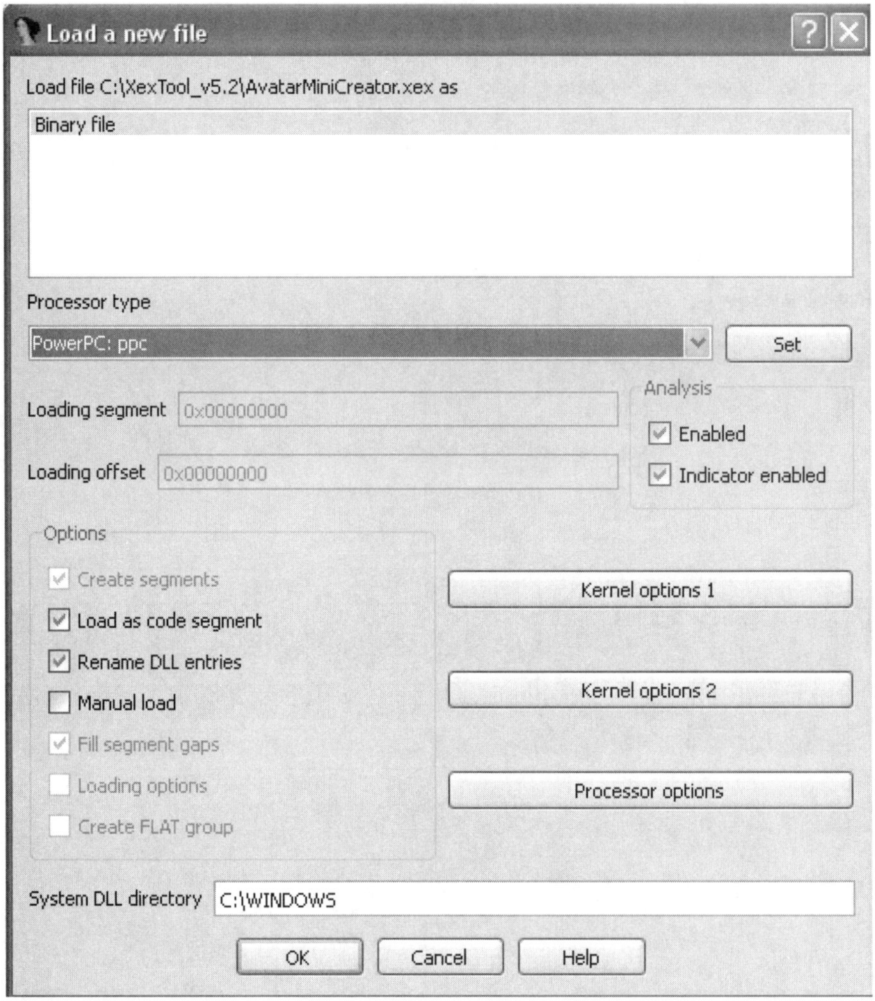

FIGURE 11.18

Selection of the power PC processor type and the highlighting of the binary file.

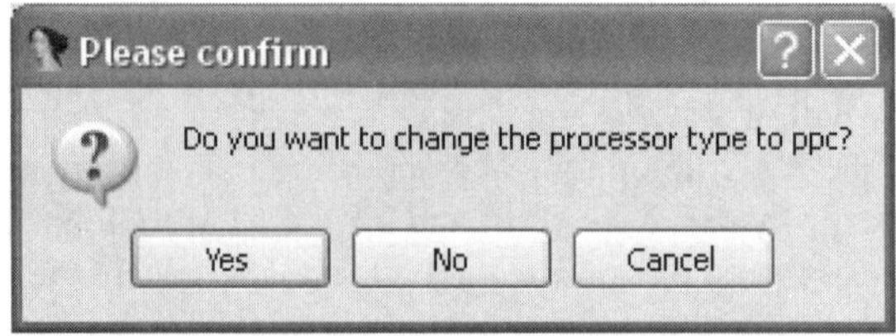

FIGURE 11.19

Notification of the change of processor type.

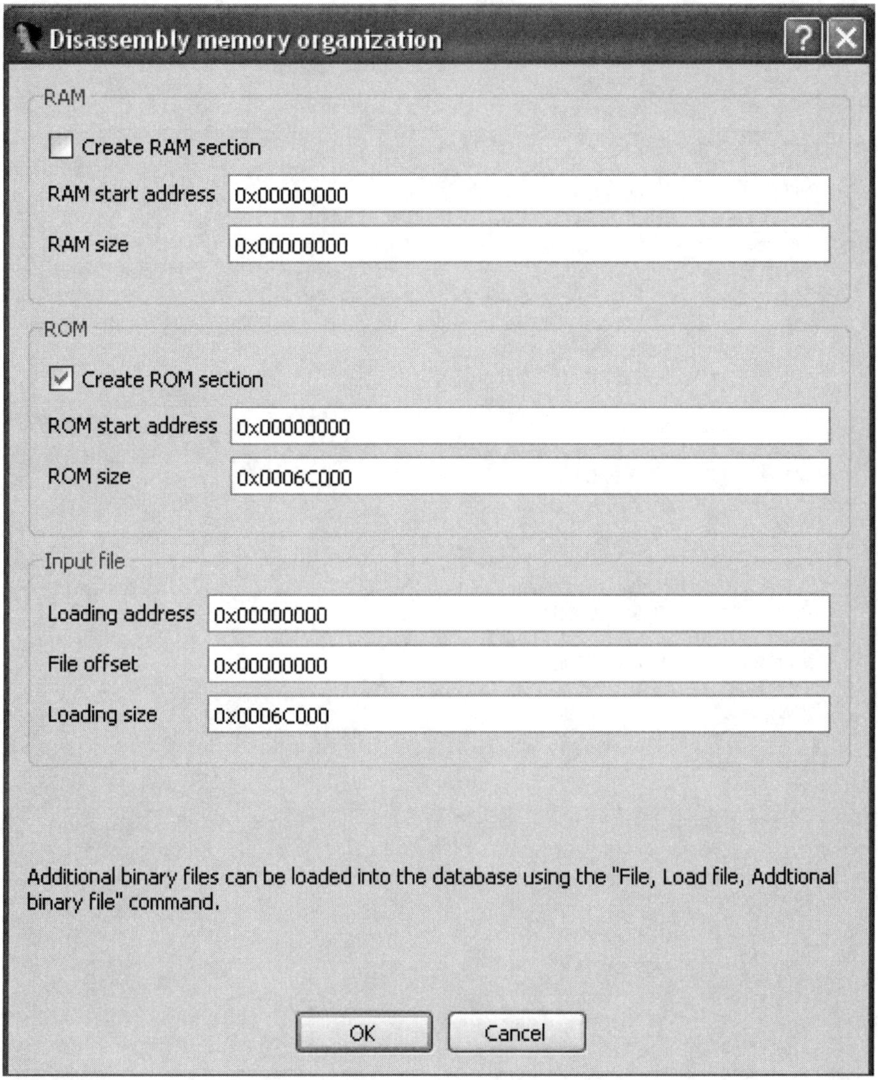

FIGURE 11.20

Dialog box of IDA Pro showing the default settings that must be changed. The loading size as well as the ROM size must be changed as mentioned above for the file to load correctly.

After the IDC file has been loaded and the information has been analyzed as code, the data is presented in a more organized structure. At this point, the end user would navigate the executable file using several methods, including the representation of the file through the horizontal bar above the view tabs, using the view tabs to locate data, or using the functions listed on the left-hand side of the working area. The information that is now presented to the end user could allow the dissection of the code, determining dependencies, remote procedure calls, and network connections.

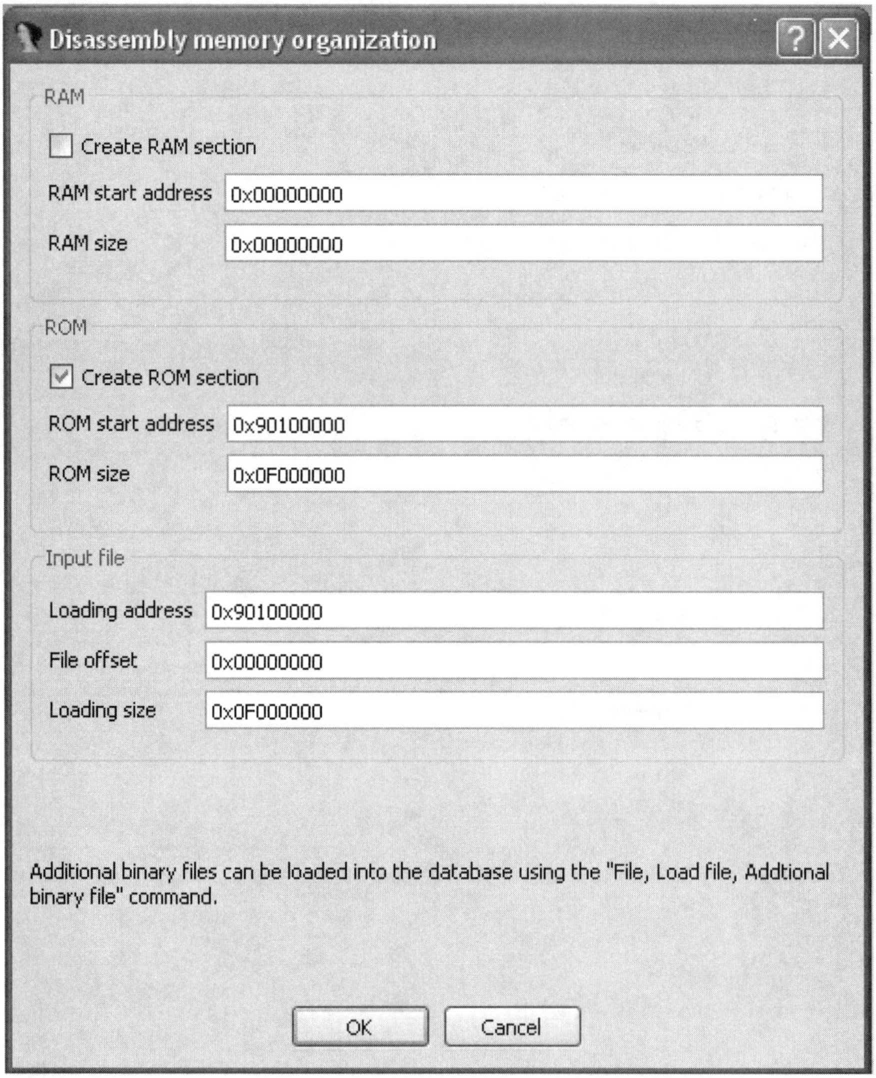

FIGURE 11.21

Load and start address with the load address that was recovered using the XexTool.

The steps mentioned above are detailed in a video that, at the time of this writing, can be located at www.youtube.com/watch?v=VroCdCE9mnY. The video details how to use IDA Pro v5.5 with the Hex-Rays Decompiler to interpret the XBOX 360 executables as code and to view the information contained within.

Using IDA Pro allows a high-end user to edit and alter data as they see fit. This is not something that may be encountered on a routine basis, but could be uncovered if

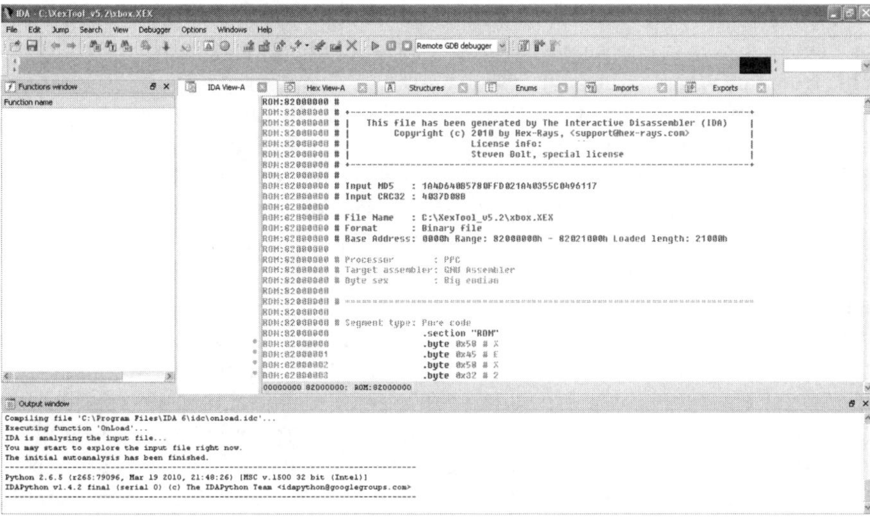

FIGURE 11.22

Initial load of the data into IDA Pro.

there were a gold build hash set provided. IDA Pro has become one of the de facto standards for the decompiling of code in order to grasp a deeper understanding of code and determine the exact function of a program and its dependencies. Because game consoles are application-specific computers, examiners may one day be faced with malware that is targeting game consoles. This day has not yet come, but the ever-evolving functionality of the machines may one day become a target of the malware community.

ADDITIONAL TOOLS AVAILABLE FOR ANALYSIS

In conducting this research, it became evident that there are far more directions that can be taken with the examination of the console and the associated executables than can be covered in a single book. The more research that was conducted, the more applications were uncovered that can be applied to the examination of the console, associated artifacts, and the executables that are on the digital media. One of the issues with the tools that are being used for these examinations is that the tools themselves appear to still be under development and as such, there is no real vetting process. Because the tried and tested forensic applications are, at this time, not able to interpret the file structure of the console, an examiner would be forced to use some of these third-party tools to conduct their examination and use the industry standard tools for verification of the findings.

The first of these additional tools allows an examiner to look inside the PIRS files that are stored on the digital media. There is no need to revisit the format of the files, but the information that is contained within the files may be of interest to determine the exact title found within the file, again, perhaps providing a linkage between victim and suspect. There is a free application called wxPIRS available from http://gael360.free.fr, which allows an examiner to extract information, including embedded files, from PIRS files. This application is simple to use and can provide further information relevant to cases, depending on the particular PIRS file that is run through wxPIRS. There are other applications available at this site as well that are utilities that can be used for examination of the console and associated artifacts.

Using wxPIRS is rather straightforward. Once the application is downloaded and uncompressed, the executable does not undergo an installation wizard and is simply launched by double-clicking on the icon. Once the application is launched, there is not a great deal to the interface. Figure 11.23 provides a screenshot of the initial screen that is presented to the user. After launching the application, the examiner, through the wxPIRS application, needs to navigate to a saved PIRS file through the **Open** option. This step requires that an examiner was able to identify and extract a PIRS file using either one of the traditional forensics tools or Xplorer360. Figure 11.24 provides a screenshot of a PIRS file after it has been loaded into wxPIRS. It has already been discussed that the PIRS, LIVE, and CON files are a custom compression format for the XBOX 360 console. Think of the wxPIRS application as the custom zip/unzip application to view the contents of these files. Once a PIRS file is loaded, the examiner would need to extract the data for further examination. There are files embedded within these PIRS files that contain executables, plain text, and other information that may be relevant.

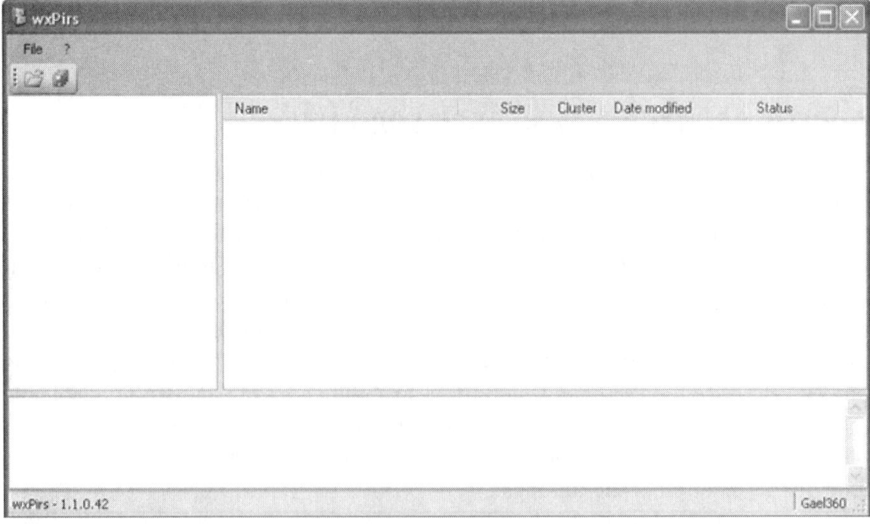

FIGURE 11.23

Initial GUI of the wxPIRS application.

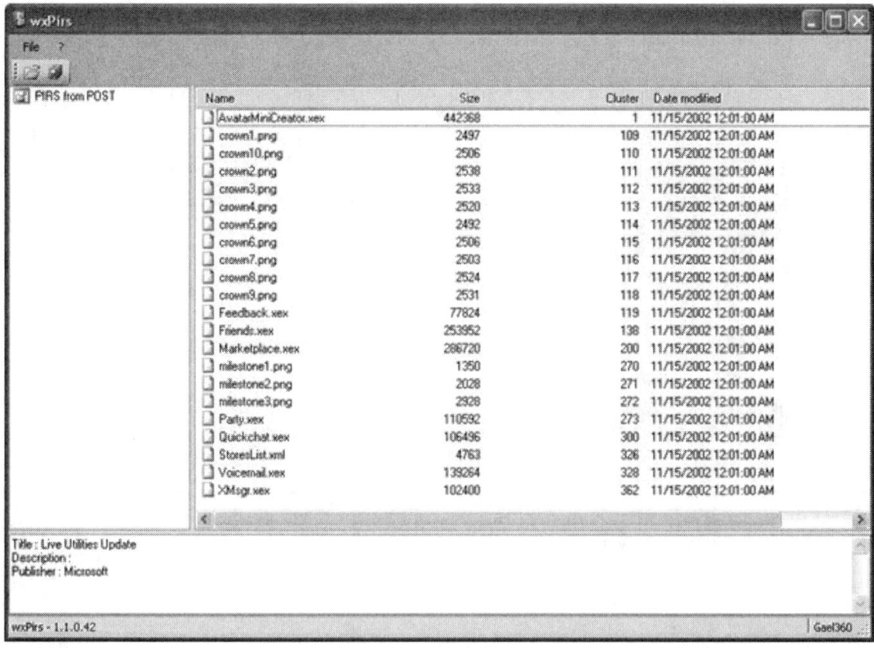

FIGURE 11.24

PIRS file loaded into wxPIRS detailing the embedded files found within. Note the entries for "friends," "milestones," and "voicemail." Under the File menu is the option to extract all the data for further examination using other applications.

Extraction is to a user-defined location, and once the process is initiated, the designated folder is populated by the files listed in the wxPIRS application with the associated information. The benefit of this application is in that it parses through the PIRS file, identifies the individual files with their appropriate names, and provides for extraction of these individual files. Figure 11.25 provides a screenshot of the extracted files. Figure 11.26 shows this same PIRS file loaded into EnCase.

Because the area of game console forensics is truly an area that is in its infancy, there are some utilities that are coming on the market that are attempting to fill the gap between traditional forensics tools and the third-party tools that have been detailed here. One such tool has been developed and is sold by Protowise Labs. Their Web site is www.protowise.com, and they have made some strides toward the development of a tool that will interpret the FATX file system, hash files, recovery deleted items, and provide for an image preview. This new utility, XFT 2.0, has entered the market, and although there was no opportunity to review the application, the company is providing an application and training in an attempt to fill the void in game console forensics. Figure 11.27 provides a snapshot of their Web page.

In addition to the lack of traditional dead box forensics analysis tools, there is also a need for online tools to capture complete online gaming sessions. As with

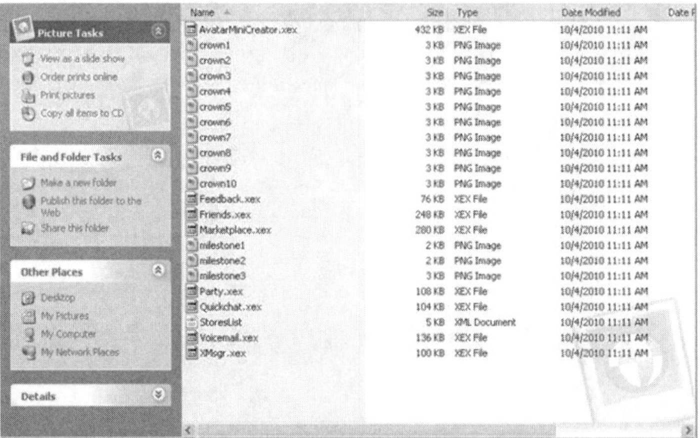

FIGURE 11.25

This is a screenshot of the extracted files. Each of these files can then be imported into other applications for analysis.

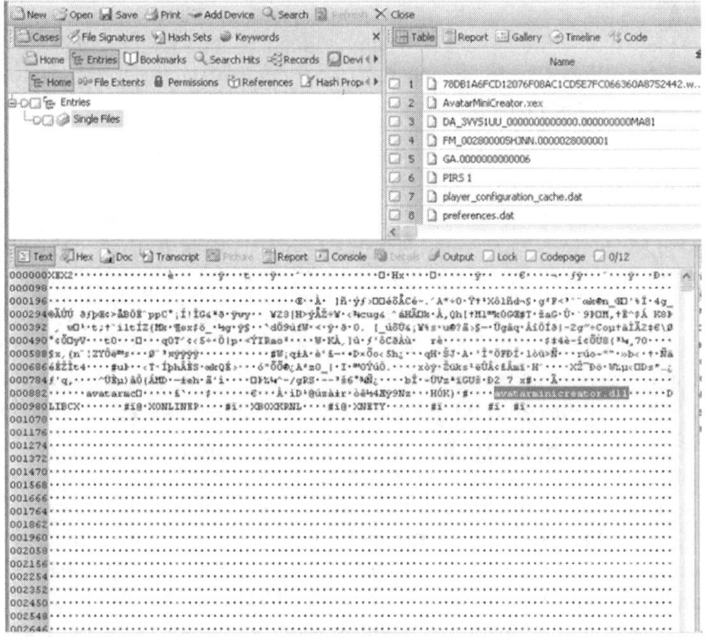

FIGURE 11.26

Continuing with the examination process, this is the header information for the "Avatar-MiniCreator" file that was extracted with wxPIRS and as viewed in EnCase. This allows for further examination.

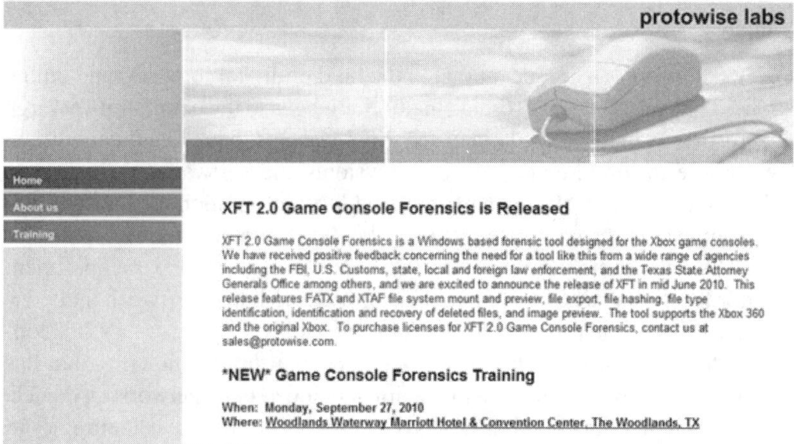

FIGURE 11.27

Screenshot of the Protowise Labs website.

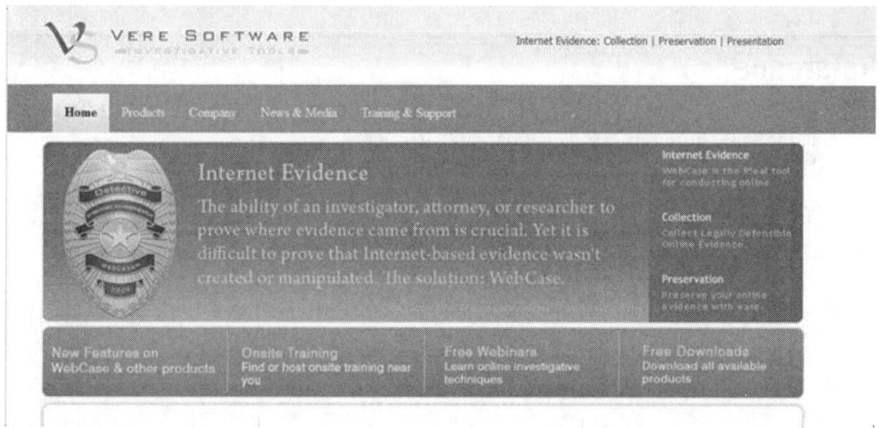

FIGURE 11.28

Screenshot of Vere Software home page.

many other online investigations, a need will arise to move toward the capturing of the network traffic, complete with geolocation of IP addresses and ISP information. At the moment, the only means to capture this information on a game console is to create a setup as outlined earlier, which takes up a great deal of room and may be time consuming in order to gather all the required hardware and software. One company that has established its dominance in the online investigative software market is attempting to fill the gap for game console investigations. Vere Software is developing a process that will provide online investigators with the needed tools to collection gaming sessions and network traffic in a forensically sound manner. Figure 11.28 provides a snapshot of the Vere Software home page.

SUMMARY

The XBOX 360 console is a unique animal in the field of digital forensics and online investigations. The console itself presents many challenges to the community at large because Microsoft has incorporated many security measures to prevent the modification of the console to run alternate operating systems and software modifications. The digital storage media for the console is a wealth of information that can provide supporting documentation to an investigation or be the source of great frustration for an examiner. There are some third-party utilities that can be used to extract pertinent information for the digital artifacts and that may provide a linkage between individuals or exonerate others. The point is that the game consoles of today are application-specific computers, designed to play network games, but the functionality that has been incorporated has moved them into the realm of being a social networking device. Faced with many challenges on a daily basis, each forensic professional struggles to stay abreast of the current information in their field. Game console forensics is an area that is evolving. Along with the evolution of the functionality of the consoles, so to must the industry evolve.

Reference

[1] WhatIs.com. "What is DCOM?" http://whatis.techtarget.com/definition/0,,sid9_gci213883,00.html (accessed October 4, 2010).

APPENDIX

Tools Used in This Research

GUIDANCE SOFTWARE'S ENCASE V. 6.16.2 (FORENSIC APPLICATION)

Available from www.guidancesoftware.com/EnCase is an industry standard in digital forensic examinations. Guidance Software provides solutions for the forensic and e-discovery needs of the industry. From their Web site:

> *Guidance Software offers eDiscovery, data discovery, and computer forensics solutions for corporations and government agencies. Validated by numerous courts, corporate legal departments, and government agencies, our EnCase technology is used by over 30,000 licensed users worldwide.*

A special thanks to Guidance Software for providing a license for their application for this research.

IDA PRO V. 6 (USED FOR DECOMPILING FILES AND DEBUGGING)

IDA Pro is a program that is used to decompile and debug various applications with support for several processor types. The application is available from www.hex-rays.com/idapro/ and is one of the leading decompilers. A better description of the application and its functionality is provided from their Web site:

> *The IDA Pro Disassembler **and Debugger** is an interactive, programmable, extendible, multi-processor disassembler hosted on Windows, Linux, or Mac OS X. IDA Pro has become the de-facto standard for the analysis of hostile code, vulnerability research and COTS validation. See this executive overview for a summary of its features and uses.*

A special thanks to Hex-Rays for providing a license for their application for this research.

X-WAYS FORENSIC V. 15.5 SR 4 (FORENSIC APPLICATION)

X-Ways Forensic is another industry tool that is gaining in popularity on the world market; it is a dominant force in Europe. The company provides training and forensic applications to the community and is based in Cologne, Germany. X-Ways is one of the products that they offer and is available from www.x-ways.net/. A more accurate description is provided from their Web site:

> *X-Ways is the leading developer and supplier of computer forensics software in Europe. Our software is used for computer forensics, electronic discovery, data recovery, low-level data processing, and IT security. Plus we offer computer forensics training and courses for our software and data recovery services.*

A special thanks to X-Ways for providing a license for its application for this research.

WIEBETECH WRITE BLOCKERS

Wiebetech is a provider of many products, from data storage to write blockers. Its Web site, www.wiebetech.com/home.php, provides a good overview of the products that are offered by the corporation, products that are used by a wide variety of industries and that have been showcased on several television shows. The UltraDock and USB Write Blocker were both used in the research for this book.

A special thanks to Wiebetech for providing the UltraDock and USB Write Blockers for this research.

ACCESS DATA'S FORENSIC TOOL KIT V. 1.70.1 (FORENSIC APPLICATION)

Access Data's Forensic Tool Kit, or FTK, is available from www.accessdata.com/, and it is yet another industry leading forensic application. A description of its products is provided from its Web site:

> *We've pioneered digital investigations for 20+ years. Our Forensic Toolkit®, cyber security and eDiscovery software solutions allow organizations to preview, search for, forensically preserve, process and analyze electronic evidence. Law enforcement, government agencies & corporations use our digital investigations solutions to address computer forensics investigations, incident response, eDiscovery and information assurance.*

wxPIRS (USED TO UNCOMPRESS PIRS FILES)

wxPIRS is an application that is available for download from http://gael360.free.fr/wxPirs.php. At the time of this writing, the application is free of charge and is one of many that are available from this site. The program is used for viewing and extracting compressed files from the custom PIRS files that are located on a FATX-formatted storage device. Consider this application a zip archive program for the PIRS files, enabling the uncompressing of PIRS files to view the files contained within.

XPLORER360

Xplorer360 is one of the few applications that have been coded to deconstruct the FATX file chains and, therefore, can present the FATX files structure in a GUI format. As of this writing, the program is available for free from several Web sites; a simple Web search will locate the application. The application is provided without support.

APPENDIX

List of Products Used to Construct the Off-the-Shelf Capture Box

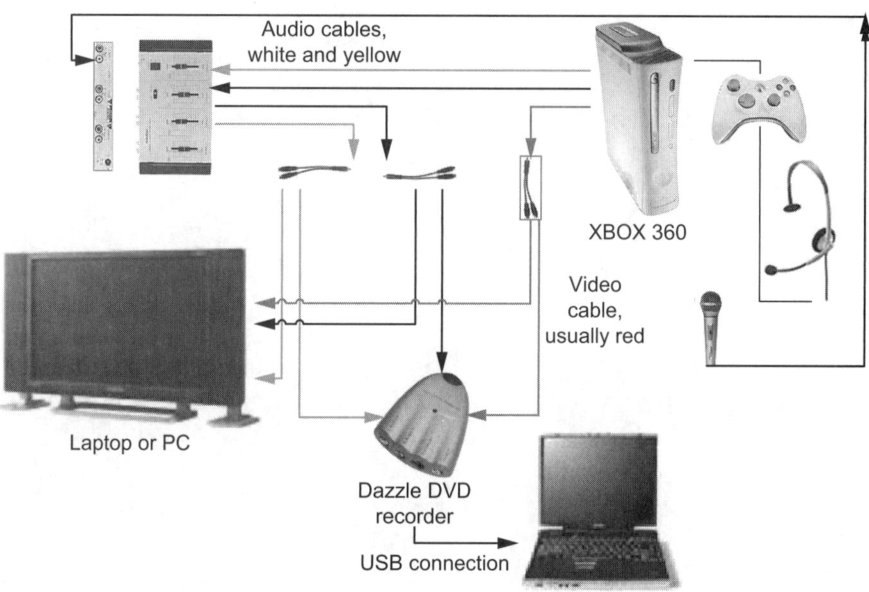

The capture box configuration that is provided is simply one example. As the research has developed over the course of the last few years, many individuals have provided alternate device configurations. Providing this information is meant to provide investigators the means to construct such a capture box should the need arise. This configuration is specific to connections using AV cables.

Items needed to reconstruct the diagram capture configuration:

- Four-channel mixing board, approximate cost $20
- One microphone, approximate cost $30
- Three AV cable "Y" splitters, approximate cost $10

- Three sets male-to-male extension AV cables, approximate cost $15
- One XBOX 360, approximate cost $200 to $500
- One XBOX Live Gold subscription, $50/year
- One video monitor, approximate cost $100 to 1000
- One USB AV video capture device and associated software, approximate cost $30
- One computer capture system

APPENDIX

Removal of the Hard Drive from the New XBOX 360 Slim and Artifacts Pertaining to Data Migration from One Drive to Another

An opportunity presented itself to examine a new Microsoft XBOX 360 Slim and document the removal process of the integrated hard drive. It appears that Microsoft has migrated away from the proprietary SATA interface in favor of a more straightforward design. The hard drive is now integrated internal to the console, but it retains the functionality of removal.

The first step in removal of the drive is to orient the console, placing the grated area in such a position that the end user can easily access it. Built into the grate is a spring-loaded latch that opens the storage location of the drive. Once the latch is opened, then a plate is removed, revealing the location of the drive. Attached to the drive is a nylon tab that, once pulled, pulls on another spring-loaded latch and allows the complete removal of the hard drive. The drive itself is still housed within a custom case, but the SATA connectors are exposed, allowing for forensic imaging once the drive is removed.

Figures C.1 through C.7 show the process of removal of the hard drive from the new XBOX 360 Slim.

FIGURE C.1

Orientation of the XBOX 360 Slim with the grate placed on top. In the middle on the right-hand side is the spring-loaded latch.

FIGURE C.2

Removal of the grate to reveal the hard drive compartment.

FIGURE C.3

A nylon tab is connected to the hard drive for removal. Pulling on the tab depresses another locking mechanism, seen here as a black tab on the hard drive. This lock is present to ensure that the hard drive stays in place, once inserted into its internal carriage.

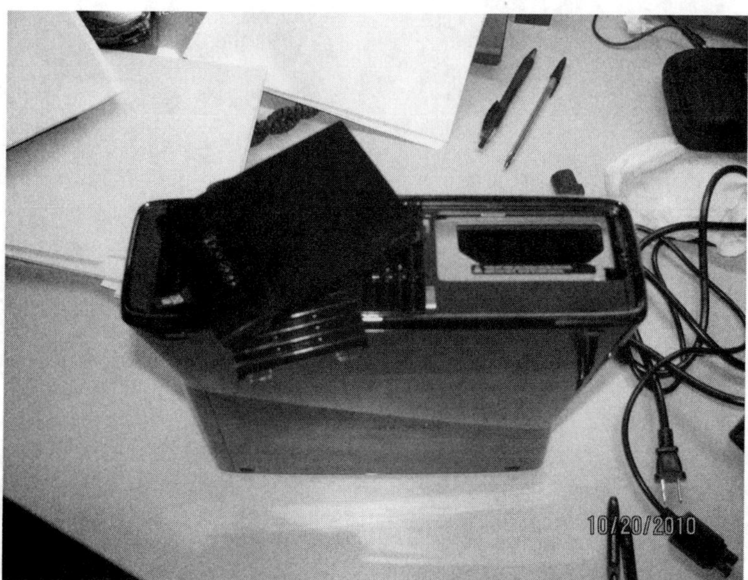

FIGURE C.4

The hard drive removed from the internal storage location.

FIGURE C.5

The new hard drive custom enclosure is a plastic housing that encases the SATA drive.

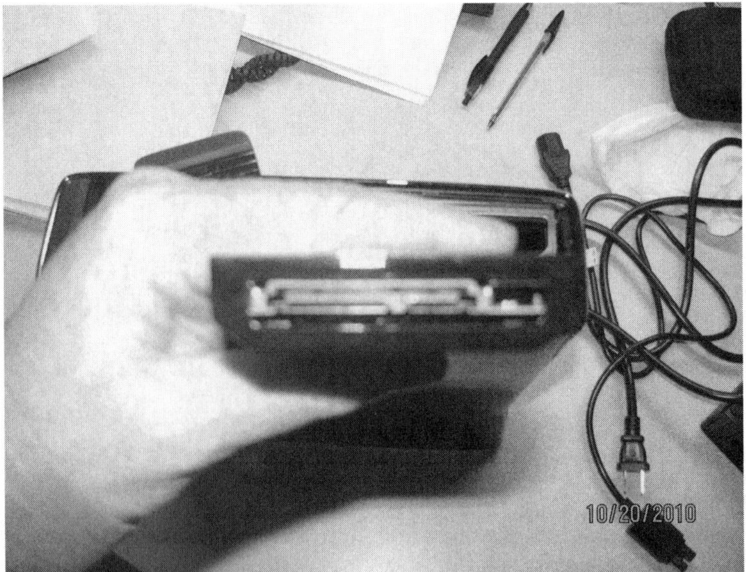

FIGURE C.6

The custom housing with the SATA connectors exposed.

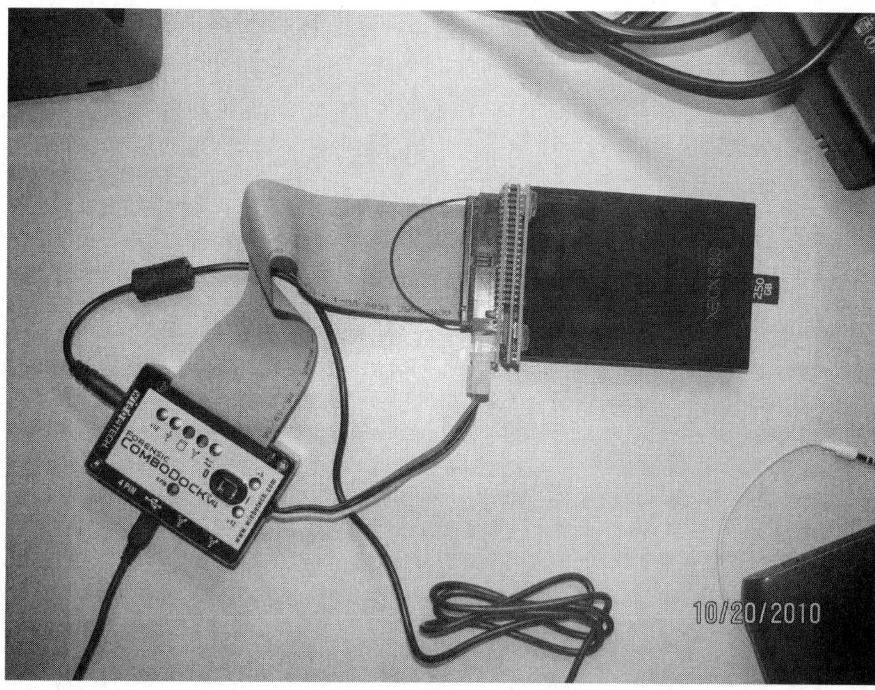

FIGURE C.7

The custom enclosure of the XBOX 360 Slim hard drive being attached to a Weibetech Write Blocker for imaging.

DATA MIGRATION FROM ONE DRIVE TO ANOTHER, A SHORT NOTE

A note regarding the data migration from drive to another seemed pertinent. The reason this information needed to be addressed is that many XBOX 360 gamers upgrade their consoles and, in so doing, they migrate the data from their old drive to the new drive. An opportunity presented itself to perform an analysis of a drive that had its data migrated to a newer drive.

The drive that had its data migrated was initially viewed using Xplorer360. None of the data from this drive, a drive that had a great deal of usage, was presented using Xplorer 360. In fact, the drive was reported as if it was a new drive from a retail package, with the exception of the default date being changed. The drive was then viewed using EnCase and some keywords were created and run against the drive. These keywords were created based on information provided by the drive's owner, which included games played, Facebook names, accomplishments, and friends lists. The results of the keyword search revealed that the information was still present on the drive. It appears that the data migration process is akin to performing a quick format on a disk drive: The data remains, but the pointers are removed.

APPENDIX

Other Publications

This research was not conducted in a vacuum, and other researchers have been working to document the artifacts that are stored on the drive of the XBOX 360 game console during normal usage by the end users. In doing so, there are several other publications that are available, and this research would be remiss if they were not at least mentioned.

Both publications are available from Elsevier for a minor fee. The first publication is entitled *XBOX 360: A Digital Forensic Investigation of the Hard Disk Drive*. From the abstract:

> *In recent years an increase in the complexity of games has subsequently demanded an upscale of the hardware in the consoles required to run them. It is not uncommon for games consoles to now feature many pieces of hardware similar to those found in a standard personal computer.*
>
> *In terms of forensics, the most significant inclusion in today's games consoles is the storage media, whether it is flash-based memory cards or electro-mechanical hard disk drives. When combined with networks, particularly the Internet, this built-in storage gives game consoles a host of new features, including the downloading of games, updating of console software/firmware, streaming media from different network locations, and activities centred around social networking and usually involving user-specific content being saved on the console's storage media.*
>
> *This paper will look at analyzing the SATA hard disk drive contained in Microsoft's XBOX 360 game console. We present our findings and provide suggested basic guidelines for future investigations to be able to recover stored remnants of information from the drive.*

The second publication addresses an area of research that is not covered in this book. There are methods that have been developed by other researchers in an attempt to gain access to the volatile memory of the XBOX 360, as well as the internal NAND storage. The article is entitled *Using a Software Exploit to Image RAM on an Embedded System*. From the abstract of the publication:

The research in this paper is the result of a court case involving copyright infringement, specifically, a request for expert evidence regarding the proportion of copyrighted data present in the RAM of a games console. This paper presents a novel method to image the memory of an embedded device (a games console) where normal software and hardware memory imaging techniques are not possible. The paper describes how a buffer overflow exploit can be used in order to execute custom code written to create an image of the console's memory. While this work is concerned with the Microsoft XBOX, the principles of vulnerability-enabled data acquisition could be extended to other embedded devices, including other consoles, smart phones, and PDAs.

Index

Page numbers followed by *f* indicates a figure and *t* indicates a table.

D